Health & Safety at Work

FOR DUMMIES®
A Wiley Brand

by Dr David Towlson, Dr Terry Robson, Vicki Swaine, *RRC International*

Health & Safety at Work **For Dummies**®

Published by: **John Wiley & Sons, Ltd., The Atrium, Southern Gate, Chichester,** www.wiley.com

This edition first published 2016

© 2016 by John Wiley & Sons, Ltd., Chichester, West Sussex

Registered Office

John Wiley & Sons, Ltd., The Atrium, Southern Gate, Chichester, West Sussex, PO19 8SQ, United Kingdom

For details of our global editorial offices, for customer services and for information about how to apply for permission to reuse the copyright material in this book, please see our website at www.wiley.com.

For general information on our other products and services, please contact our Customer Care Department within the U.S. at 877-762-2974, outside the U.S. at 317-572-3993, or fax 317-572-4002. For technical support, please visit www.wiley.com/techsupport.

Wiley publishes in a variety of print and electronic formats and by print-on-demand. Some material included with standard print versions of this book may not be included in e-books or in print-on-demand. If this book refers to media such as a CD or DVD that is not included in the version you purchased, you may download this material at http://booksupport.wiley.com. For more information about Wiley products, visit www.wiley.com.

A catalogue record for this book is available from the British Library.

ISBN 978-1-119-21093-1 (pbk); ISBN 978-1-119-28724-7 (ebk); ISBN 978-1-119-28725-4 (ebk)

Printed and Bound in Great Britain by TJ International, Padstow, Cornwall.

10 9 8 7 6 5 4 3 2 1

FSC
MIX
Paper from
responsible sources
www.fsc.org FSC® C013056

Health & Safety at Work

FOR

DUMMIES®

A Wiley Brand

Contents at a Glance

Table of Contents

Introduction

. . . .

*H*ealth and safety is a surprisingly interesting topic. It combines bits of science, engineering, management, psychology, ergonomics, law and economics, giving them a safety and health spin. So, if you've ever studied anything or had a job of any kind, you may find that much of the information in this book is familiar and accessible (though it certainly has its techy bits).

We wrote this book because a lot of people are still a bit confused or mystified by health and safety – and we don't want that confusion to continue! It's partly because health and safety is surrounded by more mythology than an ancient Greek epic, and partly because it can be hard to find the information you need unless you know exactly what you're looking for (or you're just plain lucky).

At one extreme, you may think that health and safety is just common sense (so why all the fuss?), and at the other, you may think that it's just too complicated. We have sympathy with both extremes because we've all been there. None of us started out as safety professionals (though we've always been professional . . .). We're ordinary folk (with what we like to think of as a healthy interest in fires, explosions, drugs and alcohol).

To start you off on your health and safety journey, here are a few interesting things we, as authors, have picked up along the way that you may find useful:

- ✔ Risk assessment is a core tool for health and safety. It helps you to make decisions and is a springboard for action; it isn't supposed to be an end in itself.

- ✔ Safety management systems are much easier to set up than to maintain, review and improve – people can lack the motivation for these repeat visits/checks/audits.

- ✔ Using consultants can be an efficient and effective use of resources, especially when you're dealing with something technical. But make sure that you're clear about what you want from your consultant (in terms of end-result deliverables). A good consultant can help you work out the specifications around your needs, but this process can be tricky if you yourself have no clear idea of what you want in the first place.

- ✔ Consultant fees seem only to come in units of one day, regardless of how little work is done.

✔ No two safety experts will ever agree on the detail. Don't let that worry you too much – health and safety work relies on professional judgement, and in reality you can find many ways to achieve the same end result. Take a holistic view.

✔ You get better at safety the more you do it!

About This Book

Businesses have lots of things they need to do to be successful – and making sure that the money is coming in is obviously right up there. But health and safety is also an important part of managing a business. It isn't something separate or an optional add-on – it needs to be integrated into your business's operations, but it often isn't.

In terms of health and safety, you and your business at least need to:

✔ Navigate the apparently complex laws and guidance.

✔ Discover what your priorities are – the things you must do, like write a safety policy, complete risk assessments, consult with your employees and report accidents.

✔ Work out what you can do yourself and when you may need help – and where this help may come from (for example, from consultants).

✔ Work out how to improve performance.

✔ Be sensible, proportionate and realistic (rather than striving for perfection or overreacting).

This book can help you to do all these things, using the experience, wit and humour of three safety professionals (us, your authors). We can help to make health and safety real – so you can see how it can be put into practice in everyday terms. We also introduce you (in Parts III and IV) to the wider scope of safety and health. Not all of these areas will apply to you and your business, but health and safety crosses industries, sectors and continents. It's relevant in any industry that's interested in protecting its people, so we aim to deliver comprehensive coverage of the major topics.

You may notice a few icons in the margins as you work your way through the book – these icons help you to identify the key points, take note of some useful advice and they also indicate the stuff that's just nice to know. You may prefer to skip some of the sidebars and 'Technical Stuff' icons if you're in a hurry and need the basics fast.

Within this book, you may notice that some web addresses break across two lines of text. If you're reading this book in print and want to visit one of these web pages, simply key in the web address exactly as it's noted in the text, pretending as though the line break doesn't exist. If you're reading this as an e-book, you've got it easy – just click the web address to be taken directly to the web page.

Foolish Assumptions

We assume that you're either very interested in health and safety or at least need to know the basics. However, we don't assume that you know very much about health and safety, apart from what you may have read in the newspapers. You may be a business owner, a manager or anyone who needs to get health and safety sorted in your workplace.

Icons Used in This Book

To help you sort out the important information, we use icons in the text. Here's a quick summary of what these icons mean:

This icon indicates practical advice that we've discovered along the way that can make life easier for you.

This icon points out some things that are important enough for you to take note of. You may even want to write these key points down somewhere.

This icon warns you of traps that you can fall into if you're not careful.

This icon provides you with a realistic example (sometimes from your authors' chequered pasts) that can help you to see how things work in practice.

This icon highlights technical terms. Did you really think you'd get away with avoiding the jargon? Every topic has some subject-specific terms that need a bit more explanation, so we take the time to point them out, especially when they're common words that have a special meaning in a health and safety context.

This icon notes specialised health and safety facts that go deeper into a topic than you may need to go. But you can skip these if you're in a rush and still get the point.

Beyond the Book

As you navigate your way through *Health and Safety at Work For Dummies*, you can supplement our sublime text with some extra online goodies. You can find the book's e-cheat sheet at `www.dummies.com/cheatsheet/ healthandsafetyuk`. And, by going to `www.dummies.com/extras/ healthandsafetyuk` you can find some bonus articles with detail that we just couldn't fit in the book.

Where to Go from Here

This book isn't a novel; it's a reference book. As such, you can start anywhere you like. But, if you have little or no safety knowledge or experience, we suggest that you start at the beginning, because the chapters in the first part provide a gentle introduction to the subject and focus on the key things you must do in a business to cover health and safety – the absolute basics.

Other than that, take a quick look at the table of contents or index and choose a topic that makes you smile – and get started!

Part I

Getting Started with Health and Safety at Work

In this part . . .

✔ Understand what health and safety is and its benefits to you and your business.

✔ Decide whether you need professional help or can go it alone, and take a look at your safety policy.

✔ Set the right culture – lead from the front, consult with your employees, communicate effectively with your team and train your employees to do their jobs properly.

✔ Assess your business risks using pragmatic and sensible approaches that are proportional to the risk.

✔ Create a healthy and safe physical workplace environment and give attention to your employees' welfare – that means toilets, temperature and housekeeping.

Chapter 1

Making Sense of Health and Safety in the Workplace

....

In This Chapter

▶ Understanding what health and safety is

▶ Establishing how health and safety can benefit your business

▶ Navigating health and safety terminology

....

*H*ealth and safety at work isn't a new thing. In past times, making work safer has sometimes been a by-product of not wanting to run out of a limited supply of skilled labourers. For example, gravity has always been difficult to defeat for us humans, so even the ancient civilisations (like the Greeks and Romans) thought of scaffolding and cranes (which also introduce some additional risks – choices, choices).

Things have moved on since then. Modern times bring their comforts and benefits but also new health and safety challenges for every business owner and manager. Safety standards are considerably higher today, and society won't tolerate a business that recklessly fails to protect its employees from unnecessary risks. With modern knowledge, tools and technologies, you're more capable than ever of managing these risks – but you may at times feel that you need to embrace a seemingly bewildering range of legislation and advice along the way. But not to worry – we're here to help you figure out how to rise to the health and safety challenge.

In this chapter, we look at what workplace health and safety really is, why it's important, and how good health and safety practices can help your business flourish. We also introduce you to some of the key terminology you'll see again and again as you discover more about the wonderful world of health and safety. More than anything, we want to give you the confidence to tackle health and safety issues yourself in your own organisation.

Putting Health and Safety into Context

Health and safety can be an emotive subject. It gets a lot of bad press in the UK. Every week you hear about some nonsense or other that reinforces that health and safety is out to spoil everyone's fun, ridiculously disproportionate or just plain silly. Or you hear lots of stories about how not enough was done, how someone or other must be held to account, and how on earth this can be happening again. It's enough to make you want to write a strongly worded letter to *The Times*!

But, believe it or not, health and safety professionals get just as frustrated with this as you do – and they're not out there to spoil your fun or to surround you with red tape. In fact, many rather like having fun themselves.

The next few sections offer some perspective on health and safety, so that you can understand what it's really about (and save you from believing all the bad press and silly stories).

Cutting through the hype

Quite a few (though not all) of the stories you hear in the news berating health and safety have nothing to do with health and safety. In fact, they're often down to local policies and decisions, and health and safety is simply an excuse or a smokescreen used to hide a decision that has already been made for other reasons.

As a result, in the popular mind-set, health and safety can be seen as a reason for *not* doing things. Indeed, this idea has become somewhat of a comic stereotype in the UK – with 'elf and safety' providing the incontestable, final word. But try it on your nearest and dearest and see how far it gets you: 'I'm not cleaning the toilet today – health and safety – I might fall into the bowl'; 'Kids, I'm not taking you to that birthday party today – health and safety'. You'll find that your excuses quickly wear thin!

In reality, people manage risks perfectly well when it's something they want or need to do. For example, you can apply risk management principles to oil production (the source of many modern-day chemicals, and used to make plastics and fuel your car), power generation or even simply driving a car.

The UK's main health and safety regulator, the Health and Safety Executive (HSE), became so fed up with health and safety being used as an excuse to ban things that it set up a 'myth-busters challenge panel'. It's dedicated to challenging some of the more ridiculous health and safety excuses that have been reported to them by outraged members of the public. The idea is that the panel investigates the circumstances and reports their thoughts on the matter. That is, do they think that the reasons given are really due to health and safety – or do they think that health and safety is being used as an (unconvincing) excuse?

The panel's answer is just its opinion – it isn't legally binding. So, it doesn't mean that you can enforce an appeal. But it does mean that you can challenge the reason for the apparently poor decision. (The real reason may simply be that someone was looking for an excuse not to run an event, for example. That's fair enough, and often entirely up to the decision-maker in question, but they shouldn't be calling it a health and safety reason when it isn't. They should come clean and give you the real reason.)

Many cases heard by the panel surround events that have been run for years but get cancelled or unreasonably constrained on the basis of some made-up health and safety reason.

Here are a couple of examples to brighten your day, which just goes to show how much fun it must be working for the HSE:

- **Custard pie fight:** *'A custard pie fight at a local event has been cancelled because the event organisers could not get insurance on the basis that the activity is too dangerous'.*

  The myth-busters panel concluded that this was just a case of 'over-the-top risk aversion' and there was no real danger. Instead, everyone missed out on some harmless fun.

- **A night in the museum:** *'A national museum is hosting a 'sleepover' event and has advised those attending that they can bring a foam mattress to sleep on but not an inflatable one on the grounds of health and safety'.*

  The myth-busters panel couldn't think of a convincing health and safety reason for this. Their conclusion is that the museum needs to justify it – not just blame health and safety when it isn't a health and safety issue.

According to the HSE, one of the reasons cited for disproportionate interpretations of safety requirements is a fear of being sued. With the ease of access to no-win, no-fee lawyers, people have the perception that anyone can sue for just about anything, however trivial, and get away with it. But there's little evidence that being sued for trivial things happens much in practice – the law, in most places around the world, does at least grasp the concept of reasonableness; frivolous cases usually get dismissed or thrown out (but obviously with the aid of a safety net).

Of course, the fear of being sued is not to be sneezed at, and many organisations develop unnecessarily in-depth health and safety management plans to protect their business. The nearby sidebar, 'Reclaiming health and safety', looks at the disproportionate application of health and safety regulations in more detail. It also points out that the legislation itself actually seems to be set at about the right level in the UK – which is good to know!

The UK health and safety system is largely one of enforced self-regulation. That means a legal duty exists for those who create the risk to control it, but exactly how they do it (and monitor compliance) is pretty much left up to them to decide, based on the circumstances and some hefty guidance. In effect, you're expected to have a safety management system that actively identifies, controls and reviews risks. It's a risk-based approach. In this sense, the legal duties treat you like an adult instead of telling you in minute detail precisely what to do.

Reclaiming health and safety

In 2011, there was such a backlash against perceived excessive health and safety legislation that the UK government commissioned Professor Ragnar E Löfstedt, an eminent academic who heads up the King's Centre for Risk Management, at King's College, London, to investigate the matter and to 'reclaim health and safety'. Löfstedt published his findings, concluding that safety regulation in the UK was actually about right. Of course, there were a few examples where legislation was burdensome and requirements were duplicated. The sheer amount of legislation was an issue for some, too. However, for the most part, the UK was achieving the right balance.

Löfstedt identified that the problem was less to do with the regulations themselves and more to do with the pressure people felt to go well beyond what the law required: that is, *disproportionate application*. This seems to be the case on the topic of risk assessment in particular. The original purpose of risk assessment was to assess *significant* risks, and to prioritise and manage them. Instead, some businesses have attempted to note every conceivable risk in exquisite detail, however obvious and trivial (for fear they'll be held to account if they don't record it). And, in the process, they can turn an office risk assessment, a two- or three-page affair, into a 200-page analysis that wouldn't be out of place to justify a nuclear installation or oil refinery being placed next to a hospital or school.

Unnecessarily complex risk assessments create a disproportionate administrative burden. This greatly undermines the cause of safety and encourages the view that health and safety gets in the way, tying up valuable resources in efforts that don't benefit the business.

Understanding the value of health and safety

Health and safety is something you do every day without even knowing it. (It's always nice to have a fancy name for something you've known all along.)

At its basic level, it's a survival instinct. You look before crossing the road; you walk more carefully on ice and snow; you smell milk before drinking it; and you don't accept sweets from strangers.

To some extent, even poorly performing businesses consider safety at this basic level, utilising rules they've grown up with in order to survive. But they may not do it very well, or they may just have been lucky so far.

Health and safety covers management, leadership, law and aspects of the physical sciences (physics and chemistry), engineering, biological sciences, psychology (human behaviour) and ergonomics. Science and engineering are natural bedfellows with safety because they often involve doing things that may be considered rather risky if you don't control them properly. No one wants to get blown up when testing a nuclear device, setting off explosives or designing a new-fangled industrial robot – or even while distilling their own gin. (This may also be why a lot of safety people start out in science or engineering – perhaps they simply fail to step out of the way when management is asking for volunteers to hand out the safety equipment.)

Modern health and safety isn't some strange, mystical art. In fact, you can argue that it isn't really a subject in its own right at all. Instead, it's a collection of topics brought together with a *safety* emphasis; that is, to avoid injury or ill-health. In a wider sense, health and safety is also a key aspect of business risk management.

The word *risk* can mean different things to different people, so it's possible to get a little confused. We're using it here in a health and safety context, but the word is widely used in the business world in ways that go beyond health and safety. For example, senior business executives are responsible for *corporate governance* to ensure that their companies are managed effectively (don't look so surprised). This is sometimes termed *business risk management* or *internal control*. Obviously, it's heavily skewed towards financial, market and product risk, but health and safety (and environmental) risks also feature because these too are business risks. We talk more about risks in the later section, 'Recognising hazards and risks'.

Health and safety also features in *corporate social responsibility* (when the emphasis is more on morality, ethics and social justice). Either way, health and safety is something businesses need to see as integrated into their normal activities, and not something separate.

Neglect of significant health and safety risks can bring a business to its knees in no time at all.

If you're well-prepared and motivated (which we think you may be, because you're reading this book!), you can take charge of your business's health and safety to ensure that you have your risk management under control. The first few chapters in this book give you the essential information that any business needs to understand to get started. Like most things in business, you start by working out your policy (see Chapter 2) – which commits you to going in a particular direction – and organising your workforce to implement your policy (see Chapter 3).

A core part of safety is identifying and assessing the risks that arise from your business. We look at risk assessment in Chapter 4 and some basic things you need to get right on your business premises in Chapter 5.

Safety needs to be managed – but not to worry, we cover management system implementation in detail in the chapters in Part II. The chapters in Part III take an in-depth look at a range of workplace risks that you can control to create a safer working environment – from fire- and electricity-based hazards to manual handling and stress-related problems.

Focusing on what's important

Perspective is important when dealing with health and safety. You need to get into the right frame of mind and recognise that health and safety is essential for the success of your business. But it's very easy to feel overwhelmed and bogged down. As every management guru will tell you (for a large fee), it's better to focus your efforts on a few important things and do them well, rather than to start lots of things you never finish.

Trivial tasks can get in the way of good health and safety. If you ask yourself, 'What are my main business risks?' and find that you're not controlling these – and you're instead concentrating on trivial details that have little impact – something is wrong. For example, if you're a chemical manufacturer and you aren't focused on controlling the chemicals in your factory (worrying instead about making sure that people put lids on their coffee mugs and introducing a handrail-holding training programme), you aren't doing what you need to do.

Benefitting Your Business

Plenty of people say that health and safety is good for business. Obviously, it's good for people who sell health and safety products and services, but that's not what they mean. They mean it's good for any business.

In the following sections, we look at some of the inspirational benefits of health and safety that should convince any doubters out there. You may see a lot of overlap between these strands – because one aspect can influence another – but they provide a solid overview of the benefits.

Protecting your employees

Looking after your employees is good for business. You should treat your employees with respect and common human decency – just as you would treat anyone else. This is a so-called moral imperative – doing the right thing.

People don't expect to get injured, killed or ill as a direct result of their work. However, we accept that people do, to some extent, volunteer for different levels of risk by their choice of employment. Thus, a Grand Prix racing driver or TT motorcyclist knows by the nature of his activity (and historical records) that he runs a greater residual risk of injury, even if he does what's reasonable to manage it. (*Residual risk* is just the risk that remains after you take into account the precautions you already have in place to manage it.)

Nothing is ever risk-free. It's self-evident that different industries carry different risk profiles. However, no one accepts that they *will* be killed or seriously injured at work; rather, they accept that they may have a *higher risk* that it may happen than, say, if they had stayed in bed.

This is an entirely reasonable expectation in any modern society. It may also be the case that your employees are already injured or ill – plenty of people with existing disabilities or conditions also go to work. But they don't expect their work to make it significantly worse.

A moral duty also extends beyond employees. Just because someone isn't an employee (say, they're a contractor or member of the public), it doesn't mean you can ignore them. Remember, your employees know (or should know) what the risks are in your workplace and still choose to continue to work there; now, that's understandable in a chocolate factory, but probably not in sewer-cleaning (which we are reliably informed is nonetheless hugely satisfying). But the general public going about their own business won't appreciate or understand the risks in the same way as a trained, experienced employee (for example, if you're erecting scaffolding on a busy high street), so they're more likely, unknowingly, to be exposed to danger. Interfacing hazardous operations with the public therefore requires more careful planning, because the public may have no awareness of the dangers they may be facing.

On a purely practical note, if you don't take reasonable steps to protect your employees from injury and ill-health, you'll soon be spending more time managing sickness than managing your business. So, take this on board as a valuable lesson. Be nice.

Boosting your profits

Giving attention to health and safety can make your business more profitable for all sorts of reasons. If you're a single-minded, money-fixated boss, this should be the clinching argument for you.

Done properly, health and safety can save you a lot of money. That money then stays with you and adds to the bottom line. This isn't easy to appreciate until you look at the cost of neglecting health and safety. If you manage health and safety properly, you can detect the triggers that lead to serious accidents at an early stage and then manage these issues before they cost you too much money.

Arguments about theoretical accidents that can happen may not quite convince you. It may therefore be tempting to see a health and safety department as an unnecessary expense. But that's short-sighted and, though probably not immediately, it will eventually cost you far more.

Accidents are pretty convincing when they happen. Their effects go well beyond the injured person. In terms of the financial implications, you can divide costs into *insured* versus *uninsured costs* (or *direct* versus *indirect costs*). These are just different ways of labelling costs. But, whatever you call them, even a simple accident will cost you money.

If you've ever had a car accident, you know how time-consuming and awkward it is, even for a minor scrape – a cast of thousands seems to be involved, and you never recover all the time and money involved. And, all the while you're dealing with that, you have an *opportunity cost* to think about – you lose the time that you may have spent doing other things (okay, maybe you were just going to flop in front of the telly, but it's still your time that you've lost out on).

Imagine that you're the manager of a supermarket. Your employee drives a ride-on sweeper around a corner and straight into a customer on a mobility scooter, tipping her from the vehicle into a pile of neatly stacked bottles of wine. Bottles are broken, wine is everywhere, and your trained sweeper operator (and others) slips and falls while trying to help.

The costs soon mount up: repair to the sweeper, repair to the mobility scooter, loss and replacement of product, loss of productivity (other employees helping on the scene, first-aid-trained colleagues taking time away from their posts, the cleaner on sick leave recovering), hire of a replacement sweeper and mobility scooter while the damaged vehicles are undergoing repair, conduct of an internal investigation (time is money), injury compensation, legal advice costs, increased insurance premiums . . . and before long, a seemingly simple accident has become an incredibly expensive experience.

You also need to be aware of the intangible costs. The incident may appear in local newspapers and on social media feeds. The woman on the mobility scooter may be the most hated person in the district, may have deliberately rammed the sweeper or may have had a death wish, but that doesn't matter a hoot. The supermarket may become a retail pariah if its customer services team doesn't handle it quickly. This kind of damage to your business's reputation can stretch into years of depressed sales.

The woman on the mobility scooter may develop a phobia of sweepers or supermarkets. It may even change her social life as she deals with the stress. Of course, it may all end well, so don't get too morose. It depends on how you deal with it, but it's better to stop it happening in the first place.

Some of your accident costs can be recovered from your insurer (the current law in the UK is that you need to at least have Employers' Liability Insurance), but many of the costs can't, and you'd need to cover these through the business. In fact, in one study, the HSE calculated that uninsured costs were between 8 and 36 times the insured costs (this is sometimes called the 'iceberg' model, because most of the costs are 'hidden' – in the same way that most of an iceberg is under the water level). That's a lot to self-fund and reminds you that the true cost of an accident is far more than you think. In cut-throat, low-margin businesses, it can be the difference between profit and loss, but in any case, these additional costs eat directly into business profits. If you consider, 'How much of the price I'm charging is going towards supporting my accident rate?', it can be sobering.

The preceding example outlines a small accident. If you have a fire, you can lose the whole building, and your employees may lose their jobs as a result. On the flip side, having a proactive system that foresees safety issues and manages them properly saves you from a whole world of pain and proves a very worthwhile investment. How much you invest needs to be proportionate – but you probably already know all these cost–benefit arguments if you're in business.

In one example case from the HSE, a food company invested in health and safety training for its managers and supervisors installed a formal safety management system, and set Key Performance Indicators (KPIs). It reportedly observed a significant reduction in injury rates and lost staff time (equating to a saving of around £100k per year in replacement staff), saw a 45 per cent reduction in injury compensation claims and received an insurance premium reduction. Though the programme cost around £215k, the company calculated that it had saved around £380k in total over a three-year period in reduced injuries and compensation claims. Food for thought indeed. (Find out more about this case here: www.hse.gov.uk/business/casestudy/uniq.htm.)

The HSE has several case studies demonstrating the benefits to real businesses of investing in health and safety. Check out their website for a few more examples: www.hse.gov.uk/business/case-studies.htm.

Staying legal

Many moral imperatives eventually become part of the law, because everyone thinks it's such a good idea and it should become a definite rule. Sometimes, it even gets written down by lawyers, and a new law is passed by Parliament.

Every business needs to, at a minimum, be trying to comply with the law. We take a look at the main health and safety laws in Chapter 17, and you'll find reference to specific laws scattered throughout the book.

Full compliance may take time. Most compliance is a work in progress – you start with the big things (and have in mind the spirit of the law) and get better, improving and then exceeding compliance.

Speaking the Language Like a Pro

It's nice to speak the language a little when you go on holiday to another country. Health and safety is just like that. In the following sections, we look at some of the common health and safety terms that you'll come across.

It's difficult to find universally agreed definitions for the terms we're about to introduce you to. You can find a range of definitions in fact, if you look hard enough. But the key message is always the same, and we provide you with what we feel are the most effective and helpful definitions to help you navigate your way around health and safety.

Recognising hazards and risks

Risk and hazard (and danger) can often be used interchangeably in popular talk. Most dictionary definitions use these interchangeably too, describing a hazard as a risk or a danger. That's entirely understandable because they're connected via the consideration of harm. But, because you're trying to find out about safety properly, it's a good idea to consider a proper definition in the context of health and safety, the knowledge of which will mark you out a health and safety pro.

Figuring out hazards

A popular working definition of a *hazard* is:

> *Something with the potential to cause harm.*

Now, that's interesting. The *something* can in fact be anything. An object, an activity, a process, a person, a situation, an energy source, a chemical or condition, or even a combination of things coming together (yes, don't just think of single things). This means that guns, knives, tigers, working at height on a ladder, lifting a heavy load, welding the old Mini, oil spills on the floor, the electricity flowing through your power cables and thieves waiting to mug you down a dark alley are all hazards.

Note also that hazards have the *potential* to cause harm. They may not have caused actual harm or even tried to; it's just that harm is foreseeable. It can be envisaged. That, too, is interesting, because if you can't conceive of something causing harm, it doesn't appear as a hazard to you. You don't recognise it as hazardous. So, in practice, you have to have in mind the type of harm something can cause before you recognise it as a hazard.

That's also why the same thing can be treated very differently in different physical forms. A wooden plank has very different potential for harm compared to, say, the same wood in the form of wood dust (which can enter the body through the lungs). The plank is rather difficult to swallow or inhale (though we're sure some will try, just to prove us wrong).

The final point is about harm. *Harm* is a possible consequence of a hazard. The harm may be an injury, illness or, more widely, loss to a business. A given hazard can, of course, lead to multiple types of harm (from the trivial to the serious).

In practical terms, it's best to think of *significant harm* as the line not to be crossed. The truth is, everything can cause you harm to some degree. Harm can, of course, be physical or psychological.

So, that brings us to the difficulties with hazards. Some hazards are entirely obvious. For some, for example, you share a collective innate awareness. You don't need to explain that the type of harm that may befall you from the approaching charge of a rhinoceros constitutes a hazard. But, in practice, many hazards are *contextual*, or rely on knowledge that you may not have. For example, knowledge of health hazards increases as health and safety experts explore and investigate incidents that have occurred (and thus connect the cause with the effect).

Asbestos was at one time considered a wonder mineral – fireproof, insulating and so on. Now you know differently. That's what life is like. It's not that things become more dangerous over time, it's that you discover more about what surrounds you.

In practice, then, what you perceive as a hazard is also contextual. For example, you tend to consider small parts of toys to be choking hazards only in the context of the small children who may play with them (warnings about choking hazards are typical for many toys). However, conceivably, though probably less likely, older children and even adults can also choke on them (or on, well, anything). But this thinking of hazards in context is usually helpful because it helps you to filter out the trivial from the serious in any given circumstance.

Some hazards will be obvious to everyone, some just to you, and some you may need specialist help with. Half the battle is recognition. And the battle of recognition is won by asking yourself, 'How can it cause me significant harm?'

Understanding risk

Here's a working definition of risk:

> *The chance (or likelihood) that harm will occur (when exposed to the hazard), together with an idea of the severity of the harm.*

Now, that all sounds truly beautiful. In effect, it means the chance of a *particular* harm, given that you're exposed to a *particular* hazard. Notice that different harm outcomes, and the severity of harm, may have different likelihoods (from the same hazards). You therefore tend to express risk in terms of a particular severity. For example, imagine that the chance of getting lung cancer from smoking in any one year is, on average, 1 in 10,000 (we just made those figures up by the way – this is purely hypothetical). You may also say that the chance of getting a persistent, hacking cough from smoking is 1 in 2 (again, we made that up, but you can see that as you change the harm you focus on, the risk-level changes).

When you see such figures quoted, they're nearly always averages. The real risk will change depending on your specific circumstances (in this case, you can include a number of other genetic, lifestyle and work factors when you're looking at the chances of getting lung cancer or a severe cough – some people smoke their whole life and don't develop cancer, whereas others do).

Sometimes, chance is expressed as a probability (1 = certain, 0 = never) and sometimes as a frequency (the number of times it may happen on average in a given time period). In the latter case, an example may be 0.01 per year – a hundredth of an event per year or, in more normal terms, one event in a hundred years. This latter way is the way you tend to see rare (but big consequence) events quoted – events such as major explosions or widespread flooding in populated areas. But you accept that this again is an average. You know that because of the part chance plays and that we have little reliable data (because these events are rare), the event may well occur again next year, or in 200 years, for example.

Exposure to the hazard is a necessary prerequisite for risk to have any meaning. If you never come across the hazard, it presents no risk to you, even though it has the *potential* to cause you harm.

The more you're exposed to the hazard (in terms of duration and amounts), the more likely it is that you'll be harmed, and perhaps the more severe that harm will be. For example, with noise exposure, the louder the noise and the longer it goes on for, the more likely you are to be harmed (and to perhaps become a rock legend on the way; see Chapter 16 for more on the problems with noise). But, a similar principle operates whenever you put yourself in harm's way – the longer you're there, the more likely you are to be harmed.

Sometimes, a combination of events may occur together and make a minor incident far more serious than you may have thought; for example, someone slips on an icy road and falls into the path of an oncoming truck. These events have an underlying randomness. You can predict a probability for different outcomes – how many people will be killed on the roads, for example – but you can't know exactly who will die and when. (We're not sure we'd want to know anyway, come to think of it.)

Chapter 4 dives into how to complete a risk assessment when you identify health and safety hazards in your workplace.

Balancing risk: Opportunities and threats

Risk is often viewed negatively by health and safety people and, to a certain extent, by the general public. You associate risk with bad things happening. That's understandable because safety people spend most of their efforts trying to eliminate, reduce or mitigate risks.

You don't tend to hear about the risk of success; instead, you hear about *opportunities*. In the business world, people are used to talking about risk from a positive perspective. Indeed, ISO 31000 (an internationally recognised standard on risk management from the International Organisation for Standardisation, ISO – yes, ISO not IOS, the abbreviation used is from the French version of the title) defines risk as the effect of uncertainty on objectives and notes that it can be positive (an *opportunity*) or negative (a *threat*). The definition may challenge your beliefs, but the fact remains – it's healthy to take a positive view of risk. Granted, any business should try to minimise the negatives, but doing business itself is a risk (that is, the outcome isn't certain).

Creating standards: The International Organisation for Standardisation (ISO)

Standardisation (making standards that people adopt and agree to) can sometimes be desirable. It can occur on a national, regional or global level, depending on the need. Simple examples of standards in everyday life in the UK are weights and measures – wherever you go in the UK, you know a pint is a pint and a kilogram is a kilogram.

ISO creates international standards – these are specifications or guidelines, which, if used widely and consistently, mean that everyone is working to a similar standard. ISO is made up of members from national standards bodies – for example, the British Standards Institution (BSI) for the UK and the American National Standards Institute (ANSI) for the United States. In effect, these national bodies represent ISO in their countries – and suggest topics for standards to ISO.

Although national standards bodies can unilaterally create standards of their own, they also contribute to the development of ISO standards and then transpose them for national use (that is, make them work in the national context, often with just a few simple changes to the language). This process can also work the other way round: a national standard can end up being proposed as an ISO standard if there's enough international interest.

A business can't exist or compete effectively if it eliminates all risks; it may as well give up now. Risks must be taken, accepted and managed. The level of risk depends on many things, including the context in which the business operates and the business's appetite for risk.

Chapter 2 looks at how a business can assess its risk profile in terms of health and safety.

Distinguishing between 'health' and 'safety'

Health and *safety* are terms that are usually used together, like fish and chips, bankers and embezzlement, politicians and lying. But they do have meanings in their own right. *Health and safety* is simply trying to manage health and safety risks in the workplace.

It's useful to think of health risks as longer-term threats to your health, sometimes called a *slow accident*. Safety risks, on the other hand, are more immediate things, such as being struck or cutting yourself. It's not really worth worrying too much about the distinction, except to say that health risks are far too easy to forget about, because they can take decades to do their damage. That's why you need to always keep them in mind.

Keeping things in proportion

The law is not as unreasonable as you may think. Enshrined in UK health and safety legislation is the concept of *proportionality*. The legislation expects you to manage your own risks using proportionate measures. In other words, it doesn't expect you to expend enormous effort on trivial risks (like putting lids on coffee mugs, however sensible that sounds) because the increase in safety may be marginal compared to the effort involved.

In legislative terms, you're taking 'reasonably practicable' measures so that you can weigh the cost (time, effort, resources) against the risk to help you decide what to do. On the other hand, the greater the risk, the more the law expects you to do to control it. This risk-based approach is entirely consistent with the way businesses tend to run their other affairs, such as managing financial risks, so taking this approach is business as usual.

The modern UK health and safety legal framework (see Chapter 17) is no longer prescriptive but goal-setting. In most cases, the law sets objectives for you to meet and gives you guiding principles, but it leaves much of the detail on how you achieve these objectives up to you (and yes, you may find the unwelcoming arms of the prosecuting barrister if you get it badly wrong).

Your solutions may be different from those of other businesses, even though the overall risk is managed adequately. But the law doesn't expect you to be perfect – risk control never is. In fact, living with a sense of inadequacy is probably a good thing – it means you're always thinking of ways to improve. Now, about putting lids on coffee mugs . . .

Chapter 2

Setting Your Health and Safety Policy

*T*he *thought* of doing something is often worse than *doing* it, and this reality pops up in all walks of life. For example, you may dread starting a new diet programme, or even simply getting up in the morning. Looking to the world of work, you've probably experienced at least one kind of management system audit and know full well that the initial enthusiasm for setting up the auditing programme is rarely matched as you try to stick to an auditing schedule. You can always manage to find something more important, urgent or interesting to do. But eventually, you know that you have to do it, and that sense of relief you feel afterwards makes you wonder what all the fuss was about.

And so it is with health and safety. Procrastination and being busy are your enemies, and you may conveniently find yourself in thrall to the tyranny of the urgent or the lure of the interesting – anything to avoid doing the boring and necessary.

But you have some very good reasons for taking action (refer to Chapter 1), and in this chapter we help you to start taking easy steps towards taking these important and necessary actions to get your health and safety policy off the ground. First, we help you to consider the capacity you already have in-house and whether you need any professional help (don't we all?), and then we take an in-depth look at how to develop and implement your health and safety policy.

Deciding Whether to Go It Alone or Seek Assistance

When you're in business, you have to decide what you and your team can do internally and what you may need to outsource to others. You probably already outsource your Internet provision, recruitment and cleaning. Typically, the higher the risk and/or the greater the complexity and scale of your business, the more you're likely to outsource. Just look at oil and gas, and construction – two industry sectors in which companies make wide use of sub-contractors. Typical examples of sub-contracting include risk assessments (especially the specific types, such as fire, explosive atmospheres, noise, vibration and chemicals), asbestos surveys, safety management system auditing, development of specific policies (such as drugs and alcohol), behavioural/cultural analysis and change programmes, safety checks/tests on portable electrical equipment, fire extinguisher maintenance, fire alarm maintenance/tests, and some health and safety training. In fact, you can outsource virtually anything these days. It may be a wise use of your resources, but it's a decision you should keep under review, as at some stage it may be better to develop some of the expertise internally.

Outsourcing can lead to its own problems. That's because, in terms of an employer's duty of care to its employees under health and safety law, although you can delegate tasks, you can't delegate your legal responsibilities (and the liabilities that comes with it – see Chapter 17 for more on these so-called 'non-delegable' duties). If you fail to choose contractors wisely or fail to manage them effectively and their negligence causes injury to an employee, you can find yourself liable. Working with contractors may end up being more trouble than it's worth.

If you're a manager, you may like to delegate outsourcing decisions to one of your trusted and experienced employees. Outsourcing decisions often boil down to an assessment of the level of expertise and resources held within the business. Your decisions don't have to be permanent (unlike membership of the Mafia) but can be reviewed as your circumstances change.

Some outsourcing decisions may be obvious to you, based on your existing knowledge and experience. But a systematic way of helping you decide how to proceed is to:

✔ Work out what kind of business you are – in terms of your business risk profile. By evaluating your risk profile you can discover the main types of health and safety issues that you need to deal with (and therefore the types of expertise and knowledge you may require to deal with these issues).

✔ Figure out what capabilities and expertise you already have within your business to cover those issues.

✔ Find the expert help you need if you find a gap between the expertise you need and what you have.

We cover these steps in the following sections.

Understanding the risk profile of your business

The first step to help you decide what you need to outsource is to work out what kind of business you are. Specifically, what is your risk profile?

Risk is a funny word (refer to Chapter 1 for an introduction to some common health and safety terminology and Chapter 4 for more detail on risk assessment methods). It essentially means the chances of something bad happening (and how bad it's likely to be).

A term that has crept into health and safety from the business world is 'risk profiling'. *Profiling* means building a description, picture or image of what things are like (or may potentially be like). The police have used profiling for years to create psychological profiles of suspects (no, they haven't caught you yet!). Your Facebook, LinkedIn or Twitter profile also builds a picture of who you are. Therefore, *risk profiling* is all about building a basic picture of the set of risks that your business faces and using this as a basis for decision-making. As part of this process, you may also decide what level of risk you're happy with. In the context of health and safety, your risk profile identifies the major (high-level) risks that relate to your business operations. For example, if you're a chemical manufacturer, your major risks are associated with chemicals (such as storage, use, processing, transport and so on). If you instead focus on sorting out your swish new office, you've got your priorities wrong.

Insurance companies do risk profiling all the time. A familiar example is motor vehicle insurers. They gather risk-relevant information (or factors) from you (for example, about your job, lifestyle, location and driving convictions) to estimate your overall risk. This information is used to help personalise your insurance premium. Insurers clearly take other things into account, but the assessment's essentially risk-profile based. And yes, if they conclude that you're too great a risk, they may refuse to insure you. For example, you may find it more difficult to get car insurance (or at least more expensive) if you have a history of motoring convictions, have very little driving experience or live in a high-crime area.

Financial investment companies do risk profiling too – but, when advising you on suitable products, their emphasis is more on matching your *appetite* for risk to the risks inherent in their various investment products (a bit like dating agencies, where they try to match your personal profile to your 'ideal' partner).

The health and safety risk profile of your business provides a realistic analysis of the nature, significance and potential consequences of all the health and safety threats that your business may typically face. You may decide to profile the whole of your business or you may instead decide to start by profiling part of it (perhaps a particular operation, process, building, department or site), but you ultimately need to profile your whole business to get an overview of your major risks.

Risk profiling goes beyond risk assessment (see Chapter 4). It looks at the consequences of health and safety risks, such as costs, disruption, effect on reputation, business continuity and so on (refer to Chapter 1 for the many business benefits of managing health and safety, and the business consequences of leaving health and safety to chance).

Risk profiling and risk assessment can be easily confused. The truth is that you see a good deal of overlap. The terms are also used interchangeably, so their meanings have become unclear (the Internet has a lot to answer for). This is partly because the former term is a broader (macro-level) business term that has crept into health and safety, and partly because health and safety has tended to focus on risk assessment of individual tasks, processes or substances (so it operates more at the micro-level). But the basic idea is the same – to get a handle on the significant threats that face the organisation, how likely they are, their potential consequences and what you have reasonably in place to deal with them (including the skill sets of your employees).

In our experience, risk profiles tend to be high-level summaries of the range of significant risks facing the business, whereas risk assessments tend to focus on the detail (even down to individual risk types). As a result, risk profiles draw on your existing risk assessments and also cast their net wider, looking at things like complaints, prosecutions and accident/incident data to get a broader picture of risk.

In short, risk profiles need to cover:

- ✔ **The major risks (type/level):** They collect the risks together into a 'profile' or overall picture

- ✔ **The consequences of each risk:** Their likelihood and severity (including business disruption, costs and so on)

- ✔ **The existing risk management approach:** What you already have in place to manage each risk (and how effective these approaches are)

Though there will be similarities between businesses, the risk profile of each business is unique (that is, each business has a unique set of risks in its profile).

In the following sections, we help you get a broad overview of your major risks to determine what you need help with (through your risk profile). We go into the detail of risk assessment methods in Chapter 4.

Developing your risk profile

Risk profiling (and indeed risk assessment for that matter; see Chapter 4 for more on risk assessment) can be as complicated or as simple as you want it to be in terms of managing your major business health and safety risks. Indeed, for low-risk businesses, risk profiling should be quite an easy, simple process. For more complicated businesses, the job will always be proportionately more complicated.

You first need to identify the most significant health and safety risks that your business may encounter:

1. **Compile a list of the health and safety issues that your business faces.**
   Base your list on your understanding of:

   - The activities you do (such as manufacturing widgets on a production line, delivering parcels or operating a call centre)

   - The available guidance/legislation (the things you're supposed to do, such as make sure all your dangerous machines are safeguarded)

   - Historical records of enforcement notices and prosecutions (you will have your own records of these, but remember that you can use the publicly accessible record at www.hse.gov.uk/prosecutions/; therefore, any prosecutions can be discovered by the public and your clients, and such prosecutions may affect your business reputation)

   - Accident and near-miss statistics (again, you should have your own records of these in a database or accident book – *accidents* are things that have happened that have caused some injury or loss; *near misses* are things that didn't cause injury or loss but may have done so, therefore they reveal the potential for an accident)

   - Audit findings (from your own internal audit records as well as any third-party audits from clients or auditing companies – these usually reveal deficiencies in your safety management systems that can indicate as-yet undiscovered risks to the business)

   - Complaints (these may be from the public or your own staff – either way, they may indicate risk areas such as violence, drug/alcohol abuse, reckless driving and so on)

2. **Analyse and rank these issues in terms of their *consequence potential* (their likely impact if things go wrong).** To do this, consider the following questions:

   - Given your current control measures (and your estimate of their effectiveness and reliability), are these issues likely to lead to serious loss or damage (including to your reputation)?

   - Can you quantify this loss or damage (for example, its scale, cost and so on)?

This is where you need to think about your business's risk appetite. How great a loss or damage to your reputation are you prepared to tolerate before you do something about it?

It's a good idea to discuss your risk profile with a group of your colleagues to ensure that you gather the collective wisdom of your team. (You can even make a social event of it, and provide pizza and drinks to encourage people to come along!)

Your resulting list tells you the typical risks that your business may face. You'll probably find that you already know most of them, but some may be a surprise. If your business is simple, with exposure to only general risks, it's likely that you already have sufficient knowledge and expertise to tackle most of the areas identified in your risk profile internally, instead of paying an expensive consultant to help you out. However, the more complicated and specialist your business, the more you're likely to need specialist help. (You may even already have the specialists you need within your business, depending on what you do; if so, they can help you tackle these areas of risk – after all, you hired them for their expertise.)

Maybe you don't have time to tackle all the risks that you identify yourself, or you identify a need for some additional specialist knowledge; if so, by all means bring in external resources (check out the later section, 'Selecting qualified help' for more on this). But you still need to understand what these external consultants are saying, and many consultants get a good deal of their input from you anyway. Why is that, you ask? Well, it's inescapable that you probably already know your own business risks better than anyone else – though you may not realise it yet!

Risk profiling isn't a once-only process. Your risk profile evolves, so you have to revisit it. Your risk profile changes because your risks change. At the very least, the law will change over time, and so may your manufacturing processes. If you really don't understand your business or know what you're doing, you won't be in business for much longer.

As you develop your risk profile, remember to be realistic to think about your *residual* risk – the risk that remains when you take into account all the precautions you already have in place. Don't waste your time looking at *pure risk* (the risk assuming you don't have anything in place to manage it). You'll almost certainly have something in place that makes the consequences of your risks less likely to happen and less severe. So, for example, when it comes to fire risk, every workplace has some basics in place (like detectors, alarms and fire escapes) that already reduce the risk substantially, though a residual risk remains.

Categorising your business

An alternative to creating your own personalised risk profile is to slot yourself into established risk profile categories based on a reduced set of information.

Fire risk profiling provides a risk profile based on the building occupancy type and fire growth rate (that is, the rate at which it's assumed a fire will grow, which you can calculate using figures available for some typical example scenarios). The relevant guidance (BS 9999:2008 – *Code of Practice for Fire Safety in the Design, Management and Use of Buildings*, published by the British Standards Institution) helps you even more here by suggesting risk profile categories for different building-use types, such as for an office used for administrative tasks.

By categorising your business, you can make qualified assumptions about your risk profile. Low-risk businesses are often office-based, where the risks are simple and obvious, as are the solutions. Higher-risk business environments, such as large chemical manufacturing sites and refineries, have complex risks that require careful consideration, using advanced methods to adequately analyse them.

If you have a large business site with a range of working environments, you may have a mixture of risk levels. Some parts may be low risk (such as offices) and others may be medium or high risk (like manufacturing/processing plants or storage areas for hazardous materials). In many cases, you can treat these different risk areas as separate risk profile exercises (but bear in mind that, depending on proximity, a high-risk location may have consequences well beyond the building it's operating within – an explosion may reach nearby buildings, for example).

Evaluating your own capabilities

You may feel inadequate, incapable or incompetent. That's normal in relationships (but try not to make a habit of it at work). However, the workplace is one of the few places where you can justifiably call yourself, and others, incompetent in the true technical meaning of the word, and get away with it.

Competence means being able to do the job that's asked of you to the required standard, and to achieve this consistently (achieving something by complete accident doesn't really count – that's just being lucky. Tomorrow, you may not be so lucky!).

Think of competence as being at two levels – competence at the individual level, and competence at an organisational level (or *collective competence*).

Competence presupposes that you have the necessary knowledge, experience, skill and attitude (individually or collectively). Knowledge and skill may be expressed in terms of formal qualifications, but not always. You may just need to do a little background reading, be shown what to do or practise what's required of you a little before you can master a given task.

Qualifications don't necessarily make someone good at a given thing – knowledge often needs to be backed up with both practical skills and experience.

Experience (through practise) helps you to develop your skill base (and thus extend your knowledge). Doing the job makes you better at it. For example, you get better at driving through practising. (Thieves and liars do the same!)

Most people have varying levels of competence – after all, you can't be good at everything. In addition, many people can be a little inconsistent when it comes to the things that they're good at, and they may not always achieve the standard required of them (people can have 'off' days).

When you understand your risk profile (refer to the earlier section, 'Understanding the risk profile of your business'), you're in a good position to decide whether or not you can deal with the risks you've identified yourself. To do this, you conduct a *competence gap analysis* (which assesses the difference between the skills you need to enable you to address the major risks, compared to the skills you actually have). The gap is what you need to fill – either by training existing employees or contracting the skills gap out.

It may already be obvious to you whether you already have the expertise you need to analyse, assess and control all the areas that you identified in your risk profile. If you don't personally, maybe someone else in your organisation does. If you're a tenant in a multiple-occupancy building (like an office block), you may need to coordinate some of your solutions with other tenants, such as emergency evacuation procedures (for example, when the fire alarm goes off). With this example, you actually get a helping hand – the landlord usually takes responsibility for coordinating this sort of thing and you may even discover some helpful and friendly advice indirectly through their (or their consultants') expertise.

Be confident. Most small or medium-size enterprises (SMEs) are perfectly capable of dealing with at least some of the health and safety essentials themselves. SMEs also (though not always) tend to be in the lower-risk end of business, with businesses based in offices, shops and training rooms (for example, a commercial training business). These businesses have simple, obvious risks, and, as such, business owners can apply simple solutions to their risk issues.

If you're in a low-risk business, you don't need any special skills (don't even think about wearing your underpants on the outside – it doesn't give you any special powers). You can instead use your super-powers of deduction (or, of course, this book!) to find the guidance you need to advise you on the risks you can expect to encounter, as well as tried and tested, pragmatic, cost-effective solutions. You have only to find, read and implement (see the next section, 'Navigating the Maze of Official Guidance', for more, plus Chapter 21 for some nifty tools to help you assess risk and choose controls, and Chapter 22 for advice on some helpful websites).

Even so, you may not be that confident at first because it's all new to you. You may, for example, benefit from some basic instruction or training so that you understand how every aspect of your business is connected and you can think about things systematically. Risks can be unexpectedly interconnected – it can be dangerous to try and solve one risk in isolation because you may end up increasing the overall level of risk.

Scaffolding sounds like a great solution for when you need to work at height, but you have to factor in the additional risk of erecting it. If the job at hand only lasts for a short time, you may be able to find a better alternative.

You can find a number of introductory-level courses from organisations such as the National Examination Board in Occupational Safety and Health (NEBOSH), the Institution of Occupational Safety and Health (IOSH) and the Chartered Institute of Environmental Health (CIEH) to help build your confidence. Make sure that your chosen course is suitable for your business. These courses by their nature are general because they're designed to prepare people for a wide range of issues that you may encounter in a variety of working environments. But if you don't need to know about fork-lift trucks, tower cranes or luffing jib cranes (don't ask), you may decide that a more tailored course (or part of a course) will work better for you and your business. And if you're planning to make a career in safety, you have plenty of vocational safety qualifications to choose from that can prepare you for a life in safety.

You also need to appreciate the danger of not knowing what you don't know. However, you can't allow yourself to overthink this danger. If you have the right attitude and you recognise the need to ask for help when you reach the end of your skill set (rather than allowing your ego – or any fear of being seen as incompetent – to get the better of you), you're off to a good start. Nothing in life is perfect, and you get better by doing.

Selecting qualified help

If you can, it's good to do some of your business's health and safety yourself. After all, you know your business better than anyone else and, ultimately, you're responsible for it. You're also likely to work harder to implement the solutions that work with and for you.

That said, if taking care of your health and safety responsibilities independently isn't your thing (or your team simply can't find the time in between attending parties, dealing with accident investigations and making court appearances), you may decide it's time to sub-contract in some external expertise.

You've probably used a contractor before at some stage, perhaps for home improvements – decorating, fixing the roof or building an extension – and you may have gone to reasonable lengths to identify someone suitable for the job. But if you don't find the right person, you may end up wondering if you can do a better job yourself, or realise that you're not getting the agreed outcome.

External safety people usually call themselves *consultants*; they're primarily brought in to consult with you on your business's needs. Consultation is a two-way process, so a good consultant will ask you lots of questions about how you do your work and what you want out of it. The consultant really doesn't know your business as well as you do, so this dialogue is important – and a good consultant will want to give you a service/product that fits your business. They do this by coming up with solutions that are proportionate, affordable and workable: tailored to meet your needs.

Selecting qualified help isn't as easy as it sounds, and finding a good contractor may take time and energy. It's worth finding the right people, however, otherwise you may find the entire process a waste of time, energy – and money.

You may wonder where to start, but think about selecting a builder. You'd look to who any of your neighbours use (quite easy in a multi-occupancy building – you don't even need to step outside), and you'd ask if your neighbours were happy with the work. If you don't have any near neighbours (because your mansion and estate is so vast) you may instead ask for references. You'd satisfy yourself that they have sufficient experience and a good track record for the work you want them to do.

You can take the same approach when seeking a health and safety consultant. You'll probably also check that they're a member of a relevant trade body. (For health and safety consultants, the main professional bodies are IOSH and the International Institute of Risk and Safety Management – IIRSM.) Both organisations have various membership grades depending on qualifications, experience and a commitment to continuing professional development

(CPD). For example, if a consultant is a chartered member of IOSH (they have CMIOSH after their name), it's a good indicator of their respectability and expertise, because it means that the consultant has high-level safety qualifications, has significant experience, keeps up to date on health and safety legislation, and abides by a code of conduct (they can face disciplinary procedures if they act outside of this). You may also find them on the Occupational Safety and Health Consultants Register (OSHCR) – a searchable database of consultants – but a good consultant may not be on this list if they're also a CMIOSH (being on the OSHCR isn't compulsory and it's not free either).

Don't mistake qualifications or memberships for competence. Sometimes an initial meeting (or even a telephone conversation) can help you decide if a consultant is right for your business before you sign on the dotted line.

You can't guarantee that you'll find a good consultant, but running these checks is better than sticking a pin in the telephone directory and hoping for the best. Don't expect a good health and safety consultant to come cheap either; however, if you use them only for what you need, their service represents good value (refer to the earlier section, 'Evaluating your own capabilities' to make sure that you're maximising your in-house skills). Like all professionals, you pay for both the cost of the specific job the expert consultant is doing, as well as for all the years of training that helped them to develop their expertise.

Be very clear on what you want the consultant to help you with. If you're woolly (like a sheep) about your needs, engaging a consultant becomes an expensive waste of time.

Navigating the Maze of Official Guidance

Unless you've been off-planet for a long time, you know that the world is full of far too much information for mere mortals to assimilate. Finding what you need (well, more precisely, what's useful) can be a challenge, so we've pulled together a list of the best places to start when looking for useful health and safety guidance:

✔ The law is at the top of the food chain in the UK. These laws are the bits that you must obey (even if no one understands what they say). Chapter 17 covers the way the law works and the two most important pieces of legislation that set the whole framework – the Health and Safety at Work etc Act 1974 and the Management of Health and Safety at Work Regulations 1999. You can also find all UK law relating to health and safety online at www.legislation.gov.uk/.

✔ Beneath this essential legal framework, you have layers of interpretations that cover what the law means. At the top, you have the official Approved Codes of Practice (ACoPs), which give practical advice on how to comply with the law. If you follow the advice in the relevant ACoP, it means that you're doing enough to comply with the law.

ACoPs carry special legal significance. If you're prosecuted for a breach of health and safety regulations and it turns out that you weren't following the advice in the ACoP, it's up to you to prove that you complied with the law in some other way. So, this legal significance means that, in practice, it's especially important to pay attention to any advice given in an ACoP. But ACoPs aren't for the faint-hearted. Despite offering 'practical advice', because of the language used within them these tend to be aimed more at safety specialists, so they can be difficult for a layperson to get to grips with. They can be almost as difficult to understand as the law itself (which is mostly written in the language of, and aimed at, lawyers).

All the ACoPs can be downloaded free from the Health and Safety Executive (HSE) website: www.hse.gov.uk/pubns/books/index-catalogue.htm.

✔ Beneath the ACoPs, you get official guidance (again, from the HSE, but this guidance has no specific legal status). This is the truly helpful stuff that's written in everyday language and is easy to understand. You find all sorts of guidance, including sector-specific industry guidance, as well as guidance giving practical advice about very specific legislation.

Sometimes the ACoP and the related HSE guidance is published in a single booklet, so that you get an interactive effect – for example, a specific regulation may be quoted directly as it appears in the legal text, and then a section of the ACoP interprets it, followed by a section of guidance that offers more advice. This process is then repeated throughout the booklet. You can even get 'short guidance' documents, which refer you to more detailed guidance! You can find all of these guidance documents online alongside the ACoPs at www.hse.gov.uk/pubns/books/index-catalogue.htm – again, free to download.

✔ Industry and professional bodies also produce guidance for their members. This is in the spirit of self-regulation, where those who create risks help to work out the best ways to control them. These guidelines aren't always free – check out the relevant organisations for your industry to see what's available.

Some of the best places to find guidance are the websites of those who enforce the law. In the UK, this is the HSE, local authorities (another name for local councils), the Fire and Rescue Service and, for Northern Ireland, the HSENI (the HSE for Northern Ireland). We list ten really useful websites in Chapter 22, but the HSE website (www.hse.gov.uk) is a good starting point for most things.

Regulators don't really want to be visiting places and enforcing the law if they can help it. It's much better for everyone concerned if they instead help you to avoid enforcement issues. You and the regulators want the same thing, after all – to avoid pain, suffering and death in the workplace.

If you work with the regulators, they'll work with you. But if you resist and try to evade your responsibilities, you'll get what you deserve. (It's then a pity if your colleagues have to suffer along the way.)

UK guidance is more helpful than it's ever been, but you do have to wade through a lot of it (dare we mention the pile of European guidance from the European Agency for Safety and Health at Work?). However, it's nearly all well-written, relevant and helpful. It's just that there's a lot of it! (And, we hate to disappoint you, but if you think sleeping with the guidance under your pillow will help to transfer it into your head, we can assure you it won't – we've tried.)

Preparing Your Health and Safety Policy

One of the first positive things that you need to do is write a health and safety policy (no, you don't need to wait for a passing health and safety consultant to do this).

The duty to have a documented safety policy is in Section 2(3) of the Health and Safety at Work etc Act 1974 (see Chapter 17), which states:

> *Except in such cases as may be prescribed, it shall be the duty of every employer to prepare and as often as may be appropriate revise a written statement of his general policy with respect to the health and safety at work of his employees and the organisation and arrangements for the time being in force for carrying out that policy, and to bring the statement and any revision of it to the notice of all of his employees.*

Small businesses are exempt from the above requirement – if you employ less than five employees, your policy doesn't need to be written down (although it makes sense to do so anyway).

Arrangements is of course an ordinary word that basically just means 'practical things you need to do' (like the arrangements you need to make for the New Year's Eve party). In this case, arrangements refers to the practical things you need to do to implement what you say in your statement of general policy. Regulation 5(1) of the Management of Health and Safety at Work Regulations 1999 (see Chapter 17) adds a bit more detail on what the arrangements should cover (again, you only need to write these down if you employ five or more employees, but it makes sense to write them down even if you employ fewer people):

> *Every employer shall make and give effect to such arrangements as are appropriate, having regard to the nature of his activities and the size of his undertaking, for the effective planning, organisation, control, monitoring and review of the preventive and protective measures.*

Taken together, these legislative requirements sound suspiciously like a safety management system (and indeed it is – we look at formal management systems in Chapter 6).

In simple terms, the law is saying that you need:

- ✔ A statement of your general health and safety policy – what you're trying to achieve
- ✔ The organisation to deliver the policy – who's going to do it
- ✔ The arrangements for carrying out that policy – how it's going to be done

In the following sections we explain what a statement of general policy is, and take you through writing your statement of general policy. (The later section, 'Implementing Your Statement of General Policy', looks at the organisation and arrangements aspects.)

Introducing your statement of general policy

Health and safety policies in themselves aren't really anything special. The wording and format isn't the important bit; it's the intent and commitment that they represent that makes the difference in your workplace – the process that you go through, in terms of thinking it through and crystallising your commitment and what it stands for. Don't spend too long messing with precise wording at the expense of getting your policy together in a timely manner.

The problem with health and safety policies is the terminology itself. It's easy to get confused. In this global marketplace, and with the proliferation of management standards, such as ISO 14001 on environmental management, ISO 9001 on quality management and the soon to be ISO 45001 on health and safety management systems (from the International Organization for Standardization, ISO), *policy* tends to mean a relatively short statement that commits you. It may outline your basic approach, but it isn't very long – it's a commitment by senior management to an approach. So, it has little detail but is hugely symbolic (like a mascot, but it doesn't need feeding or brushing).

> ## Policy versus statement of intent: A rose by any other name
>
> If you've been steeped in ISO management standards, you probably call your safety document a policy. If you've only ever known life in the UK, you probably call it a 'statement of intent' or a 'policy statement'. It doesn't really matter what you call it so long as you're clear – you need a statement of general policy (to set the scene) and the people, procedures and other arrangements to bring it into effect or 'make it happen'. The statement of general policy is the driving force and direction behind the action, which is why it's more important than you may think.

In the UK, the main health and safety law (the Health and Safety at Work etc Act 1974 – see Chapter 17) requires you to have a *statement of general policy*, together with the organisation and arrangements for carrying out that policy (that is, a safety management system that's driven by the statement of general policy). Your business's statement of general policy is the equivalent of what ISO management standards simply call 'policy' (refer to the nearby sidebar 'Policy versus statement of intent: A rose by any other name' for more on ISO management standards).

Currently in the UK, for very small businesses (less than five employees), you don't need to write down your statement of general policy.

If you're a sole trader, you may feel like you're talking to yourself if you write your policy down, but you may also find it helpful to have your safety statement in writing. (Some companies like to frame their statement and hang it on the wall for everyone to see, like a family photograph.)

Writing a statement of general policy

The statement of general policy is a rather simple affair for SMEs. It can be a little more involved for complicated, diverse businesses, however, in essence, it says the same thing. Think of it as a line in the sand: a statement about how you mean to conduct your business in a health-and-safety-conscious way.

The following sections look at this in more detail, considering how you tailor your statement of general policy to your business.

Considering your policy aims

If you think about the key health and safety threats to an organisation, what the boss doesn't want is jail and costs; that is, the consequences of a serious accident and any associated legal considerations. So as a starting point, your basic policy aims may be:

- ✔ Zero accidents (including zero ill-health)
- ✔ Total legal compliance

These aims are rather ambitious (some may say impossible!) and set a high benchmark for achievement, so it may be more helpful to give some clues in the policy as to how these lofty aims can be achieved. A more practical and informative document may include specifics such as:

- ✔ Prevent accidents and cases of work-related ill-health by managing the health and safety risks in the workplace
- ✔ Undertake risk assessments and ensure action is taken to remove or control risks
- ✔ Check that implemented actions have removed or reduced the risks and report findings of the risk assessments to all relevant employees
- ✔ Review assessments annually or when the work activity changes, whichever occurs first
- ✔ Allocate specific responsibilities to the individuals identified in the policy
- ✔ Maintain safe and healthy working conditions, for example by providing and maintaining safe plant, equipment and machinery, and ensuring safe storage/use of substances
- ✔ Provide clear instructions and information, and adequate training, to ensure employees are competent to do their work
- ✔ Engage and consult with employees on day-to-day health and safety conditions
- ✔ Implement emergency procedures for evacuation in case of fire or other significant incidents

These aims sound a bit more helpful (if not more long-winded) and give you something to get your teeth into. The first one still deals with your accident threat and the rest will get you a fair degree of legal compliance, and you've now got a bit more detail to work on.

A crafty approach to drafting your statement of general policy is to map it against the elements of your health and safety management system (see Chapter 6). That way, each bit of your system delivers an element of the policy. So, your health and safety management system needs to include:

- Management commitment (including resources – very important!)

- Management control – get managers to control their risks

- Consultation with the workforce – get the workforce on board

- Communication of information – make sure that everyone knows what's happening

- Competency – get everyone trained up

- Risk assessment and risk control – the core element of the whole process

- Active and reactive monitoring – check what's happening

- Regular review – learn from mistakes and improve performance

Your statement of general policy sets out your organisation's commitment and overall approach to health and safety and spells out the main objectives for health and safety performance. Performance relating to targets may be compared with previous performance, or with whatever the best practice is in your industry as a whole (that is, how good are your competitors and why aren't you just as good?).

A final and essential requirement for the statement of general policy is that it's signed by the chief executive officer or managing director – that is, signed by the boss!

Fitting your policy to your organisation

You may be tempted to simply acquire a laminated one-size-fits-all health and safety policy and save a lot of time on developing a home-grown version. You can find endless health and safety consultants who'll provide this service and even generously include arrangements for dealing with risks that you don't have. (Explain to us again why you need to know how to safely handle radioactive sources in a finance office?) The generic health and safety policy satisfies the question 'do you have a health and safety policy?' but completely misses the point. Your policy is meant to be your organisation's demonstration of commitment to achieving its health and safety aims, so 'one prepared earlier' by a third party isn't going to fool anyone.

Ideally, your statement should be written by people within your organisation. They're the ones who know the organisation and how it operates best. There's no harm in seeking external assistance and advice but try to keep that just for *assistance and advice*. That said, external advice can stop you from missing the obvious and provide reassurance and an extra pair of hands if needed. The actual content needs to be tailored to the needs of your business, and your employees should be involved in putting the policy together.

This way, you get the benefit of their day-to-day experience of the job and it's more likely that you'll get their commitment to carrying out the aims of the policy.

The statement of general policy is unique to your organisation, so it's up to you how you set it out. It needs to make clear to everyone what's expected of them to comply with the requirements of the policy, so use simple ideas and concepts. It's a legal requirement to have a safety policy, but it doesn't have to read like a boring legal document.

In a small organisation, a very simple statement should be suitable. Figure 2-1 shows a typical UK statement of general policy for an office-based business.

Health and Safety Statement of General Policy

Empty Head Trading Co. is committed to your health and safety whilst you are at work. We will:

- Properly manage and control health and safety risks in your workplace to prevent accidents and ill-health resulting from work

- Make sure that you are properly trained, given clear instructions and information and appropriately supervised

- Consult with you on any significant matter affecting your health and safety

- Put in place procedures to deal with emergencies (for example, fire and first aid procedures)

- Provide safe equipment, machinery and plant, and maintain it that way

- Make sure that any substances you use are stored and used safely

- Make sure that the conditions in which you work are always safe and healthy

Signed: Ivor Feeling, Managing Director
Date: 22nd April 2016

Figure 2-1:
An example
statement of
general
policy.

© John Wiley & Sons, Inc.

If you think the statements in Figure 2-1 sound a bit grand and sweeping, you'd be right. In reality, no business can get all of this right all the time. But a business that at least tries, and learns from its mistakes, is far better than one that doesn't. This statement effectively commits you (as a representative of your business) to doing the right thing (with legal compliance as a minimum). It's a promise, written for all to see. The act of signing the statement is considered a necessary sign of commitment from senior management.

For a small organisation, the organisation section that you prepare to support the statement of general policy probably won't contain many names, since most of the responsibilities will be allocated to a few people (see the later section 'Getting organised: Make arrangements and allocate responsibility' for more on this).

Even in larger organisations, the statement of general policy needn't be over-complicated. The statement is setting out common health and safety aims that apply broadly to all workplaces. The key difference between organisations from a health and safety point of view is the hazard profile, which is determined by the business and what people actually do. So, for example, library assistants aren't exposed to noise but do a lot of manual handling, whereas call centre operators are the reverse. Consequently, the hazard profile and the associated risk assessments determine how much content you need to include in the arrangements that accompany your policy (which we discuss in the next section, 'Implementing Your Statement of General Policy').

Implementing Your Statement of General Policy

It's all very well writing a grand statement of general policy (okay, then, it's just a page, not quite the Magna Carta). But you also need to decide how you'll carry out the commitments you make in your policy statement: what, in practice, you have to do to make it happen, and who will do it.

The statement of general policy never stands alone. If it did, it would be useless – fine-sounding words in a nice frame, but no more than that. Actions speak louder than words. Your need to implement your policy, which requires planning: people need to be organised, responsibilities need to be assigned and arrangements need to be put in place (for example, to write procedures and provide resources) in order to get things done.

Your statement of general policy and its implementation are therefore closely linked. The statement is the springboard for the action because it demon-strates the commitment behind it. Many people even make the assumption that the term 'policy' *includes* all this organisation and the arrangements required to carry it out: they may gather all of the related documentation together in one place and call it a 'policy document' or even just a 'policy' (as opposed to a statement of general policy). Perhaps people think that a thick document that covers all the details looks much better on the shelf in their offices than a rather thin policy statement. But no, the two are different but inextricably linked. Commitment should always lead to action.

The following sections look at implementing your statement of general policy, considering how to make it real (what you will do practically and who will be responsible for getting it done) and how to resource your health and safety activities.

Getting organised: Make arrangements and allocate responsibility

It's a good idea to break out all the promises listed in your statement of general policy into natural responsibilities and task groups. You can then create a table where each 'promise' is assigned to a responsible person, along with a description of what's practically required to make it happen. If you have a larger organisation to consider, you may like to distinguish between *accountability* (the person with the authority to make decisions, so typically a senior manager) and *responsibility* (the person or people who carry out the work). (In a smaller business, it's probably going to be the same person covering both aspects.)

Safety should be everyone's responsibility. If you end up lumping all safety tasks to one specific individual, it undermines that concept and people get the subliminal message that it's all someone else's job. So, if you have a *health and safety officer* (someone charged with the specific responsibilities for helping you manage your business's health and safety requirements), avoid assigning everything to them, and share the responsibilities out a little, including to yourself. This shows that you take improving health and safety in your business seriously (if a manager gets involved in an aspect of the business it shows that they think it's important – we bet you've never met a manager who doesn't know how much money's being made!). However, while it's good to get management involved, some tasks may need a specialist health and safety person. In these cases, your role is to have a clear idea of what needs to be done and find the best person to do it – as a manager, you're still accountable after all.

Imagine that you assign responsibilities across more than one individual, perhaps even to a team or task group. Your task group's list of responsibilities may look like this for the first policy 'promise' (refer to Figure 2-1 for a reminder of this sample policy):

Policy:

Properly manage and control health and safety risks in your workplace to prevent accidents and ill-health resulting from work

Responsible:

Ivor Feeling, Managing Director (overall responsibility)

Duncan Disorderly, Office Manager (day-to-day responsibility)

How this will be managed:

Risk assessments (including those for specific activity types) are the main way we identify significant risks and decide on any precautions that are needed to control them. We will review them if things significantly change (such as new ways of working).

Part of your commitment is to train your employees on health and safety (we cover this in more detail in Chapter 3). Practically, you may provide health and safety instruction as part of an induction for new employees. You may also do this for contractors who come onto your site (if it presents significant or special risks to their health and safety). If you require employees to wear any special protective equipment, they may require training that covers how to put it on properly (to make sure it's effective). Make sure that employees are properly trained, given clear instructions and information, and are appropriately supervised.

Another commitment is to consult with your employees (also covered in Chapter 3). So, you may have a safety committee (where you consult with employee representatives), or you may prefer to discuss safety issues with all employees directly, through a briefing. For emergencies (see Chapter 7), you probably also have a fire evacuation plan, protected escape routes and a muster point, together with fire extinguishers and emergency instructions posted on the wall. For minor injuries, you can provide access to a first aid kit (at the very least). And so it goes on.

We cover developing safe systems of work and emergency procedures in more detail in Chapter 7.

Consider a metal widget factory. What procedures do you think you need?

You need your general safety management system arrangements in place, including fire and first aid. But you also need arrangements to deal with the specific hazards of widget making, such as handling metal stock, operating machine tools, welding, noise, vibration, and oxygen and acetylene use, to name but a few. Therefore, you expect to find procedures for manual handling, operation of machine tools, operation of handheld vibrating tools, and storage and use of oxygen and acetylene. You don't have to write these procedures from scratch because they come out of the controls and safe working procedures that your risk assessment process delivers (see Chapters 4 and 7). But they give you the control you need to make sure that all your business activities are carried out to the necessary health and safety standards.

You need to regularly review your statement of general policy and your practical implementation arrangements. That way, you're poised to take action if your business experiences significant changes to people's responsibilities or to the way you do things, or if an incident demonstrates that you need to think your responsibilities through more carefully.

In low-risk workplaces, you probably won't need to make many such changes. However, it can make sense to schedule in a review every now and again. Think of it like going to the dentist for a check-up: you may just need to polish up your existing procedures on occasion.

In smaller businesses with a more compact management structure, you need to have distinct responsibilities for strategy and planning, day-to-day management, compliance with safe working practices, and specialist advisory and operational health and safety.

When your organisational structure is in place, you can track your policy aims down through the organisational chart to see exactly who's responsible for what. So, for example, if a policy aim is to ensure competence, it should be possible to identify exactly who's responsible for training needs assessment, training programme development and implementation of training so that you can ensure it happens.

Making sure the resources are available

Health and safety should be 'adequately resourced' to at least meet the legal minimum. In practice, resources are finite and you may have to justify why health and safety deserves them, especially if you're going beyond basic compliance.

You can make a business case for health and safety initiatives in the same way as any other area of workplace expenditure. *Cost–benefit analysis* is the fancy term used for the tool that helps you decide how much cash to spend on what.

With health and safety, the capital and running costs of a comprehensive ventilation system for woodworking machinery, for example, are easy to estimate. However, the benefits of better dust control are much more difficult. They're mostly based on reducing risk: of ill-health, of fire and explosion, of ill-health compensation claims, of enforcement action, of reduced productivity from a demoralised workforce and so on. But you're not exactly sure what the chances are of any of these happening, nor when, so it's more difficult to make a fully quantified business case. But don't let that stop you. There's more to persuasion than just financial arguments (refer to Chapter 1 for more on why health and safety makes good business sense).

Avoid the extremes and be sensible about resourcing. Because the costs that arise from poor standards of health and safety can be difficult to establish, you may be tempted to ignore them and do nothing; that is, to accept the risk. This will undoubtedly come back to bite you. Or you can take the opposite approach and automatically give anything with a health and safety label unquestioned priority, but this is likely to waste some of your valuable resources on trivia and, importantly, to divert them from other equally pressing business priorities (like product quality control or dealing with environmental pollution).

The middle path uses the available budget to adequately resource a prioritised health and safety programme wisely. If you have confidence in the rest of the policy setting and planning programme, your decisions for action will be well thought out and warrant financial backing without the need for justification from a precise cost–benefit analysis.

Chapter 3

Engaging Your Workforce with Health and Safety

. . . .

In This Chapter
▶ Introducing the concept of a positive safety culture
▶ Getting management to take charge and lead the way
▶ Committing to health and safety consultation
▶ Keeping your employees informed about health and safety
▶ Developing a competent team

. . . .

*Y*ou've probably managed a lot of people one way or another. You may even be familiar with quite a bit of management theory. And chances are, you've been on the receiving end of poor management.

The relationship between a business and its employees works within what you can think of as a 'psychological contract'. Each side of this contract has some basic expectations about how the relationship works. Some are explicitly written in the employment contract, while others are implied (that is, unwritten but reasonable expectations). Employers expect a fair day's work. Employees expect a fair wage and to be paid on time and treated with respect. When either party feels that this mutual agreement has been stretched or broken, they may withdraw from their commitment to their role, which can have a detrimental impact on a business.

To run a successful and safe business, you need to engage your team with health and safety from day one in order to create a positive safety culture. If everyone is on the same page and working together, adhering to safety rules and legislation will simply become good practice in your organisation, rather than a constant challenge.

You create a positive safety culture in part through four important Cs: *control* (through effective management), *co-operation* (through effective consultation and team participation), *communication* (by keeping your team informed) and *competence* (by training your team). Mastering these key elements can help your business to thrive and your colleagues to collaborate – and we're sure that your business will feel the benefits of an organised and motivated team in all areas of your business's operations.

In this chapter, we take a deeper look at developing your safety culture, before exploring each of the four Cs in more detail.

Developing a Positive Safety Culture in Your Workplace

You can manage your employees in a number of different ways (and if you don't believe us, check out the business section in any decent-sized bookshop). Certain approaches suit some situations better than others. For example, you don't want to become embroiled in a debate in the midst of a critical emergency – instead, you want a slick, well-thought-out action plan that you can implement in a jiffy. But regardless of how you and your team approach management, work tends to go better if managers and employees co-operate.

The relationship between manager and employee isn't a democracy, but it shouldn't be a dictatorship either. Managers need their employees to be engaged with their work, and employees need good management to succeed as part of an effective team. (Check out the nearby sidebar 'Being a fair judge of management discretion' for an example of how easy it can be to break a solid working relationship, and some tips for avoiding this.)

You need effective manager–employee relationships when it comes to managing health and safety too. That way, you can develop a successful safety culture within your organisation.

A business's *safety culture* is its collection of shared values, beliefs and attitudes about safety. It embodies the way that your organisation approaches and acts upon health and safety issues in the workplace.

You can view your safety culture on a continuum from positive to negative. *Positive* safety cultures are those that exhibit what are considered good characteristics, like everyone knowing what's expected of them, always wanting to get better (learning from their mistakes), actively reviewing the risks around them and not tolerating accidents.

Positive safety cultures tend to lead to good safety performance: work processes are well controlled and maintained, and your employees are protected from hazards. You can't assume that everyone will comply with the rules all the time, but you can be confident that if the vast majority of your employees do, any new recruits will do so too in order to fit in (refer to the nearby sidebar 'Establishing your business's culture' for more on this).

Establishing your business's culture

'Safety culture' is a concept that has been around for a while. You may also hear the term 'safety climate' (and often the two terms are used interchangeably).

When you visit a foreign country (or even another region) you become more aware of the different expectations, attitudes, customs and ways that things are done (that is, the different culture). This awareness can lead to some entertaining misunderstandings but also some dangerous confrontations. It's easy to assume that everyone else thinks the same as you and holds the same values. But that may not be true.

Culture is behind how things are done on the ground, despite what the rules say or the boss thinks. Speeding on the motorway is an often-used example of this. If you look around you, you realise that many other drivers are exceeding the speed limit for much of the time. Even if you don't mean to, pretty soon you may adopt the same behaviour, because you feel pushed along by the rest of the traffic. In the same way, when you start a new job, you're likely to follow the culture around you in order to fit in with the majority.

If the vast majority (say 90 per cent or more) of people in your organisation conform to doing things a certain way (the *predominant culture*), new people that join the team tend to adopt that way too. This works both ways – so, to effectively change the culture, you need to get the majority to comply with the new way of doing things. That takes time!

Beware of being part of a business that says it has a positive safety culture but doesn't live up to the claim. Far too many businesses have all the procedures in place but demonstrate a poor attitude when it comes to implementing them effectively – the reality is that they have a *negative* safety culture. You don't want your business to see safety simply as a procedural bureaucratic process. If you sign a document that suggests you've been trained in essential emergency procedures and yet you've merely signed it to tick a bureaucratic box on a checklist somewhere (rather than been allowed time to take in this essential item of training) you're just asking for trouble – the bottom line is that you won't be trained and you won't know what to do in an emergency. That puts people at risk. Don't allow your business to create a culture of pen-pushing and paper-chasing over genuinely effective safety management.

You develop a positive safety culture through developing four basic elements of your business, which all start with a 'C' (we look at these areas in more detail later in this chapter):

- ✔ **Control:** Where you have effective leadership, properly allocated responsibilities and accountability, and clear rules.

- ✔ **Co-operation:** Employers and employees need to work together, seeing health and safety as a partnership rather than 'them and us'. The main ways used to encourage this are through employee consultation (taking their views into account in decision-making) and participation (getting involved in the doing).

- ✔ **Communication:** Telling the right people in the right way what they need to know.
- ✔ **Competence:** Building knowledge, skills and attitudes through training.

Developing a positive safety culture is more complicated than taking these four aspects in isolation, and they also overlap to a large extent – therefore, you need to consider them together. However, these four elements do provide a good framework to start with – and you only have to remember four things!

Being a fair judge of management discretion

When considering the psychological contract that exists between management and employees – the many unspoken expectations from both sides – the way each party responds greatly affects each side's motivation to participate in being part of the cultural change you're trying to effect.

For example, imagine that you voluntarily work many extra hours for weeks on end on a major project, and then you turn up two minutes late one morning and find yourself being taken to one side for a quiet word of reprimand. You feel unappreciated; you expected fairer treatment – a bit of give and take. You decide to work exactly to your hours from now on and to not do anything more than you're contracted to do.

Now turn it around so that you're the manager. You expect people to work at least some core hours (maybe just because you need to maintain cover for the department during those hours). You also expect to be kept informed if someone is expecting to be late. You may feel that this employee is taking you for granted or setting a bad example that can undermine your authority in front of others.

Seeing things from both sides of the equation can help you to be more objective. The result in this situation is that the employee feels disgruntled and has decided to be unco-operative because he feels that the manager behaved in a petty and disproportionate way. The manager, on the other hand may feel as if they've nipped the issue in the bud so it won't happen again. However, there may be unintended consequences – the objective of nurturing an engaged, motivated and productive employee has been snatched away from the manager in one swift movement.

It's not quite that simple. You have rules and you often need to find a balance between what is right, fair, proportionate and enforceable. Some people will abuse the system too, so you can end up applying a rule that was designed for a few difficult people to the many (and this uneven approach may lead to all sorts of problem, as this example shows). But if you want the best out of people, employers/managers and employees need to work within the shared expectations of fairness, reasonableness, discretion and engagement.

Don't forget that, amidst all your roles and responsibilities, being an effective manager requires you to use your best judgement – that's why many rules allow management discretion.

Each of these four Cs hides a good deal of complexity. For example, take the whole area of control. Just having rules isn't enough – people may not follow them if they have no will to do so and they experience no consequences if they don't. Even if people do follow the rules, without a *learning culture* (with employees actively looking for hazards, learning from mistakes and building competence) you'll only get so far.

Taking Control

Your business's management needs to take *control*. We don't mean an armed coup or a takeover. We do mean making sure that, in terms of health and safety, employees know what they're responsible for, what's expected of them, what they've committed to do, and that you'll appropriately supervise and monitor their performance. But before managers can deliver on these important points, they have to show, through their commitment and visibility, that they're in charge. They have to lead.

Being an effective manager involves sustained effort, not quick fixes. You need to lead from the front and keep your team on the ball. Your employees need to feel confident that you're behind them when it comes to safety decisions, just as they need you to have their back when it comes to wider business decisions.

In the following sections, we look at how business owners and senior managers can lead from the front to implement positive approaches to safety, and how you can empower the mangers within your organisation to take charge of their teams in a way that leads to effective safety management.

Leading from the front

The one thing guaranteed to undermine leadership is not doing what you say you're going to do – or not acting in a way that's consistent with what you're urging everyone else to do.

Politicians are accused of this all the time: making a policy U-turn after an election-winning promise isn't going to win you any future followers. A health and safety equivalent is a manager designating an area in which you have to wear a hard hat and then failing to wear a hard hat themselves while travelling through this area.

Credibility is important when you're in charge; your employees look to you as a role model (like a rock star or a footballer, but without the Bentleys, mansions and fancy moisturisers). Your employees will take their lead from your behaviour, so think about the consequences of the way you behave.

Don't do as I do

This is a true story from the archives of experience from one of your authors. We set the scene at a large chemical manufacturing plant.

The previous site manager had instituted a site-wide no-smoking policy. You could only smoke in the designated smoking huts (much like a glorified bus shelter) provided outside the site. (*Note:* This was long before the law in the UK changed to ban smoking in public enclosed spaces.) This site-wide rule wasn't specifically implemented for safety-related reasons (though he obviously never allowed smoking in areas used to store and process flammable liquids – that would have been reckless and stupid); it was implemented as a general health policy (protecting other employees from the effects of smoke) that was extended to the whole site.

When the new site manager joined the organisation, an employee noticed him smoking just outside one of the side doors of the site and, as gently as he could, introduced himself and filled him in on the site rule. The site manager wasn't happy and the conversation didn't go well. All credit to the employee here for being brave enough to approach the new manager. . . .

The site manager went to find the employee again later that day. They had a much better chat, where the employee gently reinforced the fact that, although he was the boss, it was pretty difficult to enforce a rule for others when he flouted it himself.

As the boss, he was perfectly entitled to look into changing the rule, but what he couldn't do was ignore it. He realised that (which gained him some respect) and decided to keep the rule and obey it himself.

What you say and what you do need to be aligned. If you say that health and safety is important but you communicate that health and safety isn't important – by your attitude, through subtle behavioural signals or in what you say or do – it can infect your organisation's safety culture. (Check out the earlier sidebar 'Establishing your business's culture' for more on this, and also take a look at the nearby sidebar, 'Don't do as I do' for more on the importance of keeping what you say in line with what you do.)

You may have signed your name on the dotted line of your business's statement of general health and safety policy (refer to Chapter 2 for more on creating this important document), but you have to live it to show your employees that it's important. That means getting out of your office and, at least occasionally, showing your face to the troops (if you have any). A business's management team needs to be seen to be involved – not sitting outside the system it created. You also need to respond to any health and safety issues that are brought to your attention and not just ignore them – you're setting an example to everyone around you this way, plus it's good practice!

Don't forget to consider the health and safety implications that may arise from any business decisions that you make – these issues should never exist as an afterthought. For example, reducing staffing may save you money, but it may also reduce safety in a critical process. Significant changes may need to be managed using a risk assessment approach – looking at how the change degrades (or improves) existing controls and influences the level of risk (see Chapter 4 for more on risk assessment).

A business has many competing demands. Safety isn't more important than your other business activities (like delivering a product/service), but it should be treated as equally important so that you see it as something that helps you succeed.

You start by concentrating on the significant risks to your business, not the trivial ones. Just as with any area of business, you need to make effective use of the resources you have available.

Part of this is also allocating specific health and safety responsibilities to individuals. People tend to focus on the responsibilities that they're given. If health and safety is just fitted in when people have time, it won't get to be the priority it deserves. It'll become a 'rainy day' activity and may easily be neglected (refer to Chapter 2 for more on allocating responsibilities).

Empowering your managers

To empower each member of your management team (and to therefore empower all employees) you need to clearly allocate responsibilities and authority. People need to know what they're responsible for, in terms of health and safety, and you need to integrate safety into their existing roles. (This goes for anyone in any management position, whatever their title. You may call them supervisors or team leaders rather than managers – okay, you may also call them other names, but not to their faces.) Chapter 2 discusses assigning specific safety responsibilities to managers.

In the normal business planning cycle, define some health and safety priorities and objectives; make some performance targets to give you something concrete to aim at. Make a handful of *key performance indicators (KPIs)* – these are the things you've decided to monitor that are important enough to your business that you keep them under review (see Chapter 8 for more on how you can use KPIs to monitor and improve safety performance). Your KPIs need to be aligned to your statement of general policy and appropriate to your business risk profile (refer to Chapter 2). That's because this policy is supposed to set the whole safety direction for your business, defining what your business has already decided is important. Making sure that your KPIs are aligned with your statement of general policy means that every aspect of your business is working towards the same goals. Your KPIs also need to align with your risk profile (also refer to Chapter 2) because your business has identified these areas as the biggest risks to tackle.

Most businesses at least monitor their turnover and profit. In terms of health and safety, you may decide to set KPIs such as the number of accidents per month, the number of audits or inspections carried out (compared to the audit plan) or the amount of training hours completed. Each of these has associated targets – for example, for accidents you may set a target of zero (but some are more realistic than that); for inspections, you may aim for four per month.

Imagine that you run a chemical company. You may have a problem due to far too many chemical spillage incidents, which are caused by overfilling storage tanks from the tankers that turn up every day at your tanker off-loading point. Until now, you've treated each incident separately – but you've never really solved the problem.

It's reasonable to assume that something's wrong if a chemical company can't control its chemicals. If this issue continues, it's only a matter of time before something worse happens – like serious injuries, an explosion or an environmental incident. At the very least, the business is wasting its products, money and time.

To manage the situation, you may decide to set an objective that you're going to reduce such incidents, and even set a target of a 70 per cent reduction over the year. You need to develop a plan that covers how you're going to achieve this target (oh, how reality spoils the dream). This plan needs to designate someone to lead the effort and deliver on the objective. It needs to involve finding out the root causes of the spillages and recommending various solutions, like installing/maintaining high-level alarms and automatic shut-off devices. You then need to review the recommendations and make sure that you've allocated enough resources to the agreed solution that enable you to get the job done.

You need to make sure that the responsible person gives you progress updates at regular intervals – maybe you can add this to the agenda of your regular management team meetings. Track progress against these objectives just like you track everything else you do in your business.

Sole reliance on accident/incident-based KPIs is never a good idea. This type of data is reactive and based on organisational failures. KPIs and associated targets always skew behaviour – if you judge people by them, they'll try to achieve these targets in whatever way they can, even if this means subverting the system (so your employees may feel they need to hide these events and under-report just to meet the target). KPIs can work against you developing a positive safety culture unless the culture is very honest, open and free of blame.

Always remember to choose some so-called *active* measures for your KPIs – these are forward-looking KPIs (that is, they're not failure data) that can indicate underlying issues that, if treated, will stop an incident from occurring.

If you run your business in an office environment, you may suddenly discover that you've never done any kind of risk assessment. However, unless you're a very small business, risk assessments are a legal requirement (see Chapter 4). Because of your risk profile (low risk, general office work; refer to Chapter 2 for more on evaluating your risk profile) and large use of computers, you may decide that concentrating on getting risk assessments done for general workplace issues, fire and specifically for computer use need to be your initial priorities in order to become legally compliant.

A general workplace risk assessment (which we cover in Chapter 4) is designed to get you to consider the significant risks in your office, and can even help you identify your priorities (knowledge is power, so they say). Your objective here is to become legally compliant with regard to risk assessment, and your target is to complete those three risk assessments (for general workplace issues, fire and computer use) in the next month and to fix any issues identified in the subsequent two months.

This example is purely illustrative, but it's really no different from any other managing that you do (though in this case, you can't just ignore it and hope it will go away!).

Your employees need to be properly supervised – this is part of your commitment to them as a manager. When people are being watched, they're more careful to follow the rules. Supervision needs to be proportionate though: the more expertise and experience someone has, the less supervision they need, and many people can then effectively supervise themselves (that is, perform their duties without the need for help or direction) and perhaps even become supervisors themselves.

New and young employees need more supervision to help protect their health and safety – and that of other people – because employees new to the team are less familiar with the specific hazards in your workplace. Young people may not have the experience needed to appreciate the potential seriousness either – that's just part of growing up and maturing. Legislation on risk assessment directs you to especially consider young employees, for just these sorts of reasons.

Co-operating with Health and Safety

Another aspect of safety culture development involves your wider workforce – you need to ensure that everyone *co-operates*. In the UK in the early 1970s, the team behind the Health and Safety at Work etc Act 1974 recognised that the workplace needed less confrontation and more co-operation between employees and management. Now people live in enlightened times – which means that you may have to speak to your team and not just tell them what to do! In other words, you need to consult with them.

Consultation means taking on board what others say and weighing it up in your decision. Consultation doesn't take away your management role when you make a decision; it should *influence* your decision.

Consultation isn't telling people what you've already decided. Neither is it giving them just two seconds to think about a decision, big or small – you need to give people time to think about the options as part of the consultation process; otherwise, you won't get a sensible debate.

In the following sections, we consider the benefits of engaging your team in developing your safety culture and then look at how you can put consultation into practice.

Understanding the benefits of participation and involvement

When your employees are able to make a contribution at work, they feel part of the team. They develop ownership and motivation; they're more likely to comply with your rules, procedures and other control solutions if they help you to develop and implement them.

Your business can also benefit greatly from the input it receives from employees. The person who does the work often knows rather more than you do about the issues of the job (and perhaps even has the solutions taking shape in their minds – they're just waiting to be asked!).

Getting input into your risk assessments – getting your employees to do or contribute towards risk assessment, procedure development and monitoring (inspections, audits) – means that you often end up with better, more effective solutions. An employee who has partly developed a procedure for doing their work is more likely to follow it, and they have a vested interest in it being successful. Getting your employees involved with health and safety directly (by engaging in consultation processes) also develops trust and breaks down hierarchical barriers within your organisation. It's an organisational win-win situation!

Many years ago, when one of your authors was still young and innocent, he was conducting an inspection of a large machine as part of a chemical process. He normally used a checklist and hardly asked anything of the operator; the operator typically stood by the side of the machine, kicking his heels. The inspection went smoothly, until he asked the operator if there was anything to add, and whether the machine was operating okay. The operator said that it was, but that every time he put his hand under a cowling (which he pointed to) over the switch, he got a small electric shock. (Of course, your author told him not to put his hand there!)

It turned out that the wiring was faulty – something that may never have been discovered if the question wasn't asked. The operator didn't seem to think that there was anything seriously wrong with the machine (what commitment to the work at hand!). This conversation was very much in the early days of consultation, so he was probably surprised that anyone was interested (sigh).

Consultation therefore has many benefits. You can always find somebody out there who knows more than you, so why not use that knowledge and develop your ownership of a given situation at the same time.

Consulting through safety committees or representatives

You can approach consultation in a formal or informal way:

- ✔ **Formal consultation:** You have highly organised structures in place. A classic example of this is a health and safety committee and the use of representatives (the main focus of this section). You're not just providing a place for the team to retire to for tea and biscuits – your committee has a purpose, and your representatives have responsibilities.

  In a unionised workforce, health and safety committees are often formed of both union representatives and management. The purpose of the committee is to act as a forum to review anything significant that has a health and safety implication; therefore, it reviews recent accidents (and trends), new technologies, changes to staffing or processes, health and safety training arrangements, and risk identification/control arrangements and information.

  Importantly, representatives bring health and safety issues to the attention of the employer by representing the interests of employees. Managers don't always know what it's like out there on the shop floor – a voice representing employees can help to bridge that gap.

  In these days of reduced unionisation, representatives can either be *union representatives* (appointed by the union) or *employee representatives* (elected by the workforce). You may have a little of both. Legally you see some technical differences between the rights of these two types (for example, only union representatives can request the formation of a safety committee), but in practice employers are encouraged to treat them the same (it's certainly less complicated that way). Therefore, even non-unionised workplaces, with a reasonable-sized workforce, may have a safety committee.

If you want to know more about these technical differences, look at the Safety Representatives and Safety Committees Regulations 1977 and the Health and Safety (Consultation with Employees) Regulations 1996.

An alternative to representation in non-unionised (or partly unionised) workforces is *direct consultation* with each and every employee. This form of consultation is better suited to smaller workplaces. You may even have a committee *and* decide to consult directly with your colleagues, depending on your workforce.

Find a consultation process that works for you and your business, whether it's just you operating as a sole trader, you heading a small team, or you driving a large-scale operation.

✔ **Informal consultation:** You can consult informally with your employees through a number of channels. You may have a casual chat in the corridor that alerts you to a central issue, or find that discussions in performance appraisals reveal health and safety-related nuggets of crucial info.

Don't forget to involve your external contractors – you have a legal duty to consider the safety impact of your business's activities on others. You may already involve your contractors with regular project team meetings, so ensure that health and safety is part of that (see Chapter 7 for more on external contractors).

If you occupy a shared premises – like an office block used by different businesses – it makes sense to coordinate and co-operate with the other tenants in the building, and the landlord, on areas that affect you all. You can reach out in an informal or a formal way to get the collaborative ball rolling (also, it's the law – see Chapter 17 for more on the legalities here, specifically the Management of Health and Safety at Work Regulations 1999).

Formal consultation is a legal requirement. However, informal consultation is equally important, because it reflects how people more naturally collaborate. If you only do formal consultation, you're missing a trick.

In some committee meetings you may have a seemingly exhaustive list of agenda items; in others, you may not have a lot to discuss. As a manager, you need to listen to all the issues raised and consider what each person says. You normally chair the meeting too – someone with authority needs to be involved in case decisions need to be made. You don't have to be dictated to though. The decisions still belong to you (or your appointed manager). You do need to share certain information that's relevant to everyone involved, such as risk assessments and accident records, but you don't have to share every detail; you can keep some information back (for example, in situations where it's against national security to share certain information, you're protecting personal information that can't be shared without permission, or you're withholding very sensitive business information that may cause major damage to the organisation if word spreads too early).

Safety representatives on your committee also get practically involved by taking part in workplace safety inspections and investigating accidents.

As an employer, you need to allow your appointed representatives the time and resources to fulfil this role. It can't be an afterthought that gets deprioritised due to a busy work schedule.

Talking the Talk: Communicating about Health and Safety

You may think that the business world is saturated in so much health and safety information that one day it's likely to collapse in on itself under its own gravitational force, form a black hole and suck everyone in. You may look at your shelf of procedures sometimes and wonder if space is warping around it in preparation for this collapse (or perhaps your shelf is just going to cave under the weight). It may seem as if there's always more information heading your way.

Consultation and participation (refer to the earlier section, 'Co-operating with Health and Safety') involve a good deal of *communication*. Getting the information that you actually need in a format that works can be a bit of a challenge.

The following sections tackle this challenge, providing you with some tips on keeping your team informed about health and safety, as well as on communicating to your team about health and safety in writing.

Keeping people informed

Not everything is obvious: information needs to be filtered and modified so that it's understandable for – and relevant to – the audience (and it needs to be in the right language for its audience, too). All employees require basic information on health and safety when they join an organisation and whenever things change significantly thereafter.

You can view your business as an *open system* (that is, where your business interacts with, or at least is influenced by, the environment and context in which it finds itself). A system has inputs (that come in from the outside world), internal processes (what it does with the inputs) and outputs (what it produces and sends out). When it comes to health and safety, a lot of information comes your way. Legislation, official guidance and industry body guidance is produced by the bucket-load. Technology moves on, new machines are bought and expectations change on what is achievable within the workplace. Thanks to these varied inputs and pressures, finding out what affects you, keeping up to date and navigating the maze of legislation is probably not something that you look forward to doing.

Try to see mining this pile of information as another form of market intelligence activity. For example, you monitor your competitors to see what they offer; you get information from business alerts on upcoming changes to employment law or new-fangled management planning tools. Health and safety is no different – you just need to deal with it in the same way.

If you can't keep on top of the latest healthy and safety guidelines and legislation, assign someone to do this for you. She needs to get the word out to the relevant parties within your organisation so that everyone has the information that he needs to hand.

Here's one approach that may work for you or your lucky appointee:

1. **Monitor what's going on in your industry and in the wonderful world of health and safety.** Look out for new information coming through – signing up to the Health and Safety Executive (HSE) news bulletins and newsletters is a good start, but industry professional bodies also produce a good deal of guidance that applies legal requirements in a practical, meaningful way to your industry. Indeed, in some cases, the HSE collaborates with industry bodies to produce such guidance.

   Get more detail if you need to – you can access HSE guidance notes and legislation online at www.hse.gov.uk.

2. **Evaluate the relevance and significance of any information that you acquire to your business.** For example, if you notice an amendment to legislation on controlling risks at large chemical installations, it's unlikely to have much relevance if you manage a butcher shop (unless you're secretly storing 50,000 litres of petrol in your shed out the back).

3. **Tell the relevant members of your team what they need to know.** You need to share the information throughout your team (if they need this information for safely completing their work) and make sure that it's modified for the right audience (that is, the bits that are relevant for that group are communicated using the right language – whether everyday or technical language).

4. **Implement any required changes appropriately.** You may need to amend a procedure or you may need to upgrade your control measures. Follow the legislative advice to make the changes that are required in order to remain compliant.

Writing down your procedures and processes

Communication comes in many forms. Writing down the information that you expect your team to adhere to is great practice because you provide your employees with an effective reference that can be relied upon.

Your employees need to know what your responsibilities are to them (as their employer) and what their responsibilities are to you and to others. It's a legal requirement in the workplace for you to share these responsibilities with your employees. You have to display these responsibilities in your workplace on a Health and Safety Law poster (if you can't display it, you need to give the equivalent information to employees directly on an individual basis). You can buy the poster from all good bookshops or directly from the HSE website (`www.hse.gov.uk/pubns/books/lawposter-a2.htm`), and you can download the equivalent information in the form of a leaflet for free.

The poster is direct and no-nonsense; it covers all the facts, including who your on-site safety contact is. The legal framework for a business's approach to health and safety at work is encapsulated on this poster. (***Note:*** The poster is available in English and Welsh.)

To get an idea of the nature of this legal content for employers, here's a short extract from the Health and Safety Law leaflet (available from `www.hse.gov.uk/pubns/law.pdf`. The Health and Safety Law leaflet contains public sector information published by the Health and Safety Executive and licensed under the Open Government License):

What employers must do for you:

1. *Decide what could harm you in your job and the precautions to stop it. This is part of risk assessment.*

2. *In a way you can understand, explain how risks will be controlled and tell you who is responsible for this.*

3. *Consult and work with you and your health and safety representatives in protecting everyone from harm in the workplace.*

4. *Free of charge, give you the health and safety training you need to do your job.*

5. *Free of charge, provide you with any equipment and protective clothing you need, and ensure it is properly looked after.*

6. *Provide toilets, washing facilities and drinking water.*

7. *Provide adequate first-aid facilities.*

8. *Report major injuries and fatalities at work to our Incident Contact Centre: 0845 300 9923. Report other injuries, diseases and dangerous incidents online at* www.hse.gov.uk.

9. *Have insurance that covers you in case you get hurt at work or ill through work. Display a hard copy or electronic copy of the current insurance certificate where you can easily read it.*

10. *Work with any other employers or contractors sharing the workplace or providing employees (such as agency workers), so that everyone's health and safety is protected.*

Health and safety responsibilities are part of a relationship between employees and employers, so here's an equally impressive (but shorter) list from the Health and Safety Law leaflet of things that employees need to do (that's co-operation for you):

What you must do:

1. *Follow the training you have received when using any work items your employer has given you.*

2. *Take reasonable care of your own and other people's health and safety.*

3. *Co-operate with your employer on health and safety.*

4. *Tell someone (your employer, supervisor, or health and safety representative) if you think the work or inadequate precautions are putting anyone's health and safety at serious risk.*

Your business's statement of general health and safety policy, as well as all your supporting arrangements to implement it, is usually communicated to staff in writing (refer to Chapter 2 for more information). Okay, they may not read it, but they will feel the love.

Investing in Your People

The final part of the safety culture jigsaw puzzle is the people in your business. Yes, that includes you. After all, they're the people who get things done. Maybe in a hundred years' time – when artificial intelligence robots have taken over – things will be different, but for now it's humans, with all their issues, that help you to achieve your business goals. If they're going to do this effectively, your employees need to be competent at what you need them to do.

Competence is being able to do a required task consistently and to the required standard. Competence usually involves a combination of the right knowledge, attitude, training and experience. People may be entirely self-taught, or they may get external training (and qualifications).

The following sections look at how you can train your workforce into a super-competent team – and how to keep your employees' knowledge up to date.

Turning your people into health and safety ninjas

In Chapter 2 we talk about evaluating your own competence and selecting external help, and you have similar considerations here. You need to surround yourself with people who know what they're doing and can do that consistently well.

In the world of human resources (or HR), you often hear about competency matrices and competency management. HR experts talk about initial training, development and even continuing professional development (CPD), which is another way of talking about getting your skills in place and staying that way (by keeping up to date).

Usually, you develop a matrix (or table) that pits each organisational role against a set of competency elements. Different roles may require similar information on the same topic; for example, a warehouse operative's matrix may only require a certain level of awareness, while a specialist safety person's matrix may state that they need a lot more detail. A warehouse operative may need to be aware of the general hazards in the warehouse, be able to lift parcels safely and drive a fork-lift truck in an area shared with pedestrians. The first competency area may be common to all sorts of employees, but the other two areas are much more detailed and specific to the role and the activities that the warehouse operative performs.

Safety specialists have a wider role of advising the business, interpreting and applying legal standards, and working out practical, proportionate solutions in the context of your business's operational risks. Your matrix doesn't need to be that complicated – you just need to have a basic idea of what level you're expecting (or you need) certain people to operate at.

You can find a number of ready-made courses (some of which lead to national qualifications) that are intended for specific types of safety roles within a range of industries.

These courses focus exclusively on safety aspects and strategies. Here are a few examples (we don't endorse any of these specifically, but this provides you with an idea of what's popular):

- **Basic level courses:** Working Safely – Institute of Occupational Safety and Health (IOSH)

- **Supervisory level courses:**

  - Supervising Safely – IOSH

  - Award in Health and Safety at Work – National Examination Board in Occupational Safety and Health (NEBOSH)

- **Courses for people with some (limited) safety responsibilities:** If you take this kind of course, you're often on the way to being a safety professional:

  - National General Certificate in Occupational Safety and Health – NEBOSH

  - City & Guilds Level 3 NVQ (National Vocational Qualification) Certificate in Occupational Health and Safety

- **Courses for those who are heading for safety professional status:**

  - National Diploma in Occupational Safety and Health – NEBOSH

  - City & Guilds Level 5 NVQ Diploma in Occupational Health and Safety

  - MSc (a Master's degree from various UK universities)

These qualifications have become widely known and are standard progression routes for developing health and safety training. They can be completed in a traditional classroom setting, through e-learning or by some combination of the two (blended learning – but alas, it never seems to come with whisky).

Matching your business to its training requirements

Training needs to add value to your business. If it doesn't help to make your employees more effective, efficient and productive at their jobs (and so, directly or indirectly, improve profitability), you're wasting your money. Your business isn't a charity (well, okay, it may well be – charities need health and safety too), and you're not training people just for the love of it.

Training also needs to be relevant. Ask yourself the hard question – how is this training going to benefit your business? The benefit may not be immediate – most new recruits don't contribute much in the first few months. Indeed, they initially draw from your resources as you induct and train them in the way the business works. But because you want to invest in your team, you're convinced of the long-term value of this training, and this value is usually realised. That being said, you don't want to get suckered into doing safety training for its own sake.

General health and safety courses (refer to the preceding section) are designed for generalists (that is, those who are likely to come across a wide range of safety issues common to nearly all workplaces) and those who are moving into careers in health and safety (these people experience a wide range of issues and require high-level analysis and problem-solving skills to work out solutions in familiar and sometimes unfamiliar environments). (You can also get low-level versions of these courses, which are designed to get lots of people up to a basic awareness level on a range of topics, so these may be more suitable for employees who have no specific health and safety roles.)

Not everyone needs to do a full-blown safety training course. Some of your employees may only require information on a specific topic or need a bit of specific instruction. You may not have a training need in this case – perhaps your employees need to read some relevant guidance instead to fill the knowledge gap.

You need to evaluate the knowledge/training gaps in your business. You may be surprised to know that specific training is rarely mandated in law. Most of the time it's entirely up to you to decide what you need to do, depending on your business risk profile (refer to Chapter 2 for more on establishing your business risk profile).

You may prefer to design your own training for your employees – you can then target the training to your business.

You don't need to provide a recognised qualification to deliver effective training. You may simply be able to take a topic from a standard off-the-shelf course and ask your employees to complete this to ensure that any gaps in employee knowledge are filled.

If you want to target your training to your workforce, follow a systematic process. This list provides a typical training cycle methodology:

1. **Identify your training requirements.** Compare your employees' current skills with those that are needed by an identifiable role or group; for example, doing fire risk assessments.

Identifying your requirements helps you to develop proper learning outcomes/objectives – the behaviours and skills that you want to see after training; for example, the skills to identify fire hazards and evaluate current fire precautions against best practice standards/guidance/legal requirements.

2. **Devise an appropriate means to test whether your employees have met these learning outcomes.** For example, if you want employees to be able to do a risk assessment, you provide a test to assess their ability to successfully complete a fire risk assessment.

   You may also want to test their underpinning knowledge, but think carefully about what you want them to demonstrate. Some advanced testing procedures ask people to rate how sure they feel about their answers. This can help to weed out the dangerous people – those who are convinced that they're right, but are in fact wrong.

3. **Develop the content/resources and plan to deliver a lesson that's designed to meet your learning outcomes at the appropriate level required.** That is – your awareness level versus a deeper level of understanding. Partly this will depend on what your trainees already know, compared to what they need to know for their job.

4. **Deliver the training.** Typically, training is delivered in the form of traditional classroom-based training.

5. **Check to see whether the training has worked.** Ask employees to take a test to assess their new-found knowledge (refer to Step 2). For example, you may want to check whether people are actually any better at doing fire risk assessments.

6. **Aim for continuous improvement.** Evaluate the whole training process (performance, experience) by thinking about what went well and what didn't go so well to improve the training over time.

This tried-and-tested training cycle model is widely used to develop training commercially. This model should work for any business.

Refreshing employee training

You never forget how to ride a bike. Training isn't like riding a bike (okay, it is a little – people trained you to ride a bike once upon a time, after all). But training is different because it's not a one-time event. You don't use all the aspects of your training equally. You get rusty, and so you need to refresh your knowledge base – and you need to update it as new information comes to light.

How often you refresh your training, and how far you go in each refresher session, can depend on a number of factors. For example, if you never seem to use your training, perhaps the training hasn't been very relevant or you're in the wrong job.

If you've been trained on something and you use this knowledge constantly, you quickly become highly proficient and an expert on the topic. You may not require refresher training, as such; you may instead just need the occasional update on new developments.

Providing blanket refresher training is a waste of valuable resources. Get your team to justify why training is required.

If you get the stock answer – that there's a legal requirement for an annual refresher training session – check this carefully, because it may not be true. Check out the nearby sidebar 'Avoiding training for training's sake!' for a real-life example that shows how easy it can be for a business to assume that some aspect of training is essential when it's not.

Sometimes the best way of checking whether refresher training is needed is to develop a suitable test or assessment (based on the original training) and ask your potential trainees to take this test. If they do well and you don't identify any issues, you may be able to assume that refresher training isn't currently required.

If refresher training is still considered appropriate, it may not have to involve taking the full course all over again. You can instead provide the information as a quick online update, for example.

Avoiding training for training's sake!

One of your authors visited an organisation one day and got chatting to a group of five employees (maybe they thought he looked lonely). They were facing the prospect of yet another annual 'refresher training' (actually, it was more like a full training programme) on asbestos awareness. None of them ever dealt with asbestos, and all the asbestos in the building had already been identified, labelled or removed. They liked the trainer. He was jolly and good at what he did, but despite that were utterly fed up with having to go through the same stuff for the fifth year running. They had stopped listening because they knew it was no longer relevant (if, indeed, it ever had been) to them and it consisted of pointless repetition. They had been told that the annual training was a strict legal requirement — but it wasn't, it was an internal policy decision that had become distorted at some stage and was then taken as an absolute truth.

This incident may sound unlikely, but it's a surprisingly common scenario. It would have been better if someone had taken the time to work out what training (if any) the employees really needed and, importantly, would be useful to them, given their roles and responsibilities.

Chapter 4

Assessing Health and Safety Risks in the Workplace

*R*isk assessment is fundamental to health and safety. The relationship isn't quite as fundamental as the relationship between quantum field theory and theoretical physics, but it is, nonetheless, the stock in trade of health and safety experts. You'll be delighted to know, however, that risk assessment is nowhere near as complicated as quantum field theory (no matter what the experts say!).

In the words of the UK's Health and Safety Executive (HSE), 'A risk assessment is not about creating huge amounts of paperwork, but rather about identifying sensible measures to control the risks in your workplace.' After all, you want your risk assessment to lead to positive action in the workplace – and no one wants to generate mountains of paperwork!

In this chapter, we look at how you can ensure that you get your risk assessment right. It's not rocket science, but it's easy to get distracted as you perfect your assessment process and to forget the whole point – the control of your identified risks – along the way. Don't let this happen to you: set yourself up for success by considering your risk assessment carefully and taking control of any risky business. We also talk you through how to keep things covered and to protect your financial position – yes, we're talking about insurance.

Thinking about Risk

In Chapter 2 we consider the wider topic of business risk profiling in terms of health and safety. This allows you to understand the overall, high-level risks your business faces, the context in which your business operates and your business's general *appetite* for risk (appetite here means how great is the business loss, or the damage to your reputation, that you're prepared to tolerate before do something to manage your level of risk?). Risk profiling is focused more at the macro (high) level, whereas risk assessment tends to be focused on the micro (lower) level (individual tasks and processes). Information from your risk assessments then feeds into the risk profiling process.

In Chapter 1 we introduce some of the health and safety terminology that you use in risk assessments – in particular, the terms hazard and risk, which can easily cause confusion. A *hazard* is anything with the *potential* to cause harm – an object, perhaps, or an activity, action, substance or condition – anything, in fact, that can potentially hurt you. It may not *actually* harm you – but it can potentially harm you, so you need to be aware of the type of harm it may cause so that you can recognise this thing (whatever it may be) as a hazard.

A dramatic but effective example is the tiger. A tiger – a big live adult one, with lots of sharp teeth, standing right in front of you (rather than gazing out at you from the TV) – is hazardous because it has the potential to cause you harm. You may find that it just licks your hand and nothing else happens (if it's well trained, well fed and content); you may get bitten and scratched a few times before you can make your escape; or, of course, you may sustain serious injury – or even become the tiger's next meal.

Risk is closely related to hazards – it's the *likelihood* of that 'potential to cause harm' becoming a reality. Hazards can lead to lots of different outcomes – from nothing bad happening (the tiger just licks your hand), all the way to major disaster (the tiger eats you!). All of these different outcomes present different risks: different chances of an outcome happening, depending on the circumstances. Going back to the tiger in the preceding example, you can't do much about the tiger's nature – but you can influence the level of risk, perhaps by not going into the room with the tiger. By influencing the level of risk, you take better control of the outcome (see the later section, 'Controlling Your Risk Level' for more).

We become accomplished risk assessors by an early age. For example, we all learn to cross the road safely by looking out for vehicles before crossing and then choosing when it's safe enough to cross the road.

Perceiving different levels of risk

All people perceive the world around them differently – they take in information through their senses and then filter, interpret and modify it based on all sorts of things (such as expectations, memories, prejudices and experiences). Therefore, your view of the world may not be as objective as you'd like to think. For example, you may not recognise hazards and risks for what they are and, importantly, you may disagree with others about how risky something is.

Different people have different levels of what they perceive to be acceptable behaviour (they're somewhere on a scale between risk-averse and risk-taking). You therefore need to bear this in mind when you conduct a risk assessment, because everyone brings their perception of risk (perhaps unwittingly) into a risk assessment. That's because risk assessment relies to some extent on not only knowledge but also experience and judgement (albeit with cues from relevant official guidance).

Risk can also be judged differently depending on who's taking the risk – your *risk perception* may change depending on whether you're considering the risks you take yourself or the risks that others' take in relation to you (so, they still affect you; for more on risk perception, see the nearby sidebar 'Perceiving different levels of risk'). For example, you may feel differently about your level of risk if you're riding (and controlling) a motorcycle, as opposed to riding pillion on the same bike.

With a little time and research, you can work out what you need to do to create a safer working environment.

Conducting Your Risk Assessment

Risk assessment is a tool to help you identify and control risk in a systematic and prioritised way. You approach it just as you approach any other aspect of your business – by trying to manage risks properly and proportionately. Risk assessment is a legal requirement under the Management of Health and Safety at Work Regulations 1999 (refer to Chapter 17 for more on these regulations). These regulations are quite general and require all significant health and safety risks to be assessed (to help protect employees and others).

The complication is that you also have lots of laws that cover specific risks (like those arising from manual handling, chemicals, computers and noise to name but a few – all issues that we cover in Part III), and these extra laws also require specific risk assessments. This may seem rather like duplication. But where there's a specific legal requirement for a specific risk assessment, it also often partly fulfils the more general requirement for risk assessment in the Management of Health and Safety at Work Regulations 1999. So, for manual handling risk assessments for example (see Chapter 11), you don't need to do your risk assessment twice.

The output of risk assessment (that is, actually doing something to manage or eliminate risk) is far more important than the process of assessing risk. If it doesn't help you stop people getting hurt or falling ill (or at least limit the potential physical and health effects), then you're wasting your time.

The HSE recommends a five-step approach for conducting a standard risk assessment. You follow these five logical steps (this approach is much favoured by people with five fingers):

1. **Identify the hazards.**

2. **Identify who may be harmed and how.**

3. **Evaluate the risk – consider what you're already doing and whether you need to do anything more to control this risk.**

4. **Record your findings and implement your control options.**

5. **Review your risk assessment and update it if required.**

The above five-step risk assessment approach is basically always the same. The specific tools and techniques you use within each step are what can vary – selected on the basis of the type of risk you're dealing with (and its complexity). In short, risk assessment always needs to be suitable and sufficiently robust to identify the *significant* risks. However, because you need to consider all the *risk factors* (the things that influence risk), the actual tools and techniques you use may vary from the simple (which work to assess risk in a typical office) to the extremely complicated (which work to assess risk in a nuclear facility or oil refinery).

In most cases, different tools tend to be used to help make the 'hazard identification' stage more focused, efficient, detailed and systematic. For example, a simple checklist of common office hazards is a useful aid. But you can also find well-established, more detailed, thorough approaches for specific hazard types too. For example, manual handling risk assessments focus on the detailed range of factors that affect the level of risk from manual handling (such as the characteristics of the load, individual capabilities, the way you're carrying out the task and the environment you're working in – see Chapter 11 for more on manual handling). In an oil refinery, you may well be using advanced hazard identification techniques, such as *hazard and operability studies*, which focus on asking 'what if' questions – looking at how things can go wrong with your process and the potential consequences should it happen. You may also be using techniques that involve measurement or calculation to quantify the level of risk, instead of purely qualitative approaches (which rely more on judgement).

Different techniques are appropriate for different cases, the idea being to make sure that the significant risks are identified, rather than missing critical information. So, more complex risks require more detailed, complex methods to identify them, whereas simple, more obvious risks only need simple methods.

Some health and safety legislation specifies its own type of risk assessment. You need to make sure that you assess risk properly – covering all the factors that may significantly affect the level of risk. For example, the Control of Substances Hazardous to Health Regulations 2002 consider factors such as the level, duration and frequency of exposure, the number of people exposed, and so on when assessing the risk from chemicals (see Chapter 15 for more on the risks associated with using chemicals in the workplace).

When you conduct your risk assessment, you need to check whether a legal requirement exists for you to conduct it in a certain way, to take account of the very specific risk factors relevant to that type of risk. As is true in all walks of life, you need to make sure that you're using the right tool for the job. Part III of this book delves into the many different types of workplace risk that you may encounter as you conduct your risk assessment, and explores their associated legalities. Keep these in mind as you identify the hazards in your workplace. However, a good starting point is the (legally required) general workplace risk assessment. This can help you identify whether you need to do specific risk assessments (such as for manual handling or chemicals) in your workplace.

In the following sections, we take you through a workplace example of how risks can be identified and controlled. We concentrate on a simple qualitative technique before also taking a brief look at how you take a quantitative approach (don't worry, we also explain these technical terms along the way).

Using qualitative techniques

For most workplaces, a simple qualitative risk-assessment technique (following the five steps approach in the preceding section) works wonderfully well. A *qualitative* risk assessment is obtained by using your professional judgement with reference to official guidance, rather than using measurements of any kind (known as a *quantitative* risk assessment – see the later section 'Taking a quantitative approach' for more). You make a judgement on the likelihood and consequences of a particular hazard.

The HSE provides a great online tool to help you conduct a risk assessment for a low-risk office environment at www.hse.gov.uk/risk/office.htm.

Consider a small, light engineering business that makes metal components. It's moved into new premises in a business park, but staff are using second-hand machining tools. The business makes the components by following this process:

1. Materials in

2. Materials handling

3. Machining

4. Oxy-acetylene welding

5. Precision machining

6. Goods out

The business has two directors, three supervisors and 15 operatives.

The main hazards for this type of light engineering business include:

- **Machining tools:** Tools may cut/puncture, strike you and so on (see Chapter 12).

- **Grinding dust:** Dust may cause various lung diseases if you inhale it (see Chapter 15).

- **Noise:** Noise may cause hearing damage (see Chapter 16).

- **Vibration:** Vibration may cause various neurological and vascular disorders, such as Vibration White Finger (see Chapter 16).

- **Storage and use of oxygen/acetylene:** Oxygen can intensify fires and acetylene is a highly flammable gas and can explode (see Chapter 14).

- **Welding:** Welding, as well as starting fires (accidentally), can cause skin burns and eye damage from exposure to UV radiation (see Chapters 14 and 16).

- **Manual handling of equipment and materials:** Incorrect handling techniques may cause back injury, for example (see Chapter 11).

- **Ignition sources and fuel:** In other words, fire risk (see Chapter 14 for more on fire risk management).

- **Electricity:** Electricity may cause electric shock, for example (refer to Chapter 13).

The people at risk of harm due to these hazards can be divided into two main groups:

- ✓ The supervisors and operatives who handle the materials, do the welding and operate the machinery
- ✓ Everyone who works in or visits the building, including the supervisors and operatives (these people are exposed to risk from the building's electrical system, as well as the building's fire risk)

After you identify the hazards, and who may be impacted by these hazards, you need to evaluate whether anybody is likely to be harmed by them. In this case, the business is operating in new premises, so the fire precaution system and the electrical system are both state-of-the-art. The welding kit is brand new, with its own ventilation system, and the gas bottles required to power it are stored in a purpose-built enclosure. Noise levels aren't particularly high, and the use of handheld vibrating tools is minimal. However, the machining tools (a horizontal miller, a vertical miller, a grinder and a lathe) present a problem because they're second-hand, and none of them have proper guards. Also, the delivery of raw materials is a little unplanned, simply relying on whoever happens to be available to do some heavy lifting, pushing and pulling, and it's likely that somebody is soon going to strain something, or worse.

In order to manage the risk level here, you need to take the HSE's advice and implement 'sensible measures to control the risks. In this case, the business may consider the following:

- ✓ **To resolve issues with the second-hand machining tools:** You can start by finding out what the current standards are for providing safeguards for these machines. Check out the HSE website or its many publications offering good practice guidance, or turn to the EEF (the Manufacturers' Association, formerly known as the Engineering Employers' Federation: a trade body which aims to support the manufacturing and engineering sectors) for advice – or any other relevant trade body. You can also contact suppliers of machining-tool guards for their input, as they can provide you with the specifications you need to ensure safe guarding on all your machines. You may even find that some additional machine-based training is helpful. Chapter 12 looks at machinery-related safety issues in more detail.

- ✓ **To overcome manual handling issues:** You can find guidance on these concerns in the Manual Handling Operations Regulations 1992 (these cover work that involves lifting, lowering, pushing, pulling or carrying of loads). These regulations take you through a more detailed assessment to help you identify your options to reduce the risk of injury. In this case, the business may require a few handling aids (that is, equipment that helps you handle loads and reduces the risk of manual handling injuries), and it may need to provide some additional staff training. Chapter 11 delves into the details of these regulations and provides other tips on manual handling.

After you place proper guards on your machines, put your handling aids into place and train your staff as required, you'll find that you've significantly reduced the risk of injury. Job done!

In this section, we've taken you through a practical example of how a risk assessment works, using a common-sense approach. In the following sections, we take you through the more systematic (qualitative) approach, following each of the five steps we identified in the earlier section, 'Conducting Your Risk Assessment'.

Identifying hazards

You may have heard the old saying, 'if it can go wrong, it will go wrong'. That sounds a bit fatalistic, but the sentiment is that things do go wrong if you don't take steps to reduce the opportunity for them to go wrong. To identify hazards, you need to look out for what can go wrong, under the reasonable assumption that, at some stage, it will go wrong. You want to look out for any kind of hazard or way in which someone may come to harm in your workplace – before you're alerted to the dangers courtesy of an accident happening right in front of you. Hindsight is a wonderful thing, of course – so how do you make sure that you don't neglect anything and that you can prevent potential accidents before they happen?

It may be enough to walk around the workplace, perhaps with a hazard checklist to help you identify common hazards, and observe what's going on while noting potential issues. It's also useful to talk to people (if you like that sort of thing), such as safety representatives and other staff, to learn from their experiences and to take into account their concerns. You're looking for potential accidents or causes of ill-health, so any input is valuable.

In the light engineering business example from the earlier section 'Using qualitative techniques', you consider the hazard topic of mains electricity as you wander around looking at the workplace. It's present on the premises, and the potential consequences of contact with a live conductor may be fatal. However, the site is a new factory unit with a recently installed (and so inspected and tested) electrical system, so the likelihood of a shock is ordinarily minimal where it's used in most day-to-day activities (but don't forget about non-routine cases, such as maintenance work on the electrical system or equipment connected to it). If the business was operating in an old Victorian building with an electrical system in serious need of refurbishment, your judgement of the level of risk may be very different.

If your workplace is more complex, you may require a more systematic approach – for example, by tracking everyone throughout their working day, from clocking in to going home, and identifying every way in which each person may be harmed. You'd then have a complete picture of all your hazards.

This process may sound rather tedious, but techniques such as *task analysis* can help you to do this on a more manageable scale. Task analysis can sound grand but all it means is looking at the task in detail. You take a particular task, divide it up into a number of steps, consider each step separately, and use this to identify the potential hazards associated with each stage of the task – using your knowledge, observations, discussions with employees and any available guidance. This technique is commonly used for developing safe systems of work (see Chapter 7, where we look at task analysis in more detail).

If you want to take a comprehensive approach to identifying hazards, you may like to make a formal inspection of your workplace using a checklist or inspection form. This is useful purely as an aide memoire – to make sure that you cover things systematically and don't forget anything important. If you just go into an area with a blank piece of paper, you may find that you have to revisit it several times because you miss something important that you later remember to check (or you may end up missing it completely).

Checklists prompt you, but they may not cover everything, so it's always worth having extra space to note any issues you discover that aren't yet on your list.

One way of identifying hazards using a checklist is to use the 4 Ps approach. It examines your:

- ✔ **Premises:** Looking at issues to do with the building, such as floors (slip and trip issues), doors (including fire doors), obstructions/storage of materials (fire risk), level of lighting (especially emergency lighting availability), condition of access equipment (stairs, ladders and scaffolds), condition of toilets and so on.

- ✔ **Plant and substances:** Looking at work equipment (whether machinery has missing or damaged guards, and whether portable electrical appliances have been checked/tested), and whether chemicals are properly stored and labelled.

- ✔ **Procedures:** Considering whether you have written procedures for emergency evacuation, risk assessment and so on.

- ✔ **People:** Considering behavioural issues, such as whether people follow established rules (like wearing personal protective equipment – PPE – in designated areas/tasks).

Using a methodical approach to identify hazards helps you to ensure that you don't miss anything. Use whatever works for you – for example, you may have developed a checklist based on your experience of common issues that occur in your workplace or industry, so this would be a sensible approach for you.

You can find plenty of checklists available for free on the Internet. They don't all use the 4 Ps approach; they may instead group hazard types together in some other logical way. For example, take a look at the checklist developed for workplace inspections by the union UNISON, available online at `www.unison.org.uk/content/uploads/2013/06/On-line-Catalogue194653.pdf`.

Considering who may be harmed

You need to link the hazards that you identify in your workplace to who may be harmed so that you have a clear picture of the potential accident sequence that you're concerned about. If you identify the use of machining tools as a hazard, you then need to examine the particular machines that you're concerned about (for example, a lathe), and the people who may be affected (for example, the employees who operate the lathe – where loose clothing may become entangled in the rotating spindle – and other employees working nearby, who may be struck by loose materials).

 Identify the different types of people who are exposed to each hazard – this can influence your choice of control measures to reduce the risk. For example, you can use control measures such as training to protect employees, but, while this can indirectly make it safer for others, you can't easily put others, such as members of the public, through a training course to protect them.

 In the engineering workshop example mentioned in the earlier section, 'Using qualitative techniques', you may protect visitors (such as members of the public, clients or supplier sales representatives) using very simple measures, such as by excluding them from hazardous areas or making sure that they're closely supervised (accompanied) at all times. The later section, 'Controlling Your Risk Level', explores control measures in more detail.

Evaluating your risks: Do you need to do more?

Evaluating risk is simply coming to a conclusion as to whether, given the measures you already have in place, your risks are controlled to an acceptable level. These risks are your *residual* risks – the risks that remain when you take into account your control measures (assuming that they work properly, of course). For the majority of workplaces, this doesn't have to be complicated, and you can evaluate risk by listing the control measures you have in place against each identified hazard (or issue) and comparing this list to the relevant guidance or best practice (such as from the HSE). The difference between the two gives you a clue as to whether you're expected to do more to control your workplace risk.

 Some organisations prefer to use a risk rating system, such as a risk matrix, to assign a rating of likelihood (of harm) and severity (of harm) to each identified hazard and thus evaluate risk. A *risk matrix* scores a hazard's severity and likelihood by allocating numbers to these, such as: low (1), medium (2) and high (3), and multiplies the outcomes to give an overall rating, which you can then use to judge the acceptability of the risk and determine your priorities for taking further action. For example, imagine that you have an event that has a potentially fatal outcome. You assign it a 3 on the severity scale (high severity). You also decide that this event is very likely (therefore, it also has a grade of 3). The overall risk rating is therefore 9 (3 x 3).

Table 4-1 shows an example risk matrix for the light engineering business's risk assessment (refer to the earlier section, 'Using qualitative techniques').

Table 4-1	Risk Matrix for a Light Engineering Business		
Hazard	*Severity (1–3)*	*Likelihood (1–3)*	*Rating (1–9)*
Storage and use of oxygen/acetylene	3	1	3
Fire precautions	3	1	3
Machining tools	2	3	6
Electrical installation	3	1	3
Welding fumes/grinding dust	2	1	2
Noise	2	1	2
Vibration	2	1	2
Manual handling	2	3	6

Fire, explosion and electrocution all have potentially fatal consequences but are well-controlled and unlikely to be realised, so score a total of 3. The hazards presented by the use of machining tools and manual handling have less serious consequences, but they're poorly controlled and therefore more likely to cause injury, so they each score a total of 6.

Using a risk matrix helps you to establish the level of risk associated with a particular hazard and to prioritise what you need to tackle first (see the later section 'Prioritising your actions' for more).

You need to be sensible when you assign values to the likelihood and severity ratings for your risk matrix. Where you can foresee a range of different outcomes from the same hazard (think of the tiger from the earlier section 'Thinking about Risk'), the common-sense approach is to consider the typical severity of harm and likelihood, rather than the worst case. If you opt to assess the worst-case scenario rather than a typical scenario, you may skew your risk matrix towards an unlikely set of values (having decided that everything can potentially end in death) and end up selecting over-the-top control measures.

Risk matrices can be quite dangerous in the wrong hands (that is, the hands of those with little knowledge or experience), because you require informed judgement to make good estimates. If you underestimate the risk (and so ignore a serious risk inadvertently) or overestimate the risk (giving far too much priority to a trivial risk), you're wasting time, money and energy and potentially creating trouble for your workplace (see the warning on the HSE website about this: www.hse.gov.uk/risk/faq.htm – check out the 'What are risk matrices?' section). (We look at an example of a risk rating system in Table 4-1.)

A risk matrix doesn't offer a quantitative risk assessment – the numbers have no meaning in terms of their relative size and they're used purely to rank the potential hazards (enabling you to prioritise your control actions).

Recording the outcomes as you go

Putting health and safety into practice involves action rather than paper-work. However, because risk assessment is such an important tool, you want to make sure that you record how you arrive at your decisions.

Risk assessments are a means to an end (rather than an end in itself). The main legislation that requires risk assessment is the Management of Health and Safety at Work Regulations 1999 (see Chapter 17 for more on these). The purpose of your risk assessment is to identify the control measures that you need to take in order to comply with the law. You're ultimately interested in identifying the control measures rather than the process leading to them.

If you have fewer than five employees, you don't need to write anything down, but it's useful to write things down anyway just so that you have a permanent record to review at a later date. If you have five or more employees, the law says that you must write down the significant findings of your risk assessment. However, for many SMEs, this doesn't need to be a big exercise; just note down the main points about the significant risks that you identify in your risk assessment and record your conclusions and the resulting control options you take.

Maintaining effectiveness by reviewing

Few workplaces stay the same. Sooner or later, you may introduce new equipment, substances and procedures that can lead to new hazards.

Keep your risk assessments up to date and review your business's activities on an ongoing basis. Ask yourself:

- ✔ Have there been any significant changes in what your business does?
- ✔ Are there improvements you still need to make to control measures to reduce the risk further?
- ✔ Have your employees spotted any significant problems (new hazards)?
- ✔ Do you need to take on board lessons from accidents or near misses?

You need to make sure that your risk assessments stay up to date because they're working documents – and businesses experience ongoing change. Aim to review your risk assessments every year – but if you find you have a lot of updating to do, you need to do review them more often. Be guided by your experience – if you don't see significant changes from year to year, you may be able to review your risk assessments across a longer timescale.

Taking a quantitative approach

Qualitative risk assessments should do the trick in most cases if you're a small business in a low-risk environment. However, if you operate in a higher-risk industry, you may find that you need to take a more sophisticated approach.

When you conduct a *quantitative* risk assessment, you're aiming to calculate the probability or frequency of a specific event. Unlike a qualitative risk assessment (where you evaluate that the risk of an electric shock is unlikely based on your knowledge and experience), you're trying to pin down the frequency of the risk to a numerical estimate, such as once every 10 or 100 years. You can then compare these results with criteria (published by the regulatory authorities) on what's considered an acceptable or a tolerable risk.

To make this comparison of your estimates with regulatory criteria, you need suitable data to get you started. This data allows you to calculate the probability or frequency of a defined event. You mainly use quantitative risk assessments in high-hazard chemical and nuclear installations, and in the offshore oil industry, where you need to justify your safety measures to the regulatory authorities.

Imagine that you live next door to a chemical plant that uses large quantities of flammable chemicals. You probably want to be assured that the frequency of a vapour cloud drifting over the perimeter fence, into your street and exploding in front of your house is a lot less than once every ten years! The chemical plant can use data on the chances of loss of containment, and on wind speed, wind direction and possible ignition sources, to calculate the frequency of this potential hazard occurring – and to (hopefully) reassure you.

Controlling Your Risk Level

Risk assessments are a means to an end – they allow you to identify the measures that you need to take in order to comply with the law and make your workplace healthy and safe.

Thankfully, you can find plenty of guidance that covers how to manage your health and safety risks. The following sections explore how you can get your risks under control without getting carried away or leaving your business – or your employees – vulnerable.

Considering your control options

You may find that health and safety legislation aimed at particular hazards starts by telling you not to do it in the first place – perhaps it advises you to avoid carrying out manual handling operations that involve risk of injury, prevent exposure to substances hazardous to health, and avoid working at height.

It's always worth asking the question, 'Can I get rid of the hazard altogether?' Unfortunately, if you're a porter, chemist or scaffolder, the answer is going to be negative! In fact, the realities of the working world mean that many businesses, in order to keep doing what they do, are unable to simply get rid of their hazards altogether.

A more useful question to ask is, 'How can I control the risks so that harm is unlikely?' You have many more options here, including:

- ✔ Trying out a less risky approach
- ✔ Preventing access to the hazards
- ✔ Organising work patterns to reduce exposure to the hazard
- ✔ Issuing protective equipment

 The legislation that requires you to carry out risk assessments (the Management of Health and Safety at Work Regulations 1999 – see Chapter 17) also kindly provides an approach to deciding on control options. It's called the *principles of prevention* and it appears in Schedule 1 in these regulations. It's a set of principles (nine in total) that you take into account when working out the best control options (or collection of control options). At the top of the list is avoiding risks, closely followed by evaluating risks that can't be avoided. Towards the end of the list is the need to give priority to collective measures (things like guards or barriers that protect everybody equally) over individual protective measures (like protective gloves or goggles that just protect the person wearing them – and so rely on being worn properly, or at all, in the first place). At the very bottom of the list, you have instructions that you can give to employees (for example, telling them to be careful). (It belongs at the bottom of the list because avoiding risk is going to be more effective than just telling someone to be careful!) You can find out more about these principles of prevention in Chapter 17.

Creating a safe place of work needs to be your main priority (introducing collective protection that protects everyone equally), rather than keeping individuals safe by relying on personal protection. Any time you see health and safety publicity in the press, you always see pictures of smiling people wearing hard hats, eye protection and high-visibility jackets (which is meant to scream 'health and safety!'); however, personal protection should be seen as secondary – used to supplement collective protection.

It makes far more sense to put an acoustic enclosure around a noisy machine than to provide ear defenders for all nearby employees, or to put in ventilation around a sanding machine instead of providing dust masks to all your employees.

You can categorise control measures into different types. Where you have clear differences in the effectiveness of these controls (as there always are, like in the principles of prevention covered earlier in this section), they're usually arranged in a hierarchy – with the most effective control options at the top and the least effective at the bottom. In practice, you nearly always need to use a combination of methods because some can't be applied (or can't be applied 100 per cent effectively) and so must be supplemented with other methods to reduce the risk. You can find all sorts of hierarchies out there, often related to specific risk types – see, for example, Chapter 15, which introduces a hierarchy for chemical controls.

Using a general control hierarchy

One well-known general control hierarchy is published in the British Standard BS OHSAS 18002:2008 – *Occupational Health and Safety Management Systems: Guidelines for the Implementation of OHSAS 18001:2007* (see Chapter 6 for more on the management system standard BS OHSAS 18001; both standards are published by the British Standards Institution (BSI) and are available from the BSI online shop: http://shop.bsigroup.com/):

1. Eliminate the hazard (for example, by changing a process or taking action to remove the hazard).

2. Substitute the hazard (for example, by replacing a hazardous chemical with one that is less hazardous).

3. Implement engineering controls (for example, using local exhaust ventilation to extract hazardous chemicals or installing guarding on the dangerous parts of machines).

4. Use administrative controls (for example, posting signs and warnings, and creating new procedures).

5. Introduce PPE (for example, safety goggles and harnesses).

You can see how this approach prioritises the types of control measure you can use, but in practice there's often a combination in use. For example, a circular saw is protected by a range of physical guards, is operated in accordance with a strict procedure and relies on trained operators who are very aware of the risks.

Prioritising your actions

Your risk assessment programme may present you with quite a shopping list of measures that you need to take in order to adequately control your risks. Assuming that you can't afford to or aren't physically able to implement each measure immediately, how do you decide which ones to deal with first?

You can use the risk matrix that you developed to evaluate your risks for prioritising what to deal with first – in simple terms, you start by dealing with the biggest total numbers in your matrix (refer to the earlier section 'Evaluating your risks: Do you need to do more?').

It may be useful to take other factors into account too, however, such as:

- ✔ If your safety representatives or the HSE are campaigning on a particular topic (for example, slips, trips and falls), it may be sensible to move this issue further up your list as a priority to make the most of this common goal.

- ✔ If you can easily achieve some of the simple and cheap things on your list, you may decide to get them out of the way quickly rather than wait for their turn in your risk-rated list.

- ✔ If you have high-profile issues, such as asbestos, or ones that can precipitate compensation claims, such as stress, you may want to deviate from the severity/likelihood formula offered by your risk matrix in favour of much simpler methods.

Most workplaces won't need to use a matrix, as what you need to do (or at least the options to try first) is already clear from the relevant best practice guidance (including the official guidance from the regulatory authority, the HSE). Sometimes your priorities won't be clear-cut, and you'll simply need to use managerial discretion and judgement.

Following through

After you've armed yourself with a list of recommendations for control measures that enable you to improve your ability to control risk in your workplace, you need a cunning plan of action to implement these recommendations.

If your action plans are going to deliver your control options effectively, they need to identify the what, who and when:

- ✔ The exact action that needs to be taken (what)
- ✔ The person responsible for seeing that the action is carried out (who)
- ✔ The timescale or completion date for the action (when)

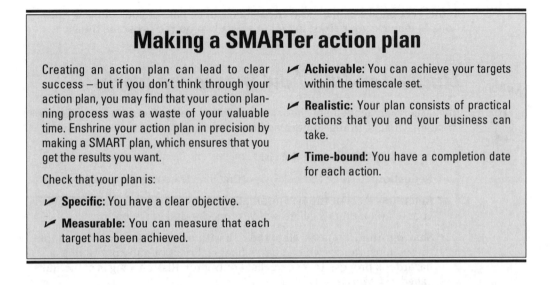

Making a SMARTer action plan

Creating an action plan can lead to clear success – but if you don't think through your action plan, you may find that your action planning process was a waste of your valuable time. Enshrine your action plan in precision by making a SMART plan, which ensures that you get the results you want.

Check that your plan is:

✔ **Specific:** You have a clear objective.

✔ **Measurable:** You can measure that each target has been achieved.

✔ **Achievable:** You can achieve your targets within the timescale set.

✔ **Realistic:** Your plan consists of practical actions that you and your business can take.

✔ **Time-bound:** You have a completion date for each action.

The implementation phase (carrying out all your identified improvements to control) of any initiative, including risk assessments, is notorious for losing momentum when it comes to actual delivery. Don't allow your business to do all the hard work and yet fail to cross the finish line!

The road to hell is paved with good intentions – if you don't convert your plans into serious action, they become useless. Check out the nearby sidebar 'Making a SMARTer action plan' for some SMART advice on keeping your plans in motion.

Transferring Financial Risk with Insurance

Unless you're living at home with your parents and enjoying their financial bounty, you probably have some kind of insurance. You can insure against just about anything – for example, accidental damage to your phone or damage to the contents of your house. Insurance cushions you against uncertainty. You know that, provided you pay your insurance premiums, you won't have to pay the majority of the potentially large sum should something awful happen.

Something awful may never happen, and you may be paying these premiums for the rest of your life without any notable benefit. However, if something awful does happen tomorrow (whether it's dropping your phone in the toilet or something far more distressing), you'll be thankful for your insurance policy. That's uncertainty for you – it's, uncertain!

In this section, we explain how insurance can be part of your range of solutions to manage your risks. In fact, it's legally required for some things.

Understanding how insurance works

Business risk management theory typically talks about four basic options for 'treating' (that is, doing something about) identified risks:

- ✔ **Avoidance:** Stop taking the risk.
- ✔ **Reduction:** Reduce the risk by putting in extra control measures.
- ✔ **Retention:** Accept the risk internally – that is, meet the costs of any loss yourself (sometimes called *self insurance*) – and carry on.
- ✔ **Sharing:** Share some or all of the risk with external parties, for example through insurance (which shares financial risk) or sub-contracting a hazardous process to a specialist contractor. Risk sharing is sometimes called *risk transfer*.

Insurance is a wonderful thing. You share, or 'transfer', your financial business risk outside of the business in order to protect your business. In reality, you don't transfer the risk itself; rather, you transfer the financial consequences. If an insured event occurs, you may find that you have some immediate costs to meet yourself – but your insurer ultimately covers some or all of the related costs. You may resent paying the premiums, but it's worth it when something happens that carries a heavy financial cost.

Claiming on your insurance policy after an insured event will more than likely increase your future premiums. Insurers may even decline to insure you going forward (for example, if you make too many claims in a given period), although being declined insurance directly is not that likely. However, you risk losing everything if an unexpected event leaves you unable to continue trading, and so you may have no choice but to make a hefty claim. Either way, you carry this additional future risk (that may impact your ability to retain affordable insurance) if you have to make a large insurance claim.

Knowing what you must insure

Most insurance is optional and a judgement call – like insuring to cover potential vet bills for your pets. You have to estimate the realistic financial consequences of a particular threat and how likely it is to happen. You can then weigh this estimate against the monthly/annual premiums that you have to pay.

In some ludicrous cases, the cost of insurance over a year can exceed the costs of replacing the goods. For example, it can be cheaper to replace a low-end freezer or washing machine than to insure it against breakdown. But on the other hand, if insurance is very cheap, it can be worth having – even if the event is unlikely to happen. It depends on what level of risk you're prepared to accept (yours, and your business's, *risk appetite*).

Some business insurances are compulsory. In the UK, nearly every employer (with a few exceptions, such as when you don't have any employees or you run a business with close family) must at least have insurance to cover compensation claims from employees who are injured or become ill as a result of the work they do for you. This is called *Employers' Liability Insurance*.

Compensation to employees isn't automatic – and if you take reasonable steps to prevent the accident or ill-health, you may not have to pay compensation at all.

Insurance companies like to sell you insurance packages – collections of different insurance policies that you may want or need. As part of an insurance package, it's pretty common to have *Public Liability Insurance*, which covers compensation claims from non-employees (that is, members of the public); *Professional Indemnity Insurance* (in case you get sued for professional negligence, like poor advice, say); and *Key Person Insurance* (to cover temporary replacement of incapacitated business-critical personnel). These insurances aren't compulsory (unlike Employers' Liability Insurance, which is), but they can be sensible add-ons to your other insurance policies.

Though you can get insurance to cover the costs of defending a criminal prosecution for a health and safety offence (or defending a civil claim for that matter), there are limits. Annoyingly for some frequent visitors to the courts (we don't mean judges or lawyers, obviously), it's rather difficult to insure against fines imposed after a prosecution, especially where it's been shown that you deliberately intended to flout the law (but failed to get away with it).

Chapter 5

Getting Your House in Order

· ·

In This Chapter

▶ Establishing a healthy workplace environment

▶ Maintaining safe buildings and equipment

▶ Looking after workplace welfare

· ·

Your workplace – the office, shop or factory where you work – includes most of the places where you're actually working (including, for some people, outdoors areas like yards, streets, fields or forests) but excludes domestic premises – that is, your private home. For the purposes of this chapter, we keep it simple and focus on standard everyday indoor work premises.

You probably don't work in a grubby, cold building with obvious signs of disrepair. Fortunately, most indoor workplaces are reasonably clean, comfortable and well-maintained. (A caring employer may even provide a toilet (actually, they have to) – and may have it cleaned regularly!)

Your workplace is expected to adhere to laws designed to provide a basic standard in every workplace. These laws set standards on things in your workplace environment that may seem pretty obvious, but are actually fundamental to your health, safety and welfare.

The relevant law in the UK is the Workplace (Health, Safety and Welfare) Regulations 1992. These regulations apply to most workplaces – and where they don't apply, it's usually because some sector-specific legislation is already in place (for example, in the construction industry) that takes precedence. Typically though, you find the same basic requirements wherever you go. After all, everyone needs regular access to water to drink (and somewhere comfortable and safe in which to drink it).

 The regulations themselves provide very little detail about what's really required. But you may find it helpful to look at the Approved Code of Practice (ACoP) that accompanies these regulations – this document provides more practical detail, and we refer to it often in this chapter. You can download it for free from the Health and Safety Executive's (HSE) website at: www.hse. gov.uk/pubns/priced/l24.pdf.

A safe workplace improves employee morale and increases productivity. You may think that providing a safe and healthy workplace is just a matter of abolishing knife-throwing in the office – but in this chapter, you discover that establishing and maintaining a healthy and safe working environment is far more complicated.

But don't be downhearted – we can help you work your way through the legislation to ensure that your workplace is healthy, safe and considerate of the welfare of your team. In this chapter, we explore these three core areas of employee well-being – health, safety and welfare – in turn.

Working Up a Healthy Sweat

Although the Workplace (Health, Safety and Welfare) Regulations 1992 don't provide a definition of what workplace health is, you can think of the relevant elements that contribute to a sense of workplace health as comfort issues, which aren't perhaps quite what you'd expect when you think of 'health' in the normal sense of the word.

Workplace health covers a broad range of issues, the main ones being:

- ✓ **Ventilation:** You provide ventilation to stop the air in the building from becoming stale and polluted.

- ✓ **Temperature:** You maintain a healthy and stable building temperature (whether by heating or cooling; apart from that one day in mid-July, you certainly need your heating on in the UK).

- ✓ **Lighting:** You ensure that employees have enough light in order to see what they're doing (even if some employers like to keep people in the dark).

- ✓ **Cleanliness/waste:** You maintain a clean office environment (which doesn't rely on fairies and sprites to spirit away the rubbish each day).

- ✓ **Space:** You allow enough room for employees to perform their work tasks safely.

- ✓ **Seating:** You provide suitable, comfortable seating (if required for the task at hand). It can be hard work standing all day.

The following sections delve into these workplace health issues in more detail.

Breezing through

One of your authors once met a double-glazing salesman who informed him that 'condensation was the biggest problem of our time'. He had naively assumed that it was nuclear proliferation, poverty or hunger – but he was wrong. Good ventilation (and, of course, double-glazing) was the solution!

Rooms that are poorly ventilated get stuffy, stale, smelly and, in extreme cases, can make you ill – so good ventilation is crucial for a healthy workplace environment. People are forever filling rooms with stuff that isn't good for them (and we don't mean food or ornaments). To consider this simply: you breathe in oxygen and expel carbon dioxide; therefore, you need to replace the oxygen that you use with more oxygen so that you don't fall asleep at your desk!

You can find guidelines on the fresh air supply rate required into a room per hour (see the ACoP document, available from the HSE, that accompanies the regulations: www.hse.gov.uk/pubns/priced/l24.pdf), but in most cases a building's ventilation is taken care of by a combined heating and ventilation system that's incorporated into the building. (Of course, you can also open a window if you feel stifled.)

In most low-risk workplaces (such as offices), general workplace ventilation (such as is provided by the combined heating and ventilation system) is quite sufficient. That's because you aren't normally generating large amounts of contaminants in the air (or producing them at high rates), so the standard ventilation system can cope perfectly well.

Unless you're working outside in a stiff breeze (the kind of breeze that seems to be a permanent feature on the Shetland Islands), ventilation becomes increasingly important when contaminants are in the air. Welding (one of the authors' personal favourite pastimes) can produce significant quantities of metal fumes; chemical processes (or any large volume of chemical liquids) can produce large volumes of vapour. Power tools can also add contaminants to the air when you're grinding or drilling through dry materials – they can quickly generate a large amount of dust. If you're doing extensive work with your power tools, you can quickly overwhelm the ability of the general room ventilation to remove and dilute the contaminating dust – before you know it, your workspace will resemble the London smog events of the 1950s.

Chapter 15 covers the significant issue of ventilating workplaces that generate contaminants, such as dust, chemical vapours or fumes.

Keeping your cool

Workplace temperature can be tricky to manage. You may have an open plan office, like many other workplaces; if so, you'll know how difficult it can be to get the temperature right. At certain times of the year you may see some of your employees wearing coats (to make a point) or short-sleeved shirts (also to make a point, though perhaps less dramatically).

Factories used to adhere to a strict minimum temperature, but modern guidelines recognise how difficult it can be to please everyone. 'Thermal comfort' is subjective – it doesn't always align with the reading on your thermometer.

A number of external factors can influence your thermal comfort (how warm you feel):

✔ Humidity levels (which may be maintained by the heating and ventilation system)

✔ Air movement (perhaps provided by the ventilation system, an open window or even a nearby fan)

✔ Activity levels (for example, consider the difference between manual labour and sitting at a desk – you feel much warmer after physical activity)

✔ Exposure to radiant heat (for example, from direct sunlight or other radiant heat sources, such as heaters and lamps)

✔ The clothes you're wearing (especially if you're wearing lots of personal protective equipment, which can quickly make you hot and sweaty)

✔ Individual perceptions of temperature (some people claim to feel the cold – or the heat – more than others; or it may be psychosomatic)

You'd probably be lucky to get the majority of people to agree on what constitutes a comfortable working temperature!

The suggested normal minimum temperature (as per the ACoP that accompanies the regulations) is 16 degrees Celsius if you're mostly sitting (for example, when you're working at a desk), which you can lower to 13 degrees Celsius if you're more active (for example, working in a warehouse, lifting parcels).

However, you won't find any mention of a maximum temperature (we're not sure why this is the case, but we suspect it's simply because it's rarely an issue in the UK, even in the height of summer). In most open-plan office environments, the issue of room temperature can be divisive, even if it's well above the suggested minimum temperature. Some like it hot (like Marilyn

Monroe and Jack Lemmon) and some like it cool. Often the thing to do is to talk to your team and get a majority view of what works in your open-plan office. You won't go too far wrong and, indeed, a majority view is probably all you can expect to achieve – you can't please everyone.

These minimum temperature guidelines don't apply in specific cases where the work environment is (or has to be) considerably different from what you'd consider comfortable. If you have a cold store (for sensitive chemicals or perishable food) or work outside during the winter months, or you work in a glass-blowing workshop or in a kitchen, it won't be practical to control the temperature in the same way. However, you can still try to get the temperature as close as possible to these guidelines.

To contend with the challenges of a hot working environment, you can try some or all of these simple tried-and-tested techniques:

- ✔ **Ensure that your buildings have good ventilation and air conditioning:** Air flow helps cool you down.

- ✔ **Insulate heat sources:** Wrap hot pipes in insulation.

- ✔ **Provide cool refuges (not just to keep your employees looking good):** Offer a place away from the heat.

- ✔ **Provide drinking water/cold drinks (why wouldn't you?):** Encourage your employees to stay hydrated.

- ✔ **Ensure regular breaks:** Make sure that people can take frequent breaks; also, see if you can vary their jobs so that they can work out of the heat at times.

Acclimatisation can also work (where people steadily adjust to a temperature). Deep mining operations rely on acclimatisation because temperatures can rocket as a result of the heating effect from the surrounding earth deep underground.

To battle the extremes of a cold environment, you can test out the following tips:

- ✔ **Minimise drafts:** Eliminate that wind-chill feeling.

- ✔ **Install shielding/lagging:** Cover up extremely cold surfaces.

- ✔ **Provide warm refuges:** Offer a haven from the cold where employees can warm up.

- ✔ **Keep your employees warm:** Provide warm clothing, such as insulated jackets, trousers, boots, balaclavas and so on.

> ✔ **Ensure frequent breaks/job variation:** Rotate tasks where possible to provide an escape from the cold.
>
> ✔ **Provide easy access to hot food and drinks:** Encourage your employees to utilise these to help stay warm (you probably already provide a kettle and microwave anyway, so not such a big ask).

Outer space presents some challenges (extreme cold and extreme heat) but technically they're beyond the jurisdiction of UK legislation, and as appealing as it seems to contemplate intergalactic travel, we don't take into account such extremities here!

Lighting the way

You need to provide good lighting so that your team can work effectively and stay healthy. The legal requirement is for lighting to be 'suitable and sufficient', a phrase that's not entirely helpful or clear but relates to the appropriateness of the amount and type of light for different areas and tasks. However, you can also find some more helpful basic guidelines on lighting intensity for certain tasks (see the HSE guidance document HSG38, *Lighting at Work*, available at www.hse.gov.uk/pubns/books/hsg38.htm), but in most cases it's *blindingly* obvious if you have enough light to do a job (have you walked into any walls recently?).

The type and amount of light required depends on the task. When you're doing detailed work – such as needlework – you need additional targeted lighting (for example, a desk lamp) as well as normal lower-intensity room lighting.

Most people prefer to work in natural daylight – but you may not be able to offer much choice on this, depending on your building design. The UK can also be rather overcast for much of the year (sigh), so you'll almost certainly need artificial lights for much of the time.

Provide high-risk areas with sufficient light, such as internal traffic crossings (for example in a large warehouse, with high or minimal windows and little natural light, to help avoid collisions between vehicles and pedestrians).

Emergency lighting is also legally required in rooms where your team are especially exposed to danger if the lights go out (for example, when operating a dangerous machine). *Emergency lighting* is lighting that's independent of the main system and is designed to kick in if your standard lighting system fails. It needs to activate immediately and automatically and to provide sufficient light for any short-term responses to the failure of the lighting system (like shutting the machinery down and walking out of the building to ask what's happened to the lights . . .). You rely on emergency lighting not only during emergencies themselves, such as during a fire (where the electrical system may be affected), but also to protect critical light-dependent work (such as in a hospital operating theatre), where failure of the lighting system may have very serious consequences.

Keeping it clean

The Workplace (Health, Safety and Welfare) Regulations 1992 also require you to keep your workplace reasonably clean and tidy (in order to make the place safe – we're not talking about being house-proud). Despite many years of training his children to put rubbish in the bin, one of your authors proved rather unsuccessful in training them to routinely empty it. Don't let that happen to you – hire a cleaner to keep your operational environment in great shape.

Rubbish mounts up, especially in the manufacturing, production and building sectors. Before long, your work environment will look unsightly – and will be harbouring easy-to-avoid hazards.

No one whose business suffered a factory fire ever said, 'I wish I'd had more rubbish stored in that building to feed the fire'. Keep your workplace clear and clean.

Staying spatially aware

When you're plotting out your open-plan office, you need to keep in mind some seemingly complicated rules that are designed to prevent you from squeezing too many people into a room. The rules don't fret too much about the size of the room: the main consideration is the amount of space that's available for people to move around in, taking into account furniture, equipment and so on.

The legal requirement in the Workplace (Health, Safety and Welfare) Regulations 1992 isn't helpfully worded. It says that you need sufficient space (floor area, height and unoccupied space) for the purposes of health, safety and welfare. However, this sounds a little cryptic. The ACoP that accompanies these regulations gives you more of a clue as to what that typically means in practice: for most workplaces, it considers that the minimum should be 11 cubic metres per person (in any calculations, this assumes a maximum ceiling height of 3 metres, so you cap the ceiling height at 3 metres if it's higher than that and use the actual ceiling height if less than that).

To put this cubic space into context, your ceiling at home is probably around 2.4 metres high, which means that you require a floor area of 4.6 square metres per person to walk around. Ordinarily this allows each person a perfectly reasonable amount of room to manoeuver, taking account of typical furnishings and furniture. But if you've got an unusually large amount of furniture in your workspace, you may need to rethink this – either by removing furniture or reducing occupancy, for example. So, if you're going for the world record for squeezing as many people as possible into an office, it will be obvious to all concerned. (If you've ever driven a classic Mini, you know all about confined spaces.) It's also accepted (in the ACoP) that certain rooms (like lecture theatres and retail kiosks) are simply not going to be able to comply with that space requirement and will therefore have much less space per person.

Sitting comfortably

Standing all day is rather tiring. So, if the job can (or needs to) be done while sitting down, the law requires you to provide chairs, and, the ACoP goes on to say, where possible, decent ones at that (specifically with support for the lower back).

You don't need to provide a chair crafted from the finest leather in order to meet your legal obligations. Sourcing decent chairs isn't difficult these days, as you can find plenty of office furniture suppliers and lower back support is almost always built into adjustable office chairs.

Not all roles require seating arrangements, and too much sitting can have negative health consequences (being linked to thrombosis – constant pressure on the thighs, such as you find with air travel – and obesity from the sheer lack of activity).

Sitting at a computer in an office-based environment usually springs to mind when you picture sitting down to do your work – we cover the important risks that you need to consider for desk-bound employees in Chapter 11.

Staying Safe and on the Move

This section of the Workplace (Health, Safety and Welfare) Regulations 1992 collects a number of physical issues together under the banner of safety. Once again, this isn't defined too clearly, other than by reference to the topics – where it becomes clear that they're commonly issues related to the fabric of your workplace buildings.

Workplace safety covers several areas, but the main ones are as follows:

✔ **Maintenance:** You need to keep your workplace in good order, as well as its equipment.

✔ **Floors and internal traffic routes:** You have to make sure that people (and small vehicles) can move around your workplace safely (though the truly beautiful people hover about a centimetre above the floor – or is that the ghosts?).

✔ **Windows, doors and gates:** Your access points need to be obvious, made of safe materials and clearly marked – especially if transparent, such as doors made from safety glass.

In the following sections, we take you through the key things you need to consider to make your workplace a safe environment to move around in.

Maintaining the working environment

Setting up a sensible system or process that contributes towards an orderly and safe working environment is easy, but maintaining these systems seems to challenge even the most well-meaning of people. Life's too short to dot all the 'i's and cross all the 't's once you're up and running – or so you may think until your working environment sinks into disrepair.

The Workplace (Health, Safety and Welfare) Regulations 1992 state that you need to maintain stuff – the workplace itself, and all the equipment, devices and systems in it – but it doesn't require you to keep things looking good or shiny. Health and safety legislation is far more concerned about things becoming dangerous if you don't look after them. Other laws exist that cover specific types of equipment that need to be maintained (for example, machinery – see Chapter 12). These specific laws apply in addition to this law.

Imagine that you own a car (this may not be hard if you do in fact own a car – or you beg, borrow or steal one when you need it). You know that sooner or later, part of your car will wear down. However, sometimes these problems don't matter – you can still pass your MOT and stay on the road if a bit of the door trim falls off, you have a bit of rust here and there (so long as it isn't structural), the carpets get a little worn or your car smells of wet dog. But if you wear down your brake pads or tyre treads, your light bulbs blow, your airbag goes wrong, your seatbelt gets frayed or your washer fluid runs out, you know that you have no choice but to fix them, because you can't do without them working properly.

The same principles apply in your workplace. You need to give special attention to anything *safety-critical* – the items (such as machinery or equipment) that can lead to danger if they fail to work or don't work properly (for example, machinery guards, emergency shutdown devices, pressure relief valves, sensors, alarms and fire sprinklers can all lead to serious consequences if they fail to operate when needed). You need to monitor the condition of any safety critical equipment and maintain and repair it (ideally before it fails, rather than in response to critical equipment failure).

Chapter 12 considers some maintenance strategies for your machinery and work equipment.

Maintaining a safe working environment goes beyond the safety of your equipment and machinery. You also need to look after the fabric of the building, such as its walkways and staircases (see the next section, 'Routing for pedestrians'), maintain the building's infrastructure, such as its heating and ventilation systems (refer to the earlier sections 'Breezing through' and 'Keeping your cool'), and maintain its kitchens and toilets (check out the later section, 'Considering Employee Welfare').

Maintenance issues are often covered by other more specific health and safety legislation too. For example, though this won't generally apply in an office, if you work in chemical manufacturing, you almost certainly rely on dedicated ventilation systems designed to control chemical exposure (see Chapter 15 for more). The laws that cover these cases require you to adhere to a rigorous inspection and maintenance regime.

Routing for pedestrians

People move around buildings throughout the day, and sometimes night, using designated walkways (scaling the walls isn't something that normally happens, except perhaps in prisons). A walkway is usually designed for pedestrians alone, but a particular area of concern arises when pedestrian and vehicle routes cross or they share the same area (such as in a warehouse). Chapter 10 looks at vehicle movements and safe vehicle/pedestrian segregation. In this section, we consider the needs of pedestrian-only environments.

You've probably fallen over a few times in your life. In the health and safety business, these incidents are referred to as 'slips and trips', and they're the number-one cause of accidents in the workplace.

Trip hazards should be easy to spot in theory. Have you ever noticed the difference when walking from a laminated floor to a carpeted one? Or when a path is uneven underfoot and you weren't expecting it?

Common causes of slips and trips include:

✔ **Slippery flooring:** You may have flooring which is slippery (polished marble) or that becomes slippery when wet. During winter, icy outdoor surfaces can make you lose your balance, and wet leaves can be treacherous!

If you're aware that the ground is slippery, you do tend to modify how you walk – therefore, surface/shoe characteristics aren't the whole story; awareness is a valuable part of the mix.

If your workplace includes areas where slippages are likely (for example, in kitchens – from spillage of cooking fat or oil), you may already have special slip-resistant flooring and ask employees to wear non-slip shoes. However, like all personal protective equipment (PPE), it should be seen as a back-up (last resort) to supplement other measures (refer to Chapter 4 for more on the hierarchy of control and principles of prevention) – you can't always rely on people wearing it, and it only helps the person who is in fact wearing it.

✔ **Walkway obstructions:** You need to keep walkways clear from obstructions (as far as possible – there is such a thing as a working mess). Machinery can eject items onto the walkway, either from height (which may strike you in the head) or by causing a slip or trip hazard (perhaps a liquid leaks out of the machine, or a solid object is discarded). Machinery may also protrude onto walkways at unexpected heights (such as low overhead piping).

To prevent trip hazards, you need to inspect and maintain walkways regularly. Your inspection should include an easy reporting procedure for employees to alert management to flooring issues.

✔ **Unsecured objects:** You can easily trip over loose flooring, trailing cables or objects on the floor. Cables running across walkways need to be managed so that they don't get out of hand and cause you to trip over them (you can get readily available mats or cable tidies for that sort of thing if you just can't avoid it) and areas where changes in the floor level occur should have good lighting (changes of floor level can really take you by surprise when you can't see properly).

You run a greater risk of tripping over or slipping up if you're carrying something in your arms that prevents you from seeing where you're going. Avoid carrying unwieldy armloads of materials around the workplace.

Falls can occur due to slips or trips, or they may happen completely independently. Falls are usually caused by uneven or shallow stairs or by standing on workplace equipment (like a chair) to reach high levels (definitely not advisable!).

The essence of the Workplace (Health, Safety and Welfare) Regulations 1992 here is that traffic routes need to be suitable for the intended use (and have to be maintained as such). The ACoP for these regulations points out that you also need to ensure that your 'traffic' routes are strong enough for the intended loads.

If you're looking at installing new flooring, you need to think ahead about likely spillages and ensure that you choose something that is non-slip and suitable for the nature of your working environment.

If you can stop the floors from getting wet in the first place, you can prevent most slips. You can take simple measures to keep your floors dry, such as:

- Using drip trays on coffee machines or for chemicals

- Having a policy of no drinks in certain areas (not just the alcoholic ones)

- Having mats and umbrella stands at the entrances when it becomes wet outside (which helps to reduce the spread of rainwater throughout the building)

- Completing cleaning operations at quiet times to reduce footfall, and therefore the chance of someone slipping

If you already have a slippery area of concern, you may need to treat it with a non-slip substance regularly. 'Slippery surface' or 'Cleaning in progress' signs provide helpful warnings – but keep in mind that these signs can also become an obstructive hazard.

Cleaning slippery surfaces can make the problem worse. One of your authors remembers being in an underground car park in Cannes, France (sadly, not courtesy of an invitation to the film festival), where the surface was regularly polished, and hearing cars losing their grip on the surface and squealing around corners, just trying to hang on. It was like being in a detective movie!

If you're lucky enough to be able to design your new building from scratch, you can eliminate potential hazards before they arise:

- Look for potential slip, trip, fall, machinery or protruding issues and try to design them out.

- Make racking areas larger so that your storage items fit.

- Ensure that walkways don't have pipes running along them.

- Check that your flooring is suitable for the area of work. Think about who will be working in each area, when they'll be working there and what they'll be doing.

- Think about abnormal situations like fire evacuation and adverse weather conditions, and consider how they can change the workplace.

Once you've put in your slip, trip and fall precautions, you need to maintain them. Ask yourself:

- ✔ Are floors regularly cleaned?
- ✔ Are spills cleaned up quickly and investigated to prevent reoccurrence?
- ✔ Are handrails/banisters for stairs in good condition?
- ✔ Are pits and holes properly covered or fenced?
- ✔ Is flooring even and free of holes/depressions?
- ✔ Can employees easily report any issues?
- ✔ Do you grit external walkways in icy conditions?
- ✔ Is the lighting good in all areas?

Asking yourself these sorts of questions will help you comply with the law – making sure that your floors and traffic routes are fit for purpose (free of obstructions, slippery surfaces, holes and so on) and that they're maintained that way.

Opening doors

Glass is transparent to visible light – light (mostly) passes right through glass. When it comes to walking into glass doors, life would be far simpler if you could see beyond the visible light spectrum and detect such transparent materials with ease. (Birds have the same problem too – you often hear of them flying into the windows of buildings with large glass facades.)

What a pile-up!

Escalators and travelators (moving walkways) aren't just for the lazy – and they're not risk-free either. If you have escalators or travelators in your workplace, emergency stops are a must. One of your authors was once travelling down an escalator to Euston's underground station. An elderly woman tripped and fell near the bottom of the escalator, and he was surprised to see a pile-up quickly unfold as people behind her then fell over her (and the people trying to help her up stumbled over her too). It seemed like an age before someone remembered the great big mushroom-shaped emergency stop button just begging to be pressed. That sorted out the problem instantly!

The Workplace (Health, Safety and Welfare) Regulations 1992 says that where it's necessary for safety (that is, where you can get seriously hurt) these transparent or translucent glass doors and panels need to be made from safety glass in case people do walk into them (because otherwise, they experience significant potential for injury when they shatter). An alternative to safety glass is having a barrier to prevent you reaching the glass in the first place (which is then no longer a safety issue because you can't reach it).

Glass doors and panels need to be clearly marked so that they're visible. In many cases, people tend to incorporate a rather artistic design (taking the opportunity to use their brand and share their corporate image) into some part of these doors and panels – which not only makes them look good but also makes their presence obvious. A clearly identifiable window or door can save you, your employees and visiting members of the public from injury. It also saves you from the embarrassment of walking into a glass door – a humiliation that reaches to the very core of your being and makes you a living legend (or the butt of many jokes).

The Workplace (Health, Safety and Welfare) Regulations 1992 also specify that doors on traffic routes that can be pushed both ways should be made so that you have a view of the area close to both sides (otherwise, you can easily be hit in the face when someone opens the door suddenly from the other side). The common way to provide for this is to fit a vision panel in the door. It's good practice to use these types of doors on main routes, even if they don't open both ways.

Considering Employee Welfare

Welfare is the final section of the Workplace (Health Safety and Welfare) Regulations 1992. Welfare primarily concerns personal hygiene and bodily needs or functions – things that, if neglected, can make you ill very quickly.

Workplace welfare covers a number of issues, but these are the main ones:

- **Toilets and washing facilities:** Not everyone can hold their bladder in check all day.
- **Drinking water:** Unless you're a camel, you need to regularly replenish your water consumption to stay hydrated.
- **Rest areas and places to eat:** You need somewhere to prepare and eat food, and take a break – and it's good to get away from the boss.

We take you through each of these fundamental areas in the following sections.

Going potty

Toilets (and associated hand-washing facilities) are something that you definitely need. Most places have quite enough toilets for most of the time. You can provide either segregated toilets (male and female in separate rooms) or unisex ones in the same room if you can lock the cubicles from the inside. (You may experience a feeling of vulnerability when seated on the throne; a locked door provides that comfort factor.)

But how many toilets are enough? The Workplace (Health Safety and Welfare) Regulations 1992 simply state that you need a 'sufficient' number of toilets, which doesn't really help at all. The ACoP that accompanies these regulations adds that you should have enough toilets so that people can use them without unreasonable delay (when you've gotta go, you've gotta go). But how many is enough? The ACoP helpfully elaborates and this information is also reproduced in the tables below. You certainly need at least one toilet (and if just the one, that toilet needs to be unisex too). And although you don't necessarily expect to waltz straight in, you also don't expect to have to queue for too long.

Tables 5-1 shows the HSE guidance on the minimum numbers of toilets for a typical workplace.

Table 5-1	Number of Toilets and Washbasins Required for People at Work	
Maximum Number of People Likely to be at Work	*Number of Toilets*	*Number of Washbasins*
1–5	1	1
6–25	2	2
26–50	3	3
51–75	4	4
76–100	5	5

Source: The Workplace Health, Safety and Welfare (Workplace (Health, Safety and Welfare) Regulations 1992) Approved Code of Practice and guidance. www.hse.gov.uk/pubns/books/124.htm. *The Approved Code of Practice and guidance contains public sector information published by the Health and Safety Executive and licensed under the Open Government License.*

Table 5-1 is applicable to your entire general workforce. However, if you have separate facilities (for example, male and female) or you provide different groups of employees with different facilities (for example, office employees and factory employees) then you treat each group separately when you apply the table.

When using Table 5-1, for every extra 25 employees (or part thereof) over 100, you add one extra cubicle and one extra washbasin.

You can substitute some of the cubicles for urinals in the case of male-only toilets, in which case you can use Table 5-2 as a guide. (For every extra 50 men (or part thereof), you provide an extra cubicle and urinal.)

Table 5-2	Number of Toilets Required for Use by Only Male Employees in the Workplace	
Number of Men at Work	**Number of Toilets**	**Number of Urinals**
1–15	1	1
16–30	2	1
31–45	2	2
46–60	3	2
61–75	3	3
76–90	4	3
91–100	4	4

Source: The Workplace Health, Safety and Welfare (Workplace (Health, Safety and Welfare) Regulations 1992) Approved Code of Practice and guidance. www.hse.gov.uk/pubns/books/124.htm.

The Workplace (Health Safety and Welfare) Regulations 1992 also say you need showers if required by the nature of the work you do. The ACoP that accompanies these regulations clarifies that showers should be provided when the work you do is particularly dirty or strenuous (so may make people sweaty) or may lead to skin contamination, for example from hazardous materials (or you may like to provide them anyway for people who cycle in or who just like to shower at any time of the day).

Drinking responsibly

Dehydration can lead to headaches, loss of energy and dizziness, and these problems increase further when you have employees working outside in warm conditions. Encouraging your employees to stay hydrated not only increases their alertness and productivity – it also improves the health of your workforce.

Employees who work 'out and about' are less likely to be supplied with water, even though the provision of an adequate supply of drinking water is one of a business's key welfare responsibilities. For those working in the office, drinking water needs to be readily available from the mains water supply.

You need to provide drinking water via a water fountain, refillable containers (like those water-coolers that are also the source of many enthusiastic conversations) or – the old, and perfectly acceptable, standby – from a mains water supply. Oh, and don't forget the cups!

Not all cold water taps are fed directly from the mains water supply, and so this water may not be fit to drink. Identify and label your drinking water taps if you foresee any potential for confusion.

Eating in style

You need somewhere to rest and eat – and this 'pop-up restaurant' can be at your desk if you like (assuming you can pull yourself away from your work!).

This rest and refuelling area needs to:

- ✔ Be clean
- ✔ Be located where food can't be contaminated
- ✔ Offer a way to heat food (usually a microwave)
- ✔ Provide suitable washing-up facilities for cleaning utensils and plates (a sink or dishwasher)

If you're often out of the office, you can use your vehicle or other places (such as parks, service stations or similar) to take a break and eat your lunch.

Part II
Managing and Implementing Health and Safety in Your Business

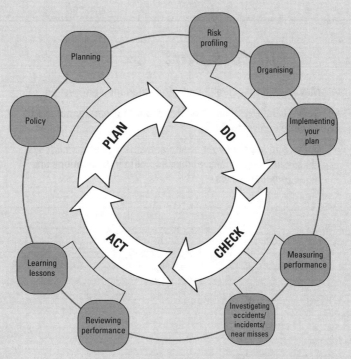

Source: Managing for Health and Safety (HSG65) published by the Health and Safety Executive, 2013: www.hse.gov.uk/pubns/books/hsg65.htm.

Take a look at some early models of accident causation online at www.dummies.com/extras/healthandsafetyuk.

In this part . . .

✔ Move to a formal health and safety management system.

✔ Develop safe systems of work, prepare for emergencies and manage contractors.

✔ Check and improve your health and safety management systems using inspections, audits, accident investigations and management reviews.

Chapter 6

Moving to a Recognised Safety Management System

....

In This Chapter

▶ Understanding how useful safety management systems are

▶ Selecting a safety management system that works for your business

▶ Using the Plan–Do–Check–Act improvement cycle

▶ Installing and certifying your safety management system

....

A cliché doing the rounds in an attempt to be witty about health and safety (a difficult job at any time) informs you that 'safety is no accident'. That's about as good as it gets in the health and safety joke department – but once you've controlled your urge to laugh out loud, the message is actually quite profound, suggesting that in order to be smart when it comes to your business's health and safety, you need a cunning plan.

This cunning plan materialises in the form of a safety management system, a comprehensive approach to ensuring that your organisation is operating in a safety-conscious manner (and that it's adhering to its legal obligations).

Every business will have a safety management system of sorts (often quite informal for small organisations), but the bigger the organisation, the more likely it is to adopt a recognised model. In this chapter, you find out how useful an effective, more elaborate recognised safety management system model is. You also discover your safety management system options, how to implement your system and how to get it certified.

Discovering Why Safety Doesn't Manage Itself

Many people think that the core business of health and safety is trying to prevent accidents (and also ill-health, if you want to be precise). One problem with this approach, however, is the term 'accident'. A common understanding (or misunderstanding) of the word is that an accident is 'an event that happens by chance or that is *without apparent or deliberate cause*'. That is, it was just a case of 'bad luck'. Although a degree of chance and unpredictability exists when an accident occurs, who the accident occurs to, the severity of the outcome and the accident sequence can often be predictable, because you already know from experience that most accidents have known causes. (The more complex the sequence, the more difficult it can be to predict – see Chapter 8 for more on accident causation and Chapter 19 for how more complex accidents can occur in the process industries.) If you're trying to run a business, you don't want the associated cost and disruption when things go wrong – but if you don't have a cause, how can you prevent future accidents?

Smart health and safety operators don't subscribe to this 'bad luck' model of accidents. They aren't hoping with fingers crossed that nothing goes wrong. They know that you can minimise the risks of injury and ill-health through sound management, planning and control, and they spend their time developing an awesome safety management system that can control the universe (or at least their workplace).

A *safety management system* offers a systematic approach to managing health and safety in the workplace. It defines organisational structures, responsibilities, policies, procedures and monitoring arrangements.

Choosing a Recognised Safety Management System

A recognised safety management system can come to your rescue and make accident prevention less of a lottery. After you put it in place it should tick over like a well-oiled machine, keeping your hazards and risks under control. You're now so excited you can't wait to get one and reap the benefits – but what does it look like and how do you make it work?

By *recognised* safety management system, we're talking about systems that conform to a recognised, published model, rather than something you just make up (which may still be quite adequate for your purposes). We look at two of these – referred to as HSG65 and BS OHSAS 18001 – in this section. But first it's worth looking at the value these systems bring.

Safety management systems are part of the more enlightened approach to health and safety of recent times (which aims to manage risks rather than slavishly follow rules and hope that nothing goes wrong as a consequence). But most new ideas are borrowed from somewhere else and safety management systems are no exception. The British Standard (BS) for quality assurance from the 1980s was based on a model that asked five simple but clever questions designed to guarantee success:

- ✔ **What are you trying to do?** You need to develop a policy.

- ✔ **Who is going to do it?** You need to set up an organisational structure to implement the policy.

- ✔ **How are you going to do it?** You need to plan and implement the policy.

- ✔ **How well is it working?** You need to set up monitoring arrangements to check the implementation.

- ✔ **What do you need to do next?** You need to review the system and improve it.

You can adapt these questions for health and safety management (or environmental management or any other function that you need to manage), where the policy is a health and safety policy, the organisational structure is just everyone in your organisation (safety is everyone's responsibility, even though some people have very specific roles to play because of the expertise that you may require), the planning and implementation involves hazard identification, risk assessment and risk control, and the monitoring and review is based on inspections and accident investigation findings.

To save reinventing the wheel, if you want a ready-made safety management system, you have two broad choices:

- ✔ **BS OHSAS 18001:2007 – *Occupational Health and Safety Management Systems: Requirements*** (published by the British Standards Institution (BSI): http://shop.bsigroup.com). This is a specification (a British Standard, in fact) for a management system, against which you can be assessed (by an accredited independent third-party organisation) and certified. It involves a lot of paperwork, external assessors and cost, but it has promotional value for your organisation.

- ✔ **HSG65 – *Managing for Health and Safety*** (published by the Health and Safety Executive: www.hse.gov.uk/pubns/books/hsg65.htm). This is the cheap and cheerful option, a more simple and straightforward model that can be implemented in-house in any type of business without too much cost and trouble.

BS OHSAS 18001:2007 (the 2007 is just the year it was last updated) sets out a model for managing health and safety. Though you don't have to do so, to utilise this standard to its best advantage you need to bring in an accredited third-party independent auditing organisation. *Accredited* means that it's approved by the United Kingdom Accreditation Service (UKAS) to audit against that standard (so the third-party organisation's auditing activities are checked and completed to a consistent standard). These third-party organisations will audit your system against BS OHSAS 18001, and if you pass their exacting checks, you get a certificate to say that you've met these standards (a process called *certification*, see the later section 'Working towards certification' for more on this). The cost is often quite reasonable (for a small or medium-size enterprise, or SME) and it can certainly enhance your image. In fact, some of your customers may insist that you have a certified management system, otherwise they won't do business with you; at the very least, it can make filling in supplier approval questionnaires a doddle, because you can lift safety information easily from the procedures you've written to answer their questions.

At the time of writing, BS OHSAS 18001 is due to be replaced with ISO 45001. But don't fret too much – good management systems are good management systems. So, if you end up with BS OHSAS 18001, it should be perfectly possible to change to ISO 45001 when it comes in.

HSG65 gives guidance on good practice and pushes the idea of risk control through active management of health and safety. However, it doesn't require certification by an outside body and the guidance is freely available.

Looking at Safety Management System Elements

All management systems are based on the fundamental business management improvement cycle of *Plan–Do–Check–Act (PDCA)*. This cycle can be used to both describe an entire management system and also describe and improve each process within it. In fact, originally PDCA was developed as a systematic problem-solving approach. So, when you use the PDCA cycle to describe how a safety management system works, it's being used to solve the 'problem' of poor (or no) safety management. Table 6-1 outlines the four stages in the PDCA cycle.

Table 6-1	The Four Stages of the Plan–Do–Check–Act Cycle	
Stage	*Problem Solving or Process Improvement Usage*	*How the Cycle Is Used to Develop an Effective Safety Management System (such as HSG65 or BS OHSAS 18001)*
Plan what you're going to do	Define the problem, identify the issues and plan possible solutions.	By creating policies, strategies and plans for controlling risk, and so on (refer to Chapter 2).
Do what you're going to do	Select solutions and implement them.	By organising people (assigning responsibilities), assessing risks, putting in precautions to control risk, training people and so on (refer to Chapters 3 and 4).

Stage	Problem Solving or Process Improvement Usage	How the Cycle Is Used to Develop an Effective Safety Management System (such as HSG65 or BS OHSAS 18001)
Check that what you're doing is working	Check that the solution(s) work as you intended (so you need to monitor and measure the outcomes).	By measuring performance (checking that risks are controlled with things like inspections) and investigating accidents/incidents (see Chapter 8).
Act to improve on what you're doing	Make any further improvements required to fix any issues that you discover in the *Check* stage.	By reviewing performance and learning lessons from accidents (see Chapter 8).

Figure 6-1 shows the PDCA cycle in a more visual format.

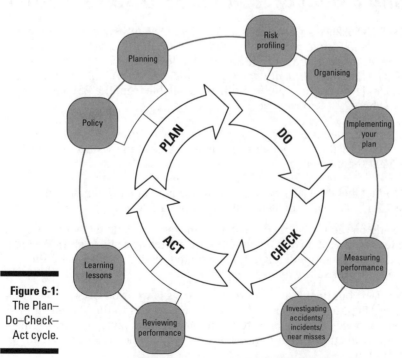

Figure 6-1:
The Plan–
Do–Check–
Act cycle.

Source: Managing for Health and Safety (HSG65) published by the Health and Safety Executive, 2013: www.hse.gov.uk/pubns/books/hsg65.htm. The Managing for Health and Safety publication (HSG65) contains public sector information published by the Health and Safety Executive and licensed under the Open Government License.

Implementing a Recognised Safety Management System

You may know about the elements that make up a recognised safety management system, but it's a whole new challenge to try and implement one. However, we're here to help you work through any hiccups you may encounter along the way.

The following sections take you through the different steps that will help you to implement a safety management system that is robust enough for the job.

We base these upcoming sections on BS OHSAS 18001, but the implementation steps can apply to any safety management system.

Taking a deeper look at BS OHSAS 18001

BS OHSAS 18002:2008 – *Occupational Health and Safety Management Systems – Guidelines for the Implementation of OHSAS 18001:2007* – provides a systematic guide for implementing BS OHSAS 18001. However, BS 18004:2008 – *Guide to Achieving Effective Occupational Health and Safety Performance* – is a more practical and user-friendly guide. Both are available from the BSI online shop: `http://shop.bsigroup.com/`.

BS 18004 recommends a process by which you work through implementing the BS OHSAS 18001 management system elements step by step, with a few extra bits at the beginning:

1. Conduct an initial review (we look at this step in more detail in the next section, 'Analysing the gaps using an initial review').

2. Decide on the scope of your safety management system (that is, the extent of what it covers, such as multiple sites or a single site). We look at this step in more detail in the upcoming section, 'Deciding on the scope of your safety management system'.

3. Develop your health and safety policy (this is what BS OHSAS 18001 calls it, but, in practice it's expressed as the equivalent to the statement of general policy that we refer to in Chapter 2). This policy describes the overall direction and intentions of your organisation (rather than all the detail).

4. Plan to control risks (largely through risk assessments that cover all activities), identify and comply with legal requirements, formulate objectives (that align with the statement of general policy) and prepare action plans to achieve those objectives (refer to Chapters 2 and 4 for more on your statement of general policy and risk assessments, respectively).

5. Allocate resources, roles and responsibilities to implement the plans in Step 4 – ensure that people are *competent* to do their job (through training), that they *communicate* appropriately and that they participate and consult with your workforce (thus ensuring *co-operation*; refer to Chapter 3 for more on these key terms and how they influence your safety culture).

   Make sure that you adequately document your procedures, processes, instructions, records and so on, and *control* these aspects where necessary (for example, if it's important to approve documents to show that they're fit for purpose and to know what the current version is; Chapter 3 also looks at the importance of control). Implement operational controls (now that you know what your risks are – refer to Step 4 – remember that these may not relate only to your internal activities but also external elements like contractor control). Sort out your emergency procedures to identify and manage emergencies (see Chapter 7 for more on emergency procedures).

6. Monitor your health and safety performance (this includes setting up inspection programmes and recording accidents), and check whether you still comply with the law (yes, it changes) and any other agreements you've signed up to (like voluntary industry codes of practice or supplier agreements). Investigate accidents and actively identify and correct 'non-conformities' (that is, areas where you no longer comply with the requirements of BS OHSAS 18001). Control your records (such as risk assessments and accident reports that provide evidence that you've actually done something, rather than just talked about doing it). Conduct internal audits to check that your systems and procedures (such as permits and risk assessments) are working as intended.

   Refer to Chapter 8 for more on monitoring your health and safety performance.

7. Conduct regular management reviews. Refer to Chapter 8 for more on management reviews.

Not all these details apply to every organisation – that's why you conduct an initial review and decide on the scope of your safety management system, to figure out what you need to do for your organisation. Sure, the basics are designed to cover every organisation – it's a standard for a reason. But how elaborate your safety management system is depends on your organisation's context – your risk profile, organisational size and so on.

Analysing the gaps using an initial review

An *initial review* is a specific type of audit that you do right at the beginning of the safety management system implementation phase (refer to the preceding section). At the beginning of the process, you either haven't got a safety management system in place at all, or the management system you have in place is ineffective (so it may have deficiencies). You use the initial review to get an idea of how far short you are of the safety management system standard that you're trying to implement.

The initial review essentially looks at the health and safety risks faced by your organisation. In practice, you compare what you currently have (perhaps something non-existent or woefully inadequate) against the requirements specified in the safety management system you've chosen.

The process for the initial review is the same whether you bring in an external auditor or do it yourself, and you look for weaknesses in your systems using gap analysis. *Gap analysis* involves comparing the safety management system in place in an organisation with the requirements of a specified safety management system to identify the areas of non-compliance (or gaps).

You use the gaps to help you plan what you need to do to implement your safety management system. If you're trying to get certified to BS OHSAS 18001 (refer to the earlier section, 'Choosing a Recognised Safety Management System'), you may get this initial status review as part of your first visit by the accredited auditor – it's a check of readiness to adopt the formal system. The auditor gives you details about the items that need to be fixed (the gaps) before you have a formal certification visit.

You can hire a consultant to do this initial review for you, but you can easily do it yourself too (as you'd have to anyway if you were working with the HSG65 system).

In your initial review, BS OHSAS 18002 and BS 18004 suggest that you look at items including:

- ✔ How you identify legal requirements (and other such requirements) that apply to your activities – and what you can do about them
- ✔ How you identify the hazards and evaluate the risks you face
- ✔ Ways to take a detailed look at the system, processes and procedures you already have in place
- ✔ Any initiatives you have for improving health and safety in the workplace
- ✔ How you investigate incidents, work-related ill-health, accidents and emergencies, and any lessons learned

This list isn't exhaustive, but it's a good start. To gather data for your initial review, you can develop and use checklists, interview people and inspect equipment and premises. But essentially you have to look at the elements of the safety management system that you're wanting to implement and see what you have in comparison to its requirements. This initial review won't do the planning for you or implement the system – it will help you decide what's needed.

The initial review is different to the routine auditing of your management system, which you conduct when your safety management system is up and running (we look at this in Chapter 8). Routine internal auditing (and the typically six to nine month *surveillance* auditing by your friendly accredited external auditor; see the later section 'Working towards certification' for more on surveillance auditing) is designed to make sure that your safety management system continues to deliver.

You can generate a simple checklist to check how well your inspection process is working. Note that the questions aren't actual inspection questions like 'Has the machine got a guard?' or 'Is the floor slippery?', but they're questions that examine the process of inspection, such as:

- ✔ Do you have a planned inspection process?
- ✔ Do staff participate in inspections?
- ✔ Have you used inspections to spot hazards in the workplace this year?
- ✔ Do you use checklists to specify the scope of each inspection?

Deciding on the scope of your safety management system

The scope of your management system has a considerable effect on its complexity. *Scope* is just a fancy term for deciding what your management system should cover – its extent. For example, if you have multiple departments/divisions or sites (perhaps even multinational sites) you may choose to implement a safety management system in a specific division or globally.

You can potentially exclude certain activities from the scope too, but that's folly if the activity in question has a direct impact on your workplace's safety or your ability to control risk.

Working towards certification

You have your BS OHSAS 18001 safety management system installed and working reasonably well. You're even doing your own internal auditing (see Chapter 8) to check that your management system is working as intended (this programme is the one that, in our experience, is always the first to fall by the wayside). You can tell yourself that you're complying with BS OHSAS 18001, but you may be deluding yourself or being too lenient on yourself.

An expert from outside your organisation can confirm that you do indeed meet that standard. That's when you may decide to get your management system *certified* (get an external independent body to verify that you have indeed conformed to BS OHSAS 18001, in this case). For a reasonable price, external accredited auditors carry out an initial *certification audit*, which thoroughly checks all your systems against the relevant standard. These checks may take a couple of days to complete for an SME, but they can take much longer for a bigger organisation. If you're lucky, you'll have very few findings and no major non-conformities (the serious show-stoppers that mean your system is rather deficient). You then get your shiny certificate.

Depending on the size of your organisation, you can then expect to receive visits every six to nine months for shorter *surveillance audits* to check that you're still doing okay. These audits are shorter because they sample particular aspects of the safety management system – therefore, they have a narrower focus. Surveillance audits may sound like they're part of a top-secret security operation, but the term simply refers to the routine monitoring audit that external accredited auditors complete in between your more extensive re-certification audits. Surveillance audits tend to focus in on specific topics or areas rather than the whole system. And, before you ask, a *re-certification audit* is a somewhat deeper, more extensive audit that samples the whole safety management system and is completed just before your old certificate expires.

Certificates are usually valid for three years, so you won't experience a larger re-certification audit for a good long while.

Management systems aren't perfect, and even accredited auditors don't expect perfection. Instead, they expect to see a system that meets a minimum standard and continuously improves as it matures.

Certification and surveillance audits aren't a substitute for your own internal audits. External auditors will expect to see evidence of a working internal auditing programme (with records of audits that you've carried out).

Having a global certification that covers all sites for your chosen safety management system standard (such as BS OHSAS 18001) may spell trouble if any single site lets you down badly. It may therefore be better to have separate certifications for each site (though this approach is more costly).

Chapter 7

Developing Safe Systems and Procedures

*R*unning your activities safely means coordinating and controlling the people, equipment, materials, location and method (sequence of events) for each task. By doing this, you create a safe system of work (when you do all these things safely, at least!). The more complicated the task, the more systematic planning you need to make sure you've thought the task through carefully.

In this chapter, you find out how to develop your safe systems of work, including using permit systems for non-routine, higher-risk activities. Because no safe system is 100 per cent safe, we also look at emergency procedures. Finally, because you'll almost certainly use contractors at some stage of your business (if you don't already), we look at procedures for selecting the right contractors and working with contractors on your site.

Developing Safe Systems of Work

A *safe system of work* is a comprehensive, formal procedure that sets out how to work safely in relation to identified hazards. It organises your people, materials and equipment, and defines safe methods for completing a specific task. Since a safe system of work is focused on a task, developing this system involves analysing the task in question to look at the hazards and how to control them (in other words, risk assessment – refer to Chapter 4 for more on this). It also looks at developing a proper procedure to describe the *methods* (the sequence of operations within the task) to instruct the people carrying out the task.

A systematic way of developing a safe system of work for a given task involves the following basic steps:

1. **Analyse the task:** For larger, more complicated tasks it can help if you break the task down into steps, analysing the hazards and assessing the risks at each step.

2. **Introduce controls and formulate procedures:** You work out sensible measures to control the identified hazards, with an emphasis on writing procedures that describe how the job can be done safely.

3. **Instruct and train people in the procedures:** You provide adequate training and instruction in the procedures that you develop in Step 2 to everyone who is required to complete the task.

4. **Check the work and procedures:** You periodically check to make sure that your procedures are still fit for purpose (and revise these procedures if required).

We look at each of these stages in the following sections and also take a look at using permit systems for high-risk tasks.

Analysing tasks

For more complicated tasks (with multiple steps), it can help to adopt a systematic method called *task safety analysis* (or just *task analysis*), where you break down a task into smaller steps and use risk assessment to analyse each step. Task analysis goes by other names too, including *job hazard analysis* and *job safety analysis*.

You don't need to use task analysis for everything – save it for more complicated tasks, as it can be quite a time-consuming process. You don't need to do an in-depth analysis for very simple, straightforward tasks (ones with few steps, where the risks are fairly obvious) – task analysis is overkill for such simple tasks. Instead, you can simply assess the risks from the whole task in one go.

The best place to start is with the job (or task). You need to thoroughly analyse the task, looking for safety issues that may arise (that is, what can go wrong).

A good systematic way to analyse tasks is to break the task down into individual steps (it's best to observe someone carrying out the task when you do this, rather than just write down what you think they do). The size of each step doesn't really matter – it's what's meaningful to you, and this often depends on your familiarity with the task. Don't make the steps too small, however; otherwise, you lose the big picture.

If you're changing a flat car tyre, you follow these steps:

1. You jack up the car.

2. You remove the wheel with the flat tyre.

3. You get the spare wheel from the boot (or wherever you store it).

4. You fit the new wheel.

5. You lower the car.

This example shows how breaking the task into steps can help you to think through each stage systematically. You can then analyse each step in turn to note any issues (that is, hazards or things that may go wrong). In terms of what can go wrong, it's helpful to ask yourself these questions for each of the steps, for any given task:

- **What is used?** This can include plant and substances, potential failures of machinery, toxic hazards, electrical hazards and so on.

- **Who does what?** Here you need to think about delegation, training, foreseeable human errors, short-cuts and ability to cope in an emergency, as well as routine operations.

- **Where is the task carried out?** As well as the normal workplace, you may experience problems caused by weather conditions or lighting, hazards from adjacent areas or contractors, and so on.

- **How is the task done?** Consider not only the standard procedures but also the potential failures in work methods and infrequent events such as maintenance, where normal safeguards may be disabled.

In the preceding example, the driver is the main person doing the task (the tyre won't suddenly change itself), and therefore the driver is at risk (they're the 'who'). Here, we take a look at each step for the car tyre example and look for the likely hazards (how the driver may be harmed, plus any other issues around changing the tyre):

- **Step 1: You jack up the car.** The jack may collapse because you've put it in the wrong place or not put it on level (or hard) ground. The car may move (because you failed to apply the handbrake). You may also be hit by other cars if you're on a busy road or motorway.

- **Step 2: You remove the wheel.** At this point you may discover that it's rather difficult to loosen the wheel bolts with the wheel off the ground (where it can freely spin, so it may have been better to loosen the bolts before you jacked the car up; this is the point of task analysis – discovering the problems with your approach). You may need to exert a lot of effort to loosen the bolts, using the wheel brace (part of your standard car-tool kit), and you may also discover that a car wheel is heavier than you think, especially with the awkward posture you have to adopt to remove the wheel. You may decide to roll the wheel to get it from

A to B, but what if you're a little enthusiastic (or you lose control of this heavy object) and it rolls into traffic?

✔ **Step 3: You get the spare wheel from the boot.** Once again, you discover how extraordinarily heavy and awkward a wheel can be when you lift it out of the car boot. And that twinge in the back that you feel when you lift the wheel is a sign of problems to come.

✔ **Step 4: You fit the new wheel.** You have to lift the wheel in place (again, it's heavy!), locate the wheel nuts and tighten these up. You then discover that this process is rather difficult if the wheel can spin freely (and the wheel brace can slip). You're also not sure whether you've tightened the wheel nuts enough (they may come loose and the wheel may fall off – a depressing waste of all that effort!).

✔ **Step 5: You lower the car.** You wind down the jack and lower the car to the ground. You remove the jack and then realise that your spare tyre is also flat (because you never bothered to check the tyre pressures or replace it after the last puncture).

This list isn't exhaustive, but you get the picture!

Formulating controls, including procedures

After you identify the health and safety problems for each step of the task (refer to the preceding section), you need to get your thinking cap on and come up with some solutions, again for each step.

The safe system of work is put in place for people to follow, so it's sensible to involve those same people in formulating the procedures. They're going to have to use the system, so it will work better if they're happy with it. Their practical knowledge can help to avoid problems that people with less experience may miss.

What your safe system of work involves depends on how complicated the task is, so it may range from verbal instructions through simple written procedures to formal permit-to-work schemes in exceptional cases. You need to think about what happens at the start of the job, such as preparation and authorisation; what planning you need as the job progresses, and the safe work methods for each bit; and what happens at the end of the job when you've got to contend with dismantling and disposing of items.

Chapter 4 (on risk assessment) introduces some general principles for controlling risks. These are termed *control measures*. But developing control measures doesn't have to be complicated. You're likely to discover, as you break down the task and identify the issues (what can go wrong) at each stage, what you need to do in order to do the job safely and efficiently.

Consider the example in the preceding section (on changing a car tyre). You can now spot a few control measures that you can implement to improve and develop a better procedure for this task.

First, consider the overall setting. Noting that you may be on a busy road, and it may be cold and dark, it seems a good idea to get an equipment list together – maybe a hi-viz jacket, a warm coat (if it's winter) and a hazard warning triangle for busy roads. A torch may come in handy too. You also need to make sure that you always have a spare tyre with you in the car (otherwise, you'll be spending a long time walking home). The tyre needs to be in good condition and properly inflated. You also need a wheel brace and a jack, and you need to be familiar with the jacking points for your vehicle.

For each step, you can adopt the following as an overall procedure:

1. Make sure that the handbrake is on (so that the car doesn't move when you jack it up).

2. Use the wheel brace to loosen the wheel nuts on the flat tyre (use a decent extending wheel brace to give you some good leverage, rather than the one made of cheese that may have been supplied with the car).

3. Put the jack in position (you need to already know the jacking points), and raise the car so that the wheel is off the ground. Remove the wheel nuts completely and slide the wheel off. Drop the wheel onto its side and position it under the side of the car near the jack (so if the jack fails, the car won't drop to the ground completely – this tactic also stops the wheel from rolling off into the night).

4. Get the spare wheel from the boot (being careful to use your good lifting technique), lift it onto the wheel stubs, and loosely screw on the wheel nuts.

5. Remove the flat tyre from its position under the side of the car and gently lower the jack. Tighten the wheel nuts further using the wheel brace (not too tight though – you need to check later that the bolts are tightened to the settings recommended by the manufacturer (you can use a torque wrench to check this).

By writing it down as a series of steps, you can see how this approach is beginning to look like a written procedure. The procedure connects the person with the tools and the task, so it's a systematic way of carrying out the task, taking account of the safest way to complete it.

(Of course, you may decide to ignore these steps and get roadside assistance insurance, which is an example of risk transfer – refer to Chapter 4.)

Training users about the system

You may have a first-class safe system of work, but it's no use if nobody knows about it. It's back to our bugbear about paperwork: many safe systems of work are stored securely in filing systems but never see the light of day in actual operations in the workplace.

People regularly object to using personal protective equipment (PPE) at work, but if you can convince them about the actual risks to their own personal health and safety then you get to the point where they wouldn't dare start work without it. We wouldn't work next to a cyanide bath without full protective gear, and we're sure you wouldn't either. It's the same with a safe system of work. If you can get to the position where the workforce can see the need for safety procedures and won't work without them, you've got it made. The self-preservation model of health and safety is the most effective one if you can achieve it.

You have to make sure that employees, supervisors and managers are all trained to make them fully aware of potential risks and the precautions they must adopt. You need to stress the point that safe systems of work are there to reduce accidents, not to slow down or complicate the job, and that supervisors play a key role in getting people to follow the system and not take short-cuts. You can even build in instructions to stop work when faced with an unexpected problem until a safe solution can be found – a clever way to prevent off-the-cuff risk-taking.

Monitoring and improving the system

Never trust anything unless you check it, and safe systems of work are no exception. Human nature is such that you may not think beyond the job that you're doing. For example, you may change your flat tyre at the roadside, but it's easy to forget that you now no longer have a spare – so part of the process needs to extend to getting a repair or replacement and, of course, checking that you have a spare before you set off (especially in a hire car or a car that you don't know). One of your authors once hired a removal van. It was only when he'd driven a considerable distance that he realised, from the performance of the van, that the rear tyre was flat. In fact, on removing it, he realised that it had worn right down to the metal banding inside! He went to fetch the spare, only to realise that this too was worn down to the wire. That's not a mistake you make twice – you improve the system to make sure that it doesn't happen again (in this case, you wouldn't hire a van from that business again, and you'd carefully check your next car or van hire!).

Smart things to keep an eye on:

- ✔ The system is still workable, it's being followed and employees are happy with it.
- ✔ The procedures are still effective and do actually make the job safer.
- ✔ Any changes in the way the job is done are picked up so that alterations to the system of work can be made.

Using permit systems to control higher-risk activities

Is a safe system of work enough? You're still relying on the co-operation of your workforce. What if you've got jobs that are so dangerous you need a tighter system of control?

The safe system of work for mowing a lawn may only need a straightforward set of instructions, but for more dangerous and complex jobs you need stricter command of the task at hand. If it was your responsibility to send someone into a petrol storage tank to complete some welding repairs, you'd certainly need to do some careful thinking to develop a plan that controlled each stage of the job without putting the operatives at risk.

This is where the *permit to work* comes in. It's a formal written document of authority to undertake a specific procedure and is designed to protect personnel working in hazardous areas or activities, or, in other words, it's a procedural way of taking every precaution possible.

Jobs that require a permit-to-work system are the ones that can go spectacularly wrong, such as:

- ✔ Working in confined spaces
- ✔ Hot work on plant containing flammable dusts, liquids, gases or their residues
- ✔ Cutting into pipework containing hazardous substances
- ✔ Working on electrical equipment

The permit needs to include the following information:

- ✔ The work to be done
- ✔ How to make the work area safe
- ✔ Any remaining hazards and the precautions required
- ✔ Checks to be carried out before normal work can be resumed
- ✔ The name of the person responsible for controlling the job

Before work begins, you may need some of the following safety precautions:

- Electrical or mechanical isolation of the plant (such as padlocking the electrical isolator in the 'off' position – the key being held by the person doing the work)
- Isolation of the machine or equipment area
- Locking or blanking off water, steam, acid, gas, solvents and compressed air supplies
- Erection of scaffolding
- Provision of temporary guards (or other like equipment) to make the job safe

The actual permit itself is a simple pro-forma (paper or electronic) which helps you to systematically and formally record the job and the necessary precautions. Table 7-1 provides a list of the typical things included in a permit, but these can vary depending on the type of job.

Table 7-1 Examples of What a Permit-to-Work May Include
1. Permit title.
2. Permit number. Reference to other relevant permits or isolation certificates.
3. Job location.
4. Plant identification.
5. Description of work to be done and its limitations.
6. Hazard identification. This includes residual hazards and hazards introduced by the work.
7. Precautions necessary. Person(s) who carries out precautions, for example, isolations, should sign that precautions have been taken.
8. Protective equipment.
9. Authorisation. Signature confirming that precautions have been taken, except those which can only be taken during the work itself. Date and time duration of the permit.
10. Acceptance. Signature confirming understanding of work to be done, hazards involved and precautions required. This can also confirm that permit information has been explained to all employees involved.
11. Extension/shift hand-over procedures. Signatures confirming checks have been made that plant remains safe to be worked upon, and that new employees have been made fully aware of hazards and precautions. New time expiry given.
12. Hand-back. Signed to certify that the work has been completed and plant is ready for testing and re-commissioning.
13. Cancellation. Certifies that work has been tested and plant satisfactorily re-commissioned.

Permits don't make things safe on their own. They're a procedure, and so they rely on people following them. That's why it's important to monitor your procedures – to check that people are following them. Otherwise, your procedures may be treated like a paper exercise – and thus add nothing to your workplace's safety at all.

Preparing Emergency Procedures

Your efforts to put health and safety into practice see you with committed managers on board, a keen competent workforce and safe systems of work for every eventuality. Job done? Well, not quite. You still need to ask yourself: 'What if something goes wrong?' You need to factor in the need for emergency arrangements, particularly with higher-risk activities.

The famous quotation 'prepare for the worst and hope for the best' is relevant here. Accident prevention is one side of the coin, and you obviously put most of your effort into that. But mitigation of consequences is important as well to make sure that an incident doesn't turn into a disaster. Quick and effective action can help to ease the situation and reduce the consequences. A common-sense approach is to concentrate on prevention of accidents and incidents first, but make sure you've early warning if they do happen and procedures to minimise the consequences arising from them.

Your emergency procedures are your backstop but, like insurance policies, you hope you're never going to need them. The smart money is on managing risks and leaving nothing to chance!

The following sections explore your emergency procedures in more detail, looking at the potential types of emergencies you may need to consider and helping you to prepare your team for the possibility of needing to leap into emergency action.

Deciding what emergencies to cover

Emergencies can take many forms and can occur on different scales so you need procedures to deal with them. So what can go wrong?

Incidents may include:

- Fire
- Bomb threats

✔ Chemical spillages

✔ Release of a toxic gas

✔ Disease outbreaks

✔ Severe weather or flooding

But this obviously depends on your organisation – what it does, where it's located and so on. Emergency situations can occur at any time, but how you deal with them can dictate whether they turn into a disaster or not. So, you need to be prepared.

Working out the details

You've thought about what can go wrong (refer to the preceding section) – now you need arrangements to deal with these potential emergencies.

You need to consider the following key elements:

✔ **What procedures to follow:** In a fire, workers exit the building and assemble at a designated place; if there's a site release of toxic chemicals, the procedure may well be the exact opposite – that is, get inside the building and away from the release.

✔ **What kit you need:** For a chemical spillage, you may use absorbent granules to contain the spill, PPE to prevent harm to those involved in the containment operation and respiratory protective equipment if the spillage gives off a chemical vapour.

✔ **Who needs to be nominated as responsible staff:** In a fire, wardens or marshals need to check that evacuation happens and a fire team may also be needed to investigate the area where you suspect the fire to be.

✔ **Who needs to be trained:** People can only know what to do if they've been trained and given information, and nominated individuals may require additional training on their specific roles within this emergency procedure. You may even have to include members of the public in this procedure, so you need to think about providing them with information on the emergency procedure (using notices or public address system announcements).

✔ **What practice you need:** You need to practise your emergency procedures to make sure that people know what action to take. If you can make people's reactions automatic, it speeds up the response, which is why you regularly carry out fire evacuation drills. You want your workforce to be like a coiled spring – ready for action at any time!

You may want to include the following details in your emergency procedures:

- ✔ **How the alarm will be raised,** including at night and during shift working, weekends and times when the premises are closed for holidays
- ✔ **What to do,** including how to call the emergency services
- ✔ **Where to go** to reach a place of safety or to get rescue equipment
- ✔ **Who is competent to take control,** including an incident controller, technical adviser and your first-aiders
- ✔ **Essential actions,** such as emergency plant shutdown, incident isolation or making processes safe with clearly identified important items (like shut-off valves and electrical isolators)

Making sure that you're always ready

You need to train your emergency personnel and to practise the plan. People will be uncertain and confused, particularly early on in an emergency when there may be little information and lots of things happening – and this can only get worse if the plan and equipment is unfamiliar. This is where your emergency situation can spiral out of control.

You shouldn't document your emergency procedures on paper that's only ever brought out in an emergency. Your people need to be trained in these procedures – to know their part in them and be allowed to practise them on a regular basis.

Test and review your plans at least every three years, especially if you know of significant changes that may affect them. A good time to review your emergency procedures is after a practice session, when you can use feedback to identify where things didn't work (for example, overcomplicated communications or a complex command structure that causes confusion).

Contracting Procedures

Safe systems of work are there to control work activities, especially non-routine and risky activities (for example, when you would need to use permits – refer to the earlier section 'Using permit systems to control higher-risk activities' for more). Perhaps one of the higher-risk things you may do is to bring a contractor onto the premises – you're not only exposing them to potentially unfamiliar risks from your activities, but they may also be exposing your workplace to risks that it isn't familiar with. In addition, the contractor may not be as competent as she thinks she is (or tells you she is).

You need to develop procedures to control any work with contractors – to help you manage selecting them in the first place and monitoring them when they're working on your site.

Selecting contractors

The quaint legal term 'master–servant relationship' is sometimes applied to the duty of care of the employer for employees. It may sound a bit old-fashioned, but it does convey the control that the employer is entitled to exercise over its employees' activities, especially ones that involve risks to safety and health. But you also have other persons on the premises that you can broadly label 'non-employees'. Within this group of 'others', contractors make up a significant proportion.

Contractors are persons that you take on to perform particular tasks without you having to worry too much about the detail. You're bringing in persons from outside the organisation to carry out specialist tasks for you. They're the experts, otherwise you wouldn't be using them – so can you just let them get on with it?

'Let contractors get on with it' was general opinion in the 1970s, until a tragic fire that involved work by contractors occurred during the construction of the destroyer HMS Glasgow and killed eight men and injured a further six. The shipyard knew of the fire risk that led to the accident and provided safety information to its own employees, but it failed to distribute safety information to contractors. The contractors (unaware of the risk) started welding and caused a very intense fire. This incident clarified the relationship between employers and contractors and demonstrated how the duty of care for employees must extend to controlling the activities of others working on the premises – the actions of the contractors placed the shipyard's employees at risk, and the shipyard company could have averted that risk by making sure that the contractors also knew of the risk, thereby controlling the risk to its own employees.

You have two problems when you have contractors in your workplace:

- ✔ The contractor is working on your premises and she's exposed to your risks.

- ✔ The contractor is working on your premises and exposing your employees to her risks.

Consequently, you need to take precautions to reduce the risks of workplace dangers to both parties and make sure that everyone understands the part they need to play in ensuring health and safety. A sensible starting point is to get a decent contractor in the first place.

The one that you wouldn't employ in a million years is the one who

- ✔ Has no previous experience or evidence of technical and safety competence in the type of work.
- ✔ Has a poor accident record and a history of enforcement actions.
- ✔ Can't supply a method statement to confirm how she'll carry out the job safely.
- ✔ Has no evidence of maintenance and testing for plant and equipment to be used on the job.

Give the contractors a good grilling before you appoint them. After such an interrogation, you end up with a contractor who can deliver. See the nearby sidebar, 'Checking out contractors' for some example questions you may like to ask potential contractors.

Monitoring the work of your contractors

When you hire contractors, you need to make sure that they're working safely and as agreed on your premises. Very often, the reason you have contractors on your site is for building and maintenance work. Refurbishment projects, maintenance and construction works constantly change your work environment. In most cases this is done by specialist contractors and you have to work round each other and co-operate. Your risks can affect them just as their risks can affect you. We limit the discussion here to what you can expect to consider when you work with building contractors (but whatever the circumstances, the same general approach applies).

Communicating and co-operating with your building contractors is key to keeping disturbances to a minimum and to ensuring the smooth running of the operation. Meeting with them before the work starts can help you to understand what's to be expected and how it will be managed.

Try to avoid directing the work of your contractors. If you don't, you may find yourself liable for any of their actions that put others at risk. You hired them because of their expertise. It's a fine balance between monitoring their work (both their adherence to agreed rules and to delivering a high-quality outcome) and telling each individual what to do. It may help to deal with a single main contact on the contractor's side – you can then discuss any concerns or issues that you have with them and leave them to translate your disquiet into actions.

Checking out contractors

A useful list of searching questions is as follows:

- What arrangements will you have for managing the work?

- Will you be using subcontractors and, if so, how will you check that they're competent?

- What is your recent health and safety performance? (Ask about any accidents and cases of ill-health, or actions that the Health and Safety Executive (HSE) has taken against them.)

- Do you have a written health and safety policy? (Ask this if the contractor employs five or more people.)

- Can you provide existing risk assessments you've completed for similar jobs?

- What qualifications, skills and experience do you have in this type of work?

- What health and safety information and training do you provide for your employees?

- If required, do you have Employers' Liability Compulsory Insurance?

One of the best approaches to protecting your employees from contractor activity (and vice-versa) is to separate them. It may be hard to separate your people from some of the activities, but where possible you need to put barriers in place to prevent access for non-construction personnel. This will hopefully prevent your employees from accidentally stumbling onto the construction site (and having to spend the weekend in a muddy field, as if they're at Glastonbury festival).

Chapter 8

Monitoring and Reviewing Health and Safety in the Workplace

....

In This Chapter

▶ Monitoring your safety management system

▶ Creating health and safety targets and KPIs for your business

▶ Inspecting and auditing your business

▶ Learning from incidents to prevent a recurrence

▶ Reviewing your safety performance to get better at what you do

....

You want to be good at health and safety, which is why you're reading this book. In practice, what you really want is to manage risks so that, as far as possible, you avoid having any accidents or ill-health next week, next month, next quarter. That's what 'good' health and safety management really is. So you need a measure of 'goodness' (performance indicators and their associated targets) and tools to measure it (monitoring systems).

Of course, nobody has a crystal ball (or one that we've any faith in) to predict the future, so the next best thing is to use the laws of cause and effect. The more you know about the causes of accidents, incidents and cases of occupational ill-health, the better the chance that you can prevent similar effects in future. That's why accident investigation to find out the actual causes, rather than who's to blame, is so important.

In this chapter you find out how to keep a close check on your health and safety systems. You discover how to get as much useful information as possible from incidents and how to use your monitoring information to get better at what you do. If you've got any shortfalls in performance identified by your monitoring and review processes, you can therefore make the improvements you need by following infallible action plans.

In this chapter we use the term 'accident' in its everyday sense – as a shorthand for accidents, incidents, cases of occupational ill-health and any other loss-causing event that you need to control.

Monitoring Your Safety Management System

If you're relying on your management system to make you good at health and safety, you need to look after it, nurture it and, above all, keep a close eye on it to make sure that it continues to work. Checking that you're managing risks in your organisation is a vital step and gives you the confidence that you're doing enough to keep on top of your organisational health and safety. It involves setting up a monitoring system that works, backed up with sensible performance measures that tell you how well you're doing.

You have two sources of data to monitor health and safety performance:

- ✔ **Reactive monitoring data:** The things that have gone wrong, such as accidents, incidents and cases of occupational ill-health, which suggest that you're not performing particularly well and need to do better. This data is valuable because you can use it to learn from your mistakes and improve for the future (take a look at the later section 'Learning from Accidents' to find out more). This data is *reactive* because it examines what has already happened.

- ✔ **Active (or proactive) monitoring data:** The things that can go wrong but haven't yet – the health and safety hazards that you can pick up from things like inspections and audits (see the upcoming section, 'Conducting Inspections and Audits'). This data is *active* (or *proactive*) because the aim is to identify problems before they happen (including legal non-compliance) and put them right before you suffer the consequences.

By using both types of monitoring, you can confirm current good performance by a low accident/incident rate and expect that good performance to continue, because effective active monitoring involves picking up potential problems before they arise. This sounds like a good start to your quest for success in health and safety management!

Using KPIs and Targets

A well-known piece of management wisdom is the old adage, 'You can't manage what you don't measure'. Unless you measure something, you can't know if it's getting better or worse, or, in this case, safer or more dangerous. If you want to demonstrate successful health and safety management, you need targets and performance indicators that can measure success.

A *performance indicator* is a quantifiable measure that you can use to establish whether you've met (or are meeting) your objectives or goals. It has an associated *target*. So, for example, you may have an objective of legal compliance, setting a target of 100 per cent (so you're always complying). Therefore, you'd phrase the performance indicator as 'compliance with relevant health and safety laws'.

Performance indicators can be from reactive monitoring (which may also be known as *lagging* indicators) or active monitoring (which may also be known as *leading* indicators). Most organisations select a small number of important performance indicators and call these *Key Performance Indicators (KPIs)*.

Your safety policy and your risk assessment system help you to set performance indicators and targets. The objectives set out in your health and safety statement of general policy give you the broad standards to be achieved, for example 'we'll properly manage and control health and safety risks in the workplace' (refer to Chapter 2 for more on your statement of general policy). But you need to make these objectives more concrete and specific, so each objective needs to be linked to your risk assessment system (which identifies risks and develops control measures – refer to Chapter 4 for more on risk assessment).

You can use your risk assessment system to frame the performance indicators that you need in place in order to control risk. You may find it helpful to ask the following questions:

- Do you have a risk assessment system?
- Do you have adequate risk assessments to cover significant risks from all business activities?
- How often do you review your risk assessments?
- Are the control measures you have in place effective?

Answers to these questions (and more) can help you to decide whether you're meeting your overall objective of managing and controlling the risks stated in your statement of general policy.

You can set performance indicators and targets for anything important that you want to happen (and make the most important ones KPIs). You need to decide yourself what your organisation needs to measure, but these performance indicators should align with your statement of general policy and its objectives. Here are some ideas:

- **To encourage meetings of the health and safety committee.** Your performance indicator here may be the number of committee meetings taking place, and your target may be at least one per month.

✔ **To involve more people in risk assessments and writing procedures.** Your performance indicator here may be the proportion of risk assessments or procedures completed or reviewed by trained front-line staff, and the associated target may be 50 per cent over a year.

✔ **To show visible management commitment by involving senior managers in safety inspections and accident and incident investigations.** Your performance indicator here may be the number of inspections conducted by senior managers, and your target may be 12 per year.

✔ **To properly document health and safety rules and procedures.** Your performance indicator here may simply be the proportion of activities that you've identified as needing a written procedure that actually have one in place, and the initial target may be 80 per cent in the first quarter of the year.

✔ **To make sure that planned workplace and equipment inspections happen.** Your performance indicator here may be the number of inspections that are more than one week late against the plan, and your target may be zero (which would be excellent work!).

✔ **To make sure that actions arising from an inspection are carried out.** Your performance indicator here may be the number of actions completed on time (to the agreed deadline), and you may set a target of 90 per cent.

✔ **To ensure that accidents are reported and investigated promptly.** Your performance indicator here may be the proportion of accidents reported within one day of their occurrence; for investigations, you may use the time between the accident and publication of the investigation report (you may then set a target of one week for this report).

Conducting Inspections and Audits

You need to measure what you're doing to control risks to make sure that you're doing it properly. A low accident rate, even over a period of years, is no guarantee that risks are being effectively controlled and won't lead to injuries, ill-health or loss in the future. This is even more important in organisations where major hazards are present. The fact that there hasn't been a major fire in your petroleum storage depot in the last ten years tells you nothing about your current control of risks. This type of historical record is an unreliable or even deceptive indicator of safety performance.

So, what does work?

Well, your two main monitoring tools are inspections and audits. The terms are sometimes confused in general use, but in the world of health and safety you find a definite difference.

The *audit* examines the various bits of the health and safety management system to see how well they work. The Health and Safety Executive (HSE) defines an audit as 'the structured process of collecting independent information on the efficiency, effectiveness and reliability of the total health and safety management system and drawing up plans for corrective action'. However, that definition is referring to a rather large audit. In practice, audits can vary widely in scope – and can look at anything from an individual process (taking less than an hour) to the whole management system (an audit that will last many days). Big, extensive systems audits tend to be infrequent (because of the effort involved), whereas smaller, more targeted audits are completed more frequently.

For detailed guidance on auditing, check out British Standard BS EN ISO 19011:2011 – *Guidelines for Auditing Management Systems*, published by the British Standards Institution (BSI) and available from its online shop: `http://shop.bsigroup.com/ProductDetail/?pid=000000000030257143`.

The *inspection* is mostly a physical check (direct observation) of the workplace. It involves walking round a part of the premises (or looking at a piece of equipment), looking for hazards or non-compliance with legislation, rules or safe practice, and taking notes. The task can be made easier and more methodical if you use a checklist. (Hopefully, as health and safety standards improve, the amount of writing becomes less.)

Inspections and audits are different. Inspections are frequent, routine, direct observations carried out mainly by employees and supervisors. On the other hand, an audit is a (usually) less frequent event that focuses on systems, procedures and processes and is carried out independently (as far as possible) – that is, it's carried out by people who have no direct responsibility for the activity being audited. Modern audits can also involve physical inspection activities (direct observation), but that's just a small part of that process; they use a combination of approaches, including reviewing documentation (procedures and records), observing people carrying out their tasks, and talking to employees (in an interviewing style).

Monitoring is part of the health and safety management system and inspections are a sub-part of monitoring, so you can even audit your inspection system to make sure that it's working properly.

So how do you get these monitoring tools up and running? The following sections look at audits and inspections in more detail.

Audits

Audits are concerned with your health and safety management system and how effective it is. Your audits gather evidence (such as records, answers to questions and observations) on what you currently do (or an aspect of what you do) and evaluate your activities against your *audit criteria* (that is, your policies, procedures, requirements and so on that say what you should be doing). If your management system conforms to a recognised standard (such as BS OHSAS 18001; refer to Chapter 6), your audit criteria will be aligned with the requirements identified in that standard. You can then note any deficiencies that you identify and devise a plan to fix them. You also identify any areas for improvement (items that aren't specifically failings, but provide opportunity for improvement).

So your audit needs to:

- ✔ Examine documents such as the safety policy, arrangements, procedures, risk assessments, safe systems of work and so on.

- ✔ Look closely at records of training, maintenance, inspections, statutory examinations and so on.

- ✔ Verify the standards that exist within the workplace by interview and direct observation.

If you're involved in audits, it's interesting to compare what health and safety standards are specified in the documentation (what is supposed to be in place) with what standards the workforce think are in place (when you talk to them and get their views on things) and what actually is in place (when you have a walkabout and see what the workplace really looks like). In the perfect workplace these should all align, but this is rarely the case.

Preparing for the audit

Like most events, the audit has a beginning, a middle and an end, so what do you need to happen in each bit?

You typically plan a programme of audits 6 to 12 months ahead of time. The areas/topics that you choose depend on your business priorities. For example, it's common to focus on higher-risk areas (that is, areas that have historically been problematic). But whatever your priorities (and especially if you're just starting out in auditing), you need to plan ahead before your audit starts. You need to think about:

✔ **The scope of the audit:** This covers physical location, business units/ departments, activities, processes and timescales. For example, are you looking at one department or a whole site? Are you looking at the whole management system (which can take many days or weeks) or a single process (individual audit sessions can be very short and focused, especially routine internal audits as part of an extensive audit programme planned over the whole year)?

✔ **Who will be required during the audit:** The auditors (especially external ones) may need to be accompanied during their visit and will need access to managers for information-gathering. The wider the scope, the more auditors you need (simple, targeted audits require a single person, but larger audits may need a team of people – all assigned different audit tasks).

Auditors need to be competent – not only technically in the areas that they're auditing (so that they know what the evidence means when they look at it), but they also need to be trained in auditing techniques.

✔ **The evidence you think you need to look at or gain access to:** You may find it helpful to develop checklists or forms to record this.

It's useful to get copies of documentation, such as procedures, before starting the audit. This will include previous audit records to check that recommended actions have been implemented.

Doing the audit

As an auditor, you need evidence to support your findings. During the audit, you can gather factual information using three basic methods:

✔ **Reference to paperwork:** The documents and records that indicate what should be happening and what has happened relevant to a given issue.

✔ **Interviews:** Word of-mouth evidence given by managers and employees.

✔ **Direct observation:** Observing the workplace, equipment, activities and behaviour.

You can copy paperwork, take photographs and provide witnesses to corroborate word-of-mouth evidence. An auditor's favourite phrases are: 'Show me' and 'Can you prove it?'

At the end of the audit:

- ✔ You give verbal feedback, which may involve a presentation to the management team.

- ✔ You produce a written report that contains a description of the evidence sampled and any findings. Depending on how the audit is conducted (for example, with a tablet or laptop), you may find that you can complete the draft audit report straight away.

Your audit findings consist of two basic outputs:

- ✔ **Non-conformities:** These are where you're not conforming to a standard you've signed up to (which may be, for example, not following one of your authorised procedures). The non-conformities are usually either *major* (a fundamentally serious failure of a safety management system element, which means that you're unlikely to meet your objectives) or *minor* (an identified weakness in the system that isn't serious but does need to be fixed). An auditor will usually assign timescales for repairing these issues for each non-conformity.

- ✔ **Recommendations for improvement:** These recommendations don't represent failings in the system, but they're things that the auditor notes as an opportunity to improve your existing systems.

Even more important is the action by managers to implement the recommendations. This is an ideal task for your review process, to examine findings from the audit, get a measure of current performance, and review progress on creating and implementing action plans. The later section, 'Improving Health and Safety Performance' looks at the reviewing process in order to implement change.

Routine audits are carried out by in-house staff (internal audits). But audits can be carried out by safety specialists from outside the organisation (external audits). You find pros and cons for each option (see Table 8-1).

Table 8-1	Pros and Cons of Internal and External Audits	
	Advantages	*Disadvantages*
External Audits	Independent of any internal influence.	Expensive.
	Fresh pair of eyes.	Time-consuming.
	May have wider experience of different types of workplace.	May not understand the business, so may make impractical suggestions.
	Recommendations often carry more weight.	May intimidate employees so you get incomplete evidence.

	Advantages	*Disadvantages*
Internal Audits	Less expensive.	Auditors may not notice certain issues.
	Auditors already know the business so know what can be realistically achieved.	Auditors may not have good knowledge of industry or legal standards.
	Improves ownership of issues found.	Auditors may not possess auditing skills so may need training.
	Builds competence internally.	Auditors are not independent so may be subject to internal influence.

Inspections

Inspections are one tool for checking that the physical standards that need to be in place are, in fact, in place. They allow senior management to keep a finger on the pulse, be made aware of falling standards and sort out issues before they become critical. They also reassure your employees that you're checking things and allow them to get involved in the monitoring process itself. If you include employees and management jointly in inspections, it helps to reinforce a positive health and safety culture.

What are the issues you need to consider in order to get an effective inspection system up and running? Think about these factors:

- ✔ **What type of inspection:** Inspections are carried out for different reasons and examine different aspects of safety in the workplace. You may need a statutory inspection to ensure legal compliance, a general workplace inspection to look at plant and premises or a pre-start inspection for an item of machinery. Your inspection programme may need to include them all.

- ✔ **How often to inspect:** Determined by type of inspection and the level of risk. For example, a general workplace inspection may be conducted in an office once a month, but once a week in a workshop because of the higher risk.

- ✔ **Who's going to be involved:** Somebody needs to be responsible for making sure that inspections take place, and you need to decide who will be carrying them out.

✔ **What level of competence:** Whoever carries out the inspection needs to know what they're doing so will need training, knowledge and experience.

✔ **What documentation is needed, such as checklists:** These are valuable tools for use during the inspection and make sure that:

- Nothing gets missed
- The same things are looked at each time
- You have a written record of the inspection and its findings

The downside of checklists is that they're a bit inflexible, so you may only get the points on the checklist dealt with and other important issues may be missed – but a competent inspection team can work around that.

✔ **How to deal with problems found:** An inspection system that identifies problems but doesn't sort them is no use to anyone. You have to make sure that action gets taken after the inspection to sort the problem as quickly as possible. You need to identify:

- What needs to be done
- Who's going to do it
- How quickly it will be done

Learning from Accidents

Your active monitoring system is looking good. Your audits are keeping the safety management system in shape and your inspections are dealing with poor workplace standards (refer to the earlier section, 'Conducting Inspections and Audits'). You're checking performance (refer to the earlier section 'Using KPIs and Targets') before anything starts to deviate from your grand safety plan by identifying:

✔ Conformity with standards, so that good performance is recognised and maintained.

✔ Non-conformity with standards, and putting them right before something goes wrong.

Reactive monitoring data arises when something goes wrong: when you experience accidents, near misses and cases of ill-health. While active (or proactive) measures (like inspections and audits) are generally better, even reactive measures can be used to help inform future decisions (so, in this sense, they can be used actively – to help prevent the same things from happening again).

In the following sections we look at how you can use accident data to improve your safety management systems, and how you can investigate accidents in your workplace. We also consider the benefits of a rigorous procedure for reporting accidents in the workplace.

Using accident data wisely

Data from accidents, incidents, ill-health and other unwanted events and situations can be useful indicators of health and safety performance to highlight areas of concern. But you need to use this data with caution because:

- ✔ It's partly random, so variations from year to year can easily be due to chance rather than any accident-reduction measures that you've introduced (so no credit for that).

- ✔ You can't observe a cause-and-effect link between accident prevention measures and the effects, if any, on accident numbers.

- ✔ Under-reporting of minor accidents limits the accuracy of your data.

- ✔ Major disasters are thankfully rare (often due to a complex series of events all coming together), therefore numbers relating to these aren't statistically significant or useful for monitoring purposes.

Despite these weaknesses, reactive monitoring is a useful tool (as long as you keep these drawbacks in mind). Indeed, looking at the overall picture of monthly, quarterly and annual incident data can help you to identify trends over time or comparisons between different groups of employees or different workplace locations.

Counting accidents has its uses for statistics and trends, but nailing down their cause and doing something about them is far more productive.

We're using the term 'accident' to include more than just those events that cause an injury. You want to prevent all those events and occurrences which may have caused an injury or damage, as well as those which did. And if you think about it, although the severity of the injury from the accident is the way you classify the significance of the accident, that's not the whole story. Obviously, a fatality at work is a tragic event and something of the highest concern, but it's the events leading to the outcome that are more use to you for future preventative action.

Consider a simple example. An employee is walking down a corridor and sees that cooking oil has been spilt outside the kitchen.

A number of scenarios can unfold here. The employee can:

- ✔ Ignore it, walk past, not even report it and leave a potential accident for someone else.
- ✔ Clean it up.
- ✔ Report it as an incident and contact who's responsible for cleaning it up.
- ✔ Just miss slipping in it and report it as a near miss.
- ✔ Slip in it, regain balance, curse and report it as a near miss.
- ✔ Slip in it, fall to the floor but with only damage to clothing (an incident report and claim form for expensive clothing may follow).
- ✔ Slip in it, bruise rear and report it as an accident.
- ✔ Slip in it, break arm and report it as a specified injury as required by law.
- ✔ Slip in it, fracture skull and colleagues report it as a fatality as required by law.

The outcome defines the significance of the incident, and quite rightly so, but is based very much on chance. So you need to take incidents such as simple spillages seriously, just in case you get a worst-case outcome.

In this example, in a workplace where minor incidents and near misses aren't captured, the first you would know about it would be when one of the reportable accident outcomes occurred. It may be a regular occurrence that the corridor outside the kitchen is contaminated with cooking oil, but the first time you would find out would be when you had your first reported accident. Obviously, you want to do better than this, but getting people to report non-damage incidents or near misses is notoriously difficult. People think that it isn't an 'accident' until someone is injured, but with this limited approach you're losing a lot of valuable monitoring information.

Emphasise to the workforce the need to report all deviations from the pre-scribed way of doing things that have the *potential* for loss (that is, it may lead to injury or damage accidents, even if it doesn't actually result in that). To encourage reporting, you may need to allay your employees' fears that they'll be blamed (if they're the ones that caused the incident).

The immediate cause of the incident – 'how it happened' – should be obvious from the description of events. The underlying causes – 'Why it happened' – can be a bit more difficult to establish.

There have been lots of theories on accident causation. We won't bore you with the detail. Some very simple events have a single cause, but current thinking recognises that many accidents are *multi-causal*, when lots of things come together all at the same time to cause the accident (which may not have happened had all those factors not occurred together).

A simple example of this is a fire or explosion (see Chapter 14 for more on fire).

Imagine that you have a gas leak in your home. You get an explosion only if:

- ✔ The gas (mostly methane) is in the right concentration range (5 per cent to 15 per cent)

- ✔ Oxygen (or air) is present

- ✔ There's an ignition source (like a spark or flame)

The ignition will only happen if these three events occur together. Each of the three events themselves will be the end result of a further sequence that explains where the fuel and the ignition source came from in the first place, and so on. So once you know where the unwanted source of ignition came from, you can take action to prevent the ignition from happening again. Similarly, when you know what caused the gas leak, you can take action to prevent a future leak.

If you're going to learn from incidents, you need to investigate and identify all significant causes. By tracking down the exact sequence of events (the causes and sub-causes) that led to the incident, you can identify the various levels of causation, including the root cause(s), understand what went wrong and put these things right so that the same incident, and hopefully many similarly caused ones, won't happen again.

Investigating accidents

You may sometimes wonder why you need to bother to investigate accidents. Before you ask, here are some of the main reasons:

- ✔ To identify the immediate and underlying/root causes, so you can try to fix it to prevent it from happening again.

- ✔ To record the facts of the incident as evidence for the future. It may be for legal reasons (some accidents need to be reported to the authorities but there may also be civil cases, prosecutions and so on) or disciplinary proceedings (because sometimes employee behaviour can fall short of what you expect).

- ✔ To help you prioritise resources/actions. Accident statistics can be used to identify trends and patterns if you've got good quality data.

The two key questions to ask when investigating accidents are:

✔ **How** did it happen?

✔ **Why** did it happen?

The answer to the first question gives you a description of how the person got run over, electrocuted, trapped in the machine and so on, therefore it identifies the hazard and the mechanism of harm by which the person was injured. That enables you to deal with the immediate cause of that particular accident. But it doesn't get to the root of the problem. You're still left with the nagging doubt that if these sorts of things can go wrong in one part of your workplace, they can go wrong somewhere else. And just dealing with each specific accident but doing no more is simply fire-fighting; it's not a systematic approach.

The second question, why did it happen, is a lot more productive. If you find out why something happened, your remedial action will be much more effective. Instead of preventing a particular type of accident, it will prevent a whole range of accidents that stem from the same underlying cause.

The harsh but fair conclusion is that the root cause of accidents is often management failings (such as missing procedures or poor training).

The following is a simple four-step accident investigation process (this process is outlined in the HSE guide HSG245 – *Investigating Accidents and Incidents*, available to download free from www.hse.gov.uk/pubns/hsg245.pdf). It provides you with a systematic approach for getting the result that you want:

1. **Collect as much information as you can about what happened.**

2. **Analyse the information to work out what the immediate and underlying causes were.**

3. **Identify the control measures you need to deal with the immediate causes, and what improvements you need to make to the safety management system to sort out the underlying causes.**

4. **Prepare and implement the action plan that will make sure the remedial actions are carried out.**

You may find that when you start to analyse the information, you don't have it all to hand, so you may need to go back to Step 1 a few times until your analysis is able to lead you to the immediate and underlying causes.

Of course, immediately after an accident, the area has to be made safe and any casualties dealt with before any investigation commences. And you also need to decide about the type or level of investigation needed. You would look rather silly launching a five-month, full scale investigation over a minor paper cut. You need to decide if your investigation is going to be:

✔ A relatively simple investigation of an incident that caused no or minor outcomes and did not have the potential to cause serious outcomes. This type of investigation may be carried out by the line manager for the area.

✔ A more in-depth and thorough investigation of an incident with serious outcomes or potential for serious outcomes. This may involve a team of investigators and include safety specialists, senior managers, technical specialists and possibly employee representatives.

But getting back to your four-stage approach. What's involved in each step?

Gathering information

The first thing you need to do is to safeguard your evidence by securing the scene as soon as possible to prevent it being altered. Also quickly get details of witnesses before they start to vanish. You can then collect the facts from the scene. It's handy to take photographs and possibly videos (most smartphones are perfectly capable of doing this), but for more serious accidents you may well need sketches, measurements and written descriptions of important factors such as wind speed, temperature, visibility and so on. If this is the case, you'll also need equipment to record this information.

Once you've thoroughly examined the scene, you need to speak to witnesses. They provide crucial evidence about what occurred before, during and after the incident and need to be interviewed carefully to make sure that you gather good quality evidence.

The following tips can help you with your interview technique:

✔ Use a quiet room or area free from distractions and interruptions.

✔ Explain the purpose of the interview, perhaps emphasising that the interview is not about blaming people, and try to establish rapport with the witness through your verbal and body language.

✔ Use open questions that begin with what, why, where, when, who and how that don't put words into the witnesses' mouths and don't allow them to answer with an uninformative 'yes' or 'no'.

✔ Keep an open mind and don't prejudge the situation.

✔ Take notes so that the facts being discussed aren't forgotten.

✔ Ask the witness to write and sign a statement to create a record of his testimony. It may seem a bit formal, but you may need it later. You can reduce the anxiety involved with this by explaining that the aim is to simply get an agreed record of the facts, not to allocate blame.

After you've interviewed your witnesses, your third source of information is the documentation associated with the accident. Depending on the particular incident, you may want to examine your:

- ✔ Safety policy
- ✔ Risk assessments
- ✔ Training records
- ✔ Safe systems of work
- ✔ Permit-to-work documentation
- ✔ Maintenance records

These documents can tell you how things should have been and, of course, the purpose of your investigation is to find out why they weren't.

Analysing information

You then need to draw conclusions about the immediate and underlying causes of the accident.

Immediate causes (*how* did it happen?) are the unsafe acts (the things that people did or failed to do) and unsafe conditions (the things wrong with the workplace, equipment and so on) that gave rise to the event itself. These will be the things that occurred at the time and place of the accident, and they can be worked out from the actual sequence of events. So, using the example of a person slipping on a patch of oil spilt on the floor, the immediate causes are the slippery/oily floor (unsafe condition) and the person walking through it (unsafe act).

Underlying (or root) causes (*why* did it happen?) are the things that lie behind the immediate causes and tend, ultimately, to be failures in the management system. A good way to get to the bottom of things is to keep asking the question, 'Why?' Usually doing this about four or five times gets you there.

Common management failings are:

- ✔ Poor supervision of employees
- ✔ Not providing the right (or enough) PPE
- ✔ Poor training
- ✔ Poorly maintained plant and equipment
- ✔ Poor (or non-existent) checks or inspections
- ✔ Poor (or non-existent) risk assessments

Some workplace accidents are complex and have multiple causes. If you have several immediate causes for an accident, you need to identify the underlying/root causes for each of these.

For example, imagine that you have an employee who is struck by a load being carried by a fork-lift truck. Immediate causes for such an accident may be:

- ✔ Failure to secure the load on the pallet

- ✔ Poor road positioning of the truck close to a pedestrian exit

- ✔ Aggressive braking by the truck driver

- ✔ An inattentive pedestrian stepping out in front of the truck

When you investigate each of these immediate causes, they turn out to have their own separate underlying causes, such as:

- ✔ The driver is not trained, is new to the workplace, hasn't worked with this type of load before and/or doesn't know how to secure the load properly.

- ✔ Your pedestrian and traffic routes aren't segregated; you have no barriers and no markings to separate the two.

- ✔ You provide no driver induction into their new workplace, so they're unaware of the layout and position of pedestrian exits.

- ✔ You give no refresher training to existing staff, so that experienced staff have become complacent.

Identifying control measures

After you discover what the problem is, you can start to formulate your solutions. You now know what the immediate and underlying causes of the accident are, so you can decide on the additional control measures that you need:

- ✔ **Fixing the immediate causes:** If the oil spill that you're concerned about is from a leaking vehicle, more leaks will occur if you only deal with the immediate cause by cleaning up the oil in the distribution depot. This can lead to more pedestrian slips and possibly more vehicle skids as well. So, although you need to do it, you're not really much further forward in terms of accident prevention.

- ✔ **Fixing the underlying causes:** If you clean up the oil spill, identify the source of the oil and rectify the failure of the management system to inspect and maintain vehicles, this will fix that particular problem before another accident occurs, and there's also a good chance that most oil leaks will be prevented in the future for all vehicles in the fleet at all locations.

Your key test of how effective your control measures are going to be is these two questions:

- ✔ If this action is taken (on the immediate causes), will it prevent this same accident from happening in exactly the same way at this location?
- ✔ If this action is taken (on the underlying causes), will it prevent other similar types of accident from happening in similar locations in the future?

You need a 'yes' answer to both questions; otherwise, you're going to have to think again about your controls.

Planning the remedial actions

Accident investigations, like all other safety initiatives, are only any use if they lead to improvements in the workplace. So you need to treat the findings from your investigation in the same way as those from workplace inspections or risk assessments – you need to implement them in an action plan. If the action plan spells out what you want done, who you want to do it and when you want it done by, it needs to be pretty difficult for your recommendation not to be carried out. You can also specify the priority as well, just for good measure, so that if there's a list of recommendations, the persons implementing them have an idea of relative importance.

Table 8-2 shows an extract from an action plan. The warehouse manager has little choice but to introduce induction training for all new drivers within a month; otherwise, there'll be naming and shaming at the health and safety committee!

Table 8-2	Sample from an Action Plan		
Recommended Action	*Priority*	*Timescale*	*Responsible Person*
Introduce induction training for all new drivers.	Medium	One month	Warehouse Manager

Obviously unsafe conditions, dangerous practices and high-risk activities must be dealt with straight away, with immediate action taken to remedy these circumstances when they're discovered. You may have to take machinery and equipment out of action, suspend certain work activities and evacuate locations. You can't leave these responses until the investigation has been completed; they have to be implemented immediately to ensure safety while the investigation's in progress.

You may be able to introduce interim control measures in the short- to medium-term to allow work to proceed while longer-term solutions are pending. For example, you can introduce hearing protection as a short-term control measure until the maintenance of a piece of machinery that is producing excessive noise has been completed. You can fit a perimeter guard around an overheating machine that would ordinarily be protected with a fixed enclosed guard while new cooling units are sourced and delivered.

Your underlying causes will often demand significant time, money and effort to remedy. Therefore, you need to prioritise and timetable the remedial actions that will have the greatest impacts first. There may be actions that have to be taken (to address a management weakness or to achieve legal compliance) that won't be as effective in preventing future accidents. These actions should still be taken, but with a lower priority.

Reporting accidents

You've seen how much you can learn from thorough accident investigation. But all this presumes that you've actually got some accident reports to work on, so you're going to need a good accident reporting system to deliver the data.

The law requires you to report certain accidents and incidents to the HSE. The Reporting of Injuries, Diseases and Dangerous Occurrences Regulations 2013 (RIDDOR) requires you to report and keep records of:

- ✔ Work-related accidents that cause death
- ✔ Work-related accidents that cause certain serious injuries (reportable injuries)
- ✔ Diagnosed cases of certain industrial diseases
- ✔ Certain 'dangerous occurrences' (incidents with the potential to cause harm)

So you have to keep a record of:

- ✔ Any accident, occupational disease or dangerous occurrence that requires reporting under RIDDOR.
- ✔ Any other occupational accident causing injuries that results in an employee being away from work or incapacitated for more than three consecutive days. (These don't need to be reported under RIDDOR unless they start to exceed seven days.)

If you're keeping an accident book, the record you make in this will be enough to satisfy legal requirements, but you may be asked to produce RIDDOR records when asked by enforcing authority inspectors.

If you need to report an accident, disease or dangerous occurrence you can complete the HSE report form online and submit it directly to the RIDDOR database. You can also use the telephone service provided by the HSE (for reporting fatal and specified injuries only).

If you want to capture all the available reactive monitoring data, you'll probably want to go further than just the legal bare minimum. You need a system to make sure that all work-related accidents get reported internally to management and you don't miss anything. The simplest system is for employees to report incidents to their immediate line manager verbally and then follow this up with an internal incident report form. But, of course, you need to be clear on what you mean by 'an accident' and what you want reported by your workforce.

Any incident that involves injury or first-aid treatment is self-explanatory. But you also have to collect information on less apparent things such as verbal abuse, which is a form of work-related violence but not an obvious 'accident'. Then you have near misses, which can start to overlap with 'hazards' in some cases. For example, you walk past a cavity that has appeared in the ground and nearly fall into it but don't. Is that a near miss (you could have fallen into it) or a hazard (a hole in the ground waiting for someone to fall into it)? Rather than lose sleep over definitions and semantics, the simplest approach is just to encourage the reporting of anything of concern to the workforce. It's better to be able to sift out what you don't want later rather than miss something important by being too prescriptive.

After you establish your incident reporting policy, you've got to encourage your employees to report incidents. Here's what really helps:

- ✔ Be clear on what incidents you want them to report (state this in a procedure/policy).
- ✔ Make it easy, quick and convenient for everyone to report incidents (don't overcomplicate it; electronic is fine, but may not be convenient for some production staff, so don't discount the convenience of paper forms).
- ✔ Ensure that everyone knows the process (through instruction/training).

If fatal or major injuries, high-cost dangerous occurrences, or high-profile incidents occur, you'll need arrangements to notify internal personnel immediately, such as senior management, human resources, health and safety management, and employee representatives. They then may need to inform external parties, such as the family of the casualty, external authorities, insurance companies, public relations advisers and so on. You need to make sure that these internal and external contact procedures are documented in the incident reporting section of your safety policy document.

You need a record of all work-related accidents that result in personal injury, which is the legal minimum.

A typical accident record may include the following:

- ✔ Name and address of casualty
- ✔ Date and time of accident
- ✔ Location of accident
- ✔ Details of injury
- ✔ Details of treatment given
- ✔ Description of event causing injury
- ✔ Details of any equipment or substances involved
- ✔ Witnesses' names and contact details
- ✔ Details of person completing the record
- ✔ Signatures

You also want separate forms for the recording of accidents and the recording of accident investigations. You don't need the personal data in the accident record included in the investigation report. A good investigation report takes a detached, objective look at the circumstance of the accident, so the personal details of those involved are not relevant to the analysis.

Improving Health and Safety Performance

Monitoring safety performance isn't enough in itself to maintain an effective health and safety management system. It's just one aspect of what you need to do to make improvements. Periodically, senior managers need to review performance – that is take a holistic view, looking at all your internal monitoring data, relevant trends and external influences (such as new legislation) – and make strategic decisions on what needs to change (or confirm that everything is in fact on track).

In most formal management systems (refer to Chapter 6), this review process is called a *management review* and it's a separate process from monitoring activities like auditing and inspections. It's quite easy with audits and inspections to get lost in the detail and forget to look at the bigger picture – whether your system is achieving the objectives that you set (and whether those objectives are still valid or helpful).

The management review draws on all the data from your monitoring activities. The review then makes recommendations, which provide you with a springboard for continuous improvement. We look at the review process and how to implement the review outcomes in the following sections.

Reviewing your safety management system

You safety management system looks good on paper and we're sure you've done your homework well, but you'd better plan to keep an eye on things just in case something changes or stops working as well as it should. This is where the *management review* process comes in – to confirm whether your health and safety arrangements still make sense. Is your safety policy still valid? Is your safety management system still working properly?

Your review process checks on safety performance. You need feedback to see if the safety management system is working properly and in the way you planned it to.

The management review usually involves the senior management team (including a safety advisor if you have one): people with a broad knowledge of the business and the power to make decisions. The frequency of your management review is up to you, but it makes sense to complete one at least annually or even quarterly (depending on how much you need to review and how quickly things change).

In general, you draw on the following items for review at your meeting:

- Internal audit findings (from previous audits over the period), including the status of any actions on findings

- Analysis of compliance with relevant legal requirements (sometimes called *legal compliance audits*)

- Analysis of compliance with other standards that you've signed up to (this may include complying with a specific customer-related safety requirement or following a voluntary code or policy)

✔ Input from consultation activities (such as safety committee meetings or from employee representatives – refer to Chapter 3 for more on these)

✔ Input from external parties, such as safety-related complaints from customers and neighbours, actions from government regulators (such as enforcement notices from HSE inspectors), or findings of audits conducted by external people (for example, customers or certification bodies)

✔ Overall performance and trends, such as KPIs and targets (which often relate to your risk management controls; refer to the earlier section, 'Using KPIs and Targets')

✔ Whether your stated health and safety objectives (part of the safety commitment in your statement of general policy – refer to Chapter 2) have been met (or how far they have been met)

✔ The status of any accident investigations (including any outstanding actions)

✔ Outstanding actions from previous management reviews

✔ Changes that may affect the management system: for example, new laws coming into force or new standards

✔ Other matters (such as recommendations that haven't already been covered in the preceding items)

As you may expect, the internal information that you have to review mainly comes from your audits of the safety management system, your accident reports/investigations and your checks on the risk control measures. This is how you keep tabs on what you're up to.

Of course, things can change outside the organisation as well. New legislation or changes in current good practice can move the goal posts and result in the need for redesign or amendment of any parts of the safety management system – or even a change in your overall direction or objectives.

Reviewing also gives you the opportunity to celebrate and promote your health and safety successes. If it's all worked wonderfully well, why not crow about it! These days you often have to report health and safety performance publicly, so it's good publicity to be able to praise yourself.

The clever thing about reviewing is that it closes the loop, so the outcomes of your review become part of your next plan and so it goes on. This never-ending cycle of Plan–Do–Check–Act (refer to Chapter 6) should iron out all the snags in your health and safety machine so that you end up with continuous improvement and better workplace standards.

Implementing change

The management review isn't an empty meeting where you chew the fat over a cup of tea. It draws conclusions and has formal outputs. In short, your management review meeting should produce decisions that result in changes to your priorities, resource allocation, safety policy (and objectives) and so on – indeed, anything that needs changing. The final stage of the process is to make certain that your recommendations feed directly into action plans for improvement.

Action plans:

- Identify the **actions** to be taken
- By responsible **persons**
- By appropriate **deadlines**

In other words, what is to be done, by whom, and when, so that you get some definitive action from your action plans.

Part III
Controlling Workplace Risks

© John Wiley & Sons, Inc.

Check out www.dummies.com/extras/healthandsafetyuk for an online article about reducing musculoskeletal disorder issues in keyboard users.

In this part . . .

✔ Stamp out stress, violence and drug abuse.

✔ Work safely at height, manage site transport operations and safeguard driving for work.

✔ Manage ergonomic risks from manual handling and computer use.

✔ Guard against machinery hazards.

✔ Take sensible precautions when working with electricity.

✔ Understand fire risks and figure out what to take into account during a fire risk assessment.

✔ Apply the principles of good practice to keep chemical hazards under wraps.

✔ Reduce the effects of noise and vibration, and protect your employees from radiation.

Chapter 9

Tackling Behaviour-Based Issues: Workplace Woes

In This Chapter

▶ Taking affirmative action against violent behaviour

▶ Reducing employee stress levels

▶ Identifying drug and alcohol misuse

*V*iolence (actual or threatened), stress (one part of the wider topic of mental ill-health), and drug and alcohol misuse or abuse are three potential workplace issues that have become increasingly recognised over recent years. Collectively, these issues are often termed 'psycho-social' by experts and they can often be connected. Violence can cause stress and vice-versa. Stress can lead to mental ill-health, anxiety and depression, which can in turn lead to drug and alcohol misuse or abuse. Drug and alcohol misuse or abuse can then lead to violence . . . and this cycle may continue without a pause unless some kind of intervention interrupts it.

In this chapter we take a look at the issues that can cause employees the most mental grief and help you to understand your responsibilities as an employer.

Lifting the Lid on Violence

Work-related violence is defined by the Health and Safety Executive (HSE) as:

> *Any incident in which a person is abused, threatened or assaulted in circumstances relating to their work.*

(You can find out more on the position of the HSE when it comes to violence at www.hse.gov.uk/violence.)

Taking a step back from this formal definition, what constitutes an incident of violence? It's all in the key words. Consider these differences:

- ✔ **Assault:** If someone punches you, you probably recognise it as an assault.

- ✔ **Threat:** If someone threatens to punch you, you may feel physically threatened, as well as anxious about what may happen next.

- ✔ **Abuse:** This is a little stickier than assaults or threats. For example, if you swear during a conversation, does that mean that you're being abusive? It may depend on the context of the conversation and who you're speaking to, but the general 'rule of thumb' is that if the listener is offended it may be construed as abuse – especially if the listener has highlighted that they've felt offended before.

Employees need to have an understanding of what language is acceptable in their working environment and who to approach if they feel that others are using inappropriate language.

If somebody is physically assaulted, threatened or abused in the workplace, she's a victim of work-related violence. Violence can also come from clients, customers, colleagues or members of the public.

Threats and assaults are usually reported, unless employees become immune to such behaviour, believe that it's acceptable or fear they won't be believed or taken seriously. Some environments have a culture where reporting is seen as a weakness, and employees may worry about their colleagues finding out. Getting employees to report abuse can be hard because, depending on the level of abuse, they may just accept it as 'part of the job' or a 'bad day'.

Reports of any type of work-related violence need to be taken seriously – taking action in response to reports of violent behaviour can help reduce the chances of future incidents of violence.

Some professions are vulnerable to external violence from members of the public, and you often see notices in public-facing premises (like post offices and hospital emergency departments) that clarify the organisation's stance on violent behaviour. These notices may make statements that begin with 'We will not tolerate . . .' and go on to state their opposition to violent behaviour and the likely consequences of such behaviour (for example, risk of prosecution). These notices act as deterrents to potential aggressors and give employees the confidence of knowing that their employer supports them.

Understanding the risk of violence in your work environment

You first need to identify whether your business is at risk of workplace violence (for example, perhaps you run a public-facing business or you're already aware of a problem in your workplace).

You can start to work this out without even leaving the safety of your office by reviewing accident/incident report forms or asking employees to take part in a survey. Depending on what kind of business you're in, the potential for violence may be obvious. It's most obvious when you're dealing with the general public, especially in circumstances where they're likely to be frustrated – for example, providing customer services (in particular when dealing with unhappy customers), enforcing the law (primarily the police) or working in a position of authority (such as teachers).

If your business deals with cash transactions or trades in high-value goods (such as jewellery and electronics), violence may be something you're very aware of. You probably already have equipment and procedures in place to manage the potential for violence, like locked cabinets, a safe for overnight storage, shutters to provide an additional protective barrier and so on.

One of the triggers for violence is stress. Unfortunately, unless you know the person, it can be difficult to tell when someone is experiencing stress (they don't grow another arm) and resolving the cause isn't always possible. We review the causes of stress and how to take steps to help manage it in the later section, 'Stressing Out'.

Risk assessment helps you to identify hazards within the workplace and should be used to establish whether your organisation is likely to experience incidents of violence. Chapter 4 covers the risk assessment process in detail.

When conducting a risk assessment to look at violence, threats and abuse, you need to address the following questions:

> ✔ **Type of organisation:**
>
>   • Does your organisation provide a service, such as caring activities or educational services?
>
>   • Does your organisation deal with cash transactions or trade in high-value goods?
>
>   • Does your organisation have a history of issues? (You should consider both formal and informal reports.)

✔ **Employees:**

- Are your employees overworked?

- Do you often hear employees complaining that customers are 'rude' or 'demanding'?

- Is your management team perceived to be unsupportive of its employees and unconcerned for their well-being?

✔ **Premises:**

- Do your premises get overcrowded?

- Is it easy to get lost on your premises?

- Would you describe your premises as unsafe (for example, do they have poor lighting or are they cluttered), unclean or inhospitable (for example, too hot or too cold)?

- Are drugs or alcohol consumed on or around the premises?

✔ **Customers:**

- Do customers have to wait a long time before they're dealt with?

- Do you often gets complaints from customers about your employees or your premises?

If you answer yes to any of the questions above, your organisation is at risk of a violent incident.

Recognising these triggers helps you to take steps to, at the very least, reduce the risk of violence, but hopefully you can prevent violence from occurring in the first place. Protecting your employees from violence helps them to feel safe at work, supported in their job role and therefore feel more motivated. Your business will also prosper because it won't receive the associated negative publicity around violent incidents, have to replace damaged property or face prosecution proceedings. Safe work makes sense!

Reducing the risk of violence at work

You can make a great start towards reducing your risk of violence at work by producing a statement or policy outlining your business's stance on violence and verbal abuse and detailing the procedures that employees should follow when handling issues of workplace violence.

Figure 9-1 shows a sample statement that covers all the bases for a suitable policy to reduce the risk of violence at work. You can adapt this policy to suit your organisation so that you can meet your duty to provide a safe work environment.

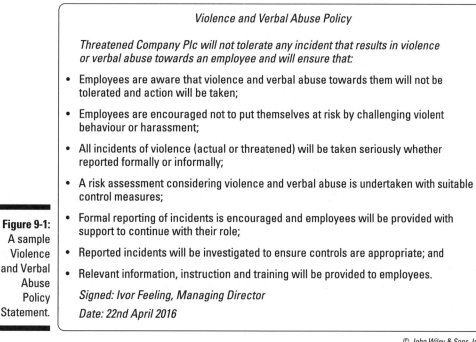

Violence and Verbal Abuse Policy

Threatened Company Plc will not tolerate any incident that results in violence or verbal abuse towards an employee and will ensure that:

- Employees are aware that violence and verbal abuse towards them will not be tolerated and action will be taken;

- Employees are encouraged not to put themselves at risk by challenging violent behaviour or harassment;

- All incidents of violence (actual or threatened) will be taken seriously whether reported formally or informally;

- A risk assessment considering violence and verbal abuse is undertaken with suitable control measures;

- Formal reporting of incidents is encouraged and employees will be provided with support to continue with their role;

- Reported incidents will be investigated to ensure controls are appropriate; and

- Relevant information, instruction and training will be provided to employees.

Signed: Ivor Feeling, Managing Director

Date: 22nd April 2016

Figure 9-1:
A sample Violence and Verbal Abuse Policy Statement.

© John Wiley & Sons, Inc.

Workplace violence doesn't always arise due to external sources. You need to be clear to your colleagues about what constitutes unacceptable behaviour on the part of managers and other employees in addition to service users or members of the public. Leave no room for doubt by providing all employees with your policy (refer to Figure 9-1 for an example), offering any required training and addressing bad behaviour quickly to nip it in the bud. You can also use signage around your premises to prevent violent behaviour from happening, although this is more common when communicating your stance on violence to members of the public (for example, on the glass partitions in customer-facing roles at banks and post offices).

Conducting a risk assessment

In the workplace, you can reduce violence from external sources through hiring security staff, installing security cameras, providing access-controlled doors, minimising queues, communicating waiting times, providing screens between staff and members of the public and installing panic alarms (with a procedure for activation). But not all staff work in nice, warm office environments. If you have employees who conduct home visits, work alone or travel to different locations for work, they may become involved in a violent incident, either by being in the 'wrong place at the wrong time' (for example, a dangerous neighbourhood at night) or because they've been targeted for high-value goods (or due to disputes with your business). In these cases, you need to evaluate how likely an incident is to occur – considering where they work (for example, places with known violent offenders) or how they work (for example, alone, in uniform, carrying laptops) – and then implement measures to prevent lone working: for example, you can require that visits are logged with a supervisor, arrange pre- and post-visit check-in telephone calls, and implement a means for confirming locations and parking in secure areas.

You can provide training for employees working in both scenarios (in-house or out-and-about), but their training needs will vary dramatically. Office-based employees will require training to defuse aggression, and non-office-based employees will require training for handling lone working issues. For specialist job roles you may need to consider self-defence training, but remember that the aim of the game is not to encourage violence but to try and defuse it.

Where employees highlight the fear of violence, quick and cost-effective solutions like reducing lone working in key locations or at key times, ensuring employees reverse park (to enable a quick exit) and updating visit diaries may be effective.

Reporting incidents

Some violent incidents need to be officially reported to the authorities (for example an injury where someone is incapacitated for more than seven days would need to be reported under RIDDOR – see Chapter 8 on accident reporting). It may also be a criminal matter (assault) and need to be reported to the police. But even if that's not the case, the internal reporting of violent incidents can assist you with identifying trends.

The HSE have produced a guide for employers called *Violence at Work*. It provides excellent advice on identifying and controlling violence and some useful case studies, for example:

> *A survey by a trade union after 12 separate shop robberies found that each incident occurred between 5 and 7 o'clock in the evening. This finding could have useful security lessons for late night opening of stores and shops.*

Looking at your incidents and establishing if you can observe any trends can assist with how you select suitable controls and help you to meet your legal obligations.

You can find the HSE's *Violence at Work* guidance here: www.hse.gov.uk/pubns/indg69.pdf.

Getting employees to report every incident, especially in workplaces where violence is commonplace (such as a customer service call centre) can be difficult. They may spend most of their days filling out forms! A good procedure in this scenario is to advise employees to keep a diary of all incidents (and possible witnesses) and copies of anything that may be relevant that they can submit with an incident report.

Digital telephone services routinely record calls ('for training purposes') and so can provide you with an additional source of incident-related evidence.

Stressing Out

It seems to be the word of the times – stress! Just over a third of work-related illnesses are put down to stress – and those are just the reported ones. People use the term 'stressed-out' regularly, but what is stress?

Some may find that deadlines are 'stressors'; some say that they perform better under the pressure of a deadline. Individuals experience stress to differing degrees and defining stressors and managing them can be difficult, especially as the stressor may not be related to work.

The HSE defines work-related stress as:

> *The adverse reaction people have to excessive pressures or other types of demand placed upon them at work.*

(You can find out more from the HSE here: www.hse.gov.uk/stress/furtheradvice/whatisstress.htm.)

The key words here are 'adverse reaction'. If your employees are stressed, you may well notice (or they'll experience) some or all of the following symptoms:

- ✔ Inability to concentrate (pay attention, you over there)
- ✔ Moodiness or irritability (which isn't normal behaviour)
- ✔ Depression or general unhappiness (when it becomes the norm)
- ✔ Nausea and dizziness (which may be accompanied by a pale complexion, but you'll definitely notice if someone hits the floor after a dizzy spell)

✔ Sleeplessness/tiredness (also known as 'bags under the eyes'; you aren't expected to monitor employees to check their sleep patterns, so this can be hard to detect)

✔ Loss of self-confidence (for people who usually have some, if not a lot)

These experiences can also be part of normal day-to-day life in small doses – for example, everyone gets tired sometimes – and mild occurrences of these symptoms may pass quickly after the pressure has lifted. However, experiencing some or all of these symptoms for prolonged periods of time can be quite debilitating, making recovery more difficult, which allows pressure to build up over time.

To minimise the impact of stress, you try to spot it early and manage it as best you can. The following sections provide tips for identifying any issues with stress in your workplace and offer guidance on tackling workplace stress.

The next two sections provide a stress-specific risk assessment (refer to Chapter 4 for the general approach to risk assessments) using a set of six known risk-factor categories – demand, control, support, relationships, role and change. We use these categories to identify the risks and to develop solutions to reduce the risks.

Identifying stressors

Tight deadlines, problems at home and a breakdown in a relationship at work are some things that may cause you work-related stress. Because everyone loves to put things into boxes (like presents), the HSE have identified six key areas associated with stress, which we share in the following list.

Work your way through this list of questions to see if your business is on top of its employees' stress levels:

✔ **Demand:** Excessive demands of the job in terms of workload (too much or too little), speed of work and deadlines, working hours (excessively long), and work patterns (for example, changing shift patterns). Consider:

• Are employees able to cope with their jobs?

• Are employees able to raise their concerns?

• Are employees able to achieve their normal day-to-day tasks in their normal working time?

- Are employees able to do the tasks allocated to them? For example, if a manager has never used a computer and you introduce a computer-based HR system, how will he be able to use it?

- Have you addressed or at least provided feedback regarding any complaints about work conditions?

✔ **Control:** Control over what work is to be done, how it is to be done, the pace of the work and the priorities involved. Consider:

- Are employees able to be imaginative about how they complete tasks?

- Are employees given the ability to impose their own deadlines on most of their work tasks?

- Can employees prioritise their work?

- Can employees work at their own pace?

- Are employees encouraged to develop new skills?

- Are employees given the chance to use their own initiative?

- Can employees decide on their break times?

- Can employees decide on their work patterns? (This doesn't necessarily mean that they can leave early or come in late but, if the work allows, are they able to move about during the day or are they stuck in one place?)

✔ **Support:** Lack of support in terms of information, instruction and training to do the work; lack of support from colleagues and managers; lack of information as to the type of support available to employees; and having no one to turn to when the pressure increases. Consider:

- Do employees get enough support and encouragement from their managers and colleagues?

- Can employees access the resources required for their job?

- Do they know how to access the necessary support, for example, online training access codes?

✔ **Relationships:** Poor workplace relationships (maybe even conflict), and in particular bullying and harassment (whether by managers, peers or even subordinates), plus a lack of policies and procedures to deal with these problems. Consider:

- Is there a bully in the workplace? Or even worse, a culture of bullying?

- Do employees actively share relevant information? (Some information is confidential but the saying 'knowledge is power' can be taken too far.)

- Are policies in place to deal with negative behaviours?

- Do employees know how to report negative behaviours?

✔ **Role:** Lack of clarity about an individual's role, the responsibilities and authority she has, and how she fits in to the larger organisational structure. No clear job descriptions or systems to enable employees to raise concerns about their role and responsibilities. Consider:

- Do employees understand their role?

- Are there clear job descriptions?

- Are employees provided with adequate information on what their role consists of?

- Can employees raise concerns if needed?

✔ **Change:** The threat of change and the change process itself, whether it's a change that affects just one worker (for example, demotion or re-assignment) or the whole organisation (for example, redundancies and management take-overs). Consider:

- Do you engage employees when change is on the horizon? Businesses inevitably change over time; even though loose plans may seem too small to share, employees who are engaged in the process can assist by providing another perspective and 'on the ground' information.

- Are employees consulted on change from the start?

- Are employees provided with support for change and given the chance to highlight areas of concern for them as individuals?

Do you think that your business has a stress problem? If you answered 'no' to any of the preceding questions, it looks as if you do.

Recognising these six areas as potential stressors early on can assist with reducing stress-related sickness and improving staff morale.

A large department store chain experienced a national increase in employees being signed off with stress by their GP. Although it had some protective measures in place, it decided to create specific workplace targets around stress. These aimed to:

✔ Raise awareness of stress and reduce any associated stigma.

✔ Prevent work-related stress where possible.

✔ Lower the level of absence due to stress, anxiety and depression.

The company undertook a stress risk assessment in all branches and collected data through return-to-work interviews, absence figures and via its occupational health team. It also included stress-related questions in its annual staff survey.

Using a working party to review all of its findings, the company identified three areas in which to reduce stress:

1. Ensuring that policies and procedures are in place for stress, bullying, diversity, sick pay, family leave and security, and so on.

2. Providing training to recognise stress that develops personal resilience, communication skills and conflict resolution, as well as job-related training.

3. Highlighting support mechanisms and ensuring that they're able to be utilised, such as referral to Occupational Health, private counselling or other mental health therapies, individual rehabilitation programmes, return-to-work interviews, support from line managers and guidance from Human Resources.

By taking action to reduce stress levels, the organisation achieved a greater understanding of stress, enabling early intervention and better employee support for when they returned to work.

You can read more about this case on the HSE website: `www.hse.gov.uk/stress/casestudies/john-lewis.htm`.

After you've established your organisation's potential for stress, you need to consider who may be harmed by stress. You may have some of this information already through sickness absence records, but to get a true reflection you can invite employees to undertake an anonymous stress survey.

The HSE provide a useful anonymous stress survey (or 'indicator tool') that you may find helpful for your organisation. You can find it on their website at `www.hse.gov.uk/stress/standards/pdfs/indicatortool.pdf`.

If your employees answer the questions in an anonymous stress survey honestly, it helps you to identify the pressure points where action is needed. You need to take action and monitor whether those actions continue to be effective at managing stress.

Managing stress using the HSE's Management Standards

In this section we look at some basic approaches for managing the HSE's six areas of work-related stress (refer to the preceding section): demand, control, support, relationships, role and change. The HSE calls its suggested solutions based on these six areas the 'Management Standards' for work-related stress.

Jobs are never stress free, and some areas of stress may not apply to some or all of your team. Whatever level of risk your team may face, you need to ensure that the level of stress is manageable and not unreasonable.

For each of the six areas of work-related stress, you can make some straight-forward changes that you can easily implement:

✓ **Demands:** Consider these points:

- Ensure that workloads, speed of work and deadlines are reasonable and, where possible, set these as part of a discussion with the employee (rather than impose them).

- Allow flexible working hours and work patterns where possible, and under special circumstances for short durations.

- If your workplace is a high-stress environment, aim to recruit employees on the basis of their competence, skills and ability to cope with difficult or emotionally demanding work.

- Allow employees to recover from high-stress situations without fear of punishment.

✓ **Control:** Allow employees to have control over how their work is done and the priorities that they have, as well as their working environment where possible (for example their lights, temperature and when they can move around).

✓ **Support:** Ensure that your employees know what's expected of them and where they can get additional support when they need it.

✓ **Relationships:** Provide clear policies concerning acceptable standards of behaviour in the workplace; don't tolerate bullying and harassment.

✓ **Role:** Establish clear lines of responsibility, authority and what the employee's role is, as well as where he fits in the larger organisational structure. Communicate these structures clearly to all employees and to others across the organisation in order to prevent any 'treading on toes'.

✓ **Change:** Explain the reasons for change and consult employees about these reasons where possible. In some situations, change is best phased in gradually to allow workers to adapt; in others, it's better to implement change quickly to minimise the impact of uncertainty. If you're looking to move employees from set desks to hot desks, for example, you can start the move gradually; however, when looking at downsizing your workforce, you may prefer not to make people wait for confirmation of your plans.

If employees have been off work with stress, or are currently off, you need to ensure that you have an effective return-to-work procedure. When employees are looking to return to work, good employer practice involves:

✓ Staying in regular contact with employees.

✓ Encouraging employees to regularly review their situation with their doctor.

✔ Implementing a return-to-work plan for your employees. This may include a phased return, lessening employee tasks for a few weeks, helping them with flexible working arrangements, and providing them with somewhere to go if they need a break and someone to talk to if they feel overwhelmed.

An effective return-to-work procedure allows you to address these issues in collaboration with your employees, which helps them to feel supported.

Wising Up to Drugs and Alcohol

Drugs (in the form of solvents, illegal drugs and prescribed drugs) and alcohol have been a potential threat to healthy, happy living for a long time. When you first consider potential issues around drugs and alcohol, you may first think about illegal drugs and drunk people (and the workplace may not be the first place that springs to mind).

However, drugs and alcohol can affect the workplace in the following ways:

✔ **Alcohol:** This can impair performance (whether consumed during the daytime, or the lingering effects from the night before).

✔ **Drugs (legal or otherwise):** Some prescription drugs can impair your ability – and illegal drugs can definitely affect performance.

✔ **Solvents:** Unintentional exposure can impair your ability to work effectively and safely. Solvent abuse may also be intentional.

Drug and alcohol *misuse* occur when someone has taken too much; *abuse* is present when physical withdrawal exists and dependency occurs. One can very easily lead to the other.

Drug or alcohol misuse or abuse doesn't just affect the user – it also impacts your business by increasing absenteeism and reducing productivity, and it raises the chance of an accident due to reduced awareness.

Tackling the misuse and abuse of drugs and alcohol will enable you to:

✔ Reduce absenteeism

✔ Increase productivity

✔ Reduce the risk of accidents

✔ Save on recruiting and training new employees

The impact of drugs and alcohol

It can be very difficult for people to recognise the difference between having a 'problem' with drugs and alcohol, and socially acceptable behaviour.

Approximately one in four workers under the age of 30 have used illegal drugs within the past year, and illegal drug use has been part of culture throughout history. *Narcotics Anonymous* exists for individuals who recognise and accept that they have an issue with drugs and who wish to change.

Legal drugs (including alcohol) can also present a significant issue, impairing abilities in many of the same ways as illegal drugs. Most people have been prescribed medicine to help their bodies overcome illness, but overuse, whether accidentally or on purpose, can have significant lasting effects, which may turn into abuse.

Alcohol is a legal drug that's socially acceptable and in some cases encouraged. Due to societal pressure and the ease of access to alcohol, it may not be noticeable that a drinking problem exists until the addiction is well established. Despite popular belief, the majority of people with a drinking problem are in work and functioning normally. Maybe you've misled your GP when asked how many units of alcohol you consume a week (this is a common deception). Or perhaps you lie to yourself – or have no idea because you don't keep track? These behaviours in themselves don't make you an alcoholic – but monitoring alcohol use can help to reduce the likelihood of addiction.

Alcoholics Anonymous (or AA) has an estimated 2.1 million members worldwide, which provides an idea of the scale of the problem.

The following sections provide advice on how to recognise that your business may have a problem with drug or alcohol misuse or abuse, and how to manage these issues in the workplace.

Looking for the signs

You may think that an employee who is drunk or on drugs is easy to spot: maybe you look out for a lack of coordination, slow movement and slurred speech.

Employees may be unable to meet their job's responsibilities due to the effects of drugs and alcohol. They may become confused and experience abnormal fluctuations in concentration and energy throughout the day; they may be irritable or aggressive; or they may behave inappropriately at work, perhaps by swearing or shouting. In the worst-case scenarios, you may identify dishonest behaviour or even theft.

To help you identify signs of a potential drug or alcohol issue, ask the following useful questions:

- ✔ Has any area of your business experienced loss of productivity and poor performance rates?

- ✔ Is an employee regularly late or absent?

- ✔ Does an employee come into work looking dishevelled, unkempt or smelling of substances?

- ✔ Have you seen an increase in risk-taking behaviour, near misses or accidents with certain individuals? If so, is there a pattern at certain points of the day?

- ✔ Is team morale decreasing, or are employee relationships breaking down?

- ✔ Are there arguments over minor issues, or are employees becoming frustrated with colleagues due to their lack of assistance?

- ✔ Has an employee changed his behaviour (usually becoming worse) or demonstrated sudden mood changes?

If you answer yes to some of these questions, you may have an issue within your organisation, and you will therefore need to address these problems (see the next section for more on how to do this).

If you have a cultural issue within your workforce (for example, a 'work hard, play hard' culture exists and encourages drug and alcohol issues or even dependence) it may take some time to address these problems.

Managing drugs and alcohol sensibly

If you identify an issue with drugs or alcohol in your business (or you think that your organisation may have a culture of acceptability or encouragement) you need to decide how you're going to tackle this in order to rid your workplace of the problem.

You need to decide your business's approach – an all-out drinking ban for your employees? No drinking in work hours? Both suggestions have their merits (although the first is perhaps challenging to enforce, not to mention rather draconian) but experience suggests that supporting employees works better than disciplining them, and so you may find a softer approach more effective in the long run.

You're trying to ensure that your workplace is a safe, healthy and happy one (and that your employees won't need to turn to drugs or alcohol to cope), so save the heavy-handed approach for persistent offenders. See if they're willing to accept help and if any of their 'triggers' for drug or alcohol use can be controlled within the workplace. (Check out the earlier section 'Stressing Out' for some tips on controlling stressful work situations.)

To help manage drug and alcohol issues, implement a simple policy that covers your aims, definitions and responsibilities as an employer, as well as your expectations from your employees. This may include:

- ✔ **The rules:** How your business expects employees to behave. Are drugs and alcohol allowed or part of the business? If not, what is/isn't allowed?

   A drink at lunchtime followed by a high-risk activity should be a 'no-no'.

- ✔ **Safeguards for your business:** Absences for treatment and rehabilitation aren't classed as normal sickness absence, and relapses are likely to occur, so you need to be clear about whether absences are to be taken as annual or unpaid leave.

- ✔ **Confidentiality:** Assure employees that they'll be treated in confidence, while highlighting that you may be required to disclose information for legal reasons. It's still illegal to use or supply illegal drugs!

- ✔ **Help and information for employees:** Where they can get help, who they should approach and what resources are available.

- ✔ **Potential for disciplinary action:** Clarify the situations in which disciplinary action will be taken (usually due to denial of drug use, gross misconduct and possession, or 'dealing' in illegal substances in the workplace). You'll also need to report anyone supplying drugs immediately to the police.

Consider implementing drug and alcohol screening where you have high-risk activities occurring, such as driving or using heavy machinery, or where you have a known drug or alcohol problem in your business.

If you do implement a screening programme, you need to screen all employees within an area of work (or all employees of the business if you're not targeting one high-risk area). Never aim your screening programme at an individual in an attempt to resolve a potential drug or alcohol problem, because you can be accused of unfair monitoring or unfair dismissal as you're obviously trying to catch the one employee out.

Some industries have legal requirements around testing for drug and alcohol misuse. For example, the Transport and Works Act 1992 and the Railway Group Standard GE/RT8070 require all rail companies to undertake testing of 'key employees' (those working trackside or on other high-risk activities).

Chapter 10

Harnessing Gravity and Managing Workplace Transport

. . . .

In This Chapter

▶ Tackling the challenges of working at height

▶ Managing safety issues with work-based transport

. . . .

*W*hen you're running a site of any size, you have lots going on. This chapter collects together a number of related issues – connected because they represent workplace environments in a state of constant change or movement. The first issue (working at height) is mostly to do with maintaining and improving the workplace. The remaining two issues relate to transport on- and off-site – which just means running around like a headless chicken (though even chickens with heads run around).

In this chapter, we look at how to evaluate whether you need to work at height, and, if it's unavoidable, we offer advice on some sensible measures you can take to make it safer. When it comes to workplace transport, vehicles and people invariably mix at some point. We look at some ways to keep them apart as far as possible and make the danger more obvious when you can't. Many people drive as part of their work these days too, so we also consider a few tips on managing the driver, vehicle and the journey.

Working at Height

Do you remember being young, not having any worries in the world and jumping from walls because you knew you could do it (even if they were twice your height)? You may take more precautions now (or perhaps not), but with the power of gravity (plus a hard surface to fall on), you know that the higher you go, the less likely you are to survive a fall without incident.

Working at height doesn't mean wearing high heels – and a fall from these heights is where you experience the full force of gravity (and discover that it can be a brutal meeting if you don't treat it with respect).

Falls from height are still the most common cause of fatality in the UK workplace. This makes working at height the most dangerous workplace activity, so manufacturers have developed some innovative designs to reduce your chances of falling and the distance you can fall when working at height.

To paraphrase the Work at Height Regulations 2005, 'at height' is defined by the Health and Safety Executive (HSE) as:

Anywhere a person could fall a distance liable to cause injury.

People tend to associate working at height with work on buildings – roofs, scaffolding and so on. But it's worth bearing in mind that the danger comes from falling vertically, so this may in fact be high up yet underground or, indeed, on a roof that happens to be fragile (so if you fall onto it, it may break and you can potentially fall to your death).

Work at height doesn't just involve going up a ladder, standing near a hole, working on stairs or using a kick-stool to access high shelves. Work at height is all about being able to fall and experience an injury, and this fall can occur over very short distances.

The following sections cover a structured way to manage the risks of working at height – avoid it if you can; if you can't avoid it, choose equipment that stops you from falling; and if you can't use this preventative equipment, choose some equipment that minimises the distance you may fall. We then look at other considerations, such as making sure that your equipment is kept in tip-top condition.

Catch me if I fall!

Bridge-building safety evolved considerably during the construction of the Golden Gate Bridge in San Francisco. The chief engineer, Joseph Strauss, was concerned about the safety of his workers and imposed one safety rule after another. He was the first to use hard hats, and he insisted on the use of safety lines. At first some of the workers refused to use safety lines and belts, but those who continued to disobey the rules were fired.

Strauss then installed the most elaborate and innovative safety device ever conceived for a major construction site – a safety net that rested under the entire bridge and was levered out by 10 metres either side of the bridge.

Avoiding, preventing and minimising work at height

Ideally, you don't want you or your employees to fall at all, whatever the height. Sounds simple enough – and you do have some ways to manage the work required so that you can achieve this goal.

To beat gravity's nasty surprises, work your way through the 'Avoid–Prevent–Minimise' mantra:

- ✔ **Avoid** work at height (where possible)
- ✔ **Prevent** falls from height (where you can't avoid it)
- ✔ **Minimise** the distance of the fall

Avoiding work at height isn't always possible but, by law, it must be avoided where reasonable to do so (under the Work at Height Regulations 2005). We don't mean that you send someone else in your place – and we're not providing you with an excuse to avoid cleaning the windows either. Instead, you can find lots of alternatives to common tasks.

Take cleaning those pesky windows as an example. Consider cleaning your workplace's upper-floor windows from the ground using extension polls (these are extendable water-fed hollow metal pipes that connect to the hose pipe at one end and have a window-cleaning brush on the other). Of course, not all windows can be reached with an extension poll (they don't reach up to the 18th floor, where we're sure you have a lovely office with a gorgeous view). The architect and builder need to have had maintenance in mind to start with, and to have designed less risky alternatives where possible. Examples of designed-in maintenance include being able to lower lighting to the ground to change light bulbs or – getting back to the windows – a window design that allows them to be opened and almost turned inside out so that you can clean both sides from the inside (we realise this also carries some additional, different risks, such as the potential for over-reaching and falling out of the open window).

Preventing falls is possible if you have the right tools for the job. The following types of product can help to prevent people and materials falling from height:

- ✔ **Scaffolding:** Specifically, scaffolding refers to guardrails (the horizontal tubes that form a 'fence' at about waist height above the working platform to stop people from falling off) and toeboards (vertical planks that run along the outside edge of the platform and seal off the bottom edge to stop equipment and materials from falling off).

✔ **Mobile elevating work platforms (MEWPs):** These are short sections of scaffold (enough to hold one or two people) on a platform that can be raised or lowered. They're mobile (so they can be moved easily from place to place) and they come in all sorts of forms and go by different names – indeed, you may already call them things like *cherry-pickers* or *scissor lifts*.

✔ **Work restraints and harnesses:** These act like a fixed dog-lead. The worker wears a harness attached to a lanyard of fixed length. The other end of the lanyard is attached to a fixed point, so the worker can't move beyond the length of the lanyard – you set the length/anchor point so that the worker can't get to a place where they're going to fall (such as a roof edge).

Scaffolding and MEWPs are known as *collective protective measures*: they're safe working platforms that protect *all* people working on them. Work restraint harnesses are an example of *personal protection* – which only protects the person wearing it.

The Work at Height Regulations 2005 state that you should give collective measures priority over personal protective measures. Therefore, wherever practical, go for collective protection over personal protection. However, because collective measures aren't always possible or practical for all aspects of a job, you may find yourself using a combination of collective and personal protective measures when you're working at height.

Minimising the distance of the fall is your final option when working at height if you can't fully prevent falls. You can use devices such as safety nets, air-bags and fall-arrest harnesses to minimise the effect of the fall – the person may still fall, but they're stopped on the way so they don't fall the entire distance. (Check out the nearby sidebar, 'Catch me if I fall!' for more on these safety devices in action.)

If you use these devices to minimise the falling distance and someone does fall, you may have another problem. You can't just leave them hanging there and expect them to magic their way out, like a workplace Houdini. You need a rescue plan to get them out! (We look at rescue plans later in this section.)

We're not saying that the only choices available are things like scaffolds, MEWPs, airbags and nets. In fact, it's recognised that those sorts of things would be considerably over the top (not to mention disproportionately expensive and time-consuming to install) for relatively light, low-risk, short-duration work. In the latter case, you can use lots of other things, like ladders and step-ups, but bear in mind that these neither prevent falls nor minimise fall distance. For larger jobs, you may be desperate to use a scaffold or MEWP but be thwarted by space constraints. Every situation you encounter may be different – but fortunately, the HSE seem to have considered this already and so they offer some helpful guidance on equipment selection online.

The HSE, in an act of outrageous philanthropy (okay, it's their job – and they do it well), have designed the WAIT Toolkit to help you decide what safety equipment is best suited to your needs: www.hse.gov.uk/work-at-height/wait/wait-tool.htm.

The WAIT Toolkit has some worked examples to demonstrate how to use it, and it's really easy to use. It asks you a few short questions, such as whether the work is heavy/light, how long it's likely to take, what access restrictions you have to work with and so on, and then it comes up with a range of solutions you can try.

Access equipment is a term used to cover all the equipment that you use to gain safe access to workplaces at height. So, it covers all the equipment we mention earlier in this section (scaffolding, MEWPs, ladders and so on). Several industry organisations and trade bodies exist that cover access equipment (for example, the National Access and Scaffolding Confederation – NASC – and the International Powered Access Federation – IPAF) and these can also be pretty helpful when it comes to advising you on suitable options, as are equipment hire companies.

You can start to select your access equipment options from the ones we describe earlier in this section, but you have many other considerations to keep in mind when you're trying to make work at height safe, including:

- ✔ **Weather conditions for outside work:** Wind speed generally increases the higher you go. Don't underestimate the power of the wind (no jokes please), for example when carrying large sheet materials or positioning materials while working at height.

- ✔ **People moving below the work platform:** You may need to exclude people from below the working platform (in addition to your platform design, you may also need to consider features such as toeboards, to prevent objects from falling from your work platform).

- ✔ **Rescue plans:** Have a rescue plan in place if you're using fall minimisation measures – you can't depend on the emergency services to save the day. (*Note:* This isn't a general statement about the emergency services' ability; but it's not down to them to resolve your workplace safety concerns, so don't abdicate responsibility and leave them to fix the problem for you. Plan ahead of time so that you and your team have all eventualities covered if you need to use your fall minimisation devices.)

- ✔ **Equipment condition:** Make sure that your access equipment is always in tip-top condition (check out the next section for more on this).

- ✔ **Training and competence (refer to Chapter 3 for more on this):** Make sure that your employees know how to use and check their safety equipment.

Ensuring that your employees can access their workplace safely (without having to precariously balance on a tightrope) is key.

Inspecting your equipment

Your life can depend on your access equipment – the equipment, like scaffolds, ladders and MEWPs, that you depend on to give you safe access to the work you're doing at height. You should therefore make sure that you keep your access equipment in good condition. This also goes for any other associated equipment that either stops you falling or catches you when you do (such as nets, airbags, fall-arrests and work restraints).

It's good practice to do pre-use equipment checks (and to include these checks in your training procedures). Those who check your equipment will need special training so that they know what to look for (for example, cuts and wear in webbing harnesses, damaged nets, and loose or missing scaffold poles). Rescue workers (who may be rescuing people trapped at height, for example, and are saved by fall-arrests, but left hanging in place) require specialist training so that they can safely rescue trapped people.

Ladders are commonly used in the workplace. You can implement some quick and easy pre-use checks for every user to do. Check for things like missing anti-slip feet, grease or dirt on the rungs, and cracked, broken, bent or missing rungs (including damaged welding on metal ladders).

You've almost certainly heard of scaffolding collapses, especially after bad weather or when a truck careers into it. The consequences are grim if scaffolding lets you down. Scaffold inspection is considerably more complicated and will require more extensive instruction and training to do the job (you can access a number of qualification schemes, such as the Basic Scaffolding Inspection Training Scheme [SITS] offered by the Construction Industry Training Board [www.citb.co.uk] for this very purpose). You need to inspect your scaffolding:

- ✔ When it's first erected
- ✔ Every week thereafter
- ✔ Following any substantial structural alteration
- ✔ Immediately after any event that can affect the stability of your scaffolding – like being struck by a vehicle

Some work at height activities may or may not be undertaken by you or your employees, so Chapter 7 considers some of the issues with contractor works occurring on your premises.

Controlling Workplace Transport

Workplace transport is an issue you're very likely to have to deal with. As a minimum people need to get to work, so you'll probably have cars coming on-site and parking somewhere. Even if you don't have on-site parking, you may well have fork-lift trucks (both indoors and outdoors) to move materials from A to B, loading bays for delivery vans to bring raw materials in and transport finished products out, with vehicles coming on- and off-site, at the very least via a trade entrance. If you're in the construction industry it's even worse, with a vast range of mobile work equipment in use on any typical site. And you may also have staff travelling to other locations by car, if not delivering goods to your other locations or to your customers' premises.

So, it would be a surprise if transport, in some shape or form, wasn't one of the hazards that you identified for risk assessment to be carried out on.

Workplace transport occurs either on-site or off-site, with differing risk management issues:

- **On-site transport** involves vehicles moving around your premises, in the process alarming pedestrians, other vehicles occupants and even their own drivers!

  On-site, your transport vehicles are operating on your premises, so you can control the environment in which your transport operations take place. You can aim for a well-organised site to combat the types of problems that are likely to occur.

- **Off-site transport** (in other words, 'driving for work') involves employees using vehicles on public highways, with all the trauma that involves.

  Off-site, your staff are on the open road (which isn't under your direct control), so the best you can do is carefully plan journeys and schedules to minimise foreseeable risks.

Moving vehicles aren't your only concern. You can hit problems before the vehicle even starts to move. It may need to be loaded, secured and any trailers may also need to be coupled to your vehicle.

In the following sections, you discover the safety problems with stationary vehicles, as well as how to get your site organised, get the right vehicles in good condition and enrol a team of capable drivers. You also find out how to look after employees who have to drive on the open road, away from your premises.

Standing still: Evaluating safety issues with stationary vehicles

You can hit problems before your vehicles even start to move, whether it's going to elsewhere on your premises or heading out onto the open road. If you're transporting goods or materials, you need to load up your vehicles, secure your cargo and couple the trailer (if it's an *artic* – a tractor and semi-trailer).

You also need to maintain your vehicles, which necessarily happens at a stand-still (and brings its own set of problems). This transport business is looking to be a bigger problem than first thought – and your vehicles aren't even on the move yet!

Keep in mind the following potential safety issues with stationary vehicles in your workplace (*Note:* This list simply flags up possible issues that may get missed if you focus only on moving vehicles. Most of these issues will be picked up using a general risk assessment approach – refer to Chapter 4):

- ✔ **Loading:** Whether you're loading your vehicles manually or using mechanical loading equipment, you have an accident risk. For example, if you need to lift crates into the back of a lorry, you have a manual handling risk; if you're using a fork-lift truck to load a flat-bed lorry, you have a collision risk.

- ✔ **Unloading:** Manual or mechanical unloading can cause you problems here too. For example, if you're using a mechanical tipper wagon (that is, a truck fitted with an open bed, hinged at the rear, that can be hydraulically lifted at the front to allow the material on the bed to be deposited on the ground behind the truck) to unload your vehicle, it may become unstable and overturn – or people may be hit by the material that you're tipping.

  Chapter 11 explores manual handling hazards (and mechanical handling solutions) and their associated risks in more detail.

- ✔ **Securing:** It's difficult to secure a vehicle properly without having to climb on the top – for example, if you want your drivers to place protective sheets over loads to prevent them from falling off when moving at speed, or to close hatches on the tops of road tankers, you need them to work at height, with the associated risk of injury from falls (refer to the earlier section 'Working at Height' for more on height-related risks).

- ✔ **Coupling:** If you're using articulated lorries, you need to connect (or disconnect) the truck and the trailer from time to time. Watch out for unsafe practices that can leave you with a runaway vehicle or trailer. Either situation can leave you with a serious or fatal injury to the driver or others, and costly damage to both vehicles and property.

✔ **Maintenance work:** You need to repair and maintain your vehicles, and if you carry out these works on your premises, you have to contend with manual handling issues, the risk of crush incidents from movement or the collapse of vehicles under repair, and the fire risk from fuel.

Moving around the workplace environment: On-site transportation

Your problem with on-site workplace transport stems from the fact that you want the vehicles on your premises to make the movement of materials easier. You also have to cater for people driving to work, coming on-site and having to park somewhere. But these mobile machines have to share the workplace with people, and if you have a collision between a person and a vehicle, the person will come off worse, no matter how slowly the vehicle's moving.

The analysis of accident statistics relating to vehicle collisions indicate two broad causes:

✔ The driver loses control of the vehicle

✔ The driver can't see the victim

To improve the control of vehicles, it helps to examine the key causes of loss of vehicle control:

✔ **Environmental conditions:** Working conditions can affect vehicle control – for example, vehicles can be hard to control in snow and ice – and visibility, such as when sunlight temporarily and unexpectedly blinds a driver.

✔ **Mechanical failure:** Problems with your vehicle may mean that the driver can't drive properly; for example, steering or brake failure may mean that the driver can't steer or stop the vehicle.

✔ **Driver error:** Errors can vary from simple mistakes to acts of gross recklessness. Driving too fast is a common problem, and you don't want your drivers to be speeding around corners and braking suddenly. And you certainly don't want your drivers to be under the influence of alcohol or drugs (refer to Chapter 9 for more on managing these tricky issues).

You need skilled drivers, because many accidents happen during complicated manoeuvring or reversing. Driver error is the usual cause of:

• Overturning – tipping the vehicle over onto its side, front or back.

• Collisions – with other vehicles, pedestrians or fixed objects.

You can think of transport accidents as happening because, in simple terms:

- The **site** is disorganised.
- The **vehicle** is substandard.
- The **driver** is incompetent.

The secret to gaining control over your transport operations is to get your site organised, make sure that you've got the right vehicles in good condition, and enrol a team of capable drivers. That way, the chances of things going wrong are pretty slim.

You need to get to grips with these three key areas if you're going to control your workplace transport and minimise the risk of accidents. We take you through some options in the following sections.

Organising your site

To organise your work site, whether you have a large warehouse or a small set-up, you need to aspire to high standards to create a site that is:

- Well-designed, so it's vehicle-friendly
- Well-maintained, so everything works as it should
- Well-operated, so you have safe systems of work (refer to Chapter 7)

When you design and construct your site, aim to make it vehicle-friendly from day one. You can eliminate or reduce the risks created by vehicle operations in the following ways:

- **Introducing vehicle-free zones:** You find them in towns and cities, so why not in your workplace? Eliminate these hazards on parts of your site by creating pedestrian-only areas.

- **Introducing pedestrian-free zones:** The other alternative is to get rid of the pedestrians (not literally!). They're the ones at greatest risk from vehicle-manoeuvring operations, so you can keep them out of the parts of the workplace where they don't need to be.

- **Installing a vehicle traffic route:** The compromise is to keep vehicles and pedestrians separate so that you can design roads and routes that keep vehicles at a distance from pedestrian walkways and other vehicles. A good way to reduce the risk of vehicle–vehicle collisions is to use one-way systems. It may also save you from too much reversing on-site as well.

- **Segregating vehicles and pedestrians:** This is the golden rule for traffic control, so your aim is to provide pedestrians with separate walkways. It's even better if you can add a barrier to the route to provide physical protection. Another good idea is to provide safe havens for pedestrians to retreat into during vehicle movements (very useful for loading bays).

✔ **Providing pedestrian walkways:** If you can't use barriers, you can mark walkways on the floor to show where the segregated areas are. These walkways are less effective than barrier segregation, but they're better than nothing.

✔ **Separating site and building entrances:** Allowing vehicles and pedestrians to use the same entrance is a bad idea. You want to avoid forcing them together and creating bottlenecks (along with the attendant safety concerns) by providing separate entrances.

✔ **Introducing speed limits:** You have to control the speed of traffic on-site, so you need to set limits, erect advisory signage and enforce these limits. You may have to get heavy and use traffic-calming measures such as speed bumps if your rules are ignored.

✔ **Improving visibility:** Seeing what you're doing is an obvious necessity, so you need to make sure that your drivers have unobstructed views from their vehicles. You can make their lives easier by getting rid of blind spots through careful traffic route design or, if all else fails, providing mirrors or CCTV.

✔ **Providing signage:** You need the site to be well signed, not just for speed limits but for any other hazards on traffic routes (such as low overheads, where you can include a maximum headroom sign).

✔ **Maintaining traffic route surfaces:** Your vehicles have to run on something, so you want good surfaces that suit the vehicles using them. Things to check include strength and stability, grip, and drainage. You don't want potholes and skid pans!

✔ **Avoiding gradients:** If you can avoid gradients, it greatly improves the stability of vehicles with a high centre of gravity (for example, fork-lift trucks with raised forks). If not, make sure that you check how the gradients that you can't get rid of may affect the stability of the vehicles that have to use them.

After you design your vehicle-friendly site – carefully planned to minimise typical transport risks – you want to make sure that it remains in great working order. Therefore, you're going to need to maintain it by providing systems for:

✔ Routine inspections

✔ Regular cleaning

✔ Repair or replacement of defective controls

The final piece of the organised-site puzzle is to keep it working effectively by providing safe systems of work for vehicle-related operations (refer to Chapter 7 for more on how to develop safe systems of work). Your safe systems of work include the site procedures and rules that you want your employees to follow. For example, you may have restrictions on times when vehicles can come onto your site (just like schools do).

Checking your vehicles

The vehicles that you use depend very much on the nature of your business. You may have all sorts of vehicles coming and going on-site, from the cars, vans and lorries that you use on public roads to 200-tonne quarry trucks that you keep on-site. And each type of vehicle has its own particular safety needs.

However, you can apply some broad principles to your whole vehicle fleet to minimise the risk of an accident.

Your vehicles need to be:

✔ Suitable for their intended use

✔ Suitable for the environment and conditions in which they're used

✔ Maintained in safe working order

✔ Driven only by suitably trained, qualified staff

✔ Inspected routinely before use

These requirements may not seem like rocket science to you – aren't they just common sense? – but don't be complacent. A huge number of transport accidents are caused by using the wrong vehicle in the wrong place, using a vehicle in poor condition or a driver operating a vehicle incorrectly (sometimes all of these at once!).

Depending on the vehicle and its use, you may also need to make sure that you've got:

✔ Seats for the driver and any passengers

✔ Seat belts

✔ Roll bars or roll cages (a frame constructed around the passenger compartment of a vehicle) to protect the driver in the event of overturn

✔ Guards to protect the driver in the event of falling objects

✔ A horn

✔ Audible reversing alarms

✔ Beacons or flashing lights

If you carry out a survey of the vehicles you have in use, you can establish what the particular requirements of each type of vehicle are and whether your vehicles comply with those standards. For example, if you use fork-lift trucks in your workplace, the HSE have published an Approved Code of Practice (ACoP) and guidance document, L117 – *Rider-Operated Lift Trucks: Operator Training and Safe Use* (third edition, published 2013) that gives guidance on training requirements for drivers and safe use of fork-lift trucks.

You may expect that work vehicles used on public roads have to comply with the Road Traffic Act 1991, and you'd be right. So, requirements that you're familiar with if you have a car of your own, such as road tax, insurance, headlights and so on, apply to your workplace vehicles if they go off-site. If your vehicles are only used on private land (such as most workplaces), they won't have to comply with the same public highway laws, but they will have to meet the legal standards for that particular workplace (in particular, the Provision and Use of Work Equipment Regulations 1998).

A vehicle is an item of work equipment. So, the Provision and Use of Work Equipment Regulations 1998 apply. These regulations have a useful Part 3 that covers mobile work equipment, so you may find it a handy reference (refer to Chapter 12 and `www.hse.gov.uk/work-equipment-machinery/puwer.htm`). Also, if you've got fork-lift trucks, they're classed as lifting equipment and so come under the Lifting Operations and Lifting Equipment Regulations 1998 as well (`www.hse.gov.uk/work-equipment-machinery/loler.htm`). If you're talking workplace law, you've also got the Health and Safety at Work etc Act 1974 and the Management of Health and Safety at Work Regulations 1999 to keep in mind (as you usually have; for more on these, see Chapter 17).

If this is all sounding a bit complicated don't worry! Your risk assessment on your transport operations will sort out exactly what safety features each of your vehicles should have for the workplace you're operating them in, and the general approach to risk assessment that we cover in Chapter 4 is adequate for this purpose.

Ensuring that your drivers are competent

You need competent drivers, and if you carefully select, train and supervise them, you're well on your way to ensuring that your team is equipped for the job.

But how do you get and keep the high-quality drivers that you need for a safe site? By making sure that your drivers are competent, fit, clued-up and properly supervised. This will help keep them out of trouble!

Here's your recipe for the perfect driver. He needs to be:

- ✔ **Competent to drive the vehicle:** You need proof of this qualification, such as a driver's license, or you may have to train and assess the driver to help him achieve this qualification. You also need to provide refresher training and re-certification. You may also want to check your drivers' licenses periodically to ensure that they don't have undisclosed penalties or that they haven't been disqualified from driving due to road traffic offences. That way, you can ensure proficiency. (If you're using fork-lift trucks in your workplace, the HSE's ACoP and guidance document L117 – *Rider-Operated Lift Trucks: Operator Training and Safe Use* (third edition, published 2013) gives guidance on training requirements for fork-lift truck drivers.)

✔ **Medically fit to drive:** You can carry out a medical examination when you recruit your drivers and repeat this exam periodically to assess health and fitness. The last thing you want is an unnoticed lapse in driving ability caused by a medical problem.

✔ **Provided with specific information, instruction and training:** You can start with driver-specific site induction training – just make sure that you've got a programme appropriate to your workplace. If you specify exactly what you want your drivers to do, they're more likely to do it.

✔ **Supervised:** You've got your safe systems of work and site rules (refer to Chapter 7), so you just need to ensure that they're followed. And make sure that your drivers don't lapse into bad practices!

Getting out on the road: Driving off-site for work

You've got a whole range of hazards to contend with at your workplace, so you expect the least of your troubles to arise when people are off-site driving somewhere. Driving is a common activity and people do it out of work all the time – so what's the problem?

Department for Transport figures suggest that more than a quarter of all road traffic incidents may involve somebody who is driving for work at the time. And in low-risk office-based workplaces, one of the few activities in which a work-related fatality may occur is when staff are driving to other sites or off to meet customers.

What factors make driving at work more risky? Consider the following:

✔ **Distance:** The further you drive, the more chance you have of an accident. But you can improve your odds by using the most suitable routes for the type of vehicle you're driving. Road traffic accident statistics confirm that motorways are the safest roads but may increase your travel distance; minor roads may be more direct and okay for a car, but present more of a problem for larger vehicles. You've also got to think about things like bridges, tunnels, level crossings and so on, which can present dangers for large vehicles. And don't forget, driving long distances without breaks can increase your fatigue levels.

✔ **Driving hours:** The longer you drive for, the more chance you have of an accident. You're increasing your exposure time and also the likelihood of fatigue, which can affect your driving ability. Your journey times need to take into account the road types and conditions and allow for rest breaks. You may even have to specify a limit for long road journeys and insist on an overnight stay after a certain amount of time on the road.

✔ **Work schedules:** Crazy work schedules are just asking for trouble, and if you expect people to drive at a time when they're most likely to feel sleepy (the worst times are between 2 a.m. and 6 a.m. and between 2 p.m. and 4 p.m.), you're increasing their risk of fatigue-related accidents.

If your business involves making deliveries, your schedules need to take this into account.

✔ **Stress due to traffic and weather conditions:** Driving isn't much fun at the best of times, and road conditions made difficult by too much traffic or bad weather can increase stress levels. But if you're smart, you can check out the traffic 'black spots' and local bottlenecks and try and avoid them by careful scheduling. Snow, ice, fog and high winds are all conditions that can increase the risk of a road traffic accident, so you need up-to-date weather reports for planning journeys and estimating travelling times. Try to use vehicles that are better suited to poor conditions, and make sure that your drivers are trained to cope with sudden bad weather.

In the following sections, you find out the smart way to manage work-related road safety to make sure that all your risks from driving for work are under control.

Developing a management system

The best way to manage your work-related road safety risk is to incorporate it into the rest of your systems for managing risk; that is, build it into your existing safety management system (for more on safety management systems, refer to Chapter 6). Therefore, road safety becomes another part of your general duty for the health and safety of your employees and third parties.

You develop your safety management system by following the Plan–Do–Check–Act model (refer to Chapter 6 for lots more on this model).

You can manage work-related road safety using Plan–Do–Check–Act as follows:

- ✔ **Plan.** How are you going to plan for managing driving at work?

  - Start by assessing the risks from work-related road safety in your organisation.

  - Produce a simple driving for work policy – this can be referenced in your health and safety statement of general policy (refer to Chapter 2) and supported with a procedure that covers things such as how journeys are organised, driver training requirements and vehicle maintenance – we look at these issues in the later section, 'Assessing risks'.

  - Get commitment from the top to show that this issue is important (you can include it as a specific point in the safety policy; refer also to Chapter 3 for more on leading from the front).

  - Sort out everyone's roles and responsibilities and make sure that people with responsibility have enough authority to make things happen (refer to Chapter 3 for more on empowering your managers).

- ✔ **Do.** How are you going to make it happen?

  - Use the outcomes of your risk assessment to prioritise your risks and specify your control measures.

  - Make sure that you've got systems to manage your risks and deal with things such as inspecting and servicing vehicles.

  - Consult with your employees, involve them in decisions to get their co-operation, and give them training and information.

- ✔ **Check.** How well is it all working?

  - Make sure you check that your policy objectives are being put into practice.

  - Use active monitoring, such as inspections and tours, to give you information on how well employees are complying with your policy.

  - Encourage your employees to report all work-related road incidents and use the reactive monitoring data to evaluate how well you prevent accidents.

- ✔ **Act.** How well have you performed and what have you learned from it?

  - Use the monitoring information to decide how effective your policy is, whether it targets the right people (that is, those more exposed to risk), and if you need to change it.

  - Keep revisiting your policy to see if it needs updating.

The risk assessment (covered in the 'Plan' stage) is a fundamental part of managing work-related road safety effectively (see the next section, 'Assessing risks', for more on this).

Assessing risks

A driving for work risk assessment uses the standard five-step approach (refer to Chapter 4) but is conveniently framed around these three areas:

- ✔ The journey
- ✔ The vehicle
- ✔ The driver

The following sections look at what can go wrong with each of these three areas in more detail, and provide guidance on what you need to do to make sure that these things don't happen.

The driver

Obvious reasons that spring to mind why a driver may contribute to a work-related driving accident include lack of ability, inadequate training, and fitness and health issues. Therefore, the areas you need to check are as follows:

- ✔ **Competency:**

  - Does the driver have the right driving licence for the vehicle he'll be driving?

  - Can the driver demonstrate relevant experience, skill and knowledge, with proof from references if necessary?

  - Was the driver's licence checked on recruitment, and has it been re-checked periodically since (for example, every six months) to make sure that it's still valid?

  - Do you keep an eye on any endorsements on your organisation's driver's licenses?

- ✔ **Training:**

  - Has the driver been provided with induction training?

  - Has the driver had additional training on routine safety checks, use of safety equipment, and breakdown safety and health issues such as tiredness?

  - Has the driver completed advanced driving or defensive driving training courses?

✔ **Fitness and health:**

- Does the driver have the appropriate medical certificate if a legal requirement exists for medical examination? (For example, drivers of heavy lorries require specific certification.)

- Do you provide regular medicals for at-work drivers who are most at risk? (For example, to check for pre-existing medical conditions.)

- Do you give reminders to staff about the eyesight requirements set out in the Highway Code?

- Do you tell staff not to drive while taking a course of medicine that may impair their judgement?

The vehicle

What do you need to check to make sure that the vehicles you use are suitable, roadworthy, have the right safety kit and are comfortable to drive? Consider the following:

✔ **Suitability:**

- When you buy new or replacement vehicles, do you get the safest ones that are the best to drive?

- Do you lease or hire vehicles if the ones that you've got aren't suitable for a particular job?

- Do you check carefully on privately owned vehicles used for work purposes to make sure that they're insured for business use and have a valid MOT certificate (if necessary)?

✔ **Vehicle condition:**

- Do you have maintenance arrangements in place and are repairs carried out properly?

- Are you doing what the manufacturer recommends for planned preventative maintenance?

- Are your drivers doing basic safety checks?

- Are you making sure that your vehicles don't exceed the maximum load weight and that goods and equipment are properly secured?

✔ **Safety equipment:**

- Do your vehicles have seat belts, airbags and head restraints, and are these fitted as standard and in good order?

- Do you provide other safety kit, such as emergency triangles, first aid kits, spare tyres and fire extinguishers?

✔ **Safety critical information:** Have you made sure that your drivers know all about:

- Recommended tyre pressures?

- How to adjust headlamp beams to compensate for load weight?

- How to adjust head restraints?

- The action to take if they think their vehicle is unsafe, and who they should contact?

✔ **Ergonomic issues:** Have you made sure that your drivers' health and safety isn't at risk from an inappropriate seating position or driving posture by:

- Thinking about ergonomics before purchasing or leasing new vehicles?

- Giving your drivers' guidance on good posture and how to adjust their seat correctly?

The journey

The perilous journey that you don't want is the one with the tortuous route and the impossible schedule, where you're under serious time pressure, and you encounter foul weather. How do you avoid that? Consider the following checklist:

✔ **Routes:** You plan your route so that hazards are avoided and you mini-mise risks by:

- Avoiding busy (for example, a town centre) or high-risk areas (for example, accident black-spots)

- Using low-risk roads such as motorways and dual carriageways

- Avoiding roadworks

In other words, you make good use of your interactive *sat nav* (satellite navigation system).

✔ **Scheduling:** With smart scheduling, you avoid travelling:

- At peak traffic times

- When drivers feel naturally fatigued (between 2 a.m. and 6 a.m. and between 2 p.m. and 4 p.m.)

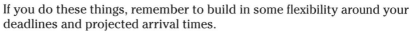

If you do these things, remember to build in some flexibility around your deadlines and projected arrival times.

✔ **Time:** You make sure you allow enough time to complete the journey safely by:

- Setting sensible journey times that take account of road types, road condition and rest breaks

- Not putting drivers under pressure to take unnecessary risks because of tight arrival times

- Letting drivers make an overnight stay, rather than having to complete a long road journey at the end of the working day

- Making sure drivers don't drive excessive distances without appropriate breaks

✔ **Weather conditions:** Imagine that you're one jump ahead as far as the weather is concerned, so you know that you have the possibility of difficult conditions, such as fog, snow or high winds. So, when you're planning journeys you make sure that you:

- Reschedule your routes if you need to

- Select and equip your vehicles properly to operate in poor weather conditions

- Instruct drivers in the actions they need to take to reduce risk

- Give your drivers reliable weather forecasts so that they can plan their journeys accordingly

- Give your drivers guidance on bad weather conditions and when they shouldn't travel

- Give your drivers advice on additional safety during bad weather

Chapter 11

Unpacking Manual Handling and Other Ergonomic Risks

*A*t some stage, you've probably twisted your back or strained a muscle (or you know someone who has). You know that the pain and discomfort stays with you much longer than is strictly polite or necessary. Bad backs, stiff shoulders and pains in the neck are all symptoms of poor handling and posture, which may be caused by workplace constraints or positioning.

Poor posture and lifting techniques can individually or together cause lifelong issues – prevention is definitely better than cure. Awkward posture causes significant stress to joints of the upper limbs and surrounding soft tissues, and pain should be taken seriously (*never* ignore it, hoping to be able to 'work through it'). Unfortunately, if you don't pay attention early on, the symptoms can be harder to overcome and you may have to manage your symptoms rather than find a solution that leads to a full recovery. People who have bad backs always lift correctly; they can't lift in any other way (but they probably used to – hence the problem).

In this chapter, we introduce you to the problems associated with poor posture and inappropriate manual handling. We take you through some helpful guidelines and training suggestions to assist with managing manual handling worries in your workplace, and we help you make sense of the postural challenges from interactions with your workspace to sitting at a desk, balancing your phone in your hands or hunching over your laptop. In no time, you'll amass the knowledge that you need to encourage smart postural practices throughout your business.

Introducing the Problem

Musculoskeletal disorders is a general term that's used to cover the many disorders caused by poor lifting and posture.

Musculoskeletal disorders make up over a third of injuries caused or made worse by work (see Figure 11-1). This means that a large proportion of your sick pay is spent on issues that you can prevent by recognising and controlling how work tasks are carried out.

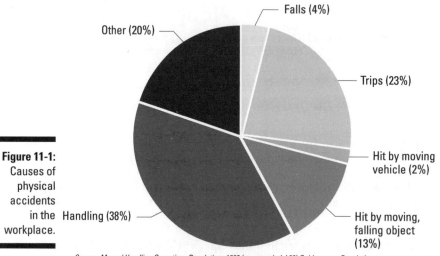

Figure 11-1:
Causes of
physical
accidents
in the
workplace.

Source: Manual Handling Operations Regulations 1992 (as amended; L23) Guidance on Regulations. www.hse.gov.
uk/pubns/priced/l23.pdf. *The Manual Handling Operations Regulations 1992 (as amended; L23) contain public
sector information published by the Health and Safety Executive and licensed under the Open Government License.*

You may think that these injuries happen only to people who lift things that are too heavy for them to manage, but you'd probably be surprised at how many people suffer pain due to poor posture alone (that is, pain caused by sitting or standing in a position that strains, twists or elongates your back). For example, you may decide to spend a pile of cash on the latest gaming computer and then spend subsequent hours playing games and creating new worlds (or whatever type of game you prefer), but if you sit slouched and hunched over while you play, such seemingly innocuous activity can lead to you struggling with a musculoskeletal injury caused by poor posture.

Back issues are a common result of incorrect *manual handling* techniques (that is, the pulling, pushing and lifting that you do to move things from place to place) and poorly designed *workstations* (that is, your work equipment and work environment). Not all workstations are desk-based; wherever you work can be classed as a workstation. An injury can be caused by a single incident or build up over time. By repeatedly lifting or sitting incorrectly you can cause wear and tear to the discs between the vertebrae in your spine – which can lead to the so-called 'slipped disc'.

Ergonomics focuses on designing equipment and processes to take proper account of their interaction with the humans that use them. When looking at a job, you need to understand where the person is positioned and where they're likely to be moving to or looking towards. For example, someone working at a ticket desk handing out pre-booked tickets may have to look up constantly from her seat as the customer approaches and talks to her, potentially causing neck ache. A simple solution here is to raise the desk and flooring so that the employee remains seated and the customer is at eye level.

Taking Practical Steps to Handle Loads Safely

Much unpleasantness can be avoided by handling loads properly in the first place. This is easier said than done: as with many posture-related things, it's easy to fall back into old habits.

Depending on your industry, you may have been on a manual handling course at some stage ('lift with your legs, not with your back' may still echo in your mind). You probably already know the best way to lift, but you may not take this approach consistently (except when you know you're being watched). Alas, it's the nature of postural training – employees may lift and handle objects correctly at work, when they think they should, but then go home and empty a dishwasher while bending their backs. If you already have a bad back, you're likely to be much more careful, because you know that a moment's thoughtlessness can lead to a lifetime of pain.

Back injuries are a common result of poor manual handling – but you can be injured in many other ways too thanks to incorrect handling techniques:

- ✔ **Work-related upper-limb disorders:** Carpal tunnel syndrome, tendon strains and sprains can be caused in the upper limbs by poor manual handling techniques. These disorders don't always involve items that are too heavy – they can be caused by over-stretching while holding something very light or an external force (such as a strong wind) causing you to tighten your grip. Check out the later section, 'Getting Comfortable with Workstations' for more on work-related upper-limb disorders caused by a poorly adapted computer workstation.

- ✔ **Muscle strains and sprains:** When stooping, moving in awkward positions or lifting items that are too heavy, you may feel muscle strains and sprains throughout the body. Muscle injuries can become even more problematic too, because the body adapts to the original injury to reduce the use of the injured muscle, which can cause problems that are just as difficult to overcome as the original injury.

- ✔ **Hernias:** The sheet of muscle that surrounds the gut becomes overloaded through poor lifting techniques, and this muscle can then distort and tear (a lovely thought!). This tear usually happens in the lower abdomen. A hernia can be a painful injury, and it doesn't repair naturally – if it's serious enough then surgery may be offered, but you often have to live with the injury for some time before medical treatment options are made available.

- ✔ **Cut or crush injuries:** These are usually caused when the load that you're moving has sharp edges, is passing through a tight space (so maybe your hands get caught in a doorway, for example) or is dropped onto your feet.

Children tend to demonstrate correct lifting techniques; they don't have the back muscles to lift incorrectly, though these muscles develop as they grow. Adults, however, don't tend to lift correctly, bending their backs and lifting with only their arms.

'Lift with your legs, not your back' is essential advice to follow if you want to avoid a back injury. Only one-quarter of your body's weight is in your legs (from your hips down), so if you bend over at the hips (rather than use your legs) your spine ends up supporting three-quarters of your body weight, plus whatever you're lifting! For example, if you weigh 12 stone, approximately 3 stone is from your hips down – 9 stone sits above your hips. The weight of the load that you're lifting, plus your own body weight, is a lot of pressure to put on your spine, which isn't designed to cope with that amount of load – your legs though, they're designed for it!

Even if you have mastered the correct lifting technique, if an item is too heavy to lift, don't lift it on your own. Either use a mechanical aid or ask a colleague to help. Lifting things that are too heavy can cause serious, irreparable injury, so check the weight with your foot or hand by pushing the item gently before you get started.

The following sections help you to assess manual handling risks in the workplace and see how you can reduce the risks of injury.

Assessing manual handling risks

You need to consider several aspects when you're lifting a load. You don't focus only on the object itself (whether it's bulky or heavy), but also where you can position it (close to your body?), where you're taking it and who may be helping you to lift it.

Reducing lifting requirements by design

Manufacturers are reducing the need for manual handling by design – think about the latest suitcases with their four wheels, which you can push along the floor using only the handle. Remember when they first put two wheels on suitcases and gave you a handle at the other end to pull it along? Ergonomic considerations have had a lot to do with developing and designing manual handling solutions that make sure that handles are adjustable in height, the handle is positioned favourably in comparison to the wheels, and the wheels can turn in all directions. In the same way, mobile phones used to be heavy and cumbersome – the first ones came with a battery pack and a shoulder strap – but through design they've become small enough to fit in your pocket.

Lifting may seem to be all about strength and heavy objects, but technique has a lot to do with it too. Lifting light objects using the wrong technique can cause an injury as damaging as lifting an object that's too heavy. You need to consider if there's a risk of injury from a manual handling task and how that injury may occur.

The following sections help you to assess manual handling risks from both light and heavy loads.

Investigating the risk factors

Before you bother with a detailed risk assessment of a manual handling task, you may want to establish whether the task poses a significant risk of injury in the first place. You don't want to waste your time assessing every single load in the workplace – only those which pose a significant risk to injury.

Your employees can benefit from a little instruction in the basic kinetic lifting technique:

1. **Before lifting:** Check the weight, centre of gravity and stability of the load. Plan the route you're going to take and establish a firm grip on your load.

2. **Doing the lift:** Bend the knees and use your leg muscles to lift the load. Keep your back upright. Keep the load close to your body. Avoid twisting, over-reaching and jerking your body while you're carrying the load.

3. **Setting the load down:** Use the same principles as when lifting: keep your back upright, keep the load close to you, bend your knees and use your leg muscles. Maintain good balance. Set the load down and then adjust its position using your body weight.

Once you identify that a load represents a risk, either due to the weight or other risk factors, you can undertake a risk assessment and decide on appropriate control measures. For manual handling tasks that can't be avoided, the Manual Handling Operations Regulations 1992 state that you need to do a risk assessment of any manual handling tasks where you have a risk of injury to your team. But in practice, as with all risk assessments, the scale of the risk assessment needs to be proportionate. The Health and Safety Executive (HSE) guidance document *Manual Handling Operations Regulations 1992 (as amended; L23) Guidance on Regulations* (www.hse.gov.uk/pubns/priced/123.pdf) gives you some manual handling charts containing weight guidelines for various lifting positions (see Figure 11-2). These weight guidelines can be used as an initial filter and may mean that you won't always have to do a more detailed risk assessment. They give you an idea of the approximate weights that you can generally lift from different positions.

To make best use of the weight guidelines in the regulations and in Figure 11-2, you observe the manual handling task, noting the zones (away from the body, close to the body, above the shoulder and so on) the lifter's hands move the load through compared to the diagram. If the load is lower than the weights provided for each zone, the load can be considered within the guidelines and therefore represents a reduced risk.

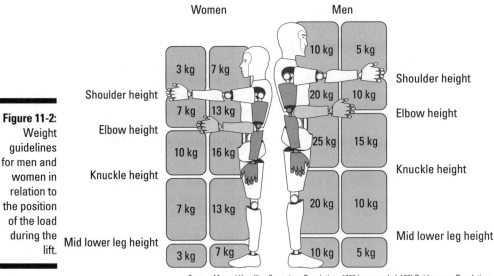

Figure 11-2:
Weight guidelines for men and women in relation to the position of the load during the lift.

Source: Manual Handling Operations Regulations 1992 (as amended; L23) Guidance on Regulations.
http://www.hse.gov.uk/pubns/priced/123.pdf.

A reduced risk doesn't mean that the load's safe. You also need to consider other issues, including who the people lifting the load are – their abilities, medical conditions and the environment they'll be using. If the weight falls under the guidelines, you must consider other risk factors (people, constraints, size and so on) to establish whether the risk increases.

Figure 11-2 provides some general guidelines about how much weight you can consider moving before it starts to become scary. Notice how the amount that you can lift reduces the further away the load is from your trunk (for example, if the load is at arm's length or if you have to bend down or stretch up to reach it). Keep in mind that these are rough guides and shouldn't be taken as an absolute value.

Though the guidelines provide advice for men and women, individuals can vary considerably in their lifting capacity. (If you turn green when you're angry and go by the name of 'Hulk', you're not likely to have a problem with lifting heavier loads!) But these are general filtering guidelines. If the task involves twisting, you need to reduce the load. The same is true if the operation is very frequent.

These guides are helpful because they show you what you can sensibly be expected to lift – they provide a realistic and practical guide. People (and not just weight lifters) lift stuff every day without doing themselves any harm whatsoever. In fact, lifting and handling can help to keep you fit and keep your muscles in good shape.

For a handy checklist of all the risk factors, check out Appendix 4 of the HSE's *Manual Handling Operations Regulations 1992 (as amended; L23) Guidance on Regulations* (the guide is very detailed but the checklist is useful, and you even get a worked example), free to download here: www.hse.gov.uk/pubns/priced/l23.pdf.

Heaving heftier loads

If the tasks are more complicated and involve bigger loads than those in Figure 11-2, you need to assess the risk more deeply – that is, you need to do a more detailed risk assessment. In the first instance, you may want to consider eliminating the need to handle such loads manually – but that may not be entirely possible.

When you can't eliminate the need to manually handle bigger loads and you see a significant risk of injury, you need to assess the risks, considering four key risk factor areas (known as TILE):

- ✔ Task
- ✔ Individual
- ✔ Load
- ✔ Environment

By breaking down the individual components of manual handling, you can ensure that all risk factors are considered and assessed. (Also, you'll be meeting your legal requirements under the Manual Handling Operations Regulations 1992.)

Tackling the task

When you assess the *task*, you look at the type, frequency and duration of movements to identify which movements are most likely to cause injury. You need to consider these potentially dangerous movements as risk factors:

- Holding loads away from the body – if you have to hold them at a distance from the body then you're unable to use your core strength or stomach muscles.

- Twisting, which places pressure on the discs in your back at a certain point.

- Stooping, for example when reaching under tables or shelves.

- Reaching upwards, above shoulder height.

- Making large vertical movements, such as from the floor to above shoulder height.

- Carrying a load over long distances – when the lift will last a long time because you have no setting-down areas.

- Pushing or pulling strenuously, such as when using trolleys or equipment with wheels.

- Dealing with the unpredictable movement of loads, where the centre of gravity of the load moves.

- Handling loads repetitively; in other words, using the same motion time and time again.

- Allowing insufficient time for rest or recovery; no down-time. For example, carrying a load over 50 metres is much harder than carrying it over 5 metres. Rest areas along the way can help.

- Moving at a work rate imposed by a process, such as when a conveyor belt forces the work rate.

Lifting in an incorrect position or making rushing, repetitive movements can impact on the task, increasing the risk of injury. For example, picking up a load at waist height is reasonably low risk within the overall 'task' factor. But picking up the same load from the floor requires you to stoop over, increasing the risk of injury significantly.

Identifying individual issues

When you assess the factors relating to the *individual*, you need to consider issues such as:

- Does the task require unusual capabilities? For example, do individuals require a certain level of physical strength or do they need to be a particular height? If so, you may need to select people with these characteristics, such as particularly tall to reach high shelving (however, tasks that require unusual capabilities tend not to be the normal, day-to-day manual handling activities).

- Do specific groups of people face higher risk of injury? For example, do people with certain health problems, or new or expectant mothers, run a higher risk of injury? Heavier weights, bending, twisting and standing for long periods can carry a higher risk of injury if medical conditions are present that may be antagonised further.

  Pregnant women release a hormone called relaxin that helps to loosen the muscles, therefore they're more likely to experience a manual handling injury.

- Does it require special information and/or training? For example, manhole covers are difficult to lift due to being sunk into the ground, heavy and awkward. Specialist equipment and training is required to ensure that you maintain a correct posture.

Individual capabilities and risk factors must be taken into account when looking at manual handling activities. Serious injuries can be caused or antagonised if you act without care and attention.

Looking at the load

The *load* in most workplaces is an inanimate object, though in some workplaces, especially healthcare, it may be a person (or even an animal). Think about:

- How heavy the load is.

- Whether the load is bulky or unwieldy, big or small, rigid or soft.

- Whether the load is difficult to grasp – maybe the load has a strange shape or the handles are poorly positioned, or it doesn't have any handles at all.

- Whether the load is unstable or unpredictable, resistant to movement, or has an unexpected centre of gravity.

- Whether the load is harmful (for example, it's sharp or hot).

- The contents of the load – for example, you may be carrying bags that may break or tear during a lift.

You need to consider the load carefully because you may not at first realise it's a risk. For example, the risk associated with handling a concrete block of 12 kg is lower than the risk associated with handling a bundle of flexible plastic pipes, each 3 metres long, that weighs the same. The flex in the pipes, the length of them and the movement caused by the bundle can cause injury from poor posture when lifting and moving. You can always handle the pipes individually, but most people will risk moving them in one go instead of handling them correctly.

Exploring your environment

The work *environment* can hamper movement and cause injury by itself, which is then exacerbated by the nature of your load (its weight and make-up) and perhaps also restricted vision (when lifting can cause issues with where to put your feet). The environment refers to things such as:

- ✓ **Constraint of your movement and posture:** For example, when you're lifting within a confined space or from fixed chairs, or the hindrance caused by certain types of clothing or personal protective equipment.

- ✓ **Slippery, broken or uneven floors, and other unstable surfaces:** For example, rickety shelving.

- ✓ **Variations in height or level:** For example, when moving up or down ramps, steps or ladders, or working with different shelving heights.

- ✓ **Temperature and humidity:** High heat and humidity can cause dehydration and significantly increase the risk of injury because muscles may not be properly hydrated. Physical exertion in high heat can also cause changes in blood pressure and fainting. Extreme cold can make objects hazardous to the touch and affect your dexterity.

- ✓ **Weather:** For example, strong gusts of wind may make loads unstable.

- ✓ **Lighting conditions:** Poor general lighting and strong variations between light and shade can restrict vision and may cause employees to miss potential hazards.

Differences in the work environment, the route taken by the lifter and the hazards they may come across on the way can increase the risks of manual handling. For example, walking outside with a large, flattened cardboard box in the wind is harder than walking from one side of the office to the other. The wind can pull the box and cause more strain on the employee.

Selecting solutions for manual handling issues

The legal requirements for manual handling require employers to eliminate manual handling where possible. This doesn't mean that manual handling is no longer allowed, but where possible you should attempt to eliminate the need for manual handling by automating or mechanising the handling activity. Conveyor-belt systems, fork-lift trucks, electric pallet trucks, cranes, hoists and other types of mechanical moving or lifting equipment provide ways to move loads without the need for you to use bodily force.

Automating or mechanising lifting can also introduce its own risks, so keep a perspective on overall risk reduction. If you introduce a machine that can't go up and down stairs when you need it to, it won't offer much practical support in the workplace.

Sack trucks, trolleys, conveyor belts, hoists and lifts don't remove the need to handle, but they make it a lot easier and reduce the risk of injury. They help by taking the weight away from individuals, reducing the distance covered by the carrier and removing environmental hazards, such as stairs. However, you still have some aspect of lifting, whether it's on and off the device or to and from it.

If you can, try to modify the task, individual, load or the environment:

- ✔ Control repetitive manual handling by introducing frequent rest breaks or job rotation to minimise the length of time that an individual employee has to perform a given task.

- ✔ Avoid stooping and twisting by changing the layout of the workstation.

- ✔ Use a table or lift to bring the load to waist height to avoid having to pick items up from floor level.

- ✔ Break down a heavy load into smaller parts.

- ✔ Use several employees to handle a large bulky load (rather than just one employee).

- ✔ Stabilise an unsteady load by securing it or placing it into a container.

- ✔ Mark up a load with an unexpected centre of gravity so that employees can see where the centre of gravity is.

- ✔ Attach handles to a load that is difficult to grasp.

- ✔ Rearrange the workspace to allow more room for the manual handling activity.

- ✔ Level an uneven floor (it may be tempting to use explosives, but you can use less destructive methods, such as ramps, filling in holes and so on).

- ✔ Supply additional lighting in a poorly lit location.

- ✔ Remove 'dead space' by moving things closer together to reduce carrying distances.

Reducing human interaction with loads reduces the chance of injury and helps you to achieve your legal obligation of eliminating manual handling where possible. However, if you have serious loads coming into your workplace, you need to establish the best solution for your business. The HSE website contains some great solutions and case studies for many industries that provide examples of manual handling solutions, and talking to companies in your industry can help you to establish best practices.

Getting Comfortable with Workstations

Workstations can vary depending on the work you do. Working on a manufacturing line often means standing for long periods of time, and the work rate is imposed by the conveyor-belt's speed. Working as a seamstress may require a lot of bending over while peering through a magnifying glass.

Most jobs now involve some type of screen usage too; whether you love them or resent their intrusion into your life, computers, laptops, tablets and smartphones are here to stay. Such screen-based devices are multipurpose tools that can help to make work, communication and play easy and fun (though try not to dwell on their tendency to distract you from essential tasks!). Even if you don't use them for work, you've almost certainly got 15 of them at home (especially if you have kids). However, these super-useful technological devices come with their own health warnings.

Work-related upper-limb disorders are muscle, nerve or soft-tissue conditions that affect the hand, wrist, arm and/or shoulder. These disorders usually start off with occasional aches, pains, numbness and tingling in the hands, arms or shoulders, but, if the case gets worse, these issues can lead to conditions such as carpal tunnel syndrome, tennis elbow and repetitive strain injury (RSI). Poor posture, developed through hunching over your keyboard or smartphone, using your device for extensive periods (they are somewhat addictive), tackling your keyboard with excessive force and repeating movements with one finger, arm or in one direction, can lead to work-related upper-limb disorders.

Ergonomic positioning is the best posture for an individual because it enables you to maintain good circulation, reduce muscle strain and provide a neutral position for the spine and head, which helps to reduce the impact on the body. If you use a desk that's too high, you may find that you experience cold fingers or a pain or discomfort in your elbows. This is because the elbow is over-bent to make the hands reach the correct typing position (like when you're poised to scare someone). The crease in the elbow reduces the circulation to the hands and causes swelling in the elbow, which on one occasion is recoverable, but if you do it time and time again you'll find that the pain and discomfort starts every time you position your elbow in a crease.

The following sections explore how you can successfully assess your workstation and take you through some tips and tricks for adjusting your workstation and associated equipment to suit you.

Assessing desktops and laptops

Working at a computer can be harmful, and anything harmful to employees must be assessed and controlled. Workstations need to be adjustable enough that employees are able to get comfortable (and what suits one person may not suit the next person). However, ensuring that employees know how to make the adjustments before they experience pain and discomfort can be a challenge. Providing training and information to employees is a start – hopefully, after employees get used to adapting their workstation they'll make the adjustments without even thinking about it. But sometimes people just want to get on with their job and don't see their health as a priority (or don't prioritise the time it takes to make the adjustments).

Hot desks (shared computer workstations) are commonplace in the modern office. As long as employees understand how to adjust their equipment, sharing workstations is a great way to maximise available office space.

Employees are more likely to make adjustments if they understand how and why they're making them. Most people adjust a car seat and the mirrors if they're driving someone else's car – the office workstation shouldn't be seen any differently. If you can't reach the controls, make an adjustment. If your back rest is at the wrong angle, make an adjustment. It's easy when you know how.

If your employees use hot-desking or share desks, they don't need to do an assessment for each desk unless each desk or work area presents significant differences (such as working on a customer service desk as opposed to in a back office).

If you want to, you can train an in-house 'assessor' to complete your business's workstation assessments. This assessor needs to physically attend the workstation and complete the assessment with each employee. However, because the process is quite straightforward, it's often easier for employees to complete a *self-assessment*. This type of assessment asks the employee to evaluate her workstation from her perspective. It usually consists of approximately 20 questions looking at all workstation equipment and the interactions that the employee has with them. You can then review your employees' self-assessments to identify and address any issues.

Because computer workstations are used by people and proper set-up relies largely on 'comfort' factors, the employee needs to complete this assessment while at his desk (whether alone or with an assessor).

Your workstation assessments, however you decide to complete them, must cover these areas under the Health and Safety (Display Screen Equipment) Regulations 1992:

- ✔ **Chair backrest:** The backrest on the chair needs to be adjustable (you must be able to tilt it) and it needs to provide proper 'lumbar support' (the rounded bit of the chair is meant to sit in the small or dip of your back and provide back support).

- ✔ **Chair height:** The chair needs to be adjustable in height (not spontaneously, obviously). You need to adjust your chair's height so that your keyboard is in line with your elbow (when your arms are relaxed by your sides).

- ✔ **Footrests:** You need to be able rest your feet upon the floor (when sitting in your adjustable chair). If you can't (perhaps because you need to raise your chair higher because of a fixed desk height), you can use a footrest.

  The height of your chair has nothing to do with your feet. Usually people have to lift their chairs to reach an appropriate height to use their keyboard (refer to the preceding point), and sometimes this means that their feet no longer touch the ground. If they don't, they require a footrest to prevent any pressure on the back of their thighs.

- ✔ **Space:** You need a bit of space to fidget and allow postural change. You need to be able to freely move your chair out from under your desk – and no, you can't store loads of stuff underneath your desk because this can limit your freedom to move.

- ✔ **Forearms:** Your forearms need to be horizontal with your keyboard. If your elbows are in line with your keyboard (you've set the correct chair height), it's likely that your forearms will be horizontal – but you don't want your elbows to bend too much or your arms to have to reach straight out for your keyboard.

- ✔ **Wrists:** Your wrists need to be in a straight/neutral position, not flexed up, down or to the side. When typing, try to 'glide' over the keyboard, and only drop your wrists when you're resting.

  People tend to rest their wrists on their desk or a wrist-rest while they're typing, which causes strain in their fingers. Wrist-rests exist for the same reasons as the arm-rests on a chair – you don't attach your arms to your arm-rests while you're typing, do you?

✔ **Screen height:** The screen height needs to be set so that your head is in a neutral position, looking forward, rather than looking up, down or to the side. This can be hard to achieve with laptops, because getting your arms and head into the right position is impossible.

When using a laptop, you either use the laptop screen as your monitor (so you need to use a laptop riser to get the height right) plus a separate keyboard and mouse (that you simply plug into your laptop), or you need to use a separate monitor (which can sometimes mean that you need to use a separate keyboard and mouse too). Laptops shouldn't be used for long periods of time on their own.

✔ **Hand-rest space:** You need enough space in front of the keyboard so that your hands have a place to rest when you're not busy typing.

A handy checklist of these factors can be downloaded free from the HSE here: `www.hse.gov.uk/pubns/ck1.pdf`.

Laptops are tricky to assess. You shouldn't use laptops without accessories (such as a separate monitor, mouse or keyboard) for long periods of time because they don't enable users to achieve an ergonomic posture.

Considering solutions for all workstations

Your employees need to know how to adjust their work equipment correctly. On their first day of work with you, they're shown how to log on to their computer, what they're required to do and how, and where to get a cup of tea . . . but when do you say, 'By the way, you adjust your chair like this'? We're pretty sure that your employees are usually so busy getting on with their jobs that when they're in pain or they have a headache, their posture isn't the first thing that comes to mind – and sparing a minute to navigate the many levers on an ergonomic chair isn't going to be at the top of their priority list. However, it should be a priority because, as well as improving posture and minimising the risk of pain or injury, sitting comfortably can make you more productive.

When training employees to adjust their own workstation, make sure that you cover:

✔ What good posture is.

✔ How to adjust chairs and other equipment.

✔ How to organise your workspace to enable you to work comfortably.

If you're often on the phone, keep it close to you so that you don't have to reach for it each time it rings. It sounds like such an obvious solution, but people often forget to do this. (The same applies to any files you regularly reach for – and the location of your cup of tea.)

✔ How to adjust your screen and lighting to avoid reflections and glare (for example, by tilting the screen or using window blinds).

✔ When to take breaks/change your activity – not extra tea breaks, sadly, but opportunities to get the blood flowing again and do other work.

Don't save up all of your printing for collection at the end of the day; split your day so that you move around more (you can not only collect your printing but also take breaks from your desk to make a cup of tea, visit the bathroom, chat to a colleague in person rather than send an email . . . the list goes on).

✔ How to report any problems that you experience, whether with equipment, software or ill-health.

✔ How to apply for an eye test. If your employees use a computer for at least one hour per day continuously, you must provide them with a free eye test – this is a requirement of the Health and Safety (Display Screen Equipment) Regulations 1992. If the eye test shows that your employee needs glasses for screen use, you can purchase the glasses required or make a contribution towards your employee's glasses (usually £50).

Evidence suggests that there's no link between staring at screens (TVs, monitors, laptops, tablets and so on) and eyesight deterioration.

If your employees need to use a phone and keyboard at the same time (for example, keying information into a computer system when taken from a phone call), you need to provide a headset to prevent them from putting the phone in the crook of their neck (not a good look – and not ergonomically sound, either).

A document holder may be useful if your employees regularly refer to paperwork or have to input data from paper-based documentation.

Why sit when you can stand?

Sitting in a static position for eight hours a day is bad for you, and innovative ideas keep emerging to get us moving. In Japan, companies regularly stop employees working to do two to three minutes of exercise at their desk – okay, so this may be a little way-out for your safety culture, but stand-sitting desks enable the user to change positioning throughout the day. You can either install electronic desks or add a section to the top of a standard desk. These are fantastic inventions that enable changes in posture in the workplace, but they must be given serious thought as chairs can get in the way and employees will need to be shown how to use the adjustable desks and be clear about the benefits. Standing for long periods of time isn't good for you either; it's having the option to change position that provides the benefit.

You may want to encourage your employees to take charge of their wellbeing by doing some gentle exercises while sitting at their desks. The following exercises can be easily completed without breaking into too much of a sweat:

✔ **Neck and shoulder exercises:**

- Move your head towards one shoulder and then the other.

- Place your chin on your chest, and then move your head back to look towards the ceiling.

- Raise and lower your shoulders, and then slowly roll them backwards and forwards.

✔ **Eye exercises:**

- Blink your eyes regularly – consciously doing this helps to keep them moist.

- Look up, down, left and right (be gentle – you don't want to strain your eyes) while keeping your head still. Close your eyes and open them again.

- Move your eyes away from your computer monitor and focus on something else for a short time. If possible, look out of a nearby window and focus on something in the distance. (You never know what you may be missing outside!)

✔ **Fingers, wrists and arm exercises:**

- Extend your arms outward, stretch your fingers out, count to five and then make a fist. Hold your hand in a fist for five more seconds and release.

- Extend your arms outward, bend both of your wrists down, allow your fingers to relax and then wiggle your fingers for a count of five. Do the same with your wrists bent up.

- Drop your arms down by your side, shake your arms gently and relax.

✔ **Feet exercises:**

- Stomp your feet (quietly!) up and down, one at a time.

- Clench your toes up (with your feet remaining flat on the floor). Hold for a count of five and release.

Don't be static, or ignore any issues with your workstation. Adjust your equipment and make sure that everything you need regularly is close by in order to avoid overstretching – save the stretching for the preceding exercises!

Chapter 12

Working Safely with Machinery

*M*achinery safety is a major topic in health and safety. The history of health and safety started with the Industrial Revolution – which started with new machines invented to mass-produce goods in factories; factories used water power then steam power to drive the machines; and machines employed power to generate force and movement, both of which can be detrimental to humans who come into contact with them.

You can find a wealth of information on machinery accidents stretching back to the start of the Industrial Revolution. The only consolation is that, as a consequence, machinery hazards and their associated controls are clearly understood. You can't plead ignorance on the topic, and the standards that you need to adopt to prevent machinery accidents are firmly established.

On the plus side, you know your machines better now and how they can cause you problems. They're machines; they're going to behave predictably, so you can use the engineering principles that created them to make them safer. Backed up, of course, with your 'soft' human controls, just to make sure.

In this chapter you find out what sorts of safety problems your machines may bring you and how you can keep them under control. You take a look at different approaches to maximising employee safety – so by the end of this chapter, you'll have a system for controlling machinery safety that's ticking over like a well-oiled machine!

Getting to Know Your Machinery's Hazards

Before you start to examine your machinery, it may be useful to clarify what a machine is. *Work equipment* is a broad term that covers any machinery, appliances, apparatus, tools or installations for use at work. A *machine* can be defined as an apparatus that uses mechanical power and has several parts, each with a definite function, that together perform a particular task. The key points are the use of mechanical power and the inclusion of a number of component parts. The significance from a health and safety point of view is that a machine has enough power to cause injury and is complex enough to be able to do this in more than one way.

If you're standing in your workplace and you take a look around you, it may reveal that your business needs lots of different machines to deliver your product or service – or that you don't have many at all! The nature of the machinery around you is dependent upon what you do. If you're in the construction industry, you may use cement mixers or circular saws to build new homes; if you ply your trade in manufacturing or maintenance workshops, you may see bench-top grinders and pedestal drills deployed to create any number of things; if your business tackles the great outdoors, you may find that lawnmowers, hedge-strimmers and chainsaws form part of your horticultural toolkit. Even offices have their moments, with machines such as photocopiers and document shredders waiting to cause problems.

The lowly office paper shredder can show a little aggression. One of your authors investigated an accident whereby an office employee was almost garrotted when his tie was pulled into this belligerent piece of machinery. Swift action to shorten the tie with a pair of scissors saved the day!

As with many office machines, the paper shredder deserves a little respect – you may not be dealing with heavy-duty machinery or feel particularly in danger when you're using it, but it can still be dangerous. You can get drawn into the machine just like the paper does (as in the preceding example), and it has some nasty blades to introduce you to if you do (we discuss mechanical hazards like this in more detail in the next section, 'Drilling down into mechanical hazards'). It's also powered with electricity (which may cause an electric shock; we talk about non-mechanical hazards in the upcoming section 'Battling against non-mechanical hazards'), and you may even have issues related to the need to lift and carry the paper waste that's generated (check out Chapter 11 for more on manual handling).

Figure 12-1 shows a common bench-top grinder that you may find in a manufacturing-oriented workplace. Can you spot any ways in which your workforce may get injured while using this machine?

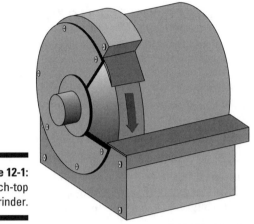

Figure 12-1:
A bench-top
grinder.

The bench-top grinder presents a number of hazards to your workforce. If you make contact with the rotating abrasive wheel, it may take a layer of skin off (ouch!). If your fingers get too close to the gap between the wheel and the tool rest (where the arrow is pointing in Figure 12-1), they may be pulled in and crushed. If the wheel itself isn't used properly and it bursts, you can get a nasty injury from the resulting fragments of the wheel. And because the wheel is mounted on a spindle, it's possible to get loose clothes or hair entangled in it. These mechanical hazards quickly add up to a situation that goes beyond the initial 'ouch'!

You've also got the possibility of electric shocks (because the machine runs on electricity), burns from the piece of metal being ground and heating up, and problems from inhaling the dust that the machine produces, as well as issues presented by the noise that the grinder makes. Your routine item of workshop machinery is looking a bit more exciting – and scary – now.

Your cursory examination of these familiar workplace machines reveals two different types of machinery hazard in the workplace:

- ✔ **Mechanical hazards:** Hazards that arise when machines generate the force and movement required to complete a task, such as a rotating grinding wheel, circular saw blade or drill bit. This force and movement may cause machine operators to be hit, crushed, cut or trapped, or to become entangled in the machine.

- ✔ **Non-mechanical hazards:** Hazards that don't arise directly from contact with dangerous moving parts. Examples include electricity, dust and noise.

In the following sections, we explore these two types of hazards in more detail.

Drilling down into mechanical hazards

Mechanical hazards come in many shapes and sizes depending on the nature of your machine, but they commonly involve some of the following:

- **Crushing:** Part or all of the body is trapped between two moving parts of the machine, or one moving part and a fixed object. For example, a hydraulic lift collapses, crushing a person underneath it.

- **Cutting (or severing):** Bodily contact is made with a moving sharp-edged machine part, such as a blade (for example, the blade of a bandsaw).

- **Drawing in (or trapping):** A part of the body is caught between two moving parts and drawn into the machine, for example, at 'in-running nips' where two counter-rotating rollers or gear cogs meet.

- **Entanglement:** Loose items such as clothing or hair get caught on a rotating machine part (like a drill-bit or lathe) and the person is drawn into the machine.

- **Friction and abrasion:** Bodily contact is made with a fast-moving surface that may be smooth (for example, touching a spin dryer, which can cause a friction burn) or rough (for example, touching a belt sander, which may physically abrade the skin).

- **High-pressure fluid injection:** Fluid is ejected at very high pressure from the machine and it penetrates the skin (for example, hydraulic fluid escaping from a burst hydraulic hose).

- **Impact:** The body is struck by a powered part of a machine (this is similar to crushing, but without a fixed structure to trap the person; the speed and weight of the object does the damage).

- **Shearing:** A part of the body (usually the fingers) is trapped between two parts of the machine, one moving past the other with some speed. The effect is like a pair of scissors, shearing off the trapped body part.

- **Stabbing, punctures and ejection:** The sharp parts of the machine (or parts or materials ejected from the machine) penetrate the body (for example, *swarf* – the filings of metal produced by a machining operation, which are often thin and sharp), sewing machine needles, abrasive wheel fragments or nails from a nail gun).

The force and movement generated by machinery can strike, crush, cut, entangle or trap operators, which is why mechanical hazards need careful consideration.

Battling against non-mechanical hazards

You don't just have the mechanical hazards to worry about: machines are also often powered by electricity, they can be noisy, they may heat, cool or generate radiation, or they may produce dust and fumes. You need to factor in these non-mechanical hazards as well as the mechanical hazards, even if they don't at first seem obvious when compared to the alarming severing and crushing that you have to consider with mechanical hazards (and that's just for starters; refer to the preceding section for the many horrors you have to contemplate when evaluating mechanical hazards). Non-mechanical hazards can be just as dangerous and problematic as mechanical hazards, however.

Non-mechanical hazards include:

- ✔ **Electricity:** For example, powering a bench-top grinder.

- ✔ **Extreme temperatures:** For example, from heat generated by an induction heating machine.

- ✔ **Fire and explosion:** For example, from wood dust ignited in a woodworking machine.

- ✔ **Hazardous substances:** For example, generated as fumes from heated plastic in a moulding machine.

- ✔ **Ionising radiation:** For example, generated by an X-ray machine.

- ✔ **Noise:** For example, from a bench-top grinder used to sharpen tools.

- ✔ **Non-ionising radiation:** For example, from the laser in a cutting machine.

- ✔ **Vibration:** For example, from a hand-held sanding machine.

Your machines are likely to be powered by electricity, produce noise and may vibrate. You may find that hazardous substances are used or produced as an integral part of the process, such as a metal-cutting lathe using cutting fluid or a robot welder producing welding fumes. X-ray machines, laser cutters and infra-red welders use radiation as part of their operation. And if your machine produces heat and uses flammable materials, you may even have to contend with the risk of fire and explosion.

So, as well as the force and movement associated with the operation of a machine, you have to consider the hazards associated with its power supply and the energy and substances produced by its mode of operation. These hazards may be less obvious than the mechanical hazards, but they can equally cause injury or ill-health for the operators.

Controlling Machinery Risk

Machines are hazardous, and therefore you want to feel secure in the knowledge that you're taking the measures that you can to use safe machinery. You can't guarantee your employees' safety – but you can definitely make your best effort to ensure their safety.

If a machine has a *CE mark,* it has been assessed (before being placed on the market) to make sure that it satisfies the legal health and safety requirements in order for it to be sold within a given market. If you buy a new machine, you can find its CE mark. The manufacturer (or importer) adds the CE mark to show that the machine has been assessed against all relevant safety standards, has the documentation to prove it, and warrants its five-star rating.

CE stands for *Conformité Européene* – which is French for 'European Conformity'. This is a declaration by the manufacturer that the machine meets the requirements of the applicable *European Directives*; in other words, that the machine meets the necessary safety standards. These are called 'essential health and safety requirements' and cover all the essential aspects of the health and safety of a machine, including protection against mechanical and non-mechanical machinery hazards (refer to the earlier section 'Getting to Know Your Machinery's Hazards' for more on these).

A CE-marked machine should be pretty safe to use because its design and method of operation has been assessed. However, what hasn't been assessed at this stage is the task, process and location that the machine will be used for. The Provision and Use of Work Equipment Regulations 1998 acknowledge this and require the employer to ensure that work equipment is suitable for the purpose for which it's used or provided. Although risk assessment isn't a stated requirement of these regulations, it is required by the Management of Health and Safety at Work Regulations 1999 and implied in order to achieve compliance with the Provision and Use of Work Equipment Regulations 1998.

The risk assessment methods that you find in Chapter 4 are perfectly valid for use with machines and enable you to identify the hazards, the persons at risk and whether the controls in place are suitable.

In the example of the bench-top grinder introduced in the earlier section, 'Getting to Know Your Machinery's Hazards', we noted several hazards, including the possibility of contact with dangerous parts, things flying out of the machine, electrocution, burns, dust and noise. What's the best way to control these hazards? You can deal with these simply by protecting the danger areas with appropriate safeguards, using personal protective equipment, checking the machine regularly and controlling who uses it, which gets you well on your way to safe operational behaviour.

Here's a comprehensive list of control options to deal with the risks presented by the bench-top grinder:

- ✔ Use fixed enclosing guards around the motor and part of the abrasive wheel.

- ✔ Place adjustable polycarbonate eye-guards over the exposed part of the wheel.

- ✔ Adjust the tool rest to minimise the nip point between the tool rest and the wheel.

- ✔ Restrict use to trained operators only.

- ✔ Provide eye protection to all employees that use the machine (it needs to be impact-resistant).

- ✔ Provide hearing protection and dust masks (if required) to all employees who use the machine.

- ✔ Conduct routine inspections on the machine and portable appliance testing to make sure that the electrical parts are safe.

You're using fixed guards to fully enclose any dangerous parts, using an adjustable eye-guard for the parts that can't be fully enclosed, adjusting the tool rest to get rid of that nip point at the wheel, providing personal protective equipment for eyes, ears and mouths, and implementing an electrical inspection process to keep the electrics safe. Job done!

Making Safeguards Count

Not all protective measures are equal when it comes to dealing with access to the dangerous parts of your workplace machinery. In the preceding section, 'Controlling Your Machinery Risk', we took you through a risk assessment for a bench-top grinder, from which we identified a number of control options you can take to protect your workforce from injury. In this section, we look at machinery control options in more detail in order to ensure that you're able to maximise their effectiveness.

The Provision and Use of Work Equipment Regulations 1998 give you the control options in a hierarchy that starts with a solid, foolproof, rigidly fixed enclosure (the fixed enclosing guard) and ends with reliance on your operators to be careful and safe. You can see why it's a hierarchy! The aim is to protect your workforce from the dangerous parts of your workplace machinery. This hierarchy suggests guards that you can put in place to act as a barrier between your employees and your machinery. We present this list in order of decreasing effectiveness:

1. Use fixed enclosing guards that physically prevent contact with the dangerous parts of the machine.

2. Provide other guards or protection devices such as interlocked guards, adjustable and self-adjusting guards, and trip devices (such as pressure mats). These guards only prevent access to the dangerous parts when they're in place, and the trip devices rely on stopping the motion of the machine before the dangerous parts can be reached.

3. Introduce protection appliances such as jigs, holders, push-sticks (a short stick – which may be shaped so it doesn't slip off the workpiece – or a block that you use to push the final bit of the workpiece through) and so on to reduce the need for the operator to work near the dangerous parts.

4. Provide information, instruction, training and supervision so that the operator works carefully to avoid contact with the dangerous parts.

The idea of a barrier between you and the dangerous parts of a machine to protect you from injury is eminently sensible. And the more robust and fool-proof the guard, the better.

You use the hierarchy to examine each option in succession to decide whether it's feasible and effective. For example, fixed guards may be too restrictive for production machinery, and adjustable guards may not give enough protection. And what you choose needs to be guided, as ever, by your risk assessment.

The preceding section's example of the bench-top grinder revealed many of the items in this hierarchy (following this order of effectiveness) in order to make the grinder safe to use.

What you likely find in practice is that you use a combination of safeguards to prevent access to dangerous parts – rather than just one aspect of the hierarchy.

If you're using a circular saw, you may use the following safeguards:

- A fixed guard that's fitted around the motor and the bottom of the cutting blade.
- An adjustable top guard fitted above the blade.
- A push-stick, to keep fingers safely away from the saw blade.
- A strict information-sharing, instruction, training and supervision process.

In the following sections, we explore each of the four areas from the hierarchy in more detail so that you can ensure you're maximising the available control options for each of your workplace's machines.

Fixed guards

A *fixed guard* is a physical barrier that prevents you from coming into contact with dangerous moving parts. The guard may fit the machine quite closely (an enclosing guard), or it may be a fence around the machine (a perimeter guard). You may have openings in the guard to allow raw material to be fed into your machine – which is probably necessary if you want any output from it! But you also need to make sure that your operators can't reach in and contact the dangerous parts.

The benefits of a fixed guard include:

✔ You can completely prevent access to dangerous parts.

✔ It's fixed in place, and therefore more likely to remain in position than an interlocked guard (where the interlocks can be disabled) or an adjustable guard (which may be incorrectly adjusted).

✔ You require a tool to remove it from the machine, so it can't be taken off easily.

Doesn't that sounds perfect? With your fixed guard in place, surely you've protected your employees from the dangerous parts of your machines? Actually, not quite – before you pop the champagne, you need to consider a few potential issues with the fixed guard solution.

The main problem with the fixed guard is also its main strength; that is, it prevents easy access into the machine. So, if you require easy access into the machine to operate, set or clean your machine, a fixed guard is no good. And if you try to fit one, the operator may leave the guard off anyway if it's interfering with machine operation.

Fixed guards are often made of sheet metal for strength – but if you box in your machine, you block visibility of the machine, plus the sheet metal can cause overheating. However, you can use Perspex (a transparent plastic often used as a lightweight, shatter-resistant alternative to glass) or mesh (steel wire with a small mesh-size to stop fingers poking through) instead of metal to enable a cooler machine, a clearer view and yet (with mesh at least) the access you require to operate, set and clean your machine.

Other types of guards and protective devices

The fixed guard presents a barrier between operator and hazard, has moving parts, is difficult for the operator to interfere with and is virtually maintenance-free. But, despite its advantages, it also has limitations and therefore you need to be prepared to consider other options such as interlocked guards, which can be opened when the machine isn't moving; adjustable and self-adjusting guards, which rely on the operator to keep them in place; and trip devices, such as pressure mats, which stop the machine if the operator approaches the dangerous parts.

Interlocked guards

The interlocked guard comes to the rescue when you're wrangling with the access problems of a fixed guard (refer to the earlier section, 'Fixed guards'). An *interlocked guard* protects the dangerous parts of the machine but can be opened if the operator needs access. Of course, to prevent the operator being injured, opening the guard must stop the machine moving; also, the guard mustn't be able to open unless the machine has stopped. You'll be familiar with this arrangement from your washing machine or spin dryer. An interlocked machine guard is designed to be removed as a normal part of routine machine operation, but it stops the machine when opened and doesn't allow the machine to restart until the guard is back in place.

The reason why you don't cook your hands in your microwave oven is because the hinged door on the front (which allows easy access) is interlocked. The power to the microwave generator is shut off when you open the door – so before you put your hands in.

The selling points of an interlocked guard are:

- ✔ The power to the machine is disabled when the guard is moved/opened, and the machine won't operate until the guard is back in place.
- ✔ The guard either remains locked shut until it's safe for the guard to open, or the act of opening the guard stops the dangerous parts from moving and disables the power to the machine.

Lots of machines are fitted with interlocked doors. When you open these doors the moving parts stop, such as with your humble office photocopier. If your machine can't be stopped immediately, the interlocked guard (or door) locks itself shut and can only be opened after the danger has passed (for example, as with a domestic washing machine: when you're waiting for that quiet click – which means that you can open the door and retrieve your clothes – that's an interlocking door mechanism at work).

The snag is that interlocked guards don't have the permanence of a fixed guard (refer to the earlier section, 'Fixed guards'). It's often possible for a determined person to disable interlocks, bypass the system and operate the machine with the guard open. If your employees feel under pressure to meet a deadline or deliver on a quota, they may try to operate around the interlocked guards, so you need a robust interlock system, strict rules about use and close supervision, just in case! You may also need to get to the root cause and try to avoid production pressures in the first place.

Adjustable and self-adjusting guards

If you can't prevent access to the dangerous parts of a machine, adjustable and self-adjusting guards are an option.

An *adjustable guard* allows access to the dangerous parts of the machine but relies on the operator to position the guard to give protection. Many adjustable guards are designed so that the workpiece can be observed during the machine's operation.

A *self-adjusting guard* adjusts itself to accommodate the passage of material, so it's designed to prevent access to the dangerous parts until it's opened by the passage of the workpiece at the beginning of the operation, and it then returns to the safe position on completion of the operation.

These guards are by no means perfect, and they rely on operator co-operation. But they may be your best choice on production machines (that is, machines that are making articles where the operator is using sharp or abrasive cutting tools and needs to see how the shape of the article, or workpiece, is changing), such as woodworking and metalworking machinery. Here, a workpiece has to be fed into the machine or manipulated during machine use, so the operator can set an adjustable guard to a range of positions, depending on the nature of the workpiece and the nature of the task. An example is the top or crown guard on a bench-mounted circular saw: you can set this at a range of heights depending on the size of the wood that you're cutting.

A self-adjusting guard (sometimes called a *retractable guard*) also prevents access to the dangerous parts of a machine – it's spring-loaded or linked to other machine parts. As the machine operates, the guard adjusts automatically to fit the workpiece. It doesn't require your machine operator to set the guard to the right position. A common example of this is on modern hand-held circular saws. When the circular saw isn't being used, the spring-loaded, self-adjusting guard completely covers the lower part of the cutting blade. But as you push the saw into the wooden workpiece, the spring-loaded guard is pushed back (retracts), only covering the bits which haven't yet entered the wood.

Although you see some flexible benefits when using adjustable and self-adjusting guards, you also have some notable downsides to consider:

- ✔ They don't completely prevent access to dangerous parts.
- ✔ They're very easy to defeat.
- ✔ They rely entirely on operator competence.

Trip devices

Trip devices don't put a physical barrier between the operator and the dangerous parts of the machinery, unlike the other guards discussed in this chapter. Instead, they use a sensor that can detect the operator and then stop the machine.

If you're using a drilling machine, you can't fully enclose the drill bit with a fixed guard because otherwise you won't be able to drill anything! An adjustable guard is an option, but you're relying heavily on your operator taking the time and effort to set up properly and use the guard every time the machine is used. You can see how the lure of production bonuses can quickly over-ride any time-consuming safety measures, but you've already come across this problem in relation to interlocked guards, and the need to get to the root cause and try to avoid production pressures. So, a trip device is an effective compromise.

With a trip device (in this case, a trip bar or wand), the drill bit isn't guarded, so the operator can still get a loose sleeve entangled around the rotating drill or *chuck* (that is, a specialised clamp used to hold a rotating drill bit). However, as the operator's arm bends around the rotating part, it touches the trip wand next to it, which stops the drill from rotating.

You can't allow any run-down time with this device, otherwise the operator will have a broken wrist before the machine can stop. The trip device needs to be designed to stop the rotation dead within a one-quarter rotation of the drill. The operator may still become entangled in the machine, but will experience far less (if any) injury.

You can find a number of different types of trip device that can help to minimise injury from machinery when a barrier isn't an option:

- ✔ **Pressure mats:** These mats are placed on the floor around an item of machinery such as an industrial robot (the type used, for example, for paint-spraying on a car production line). If a person stands on the mat, their weight activates the trip and the robot stops moving.

✔ **Trip wires:** These wires run along the front of a machine or along the side of a conveyor system. They're positioned so that if an operator moves towards the dangerous parts of the machine, they touch the wire, causing it to move and quickly stop the machine. They need to be positioned carefully so that anyone heading for the danger zone will trip the wire.

✔ **Photoelectric devices:** These devices shine beams of light across an access point. If the light beams are broken, the machine stops.

Trip devices aren't perfect; they:

✔ Don't provide a physical barrier to prevent access.

✔ May be overly sensitive, leading to frequent trips that encourage the operator to bypass or disable them.

✔ Are more complicated than simple physical guards and may therefore fail more frequently, which encourages misuse.

Protection appliances

Many safeguards look at protecting employees from dangerous moving machinery parts – but how about keeping out of harm's way by putting some distance between yourself and the machine? *Protection appliances* are pieces of equipment that allow an operator to do just that – to keep their hands away from dangerous machine parts. Protection appliances include clamps, jigs and push-sticks.

If you're cutting wood on a circular saw, the dangerous saw blade is buried in the wood for most of the cut, with the exposed top covered by a crown guard. The main threat to the fingers comes when the last bit of wood has to be pushed through the blade. This is where the push-stick comes in. It keeps the operator's fingers away from the blade and prevents a nasty laceration.

Training your team

Guards and protection devices are your best safeguards to make machinery safe. They are technical control measures, but you can also develop measures that rely on the safe behaviour of the individual:

✔ **Training:** Providing the knowledge

✔ **Competence:** Developing the expertise through experience

✔ **Information:** Accessing the facts

✔ **Supervision:** Offering the incentive to behave safely!

A familiar cause of machinery accidents is not knowing what you're doing. Some people take pride in not reading the instructions unless forced to – they may sometimes see referring to the manual as a personal weakness. But making sure that you know how your work equipment works is an obvious requirement. Knowing how dangerous machinery works and how to keep it safe is even more critical. Therefore, you need to inform, instruct and train your workforce.

How much training you need to do depends on the level of danger:

✔ For low-risk equipment, reading the instructions supplied by the manufacturer may well be enough (such as 'don't put your tie in it' if you remember the earlier assessment – in the section 'Getting to Know Your Machinery's Hazards' – of the lowly office paper shredder).

✔ For an industrial shredder that shreds wooden pallets, you obviously need to do more. If disaster strikes, you'll have more to worry about than a shredded tie! All your operators need to be provided with specific training regarding how to safely use the equipment, as well as written information. You also need to check in with your employees to make sure that the training has been understood. (For more on training and assessing/testing training outcomes, refer to Chapter 3.)

You need to train your managers as well as your workforce (the people primarily using the machinery). Your managers need the information, instruction and training to allow them to manage the risks from your machines. You need to make sure that they understand the principles that lead to safe use of the equipment.

Maintenance staff also need to be competent. These are the people who have to repair the machines and keep them running.

Your maintenance staff require specific information, instruction and training so that they:

✔ Can undertake any maintenance activities with a minimum of risk to themselves and others

✔ Understand how to maintain the equipment and are able to keep it in safe working order

Some items of machinery are so dangerous that you need to make sure your operators have special training to use them; for example, chainsaws, woodworking machines, power-presses and abrasive wheels have a long history of accidents and have been subject to previous specific legal requirements for the training of operators.

The Provision and Use of Work Equipment Regulations 1998 set out the legal requirement to provide training for people who use work equipment (including machines) and also for those who manage or supervise its use. Chainsaw operators get a specific mention in the Approved Code of Practice for these regulations, which specifies the level of training required, depending on the level of risk of the chainsaw work being carried out.

The training should cover:

- ✔ Dangers arising from the chainsaw itself
- ✔ Dangers arising from the task for which the chainsaw is to be used
- ✔ The precautions to control these dangers, including the legal requirements

Using Your Machinery

Your biggest problem with your machinery is that people may be injured by the hazardous bits. Your best safeguard is to make your machinery safe through protective measures, such as using guards and protection devices (refer to the earlier sections, 'Controlling Machinery Risk' and 'Making Safeguards Count' for more on your options here). But even with the best will in the world, and rigorous consideration of the safety options available, you may experience cases where these protective measures aren't enough on their own. You may then need to be choosy about who you allow to operate the machinery, particularly where you have a risk of serious injury to the operator or to others.

The following sections cover the final pieces in the puzzle when it comes to using workplace machinery safely – restricting use of your machines and maintaining machine condition.

Restricting machinery use

You need to restrict machinery use to competent authorised employees only; that is, employees who have received sufficient information, instruction and training to enable them to complete the work safely. And, as well as machine operators, you also need to consider the people who repair, maintain or service your machines.

You may also have to be very careful if you employ young people (anyone under 18 years old) to operate machinery. They may lack experience, training and awareness – which is fair enough, as they're young. You need to restrict their access to nasty machines such as power-presses and woodworking equipment.

Power-presses are machine tools used to change the shape of a workpiece by the application of pressure, and these are among the most dangerous machines used in industry. Accidents involving power-presses are usually caused by trapping under the tool as it comes down onto the workpiece and often result in amputation or serious injury.

Woodworking machines use high-speed sharp cutters that are often exposed to enable the machining process to take place. Many machines are still hand-fed; therefore, the hands of the operator are constantly exposed to danger.

You need to carefully control the use of these types of machines by young people, and make sure that they can't use a dangerous machine unless they have the necessary maturity and competence; in other words, they're sensible and trained. During their training period you can let them operate the machine, as long as they're supervised by a competent person. You may also require strict supervision after training if the young person in question turns out not to be sensible. Note the importance of employing competent staff who you can rely on to make accurate judgements on the skills, maturity and supervision needs of trainees.

Maintaining your machinery's condition

Machinery can be dangerous if it's not looked after properly, so you need to maintain it to protect your machine operators. A variety of tasks come under the wide umbrella of maintenance, ranging from repairing and replacing broken items to cleaning and painting. It's often necessary to carry out work in areas with restricted space, poor access, limited lighting and generally unpleasant working conditions, so you need to protect your maintenance staff from injury as they carry out this type of work.

As well as selecting safe machines and operating them safely, you've also got to keep them safe. You need to consider the dangers from machinery accidents caused by equipment breakdown or failure. Remember the bench-top grinder in the earlier section 'Getting to Know Your Machinery's Risks'? Even if your machine is safe to use and you have all the guards and protective measures in place that you need, you still have to deal with the possibility of the abrasive wheel disintegrating if you don't adequately maintain the grinder.

When it's new your machinery may work fine, but as it gets older it may break down more often, develop faults and generally wear out. However, you don't want your machines to expire in a dangerous manner.

Much early safety legislation was a knee-jerk reaction to boiler explosions, crane collapses, hoist and lift failures, and so on. These disasters were principally caused by equipment failure, so the solution was regular statutory inspection, examination and maintenance to prevent such failures. In other words, getting plant and machinery properly looked after to avert even more disasters. So it's well established that you have to keep your machinery in tip-top condition.

If a machine failure doesn't cause you major safety problems and you can live without it until repair, doing nothing until your machine breaks down can be a viable option (the reactive approach). However, in most circumstances you want to have some control over the reliability of your machinery, so the proactive strategies for maintenance are:

✔ **Planned preventative:** Be organised, carry out your servicing work at prescribed intervals and replace parts irrespective of their condition. That way, your machines are always in first-class condition. For example, you may decide to change the oil in an engine every year regardless of the amount of use that the engine has received.

✔ **Condition-based:** Check first, and then carry out servicing and only change parts where inspection shows deterioration. That way you only replace what needs replacing. For example, you may inspect the brake pads on a car every 10,000 miles but only change them when they show signs of heavy wear.

Chapter 13

Shocking Truths: Electrical Safety

- -

In This Chapter

▶ Introducing electricity, the hidden hazard in your workplace

▶ Taking control of the dangers posed by electricity

- -

*U*nless your workplace happens to be a heritage museum, it's going to be powered by electricity. Electricity is ever-present, invisible, taken for granted and often overlooked as a workplace hazard – and when all your electrical equipment is working fine, you have nothing to worry about. But electricity is a serious workplace hazard that can electrocute, burn, start fires and even cause explosions (hence the overused cliché, 'the silent killer').

Assessing the risks from electricity is quite straightforward (refer to Chapter 4 for more on risk assessment), if you know what you're doing. Because the hazards are well-known, the more difficult part is working out how people may be harmed by it – the situations in your workplace where they may come into contact with live electrical conductors (whether by accident or through faulty equipment – and remember, the effects can be lethal).

In this chapter you find out what's going on behind the scenes with your workplace's electrical equipment and why you need to keep a close eye on it. We then give you the tools you need to put a sound electrical kit in place, enlist competent people to keep an eye on your electrical issues, and implement an inspection and maintenance system that keeps your electrical systems free from danger.

Keeping Current on Electrical Hazards

You're protected from electricity when the metal conductors that it travels in (usually wires) are protected by thick layers of insulation. The danger arises when people come into contact with these conductors, or with any metal that may come into contact with them (such as the metal case around your washing machine).

Electricity essentials: An introduction

It's a bit difficult to visualise an 'invisible' hazard. Things like vehicles and machinery are much easier. But if you're going to prevent electrical accidents, you have to understand a little bit about what electricity is.

Electricity is the flow of electrons through a *conductor* (a conductor is a material that allows electrons to flow through it, such as a metal; a commonly used conductor is copper wire). *Electrons* are particles of electrical charge. Electricity flows along a path from its source (such as a battery) to the equipment using it and back again – this path is called a 'circuit'.

If you can create a supply of electrons from a battery or a generator, they can flow through a metal wire. They can also produce heat and light, and drive machinery in the process.

Although water and electricity don't mix well in the real world, you may find it useful to think of a source of electrons flowing through a wire in the same way that you consider a source of water flowing through a pipe. Using that analogy, consider the following characteristics of electricity:

✔ The water *pressure* forcing the water through the pipe is analogous to the concept of *voltage* in electrical systems.

✔ The *rate* of water flow through the pipe is similar to the *current* in electrical systems.

✔ The pipe diameter that *restricts* the flow of water through the pipe is analogous to the idea of *resistance* in electrical systems.

The science behind how electricity works is rather complex – if you'd like to brush up on a few basics, the nearby sidebar 'Electricity essentials: An introduction' has got it covered.

The problem with electricity arises when the flow of current moves through a person, not through a wire or other type of conductor:

✔ The greater the *voltage* (that is, the measure of the electrical pressure that's forcing electricity through the conductor), the greater the flow of current through the person (the *current* is a measure of the rate of flow of electricity through a conductor).

✔ The lower the *resistance* of the person (that is, how much a component in the circuit resists the passage of electricity), the greater the current flow through that person.

So how exactly is electricity dangerous? For a start, it can have a number of adverse effects, including:

✔ **Electric shock:** This occurs when a person touches a live conductor and the electric current passes through his body to an earthed surface, where the electric current leaves the body. The greater the current, the worse the effects, and electricity may need only to flow for a fraction of a second to cause death.

- ✔ **Burns:** The electric current causes overheating as it passes through the skin and the internal tissues of the body. You can experience electrical burns both directly (as current passes through the body) and indirectly (from equipment overheating and exploding).

- ✔ **Fire and explosion:** Electrical equipment may be faulty and overheat, leading to a fire, or the system may be overloaded and overheat as too much current passes through it. If a flammable atmosphere is present, an electrical spark can cause ignition of the gas (followed by an explosion).

- ✔ **Arcing:** This occurs when a strong current is able to jump a gap in a circuit or between two electrodes. High-voltage power lines can arc through the air across distances of over 10 metres and cause effects such as electrical burns and shock as a result of being struck by the arc.

- ✔ **Secondary effects:** Any sort of injury that results indirectly from receiving an electric shock. For example, a powerful electric shock causes violent muscle contractions that can throw you across a room, but even minor shocks may cause you to lose your balance and fall, perhaps off a ladder or into an object, thus causing indirect injury.

The following sections explore some of the many ways in which electricity may represent a hazard in your workplace, taking you through the perils of portable electrical equipment, the worries of working at height or underground, and the dangerous mix of electricity and water.

Plugging in electrical equipment

One of the biggest electrical problems in most workplaces is the use of portable electrical equipment, such as computers, kettles and electric heaters.

Your main problem with portable electrical equipment is that each item has a flexible insulated electric cable (used to connect it to the mains and with a plug attached to it), and it can be moved around the workplace. Therefore, it can also be easily damaged, easily tampered with and difficult to keep track of. Not all cables are permanently connected to the equipment, so you may also need to keep track of connecting leads.

As you may expect, a high proportion of electric shock accidents in the workplace involve portable electrical equipment. Here are just some of the reasons for such incidents:

- ✔ Using the wrong equipment for the job, such as portable lighting that can produce heat or a spark in a flammable atmosphere.

- ✔ Working in the wrong environment for the equipment; for example, wet, damp or humid conditions (find out more about these issues in the later section, 'Dealing with environmental hazards').

- Misusing (or extremely misusing!) electrical equipment, such as routing electrical cables under office furniture, where the insulation can become damaged and expose live conductors.

- Mistreating electrical equipment, for example by pulling the plug out by tugging at the flex; carrying the tool by the flex; or allowing the flex to be pinched, trapped or crushed.

- Allowing unauthorised personnel to carry out repairs (the later section 'Hiring electric professionals' guides you towards picking the right team for the job).

- Allowing poor repair work to take place; for example, taping up a split flex with insulating tape.

- Continuing to use faulty and defective equipment.

- Ignoring chemical damage to the flex; for example, by corrosive wet cement.

- Failing to routinely inspect, test or maintain electrical equipment (discover more on this in the later section, 'Inspecting and maintaining your electrical equipment').

Portable electrical equipment can be problematic, whether it's your kitchen kettle or the charger for your laptop. If you aren't aware of the hazards and you don't take measures to control them, you may be exposing your employees to the risk of electric shock.

Working overhead and digging deep

Electricity is dangerous but it still has to be supplied to your workplace. The best place to put electricity supply lines is either overhead and out of reach, or buried underground, out of harm's way. That's fine until you need to work at height or you start to excavate holes. As you may expect, these activities greatly increase the risks associated with electricity.

Most overhead power lines are *uninsulated* (that is, they're bare conductors); however, because they're overhead and out of reach at a safe height, they don't present a day-to-day risk (unless you're a stilt walker carrying a long scaffold pole).

If you're working near these power lines, you need to be aware of the following hazards:

- **Electrical arcing:** Arcing happens when the voltage is great enough to force an electric current to cross an air gap from the power line to a person nearby. Direct contact with the power line isn't necessary and electrocution occurs as the electric arc passes straight to the person.

✔ **Electrocution:** Electrocution can happen through direct contact – at height, this contact may occur as people work on roofs, scaffolding or elevated platforms close to overhead power lines. Anyone operating cranes and excavators or handling equipment such as scaffolding poles, metal ladders or pipes can also be at risk due to possible contact with, or arcing from, overhead power lines.

Underground cables can cause you problems because they're concealed, frequently close to the surface, sometimes found in unexpected locations, and often poorly protected. You can damage cables during excavation work by crushing or penetrating them using hand or machine tools. Pneumatic drills and mechanical excavators are good at this because they're powerful enough to easily penetrate the insulation on buried cables, thus making contact with the live conductor and providing a conductive path directly back to the operator.

Choosing your mains power supply: AC or DC?

Electricity is the flow of electrons through a conductor (refer to the earlier sidebar, 'Electricity essentials: An introduction'). Therefore, you may expect the current to always flow in the same direction. This is correct in some electrical systems, particularly the ones powered by batteries – this kind of electrical current is called *direct current (DC)*. However, in domestic houses and workplaces, you generate the mains supply in a way that causes the current to flow forwards and backwards through the circuit. This is known as *alternating current (AC)*; the current flow alternates at a fixed frequency, measured in cycles per second (unit: hertz).

In the UK, you don't have many choices when it comes to your electrical supply. That's because it is set and provided by the electricity generator and supplier (most people don't tend to generate their own electricity and, in any case, much equipment is designed to work at standard voltages). But even so, you do have some choices. Standard mains electricity is supplied at 230 volts, 50 hertz. This cyclic variation is not particularly good for driving large electric motors and other heavy electrical loads, so in your workplace you may find three-phase 415 volts systems powering your electrical machinery. The three-phase voltage waves follow each other one-third cycle apart and produce power that's continuous and constant; feeding three separate electricity supplies to the motor produces a steady current and is more efficient (although the explanation for this is beyond the scope of this book). However, the important health and safety issue is that the additional hazard of three live conductors can result in an electric shock at 415 volts, nearly twice the mains supply of 230 volts, which is likely to be lethal.

The choice of supplies in your workplace can present you with different levels of risk. Shock injury from DC is generally a lot less severe than from AC.

If you're excavating close to underground cables, you need to consider the following hazards:

- ✔ **Arcing currents:** If you damage a live cable, you can get arcing currents that rapidly generate high temperatures with associated explosive effects, fire and flames, and the risk of severe, potentially fatal burns to your operatives.

- ✔ **Direct electric shock:** This can occur following contact with buried cables, where the insulation has already been damaged and it exposes a live conductor.

Dealing with environmental hazards

You need to consider the general environment in which you use electrical equipment. If your equipment is exposed to a harsh environment, it needs to be tough.

Water poses a significant environmental hazard when you're working with electricity, because water conducts electricity. If your electrical equipment gets damp, you can find your electric current taking all sorts of strange routes instead of through the insulated conductors you provide – which is where you want it. If the electric current deviates from its insulated route and finds its way to the outside of the equipment, anyone touching that equipment may potentially be in electrical contact with a live conductor and able to receive an electric shock.

You use metals for your electrical wiring because metals are the best conductors. However, they're also prone to being dissolved by acids or other corrosive substances.

If you run an electroplating business, you work with conductive and corrosive fluids that can generate humid and corrosive atmospheres. This environment is about the worst you can get for an electrical system thanks to the following hazards:

- ✔ The risk of corrosion and damage to any uninsulated or unprotected parts. Corroded electrical components and connections won't conduct electricity as effectively, may affect earthing and can cause overheating.

- ✔ The possibility of fluids or water vapour getting into your electrical components and increasing the risk of electric shock to anyone who touches their surface.

In a humid or corrosive environment, you need to make sure that your electrical equipment is designed and constructed to survive – for example, by using water- and corrosion-proof enclosures, insulations or coatings.

You also need to consider other environmental factors, such as:

- ✔ **Weather:** Your equipment and cables may need to withstand exposure to rain, snow, ice, wind, dust and lightning.

- ✔ **Natural hazards:** You need to protect your cables from natural hazards, such as solar radiation, plants and animals (which includes gnawing of cables by rats).

- ✔ **Extremes of temperature and pressure:** You may be operating heating or refrigerating equipment or even just need to cope with the heat generated by electric motors.

- ✔ **Dirty conditions:** Your equipment won't work too well if it gets contaminated by liquids or even solids.

- ✔ **Flammable atmospheres:** These get a mention because your electrical equipment can act as an ignition source and cause an explosion.

You also need to consider more commonplace hazards, such as mechanical damage. Simple problems like abrasion can be caused by mechanical movement, which may damage your protected electrical cables – but you can easily resolve this kind of problem by using an *armoured* cable (that is, a cable protected by a steel wire braid).

Preventing Danger: Controlling Your Electricity Risk

You can anticipate and avoid problems with your electrical systems following simple methods if you know what you're doing.

Fortunately, you don't need to figure it all out for yourself: your electrical systems are strictly regulated by the Electricity at Work Regulations 1989. These regulations tell you what you need to do to keep your electrical systems safe; or, to use their quaint terminology, 'to prevent danger'.

One of your first concerns is how to reduce the risk of electric shock. You can do this through:

- ✔ **Good design:** That is, providing equipment that's fit for purpose – designed for the purpose (and environment) for which it's used.

- ✔ **Insulation and barriers:** Protecting people from live conductors.

- ✔ **Protective systems:** Using one (or many) systems that protect people from the dangers of electricity by halting the power supply.

- ✔ **Effectively trained staff and contractors:** Building a competent workforce and ensuring you have competent contractors on-site.

- ✔ **Safe systems of work:** Enabling you and your employees to do your jobs safely.

- ✔ **Adequate inspections and maintenance:** Keeping your electrical kit in good condition.

You also need to put provisions in place to provide swift first-aid in case anything goes wrong.

In the following sections, we look at these areas in more detail to help you see how a combination of good electrical hardware, sensible procedures and people who know what they're doing can safeguard you from the lethal effects of electricity.

Keeping your electrician happy

A good starting point is to get the right kit in the first place. Or to carefully select your electrical equipment to make sure that it's suitable for:

- ✔ The electrical system that you're going to use it in

- ✔ The job you want it to do

- ✔ The environment where it will be used

You need to make sure that your equipment has sufficient electrical strength and capability so that it doesn't give rise to danger. And not only danger from normal currents, but danger from overloading sockets with too many appliances (where too much current passes through the cables) and also *fault currents* (that is, short circuits that cause a sudden high current surge). So, in other words, your cables have got to be tough enough to do the job required. You've got to use them within the manufacturer's rating and in accordance with any instructions supplied, as you may expect; otherwise, you're asking for trouble!

Covering up your conductors

Danger arises from electricity when people come into contact with live conductors – your standard UK mains supply, at 230 volts, can be dangerous in this way. Therefore, the conductors in your electrical systems need to be covered with insulating material or kept in a safe position to prevent danger. In other words, you need to make sure that nobody can touch the conductors (the conducting wires and cables), or you need to keep them out of harm's way.

'Out of harm's way' means locating your cables

- ✔ Overhead (for example, temporary cables to a construction site brought in at height)
- ✔ Underground (for example, buried and protected from damage in a trench)
- ✔ Behind barriers (for example, in a protective conduit)
- ✔ In a secure enclosure (for example, within the casing of an item of electrical equipment)

Refer to the earlier section, 'Working overhead and digging deep', for more on the hazards presented by overhead and underground cables.

Insulation is your preferred method for protecting live conductors. But if you're running an electric railway system or you have overhead cranes in a factory, you may have no choice but to run bare cables (for example, because you need to make continuous electrical contact with a live conductor to power the equipment). You need to make sure that people don't touch them by:

- ✔ Making them safe by position – that is, you locate them at height so that they can't be easily accessed.
- ✔ Erecting barriers or securing enclosures to prevent direct access to and contact with the conductors.
- ✔ Developing safe systems of work for people working nearby so that they have no need to work within reach of the cables.
- ✔ Erecting warning notices to alert personnel to the fact that conductors are exposed and live.
- ✔ Providing specialised training so that any persons who need to work near live conductors are competent to do so.

If you've got insulated conductors, you need to make sure that the insulation doesn't get damaged; otherwise, you're no further forward. Cables that trail along the ground where people or vehicles are present, such as on a construction site, are at risk unless you protect them from damage by running them inside a ramped cover. Electric cables connected to portable tools are prone to this kind of damage. The Electricity at Work Regulations 1989 state that 'no electrical equipment shall be put into use where its strength and capability may be exceeded in such a way as may give rise to danger', which means that your electrical equipment needs to be tough enough to withstand foreseeable damage.

You can damage insulation by contact with chemicals such as solvents, oil and petrol; for example, when they're stored in a garage. You need to protect cables running through places where the insulation can be damaged – and thus expose live conductors.

Using protective systems

You can find a few clever ways to reduce the risks from your electrical equipment. You can take action to stop the power quickly if you hit a problem, make sure that you can't get a shock from the casing, guarantee that the equipment is *dead* (meaning neither live nor charged, and therefore safe to the touch) before you work on it, or, if all else fails, minimise the severity of any shock that may happen.

A *protective system* is designed to prevent danger arising when any conductor (other than a circuit conductor) becomes charged.

Typical protective systems include:

- ✔ **Fuses:** A *fuse* is a weak link in the circuit (see the earlier sidebar, 'Electricity essentials: An introduction' for more on circuits). In other words, if you get a surge of current, the power disconnects quickly (because the fuse wire melts) before any damage is done to the electrical equipment.

- ✔ **Miniature circuit breakers (MCBs):** MCBs are another weak link in the circuit. *MCBs* are electromechanical devices that work in a similar way to fuses to protect equipment from current overload (except they're more sensitive, can be re-set and they don't melt). Like fuses, their main purpose is to protect the equipment/appliance and the wiring, rather than the user.

- ✔ **Earthing:** If you get an electrical fault in equipment with a metal case, the fault can make the case live. Anyone touching the live case can get a shock as the current flows through the person to earth. *Earthing* helps with this. It involves connecting all the metal parts on equipment that can become live to a low-resistance 'earth' wire. If a fault occurs that makes the case live, the current flows to earth. Because the current that then flows to earth is quite large (low resistance means a higher current), it will blow any fuse in the circuit, cutting the power. If someone then touches the faulty equipment after that point, the power is already cut off, thus removing the danger.

✔ **Isolation:** You can isolate your power supply by manually enforcing a break in it, which cuts the power. If all you do is switch off the power, it's rather too easy to switch it on again (accidentally or otherwise).

Isolation is where you physically remove electrical power from a circuit or system. You can padlock isolators in the 'off' position. Tags can be used in combination with locks (this is called *Lock Out, Tag Out* – or LOTO for short, where the isolated power sources are locked and a tag is placed on the lock to identify the person who's initiated the LOTO process). But you can also remove fuses or otherwise create an *air gap* (a physical break that prevents the conduction of current) in the circuit so that equipment can't be re-energised until work has finished.

✔ **Reduced voltage systems:** You can *reduce the voltage* so that less current flows during an electric shock incident. In the UK (where the mains supply is 230 volts), you can use a transformer to reduce the voltage to 110 volts for portable power tools (and they still work efficiently enough). And by clever wiring, you can make sure that the shock voltage can never be more than half this; that is, 55 volts. By reducing the voltage from 230 volts to 55 volts, you make any shock current less than a quarter of what it was. This is standard practice on construction sites.

You can also use reduced voltage systems (if they'll do the job) that operate at even lower voltages (for example, your laptop power supply can be transformed down to 50 volts) and very low voltages (such as a 12-volt battery supply). These latter systems present very little risk of electric shock injury.

✔ **Residual current devices (RCDs):** *Residual current devices* are sensitive and fast-acting. Fuses and MCBs can protect equipment against damage from a surge of current, but they don't act quickly enough to do the same for humans. This is where RCDs come in. These are specifically designed to protect human life in the event of an electric shock. They're very sensitive to any current imbalance in a circuit and can quickly break the circuit. They are now commonplace – either as plug-in devices (between the appliance plug and the socket), incorporated into the appliance plug itself, or directly fixed into the electrical supply's distribution 'consumer unit' (sometimes, for historical reasons, called a 'fuse box'). RCDs are especially important in higher-risk environments, such as for equipment being used outdoors or electric shower installations (a wet person, plus faulty wiring, equals a big mistake).

✔ **Double insulation:** *Double insulation* is a specific equipment design that doesn't require an earth connection (so, extra measures are taken to make sure that things like casings can't become live). You can make sure that the equipment's casing isn't made of metal (for example, using plastic instead) or ensure that loose live wires inside the equipment can't possibly touch the casing and make it live (if it is made of metal).

> Possible solutions to the latter situation include providing two layers of insulation for electrical conductors (rather than just one) or adding extra-tough layers of insulation.
>
> In your own home, you may have noticed the rise of plastic-cased kettles (which don't require an earth) in addition to metal-cased kettles (which do).

A combination of these protective systems may be used. For example, in the UK, you generally find the fuse incorporated into the plug of portable appliances. But your fixed electrical installation in your home may include circuit fuses, MCBs or RCDs (or a combination of these systems).

Hiring electric professionals

Electricity is dangerous – and no matter what you do to safeguard the *hardware* (the electrical equipment and wiring), you still need to contend with the *software* element (that is, what the people in your workplace, and your sub-contractors, get up to).

Whenever your work on electrical systems creates danger or risk of personal injury (which is probably most of the time!), you need to ensure that you only enlist competent and professionally trained people to do the work.

The Electricity at Work Regulations 1989 require that people who work on electrical systems are *competent* (or are at least properly supervised by a competent person) – that is, they need technical knowledge and experience in proportion to the danger and nature of the work.

What does this regulatory advice mean in practical terms? You can think of competence as a combination of knowledge (from appropriate training), experience (from doing the job itself) and understanding (developed through a combination of the two). (Chapter 3 explores more about competency and training.)

You may have to decide how much personal knowledge and experience your team needs to do the job, and this depends on how complicated the work is. But in some cases you may get away with providing appropriate supervision (by a competent person!).

For example, you can allow apprentice electricians to gain experience of electrical work, providing you supervise them properly. Without this, of course, they'd never be able to get the experience they need to be competent!

The basic training requirements for competent electricians are well-established – an industry-recognised Level 3 qualification such as an NVQ combined with an apprenticeship is a popular route to becoming an electrician. This combines learning on the job with study at a college or training centre. It normally takes two to four years to become fully qualified.

Working out safe systems of work

Whatever technical measures you put in place to safeguard your electrical equipment and systems (refer to the earlier section, 'Using protective systems'), people still have to work with them, so you're going to have to back up your technical measures with safe systems of work. You need these safe systems when working on or near electrical systems creates risk.

A *safe system of work* is a formal procedure that results from examining a task to identify all the hazards, and then establishing safe methods to ensure that the hazards are eliminated or the risks are minimised (refer to Chapter 7 for a general approach to developing safe systems of work).

Here are a few examples of safe systems that help you to avoid specific risks:

✔ **When you're working with live electrical systems:** The Electricity at Work Regulations 1989 advise you not to work with *live* electrical systems (that is, to make sure that the power is effectively isolated and the system is de-energised if necessary). However, sometimes you can't avoid working with live electrical systems. So, in effect, live work is prohibited except in special cases.

Where live work *is* justified (you have no alternative), the regulations state that you need to have safe systems of work in place to make sure that the live work is completed safely.

Your safe systems of work is likely to include:

- Formally controlling the work using a permit (refer to Chapter 7)

- Employing competent people to do the work (refer to the earlier section, 'Hiring electric professionals')

- Providing insulated equipment, tools and clothing to protect against contact with live conductors

- Working in dedicated work areas where possible (such as a purpose-built electrical test workshop if the testing must be done on live equipment to be able to detect the fault)

Examples of where live working may be justified include undertaking maintenance, checks or repairs on a busy section of electric railway track, or work in the electrical supply industry, particularly with live cable jointing, where it would be disproportionately disruptive and costly for the live conductors to be isolated for the period of the work.

✔ **When you may strike a buried power cable:** Any time you start digging holes in the ground you face the possibility of striking a buried power cable. They can lie close to the surface, and you can sometimes find them where you don't expect to. You can easily damage them during excavation work if you're using pneumatic drills or mechanical excavators, so you need a safe system of work to ensure that you steer clear of live cables.

This kind of safe system normally involves:

- Reviewing consulting plans to show the location of known cables

- Using cable-locating devices to find the cables manually and confirm their expected location or find unidentified cables (in case plans are wrong or out of date)

- Practising safe digging techniques to expose cables carefully (using hand tools, spades and shovels rather than forks, picks or pneumatic drills)

✔ **When you may make contact with overhead power lines:** Most overhead power lines are uninsulated, so if you get too close (whether in person or with a conducting pole) you face the risk of electric shock. If you need to work near overhead power lines, the best solution is to divert the lines away from where the work is to take place or make them dead (by having them isolated from the electricity supply).

If these two options are impracticable or too costly, you need to put a safe system of work in place, which may include:

- Obtaining a permit-to-work to make sure that the work is tightly controlled and authorised (refer to Chapter 7 for more on permits)

- Erecting barriers to prevent access to the power lines

- Using signage and goal posts to warn approaching vehicles (see Figure 13-1)

- Assisting reversing vehicles

- Using non-conducting equipment such as fibreglass ladders to make sure that inadvertent contact with overhead power lines won't conduct electricity to the employee

Figure 13-1:
Passage of plant beneath lines (or 'goal posts').

Source: The Safe Use of Vehicles on Construction Sites (2nd edition, published by the HSE, 2009); www.hse.gov.uk/pubns/priced/hsg144.pdf. The Safe Use of Vehicles on Construction Sites document contains public sector information published by the Health and Safety Executive and licensed under the Open Government License.

The preceding examples demonstrate circumstances where you may encounter work on or near live electrical conductors. But in most everyday scenarios, the equipment can first be isolated and de-energised (that is, made dead), making the work much safer.

Inspecting and maintaining your electrical equipment

If you don't look after your electrical equipment, you may find that it won't be long before it starts to deteriorate.

The only way you're going to keep on top of your electrical systems and equipment is to check them to ensure that they're up to standard – and to repair them if they're not. Therefore, you need a preventative *maintenance programme* that includes a regular inspection of your equipment.

Your aim is to test and repair equipment before it develops a fault that can lead to danger.

How often do you need to inspect your electrical equipment? Well, that can vary from item to item, and is dependent on:

- ✔ **The manufacturers' recommendations:** After all, they should know how often you need to check it over – they made it!

- ✔ **Your experience from use:** How often you find problems or faults can indicate how often you need to inspect it for issues.

✔ **What sort of equipment it is:** Some things need to be checked over and and/or replaced more often than others. For example, you're probably going to change your computer for a new, state-of-the-art one well before its electrics are likely to become dangerous, whereas that small concrete breaker that you use on a construction site – which gets a lot of rough use in a harsh outdoor environment – needs to be checked far more often.

Your regular inspections need to be followed by repair or replacement of the equipment as required. It's also useful to keep records of all inspections, maintenance, tests and repairs to show that you're doing this and to flag up any trends.

Your main problem is likely to come from portable electrical equipment (refer to the earlier section, 'Plugging in electrical equipment'). It's easily damaged, easily tampered with and difficult to keep track of.

It can be tricky to decide on how often to inspect and test your portable electrical equipment, but you can find some useful examples in the HSE guidance document *Maintaining Portable Electric Equipment in Low-Risk Environments,* INDG236 (published in 2013 by the HSE and available free for download here on the HSE website: `www.hse.gov.uk/pubns/indg236.pdf`).

For example, it suggests that earthed equipment (such as kitchen kettles) should be visually inspected every 6 to 12 months and tested every 1 to 2 years. Brand new portable equipment purchased in the UK will also have a fitted plug and have been inspected by the manufacturer.

You have different types of inspections and tests that you can use on portable electrical appliances to keep them safe:

✔ **User checks:** You can get your staff to visually inspect electrical equipment routinely before use. This is important for portable electrical equipment that's used in environments where damage can easily occur (such as a power tool used on a construction site).

A user check doesn't involve any form of dismantling; users check the equipment by careful visual inspection.

✔ **Formal visual inspections:** These formal checks verify that the equipment appears to be in a safe condition. You need to open the plug (if possible) to check that the connections are still secure and that the correct fuse is fitted.

As you may expect, you need to identify a competent person to do this inspection (refer to the earlier section, 'Hiring electric professionals').

✔ **Combined inspection and testing:** The main problem with a visual inspection is that it's visual; therefore, it doesn't pick up invisible things like deterioration of the insulation or a defective earthing pathway. To identify these sorts of issues, you need to utilise testing equipment.

If you plug a standard item of portable electrical equipment (such as electric drills, extension leads, office equipment and portable grinders) into a portable appliance test meter, it runs the tests automatically. If you have equipment that's a bit more complicated and needs detailed technical understanding (such as electro-medical equipment), you probably need the advice of a competent electrical expert (refer to the earlier section, 'Hiring electric professionals' for more on finding and training the right people for the job).

Conducting a visual inspection of a portable appliance

Things to check during routine visual inspection of a portable appliance include:

✔ Body of plug is intact and secure

✔ Outer sheath of flex covers inner cores into body of plug

✔ Plug cable clamp appears to be tight

✔ Flex appears fully insulated, with no splits or severe kinks/pinches

✔ Body of appliance is intact

✔ Outer sheath of flex covers inner cores into body of appliance

✔ Appliance cable clamp appears to be tight

✔ No obvious scorch marks to plug or appliance body

✔ Plug and appliance are not excessively soiled

✔ Plug and appliance are not wet

If you want the full details, you can refer to the HSE guidance leaflet *Maintaining Portable Electric Equipment in Low-Risk Environments,* INDG236 (published in 2013 by the HSE: `www. hse.gov.uk/pubns/indg236.pdf`) to get specific details on user checks, visual inspections and portable appliance tests.

Chapter 14

Fanning the Flames: Fire Risk

· ·

· ·

*Y*ears ago, people had good knowledge and experience when it came to fire. People used fire to heat their houses, cook their food and warm their baths . . . but now, except on perhaps bonfire night or in a cosy nook at the village pub, people rarely experience an open fire. As a result, people may not fully understand or appreciate the dangers that fire can present.

You need fire precautions in commercial buildings: you see signs, extinguishers and other evidence that commercial businesses take fire safety seriously and so you generally feel safe. When people experience a fire, they may think 'someone will put it out', and people often think they have longer to get out of a building than they really have. But knowing how fast fire spreads, how quickly your view can be restricted and how people react to fire is key to ensuring that you keep people safe.

In this chapter, we introduce you to the dangers presented by fire, including how they're caused in the workplace environment and who's responsible for fire safety in your workplace. We then take you through how to assess fire risk before providing some prevention and protection options for you and your business.

Playing with Fire

Inadequate fire management can have serious consequences. Over half of businesses who experience a major fire either don't re-open or fail within two years. Minor fires can also have a significant financial impact:

✔ Costs of repairing or replacing damaged buildings and plant

✔ Uninsured costs of clean-up operations after a fire

   ✔ Costs arising from damage to the environment

   ✔ Costs associated with the investigation of a fire

   ✔ Costs of defending a civil claim (from those who experience loss or disruption due to your fire – for example, the shop next door can't receive customers or deliveries)

You may also have to contend with some hidden costs following a major fire, such as the adverse effects of negative publicity and loss of 'corporate image'. Employee morale and motivation can also be affected by fire disruption.

Are you hot on what you need to do in the workplace to fathom out your fire hazards? If not, don't worry: we're about to explain your responsibilities in the workplace when it comes to fire, how fire arises, what kinds of fire you may experience in your workplace, how fire spreads and what tends to cause workplace fires.

Taking responsibility for fire risks

Most people think their landlord is responsible for managing fire safety within their workplace, but it's actually the *occupier* (the person who controls the work within an area, whether part of a floor space or the entire building, who may be a tenant or the premises' owner) who's responsible for their work area. That means you!

In England and Wales, the Regulatory Reform (Fire Safety) Order 2005 (it differs slightly for Scotland and Northern Ireland) refers to a 'responsible person' which, in a workplace, is the occupier. If you share your building with other businesses you need to work together, though landlords generally have responsibility for common areas (that is, areas that are used by multiple occupants such as stairways, toilets, receptions and so on).

This Order requires that, for your premises, you're responsible for:

   ✔ Reducing the risk of fire starting and spreading; so, for example, you need to separate combustibles like cardboard from ignition sources, keep escape routes clear and be sensible about wall coverings, including noticeboards, which can easily spread fire.

   ✔ Providing good escape routes, so you need enough fire escapes for the number of people in the building.

   ✔ Making sure that you keep escape routes clear, so check that they aren't blocked, locked or inaccessible.

✔ Supplying fire-fighting equipment – such as fire extinguishers, fire blankets and so on – on escape routes to enable escape if required.

Fire-fighting equipment needs to be used with safety in mind, not heroics – check out the later section, 'Don't be a hero! Fighting fires to make your escape' for more.

✔ Installing fire detectors and alarms so that people have plenty of time to get out of the building.

The Health and Safety Executive (HSE) provides a useful case study to help you understand how quickly fire can cause destruction in and around the workplace. A warehouse that stores various materials in drums, including oxidising materials, solvents and other chemicals, experienced a fire that, due to the products on site, caused an explosion that broke the glass in the site gatehouse. A second explosion occurred some 15 minutes into the incident, which blew out a roller shutter door that hit the wall of a building about 10 metres away.

The solvent-filled drums started to explode in the intense heat of the fire; some were propelled several hundred feet into the air, hitting a building 30 metres away and starting another fire.

Approximately 3,000 residents were evacuated from their homes following this incident.

The subsequent investigation found that the lack of segregation in the storage of a range of chemicals led to the rapid and violent spread of the fire.

For more on this case, review the case study information at `www.hse.gov.uk/comah/sragtech/casewarehouse.htm`.

It is vital that you segregate chemicals to reduce fire spread, ensure that minimum amounts are kept on site, store chemicals as per the manufacturer's instructions and utilise suitable storage facilities (for example, flame-resistant cupboards and separate buildings). By controlling your chemicals, you can reduce the impact on the business and the surrounding areas.

You also need to instruct and train employees on what to do if there's a fire, and make sure that you appoint someone to help you with checking the fire routes, being sure to maintain the fire alarm and detection system, and monitor fire drills or fire incidents to help with the investigation.

Getting to know the fire triangle

You can prevent fire in a number of ways, but first you need to start at the beginning – not by rubbing two sticks together, but by understanding what fire needs to ignite and continue to burn.

You need three things for a fire to start and burn:

- ✔ **Fuel:** Such as wood, paper, plastic or petrol.

- ✔ **Oxygen:** Usually from the air, but also from gas cylinders or oxidising agents.

- ✔ **Heat:** From ignition sources such as open flames, friction, chemical reactions and sparks from electrical equipment.

A fire needs all three components to start. An easy way to remember this is to draw a triangle: the _fire triangle_. Along each side of the triangle you write one of the following words – 'Fuel', 'Oxygen' and 'Heat' (see Figure 14-1).

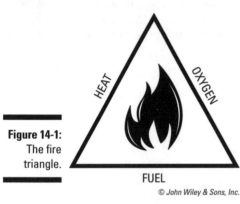

Figure 14-1:
The fire
triangle.

© John Wiley & Sons, Inc.

The five stages of a fire

If you've ever started or watched a fire, you may have noticed that it goes through five different stages (this is similar to the five stages of rage when you've just been told you have no more beer left in the fridge after you've settled yourself in to watch the big match):

- ✔ **Induction:** The start of the process, where fuel and heat come together.

- ✔ **Ignition:** Where the flame starts to flicker and the temperature increases.

- ✔ **Fire growth:** The fire grows and spreads if it has enough fuel, oxygen and heat.

- ✔ **Steady state:** The temperature stabilises as the fire consumes all the fuel.

- ✔ **Decay:** This stage begins when either the fuel or oxygen has been consumed; the fire can then extinguish and gradually cool down. Although be warned – it can re-ignite if fuel or oxygen are added.

Ignition can take milliseconds or it may take some time to occur following the induction process. Fire growth speed and the steady-state timeframe depend on the availability of fuel and oxygen (the heat being within the fire). Once all the fuel or oxygen has been used up, decay begins to occur; however, if fuel or oxygen are introduced (by the opening of a door or collapsing of a wall) the fire will reignite.

Remove any one of these three things (fuel, oxygen or heat), and the fire will go out.

Classifying fire types

If you look at a modern fire extinguisher, it tells you what type of fire it can put out (no, it won't actually speak). It may work on just one type of fire or on several types. Usually, it references classes of fire, such as 'A', 'B', 'C' or even 'ABC'. You need the right extinguisher for your fire type, otherwise you can make the fire much worse.

Here are the different types of fire class:

- ✔ **Class A** fires involve organic solids, like wood, paper or plastics.
- ✔ **Class B** fires involve liquids or liquefiable solids, such as petrol, oil, paint or wax.
- ✔ **Class C** fires involve gases, such as LPG, natural gas and acetylene.
- ✔ **Class D** fires involve finely divided metals, such as zinc and magnesium powders.
- ✔ **Class F** fires involve cooking fats and oils (if you run a chip shop, you know all about this hazard).

You probably noticed that Class E fires seem to have been missed off this list. However, they've not been forgotten – just reclassified. *Class E* fires used to denote electrical fires. But some bright spark (oh yes) figured out that you just need to turn the power off and, hey presto, your Class E fire becomes a Class A fire (mainly caused by plastic these days).

Knowing which fire class you're dealing with is essential. We look at which fire extinguishers work for each class of fire in the later section, 'Don't be a hero! Fighting fires to make your escape'.

Working out how fires spread

Fire is adept at spreading through buildings. It spreads in four main ways:

- ✔ **Conduction:** Stick a metal poker in a fire or a pan on the stove and you can soon get a practical demonstration of conduction as the heat moves up the handle. Fire can spread in this way in buildings through the services (like metal pipes) or supports (like steel joists) that go through different sections of your building (for example, that connect floors and walls).

✔ **Convection:** Hot gases rise, moving around the enclosure (ceiling), escaping through voids (usually tops of doors, vents) and eventually filling the room because the gases can't escape fast enough. Hot smoke and gases from a fire can heat up the ceiling and surrounding areas, causing fires to ignite. Fire loves tall buildings with their ready-made ventilation shafts and stairwells – it's so easy for fire to travel up the building, consuming everything in its path like Godzilla on a night out.

✔ **Radiation:** Burning materials emit a considerable amount of radiant heat, which you can feel from afar. Therefore, even materials that appear to be nowhere near the source of a fire can get rather hot and burst into flames. A soft toy placed one metre from a fire (but not touching it) can still catch fire.

✔ **Direct burning:** Fire can travel onto the next item by touching it. The fuel is next to the fire and doesn't get drawn-in, but the fire grows and then touches the fuel, causing it to ignite.

Fire can spread using one or all of these methods, so you must ensure that fuels are separated, voids are filled in and items that can be fire-resistant are. Furniture should always be fire-resistant so that there's an opportunity to slow the fire down.

Discovering common causes of fire

Fires in the workplace can be accidental or deliberate. The most common causes of workplace fire include:

✔ **Electrical equipment:** Faulty wiring, overloaded electrical systems, misused equipment and incorrectly used electrical equipment (for example, equipment used in an inappropriate environment) can lead to workplace fires.

Flammable atmospheres must have specialist work equipment that's intrinsically safe (won't create sparks) and has an *EX rating* (which means it is intrinsically safe). If you need to use any electrical equipment in these areas or any equipment that may cause a spark, you must ensure that it's rated and is well-maintained.

✔ **Arson:** Hopefully you won't be a target, but many workplace fires are started deliberately – a disgruntled employee or customer may want revenge for some known or unknown act, or your premises may just be in the wrong place (that is, your business may be the victim of wanton vandalism).

✔ **Hot work:** Hot work includes any process involving the use of naked flames (for example, welding and soldering) or that creates a significant ignition source (such as cutting or grinding). Any work activities using naked flames must be closely controlled, and monitored and performed by experts who have the appropriate fire extinguisher to hand.

✔ **Smoking:** In particular, you need to be aware of the dangers from carelessly discarded cigarette ends; sometimes they end up in bins when they haven't first been properly extinguished.

✔ **Cooking appliances:** Be careful not to leave appliances unattended and look out for cooking-oil spillages.

✔ **Heating appliances:** During the winter months employees may start to use portable heaters which, if controlled correctly, is fine, but if they're not controlled (such as not purchased from reputable sources, or they're hidden under a desk) they can cause fires by overheating or having contact with fuels.

✔ **Poor use and storage of flammable liquids and gases:** Static sparks may be generated that can ignite a flammable vapour, such as petrol or acetone.

Assessing Fire Risk

Fire risk assessment is a specific type of risk assessment, designed to help you identify and control fire risks so that your building doesn't burn down and, even if it does, everyone escapes with their lives (we cover general risk assessment approaches in Chapter 4).

Fire risk assessment takes the same five-step approach as other workplace risk assessments:

1. **Identify your fire hazards (looking for ignition, fuels and oxygen sources).**

2. **Decide exactly who is at risk, including any vulnerable people who may need additional help.**

3. **Evaluate the fire precautions already in place and decide if you need to do more.**

4. **Plan and implement any extra precautions that you require.**

5. **Review your risk assessment regularly and following any incidents, or if you have any reason to suspect that your risk assessment is no longer valid (such as new machinery, more chemicals and so on).**

Once you've completed your fire risk assessment, you know what actions you need to take to reduce the chance of a fire in your workplace and be able to better protect your employees, premises and business.

Tell your insurer about your fire risk management plans: you may get a reduction in your premium (but don't count on it).

The following sections cover how to identify fire hazards and who can be harmed in more detail. We also look at temporary places of work, such as refurbishment areas.

Considering the burning issues

To identify fire hazards, you go back to the fire triangle (refer to the earlier section, 'Getting to know the fire triangle'), which consists of three elements:

- **Fuel:** You probably have paper (because the paperless office never truly arrived), cardboard and furniture in the workplace that can burn, but you may also have gas (in kitchens, boilers or canisters) or chemicals that are also flammable and can serve as fuel sources.

- **Oxygen:** This life-giving gas is in the air and all around us (thank goodness – though not ideal when it comes to fire), pushed through ventilation systems, and may be created when certain chemicals oxidise (which create oxygen when burning . . . a bad combination).

- **Heat:** This usually arises from electrical equipment that's faulty or misused and overheats or causes a spark; lightning strikes; cooking activities, where heat sources are left near combustibles; and smoking.

Spotting these sources is reasonably easy – walk around your workplace, look at what you have, check under desks and speak to employees to see if they have any stories about smouldering appliances or equipment that heats up when it shouldn't.

If you create a flammable atmosphere as part of a normal process (perhaps by introducing vapours, gases or dust to the air which, if ignited, will set alight), you need to make sure that all electrical equipment within the vicinity is suitable (it must have an EX rating, which shows it is intrinsically safe, according to the atmosphere). Otherwise, you're just asking for trouble.

Establishing who's at risk

Consider how fire or smoke may spread in your building and how this can affect the people who work there (your building's *occupants*).

Identify who may be at risk. Think about the premises over all hours of the day and whether you have people working on their own (cleaners and maintenance employees, for example), or you have young, elderly or disabled people who may need help getting out of the premises.

You can generally group together the needs of different people on your premises; however, some individuals may need additional support to get out of the building, for example wheelchair users or those with hearing impairments.

Evaluating what you have in place

Write down everything you know that you have in place. Fire doors, alarm systems, evacuation plans . . . anything that references fire is relevant (you can find plenty of examples in the later section, 'Selecting Options for Fire Prevention and Protection'). Ask yourself: 'What is your building made of (wood, steel)?' and 'Do you need additional fire resistance?'

Plan and implement extra precautions

If, as part of the evaluation of your existing fire safety measures (refer to the preceding section), you establish that you have areas that require improvement, you need to put a plan in place that has realistic timeframes, allocate responsible people, and ensure that implementation takes place.

Review your risk assessment

You need to review your risk assessment regularly. Following your first fire risk assessment, you need to decide how often to review it (maybe quarterly or six-monthly, depending on the time-frames in your action plan). You may also base this review period on how likely you are to have a fire (high-risk workplaces should never wait over a year), how often you review your other risk assessments, and how often you conduct any other fire checks that you have in place (a daily/weekly walk-around, perhaps).

If anything changes (maybe your work equipment, amount of people, or chemicals) within the workplace, or you experience an incident, you must review your risk assessment as soon as possible.

Changing workplaces

You can assess fire risk with confidence when your workplace remains the same, but what if you need to get a building contractor in to provide a new entrance to your building, or build a second office block for your expanding business? You face a different challenge when it comes to assessing the risk of fire during temporary building works.

Your building contractors are storing flammables and combustibles, and increasing the ignition sources within the workplace. To make matters worse, because of the dust in the area, you've probably decided to cover and isolate the smoke detector heads for a short period to prevent false alarms. Not to worry though – through clear communication with your building contractors, you can keep ahead of the game and ensure that a fire doesn't occur.

To ensure that you keep the workplace as safe as possible, you should look to take these simple steps:

- ✔ Testing all electrical items before they come on site

- ✔ Storing flammable liquids in a fire-resistant cupboard

- ✔ Controlling hot works (like welding) through a 'permit-to-work system' (refer to Chapter 7), which includes monitoring following completion of the job to ensure that the area doesn't overheat and set fire to combustibles, like cardboard and paper

- ✔ Separating combustibles from ignition sources

- ✔ Ensuring that stored equipment and materials are not on walkways and so on – in other words, good housekeeping

- ✔ Preventing smoking on site, and only allowing smoking in designated areas

- ✔ Ensuring that the site remains secure when not occupied

Given that the nature of a building site changes quickly and the work areas can differ, you need to ensure that the site is monitored and regularly inspected. Talk to your building contractors to get to know what's happening on-site too.

Your building contractors need to provide you with a fire risk assessment for the job – this may be a document that they frequently update (because so many changes can occur).

Selecting Options for Fire Prevention and Protection

You know the saying 'prevention is better than cure'? Well, this is exactly how you need to consider fire risk management.

After you've identified all your fire hazards, you need to know what measures have been put in place for both prevention and protection from fire. The way your building is made, the location of different extinguishers, and automatic fire doors are some examples of these measures; they can all have an impact on fire safety, but only if they're maintained.

In the following sections, we go through the options available to assist you with protecting your employees, other occupants and your workplace, along with some useful checklists.

Controlling fuel and ignition sources

Your first line of defence is to stop the fire from starting in the first place. You can turn to the fire triangle for this (refer to the earlier section, 'Getting to know the fire triangle'). You know what fuel and ignition sources you have on site thanks to your risk assessment (refer to the earlier section, 'Considering the burning issues'). Controlling fuel and ignition sources and ensuring that they remain separate is the best way to prevent a fire from starting. In essence, you're trying to prevent the elements of the fire triangle from coming together – and removing all the oxygen isn't an option!

You need to control these sources, but don't fret – we offer some simple guidelines on what to look for:

- ✔ Are flammable liquids, solids and gases kept in separate fire-resistant stores?
- ✔ Do you have suitable signage on the stores?
- ✔ Do you test electrical equipment?
- ✔ Are employees told to undertake visual checks on wires before use (to look for faulty electrical wiring)?
- ✔ Do you control hot works (welding)?
- ✔ Do you have a suitable bin for cigarette ends in your designated smoking area?

✔ Are cooking appliances used carefully and under close supervision?

✔ Is your housekeeping of a good standard (that is, are there mounds of waste paper, are corridors used for storage, are chemicals spilled)?

✔ Do your fire doors remain closed (not wedged open) or on automatic closers?

✔ Do your fire doors close entirely when shut?

✔ Do you provide fire extinguishers?

✔ Do you undertake workplace inspections to look for fire hazards?

✔ Is the building secure (no incidents of arson, or people having access to the building without your knowledge)?

These guidelines can work as a simple checklist when you're establishing your fire controls so that you don't miss anything important and you can prevent a fire from starting. If you can answer 'yes' or 'not applicable' to each item, then you're in control; if you see any 'no' responses, you need to put in some control measures, such as maintenance, installation of items (signs, cigarette disposal bins and so on) or implementation of routine fire checks for employees.

Building barriers to limit fire spread

After you do what you can to prevent the fire, you can look to stop a fire spreading should it start. Blocking fire and smoke using fire-resistant walls, doors or mechanical measures (such as dampers in shafts and fire curtains in open spaces like theatres) can contain the fire to a single area, which hopefully means that the fire will decay or be extinguished in this one spot and thus not affect any other areas of your workplace.

Consider this scenario. A fire starts on the ground floor of a large, open-plan, multi-storey building that has open stairwells. Convection drives the hot smoke from the fire upwards. The smoke fills the ground floor of the building and then rises up each level via the open stairwells. Each stairwell, in effect, becomes a chimney. The hot smoke then fills the upper storeys of the building. The fire can't be contained and it spreads throughout the building.

In this situation, the building is likely to be destroyed or suffer severe damage. Any people in the building, especially in the upper storeys, may become trapped and die as a result of fire and smoke inhalation – they don't have time to escape and their escape routes (the stairwells) are full of smoke and flames.

This sombre example may help you appreciate why buildings are split into several compartments, each surrounded by fire-resistant materials.

Fire doors are a key element to these 'compartments' but only if they're closed. They must be self-closing and be fitted with a vision panel (this enables you to see if there's a fire on the other side of the door). A common type of fire door is held open by magnets, which release when the fire alarm is activated.

Where you erect internal fire-resistant walls or partitions, make sure that they reach to the ceiling and floor of the room. If you don't factor this into your building design, the fire can spread to the next room through the area between the top of the fire resistant wall and the original ceiling.

You may have ducts that run the entire length of the building. These ducts are scarily good at spreading fire everywhere. But they're often fitted with automatic closures that can activate during a fire alarm. These automatic closures are now part of the requirements for new-build buildings, but they may not have been fitted in older buildings. If this is the case, control measures for these areas must be maintained and monitored more closely.

Alarming yourself in the night

Just like grudges or unrequited love, fires that burn undiscovered for a long time are more likely to hurt people or block their escape, so you need to make sure that you can notify the people within your workplace quickly if a fire breaks out.

If your workplace is small (your boss probably calls it 'cosy') and employees can easily see from one side to another, you may not need automatic fire detection: you can notice a fire easily and someone can quickly raise the alarm. One way of raising the alarm manually is by shouting 'Fire!' to alert colleagues to the impending danger. But this doesn't really work in noisy areas (like construction sites), even if they're small. For smaller noisy areas like this you can use a hand bell, whistle or air horn.

But in most workplaces, you find automatic fire detection and alarm systems with, as a back-up, manual call points (otherwise known as *break-glass points*) on the final exit doors. *Manual call points* are the red boxes with a small 'glass' section in the middle, which can be easily broken. These systems are best for detecting fire and quickly alerting you to the danger.

You can detect fire in two main ways: from smoke and heat. Generally, *smoke detection* is put in most places (it's reasonably cheap and easy to install), but smoke detectors can be problematic when you have a chance of steam (near shower rooms and kitchens, for example), and they can easily be triggered by accident. You need heat detectors in these areas, which activate when there's a significant increase in the room temperature (usually 10 degrees Celsius) or when a set temperature is reached. They don't detect smouldering (we're not talking romance), so they may take some time to activate.

Selecting the right option for your premises should be easy, as long as you understand your premises. If you're planning to bring building contractors on-site to make changes to your workplace, you need to work with them so that you understand the potential impact they'll have on your workplace before, during and after the works have been completed (refer to the earlier section, 'Changing workplaces' for more).

Because everyone loves choice, you can have different types of alarms:

- ✔ **Audible:** A noise that's heard throughout the building can come in many forms – for example, sirens, bells or verbal instructions over a public address system.

- ✔ **Visual:** These can be used if noise levels are high or as a supplementary measure for those with a hearing impairment – for example, strobes, flashing lights, message boards and video screens.

Whichever type of alarm you have, you need to be able to hear or see it throughout the workplace, it needs to sound the same throughout the building, and you need to have a back-up power supply in case you're unlucky enough to have a power cut at the same time as a fire!

Don't be a hero! Fighting fires to make your escape

Fire extinguishers are now all coloured red. That may seem rather boring (we quite like red, but maybe purple would be an interesting change once in a while), but it serves a purpose because apparently it can help you to recognise fire extinguishers quickly (though, disappointingly, Klingons can't see the colour red, so they may not be a great help in a fire, *Star Trek* fans).

You need to place fire extinguishers at strategic points in your buildings and on exit routes. But they're not put in place for you to become a hero or designed to put out large fires – they're purely intended to help you clear your path and escape from the building.

You need to use different extinguishing agents for different types of fire (refer to the earlier section, 'Classifying fire types'). The main fire extinguishing agents consist of the following:

- **Water** is the most effective extinguishing agent for Class A fires. The small jet sprays water to cool the ignited material.

  Don't use water extinguishers on electrical equipment or flammable liquids. Water conducts electricity, so you may end up having casualties for different reasons (refer to Chapter 13 for more on electric shocks and other electricity issues). Flammable liquids generally sit on top of water, so the water will just pass through the flame, making no difference at all.

- **Foam** is particularly good for Class B fires and can also be used on Class A fires. The foam forms a layer on top of the burning liquid, preventing oxygen from reaching it (and thus breaking up the three essential elements of a fire – refer to the earlier section, 'Getting to know the fire triangle'), and using foam can reduce the risk of a fire re-igniting.

- **Dry powder** is effective on Class A, B and C fires. It can also be used on live electrical equipment. The powder has a smothering effect on the fire, but offers little or no cooling, so once the powder has moved you face the risk of re-ignition.

  Given that they work on so many classes of fire, you'd think they'd be beneficial everywhere, but dry powder extinguishers are very messy to use, even on small fires, and attach particles to objects, which draw in water (so wreck everything they touch).

- **Specialist powders** have been developed for use on Class D (metal) fires. You can get a variety of specialist powders, depending on the metals concerned.

  Specialist powder extinguisher operators require formal training on the control, process of extinguishing and dangers associated with using them. They aren't just a point and spray option.

- **Vaporising liquids** produce a heavy vapour that extinguishes the fire by excluding oxygen. They're safe to use on Class A and B fires and effective on fires involving live electrical equipment.

- **Carbon dioxide (CO_2)** is very good for use on live electrical equipment (the gas can get right inside the equipment). It also works on smaller Class B fires by smothering and displacing the oxygen. You do, however, have the risk of re-ignition due to little or no cooling.

  Discharging CO_2 gas can be very noisy and may alarm users, and the discharge horn can get very cold (so, training may be useful for these extinguishers).

✔ **Wet chemicals** are used on Class F fires. These chemicals are an alkaline liquid solution that reacts with the hot fat/oil to produce a soapy layer that traps vapours, excludes oxygen and provides some cooling.

✔ **Fire blankets** are used on fat or solvent fires to smother the flames and exclude oxygen. Location is critical as they need to be readily available. You need good technique too (like many things in life) to ensure that you place the blanket safely onto the fire without burning your fingers.

You may also have sprinkler systems (automatic) or fire hoses, both of which use water.

When you're using a fire extinguisher, you must point the contents at the 'heart' of the fire. Don't waste your time or extinguishing agents on 'fanning the flames' as this won't help you to extinguish the fire.

If some of your employees have special fire duties (like fire marshals) or are more likely to encounter fire (like chefs) it makes sense to give them specific training on how to use portable extinguishers. Okay, extinguishers do have instructions on the side and they're not difficult to use, but in the heat of the moment (sorry) it's easy to panic and forget that the instructions are right in front of you, and anyone can benefit from a few tips.

In England and Wales, under the Regulatory Reform (Fire Safety) Order 2005 (similar requirements exist in Scotland and Northern Ireland's legislation), extinguishers, fire blankets, hoses and sprinkler systems all need regular inspections and planned maintenance carried out by someone who knows what they're doing (that is, a *competent* person who's trained for the job).

Emptying the building: Emergency evacuation procedures

Employees can be spread throughout the building in different areas – on the roof, in the basement, in the office and so on – and all employees need to be able to get out of the building quickly if you have a fire. You can't rely on lifts either (though you can get some specially protected types that fire-fighters can use) because you can get trapped in them if the power is cut by the fire.

Getting out of a building during a fire is easier said than done. Your escape routes need to be well-designed. Consider the following advice for your fire escape routes. They should:

✔ Take you the entire way out of the building from wherever you are in the workplace and into an area that isn't enclosed (rather than an enclosed courtyard or a back car park that's only accessible through the underneath of the building).

✔ Consider how far you need to travel to escape (the travel distance); the higher the fire risk, the shorter you want the travel distance to be.

✔ Be wide enough for the number of people you have on your premises. This allows a good flow of people (no getting stuck), and you probably need several alternative routes to achieve this, depending on the fire risk. For example, a low-risk workplace with, say, only ten people may have one exit and a fairly long travel distance. This distance is no good for a high-risk workplace with 200 people, where you instead require several alternative exits with much shorter travel distances.

✔ Be clearly signed with the 'walking person' sign with green and white pointing arrows (the figure used to be running, but now it's walking – running doesn't set the right 'don't panic!' tone).

✔ Be well lit (but not by fire). Your exit routes need to include emergency lighting in case of power failure.

✔ Not be used as a storage dump. Your exit routes need to be kept clear and tidy so that people can pass through easily.

✔ Have doors that are easy to open in a hurry (for example, unlocked and with push bars), are wide enough to allow free-flowing escape and open in the direction of travel (so that you don't have to pull a door back onto yourself).

You need to have a place where everyone gathers after escaping the building (usually called an assembly point or muster point). This point needs to be out of the way of fire engines and located where you can move people further away if required (you can move people to a designated new location or direct a person with a sign to move the people according to the crowd's requirements). Depending on the size of your workforce, you may use a single person to undertake this (with a loud-hailer and a sign) or multiple fire marshals (after they've received the instruction).

The following sections consider establishing your fire evacuation procedure and evacuating people with disabilities.

Putting a procedure into place

After you figure out your escape routes, you can start to put your fire evacuation procedure together. Put simply, your procedure for employees is 'sound the alarm, get out and stay out' (only in emergencies, of course).

A simple fire procedure should cover the following:

✔ What employees should do in the event of discovering a fire

✔ What employees should do in the event of hearing the fire alarm

✔ Actions employees shouldn't do (collect personal belongings, use lifts and so on)

✔ Where employees should assemble once they have left the building

If your building is complicated (like a theatre) or some people need assistance to escape (for example, people in care homes, or, er, prisons), this simple procedure won't work, and you therefore require a more sophisticated evacuation procedure.

In these cases, after you sound the alarm, designated employees (fire marshals, hospital staff, ushers or even a dedicated fire team) carry out special duties (always without putting their own lives in danger). These people require special training on the evacuation procedure and the extent of their role, as well as on using any specialist equipment, like evacuation chairs.

High-risk workplaces such as airports have their own fire-fighters on site to deal with emergencies.

Most premises have fire marshals who 'sweep' an allocated area for people and report back to a central fire marshal if the area is clear or if people are still there. This information can be reported to the fire service so that they have a clear picture of who's still in the building and may need rescuing.

Fire drills are a great way to practise these procedures and ensure that your team performs its roles effectively. Debriefing after fire drills can help you identify any areas for improvement.

If you have a small staff team (under 20 people), and have a good system for signing in and out of the building (so no one has nipped out for lunch without first signing out), then a simple roll call can confirm that all have escaped. However, this system relies on everyone using it properly.

Assisting people with disabilities out of the building

People with disabilities, whether employees or visitors, must be assisted out of the building during an alarm. When this person is an employee, you need to develop a highly personalised evacuation plan (a Personal Emergency Evacuation Plan, or PEEP). The PEEP outlines the procedure that the disabled person needs to take, the equipment available for use, and who (if needed) can assist. If you have visitors, or other situations where you may not know if the person is disabled, you can develop a General Emergency Evacuation Plan (GEEP), which gives you basic control measures (such as employees escorting visitors, and fire marshals understanding the likely location of people and the procedures available).

You can find many products on the market to help those with disabilities escape from buildings during emergencies:

- ✔ People with hearing difficulties can use vibrating pillows in hotels, pagers in workplaces or a buddy system (a friendly colleague) so that they aren't left alone.

- ✔ People with eyesight problems need to be assisted by another person or a guide dog, and taken through the evacuation route (as it may be unfamiliar to them).

- ✔ Wheelchair users may need to use fire-rated lifts, evacuation chairs or sheets to evacuate.

Further information is available online at www.gov.uk/government/publications/fire-safety-risk-assessment-means-of-escape-for-disabled-people.

If full evacuation isn't required immediately, you can move people to a 'safe place' (usually the next compartment of the building or a 'refuge area'), but you must have a way of communicating with them and have a plan to get them out of the building that doesn't include the use of the fire service.

Chapter 15

Getting the Chemistry Right: Controlling Hazardous Substances

. . . .

In This Chapter

▶ Establishing the risks from substances hazardous to health

▶ Controlling the risks of working with chemicals and other hazardous substances

▶ Containing asbestos and managing its removal

. . . .

*J*ust like tax collectors, chemicals are everywhere. Some are natural; some are *anthropogenic* (an impressive term for man-made); some are hazardous; and some are harmless. They may be single substances (like sodium hydroxide, used to clean drains) or mixtures (like paints – or even whisky and soda, or rum and cola . . .). They may even be transformed or produced by a *process* (a chemical reaction) in your workplace.

Chemicals can display all manner of special (and sometimes alarming) qualities – they may be explosive or flammable (refer to Chapter 14), or corrosive to the skin and eyes, as well as being dangerous for the environment. This chapter is mainly concerned with chemical substances that are hazardous to human health.

In this chapter, we will look at identifying chemical substances in your workplace and how they can affect employees.

Assessing the Risks to Health from Chemical Substances

Hazardous chemical substances come in many forms and some can have serious effects on human life. A *hazardous substance* is a substance that can cause harm to health (that is, cause physical harm).

You need to make sure that you know what you're getting yourself into when you're working with hazardous chemicals and, more importantly, how to manage hazardous substances properly if you can't live without them. Chemicals are jolly useful – you'd really miss them if they weren't there. For example, cleaning products, clothes-washing powders and liquids, hair sprays, and alcohols are just some of the hazardous chemicals you can find around the house. However, the benefits to you (or society as a whole) mean that they're worth the effort of managing.

The likelihood of harm caused by a substance depends on relatively few things. Here are the main considerations you need to keep in mind:

- ✓ The nature of the substance itself – what kind of damage is it capable of? Is it corrosive (likely to cause chemical burns – for example, acids), toxic (poisonous), an irritant (likely to cause an inflammatory reaction – for example, dermatitis) or harmful (likely to cause harm of some other sort – for example, respiratory sensitisation that may lead to asthma)?

- ✓ Whether the substance can get into your body in some way (we call that a *route of entry,* and discuss these in the later section, 'Getting under your skin: Routes of entry'). In the majority of cases, this entry route depends on the physical form of the substance – dust or a solid lump, liquid or vapour, and so on.

- ✓ How much of the substance you're exposed to (the amount, or its concentration).

- ✓ How long you're exposed to the substance for (seconds, minutes or hours versus months or years) and how often you're exposed (once in a blue moon, or every day?).

You're looking to avoid *significant* exposure to hazardous substances; in other words, to ensure that the use of the substance is controlled so that the person using it isn't harmed by it.

Don't just think of exposure in the context of *intentional* work – that is, when you're deliberately working with chemicals. You may also be exposed to chemicals *incidentally* (that is, it's not a major part of your work – you just encounter a few chemicals now and again in passing) or even *accidentally* (you don't work with chemicals at all but someone may spill a whole bottle of bleach near you). For example, asbestos was used in the UK in almost everything (except perhaps tinned spaghetti) until 1999, when its use was banned entirely (amosite and crocidolite asbestos had already been banned in 1985). Therefore, if you work on building maintenance, electrical or plumbing jobs, you're likely to encounter asbestos at some point (perhaps when lifting floorboards, removing ceiling tiles or drilling). (You can find out more about managing the risks associated with asbestos in the later section, 'Getting to Know Asbestos'.)

The dangers of working with lead

The Control of Lead at Work (CLAW) Regulations 2002 require employers to prevent, or, where this isn't possible, to control employee exposure to lead. Working with lead causes a number of symptoms, including headaches, stomach pains and anaemia, and sometimes brings on more serious health effects, such as kidney damage, nerve and brain damage, and infertility.

The Control of Substances Hazardous to Health (COSHH) Regulations 2002 outline the need to undertake assessments of hazardous substances within the workplace. They don't cover asbestos, lead or radiation – why? Because these have their own specific regulations, which you find online at www. legislation.gov.uk/. You can find out more about asbestos later in this chapter in the section 'Getting to Know Asbestos', discover the essentials of radiation in Chapter 16, and introduce yourself to the issues around lead in the nearby sidebar, 'The dangers of working with lead'.

Assessments completed under COSHH are called, unsurprisingly, COSHH assessments, and these assessments follow simple steps – just like any other form of risk assessment. You need to look at the specific risk factors (which we cover in the upcoming sections), such as how it enters the body, relevant to the substances. The HSE have produced a simple e-tool to help you (http://coshh-tool.hse.gov.uk/), but if you prefer to do it yourself you need to follow these steps:

1. **Identify the hazards.** Look around your workplace, talk to employees and establish the hazardous substances that they can be exposed to. The primary information sources here are labels and safety data sheets (see the next section for more on these).

2. **Decide who may be harmed and how.** How can employees be exposed to a hazardous substance, what type of contact may they have, how often do they have contact and for how long?

3. **Evaluate the risks and decide on precautions.** Can you eliminate the use of the substance(s)? Can you replace it with another less-hazardous substance? Can you change the process to make it safer?

4. **Make a record of the findings.** Employers with five or more employees must record in writing the main findings (refer to Steps 1–3) of the risk assessment. This record provides proof that the assessment was carried out.

5. **Review the risk assessment.** A risk assessment needs to be reviewed regularly to ensure that safer alternatives aren't available, the control measures are still in place and the information on the assessment is still relevant. You never know, the chemical manufacturers may have made a hazard-free version!

In the following sections, we look at the risks to health from chemical substances in the workplace, including finding sources of information for the hazardous substances you use, and understanding the risks of ill-health and over-exposure to chemicals.

Staying informed with labels and safety data

When you buy chemicals, they're usually supplied in packages or containers. These containers are labelled with the product information and you're also supplied with (or can ask for) a safety data sheet (check out the nearby sidebar 'Labelling and safety data sheets' for more on these).

European countries use an agreed system for classifying hazardous chemicals and communicating bad-news safety data to the user – the *Globally Harmonised System of Classification and Labelling of Chemicals (GHS)*. Sadly, it's currently far from 'globally' harmonised – it's a nice aspiration though, just like the gift of world peace, eradication of poverty and a pair of slippers for Christmas. Despite this, the GHS provides plenty of jolly useful data for you, and, with large global companies, they now only produce one set of labelling and safety data sheets rather than different ones for different countries.

Suppliers have to meet the following minimum requirements on their labels for hazardous substances:

- ✔ **Contact information:** Name, address and telephone number of the supplier.

- ✔ **Product identification information:** The name of the substance, plus any unique numerical identifiers assigned by the supplier to help them identify each substance. For example, a paint manufacturer may have many different paints, so instead of matt white and gloss white they use different numbers to identify each one.

- ✔ **Name(s) of the hazardous constituents:** The ingredients that are harmful to health.

- ✔ **Hazard pictograms:** The weirdly exotic symbols that depict the hazard associated with the substance, so you can see at a glance the main hazard(s). Since these are commonplace now in supermarkets (for example, on cleaning products) and home improvements stores (for example, on paints and solvents), you may easily recognise them. See Figure 15-1 for an example.

- ✔ **Signal words:** A word (or words) that outline the hazards associated with the substance so you can understand quickly how hazardous a substance is (like 'Danger' or 'Warning' – not a secret message to get into a club or anything).

✔ **Hazard statements:** These describe the nature of the hazard (in fact, the nature of the harm usually) and are mostly self-explanatory. For example, 'Flammable liquid' and 'Vapour'.

✔ **Precautionary statements:** These are quick bits of safety advice that cover areas such as protective equipment and first aid advice.

✔ **Supplementary statements:** Anything extra that may be relevant.

Figure 15-1:
A hazard pictogram showing that a substance is flammable.

© John Wiley & Sons, Inc.

Labelling and safety data sheets

If you really can't get to sleep at night, you may want to review a useful document from the European Union (EU) that fully describes the GHS system. You can download it for free here: `http://echa.europa.eu/documents/10162/13562/clp_labelling_en.pdf`.

The label provides quick, direct advice – so you can easily say to yourself, 'Blimey, that's dangerous then.' Complementing this label is the more detailed safety data sheet, which is also 'globally harmonised' – containing 16 standard sections (the headings are prescribed by law, so forgive the clumsiness of some of them). In essence, the safety data sheet tells you what the substance is, what to do if things go wrong, how to stop things going wrong in the first place, and, finally, other stuff that may come in useful someday.

The 16 sections are as follows:

✔ **Identification of the substance/mixture, and of the company/undertaking:** Name, address and emergency contact phone numbers. The emergency number is for notifying large spills, addressing medical issues (like glue sticking fingers together) and for medical professionals to use (for example, at hospitals).

✔ **Hazards identification:** A summary of the most important features, including likely adverse human health effects and symptoms. Usually, this tells you immediately if any hazards exist with the substance.

✔ **Composition/information on ingredients:** Confirmation of chemical names, their hazardous nature (such as irritant, toxic and so on) and the approximate concentrations of ingredients.

(continued)

(continued)

- ✔ **First-aid measures:** This section is separated out to cover the various risks individually; the specifics need to be practical and easily understood.

- ✔ **Fire-fighting measures:** Emphasising any special requirements, especially if certain extinguishers can't be used on the substance.

- ✔ **Accidental release measures:** This mainly covers spillages, and the related safety, environmental protection and clean-up issues.

- ✔ **Handling and storage:** Recommendations for best practice, including any special storage conditions or incompatible materials. Very useful to know, especially if the chemical has temperature conditions or other restrictions.

- ✔ **Exposure controls/personal protection:** Any specific recommendations, such as particular ventilation systems and personal protective equipment (PPE) requirements. This section also gives you the specifications of the required PPE, such as the type of face mask required. Here you also find data such as 'Workplace Exposure Limits' – we look at those in more detail in the later section 'Exposing exposure limits', as they're quite important where substances can be inhaled (the most common route of entry in the workplace).

- ✔ **Physical and chemical properties:** Things like physical form, boiling point and solubility properties.

- ✔ **Stability and reactivity:** Conditions and materials to avoid.

- ✔ **Toxicological information:** Quite detailed toxicological data, on which it's decided if the chemical is irritant, harmful, toxic and so on. The levels are derived from the potential short-term and long-term effects, routes of entry and symptoms, and how it can affect employees. This can help you establish who can be affected and how.

- ✔ **Ecological information:** The environmental effects of the chemical.

- ✔ **Disposal considerations:** How to get rid of the chemical properly.

- ✔ **Transport information:** Only relevant if you're thinking of transporting the chemical somewhere else off-site. But, in the EU at least, you probably use a dangerous goods safety adviser to tell you about this specialist area.

- ✔ **Regulatory information:** That is, labelling the chemical with any relevant global laws or EU Directives.

- ✔ **Other information:** If you don't think there was quite enough information in there already, fear not – there's a final catch-all section for anything you may have missed.

If you still can't sleep, you can also find some detailed guidance on safety data sheets from the EU here: `http://echa.europa.eu/documents/10162/13643/sds_en.pdf`.

In many everyday cases you don't need specialist chemical knowledge to assess the hazards of using a chemical. The idea behind the labelling and safety data sheet is to give you the information in a much simpler way. It's not a perfect system, but it's much better than the alternative. You don't need to know what all the different categories are – you just need to be able to read the label and the safety data sheet (oh, and ask the supplier if you're not sure – their number is on the safety data sheet for a reason).

Reviewing the label and safety data sheet doesn't constitute a chemical risk assessment. It's just the main source of information on the chemical. These sources are fairly generic. You need to take account of how you actually use (or create) the chemical (what its physical form is, the amounts you use, the processes you use it for, who's exposed to it and so on). For example, some chemicals become more hazardous when mixed with other chemicals – such as adding bleach to a toilet at the same time as using another toilet cleaner.

Getting under your skin: Routes of entry

Chemicals can get into your body in different ways. In most cases, the routes available depend on what physical form the chemical is in.

Hazardous substances may take one of four main routes of entry into the body:

- ✔ **Inhalation:** Breathing in the substance, where it either stays in the respiratory tract or enters the lungs.

  In practice, this is the most likely route of entry in a workplace (and the lungs are probably the most vulnerable) as many processes either use, involve or generate airborne substances – gases, fumes, dusts, mists and vapours.

- ✔ **Ingestion:** Swallowing the substance. Although someone may consume a substance directly, it's more often transferred through contaminated foods and drinks, and on fingers.

  This is unlikely to be a major issue in a workplace unless the substance is highly toxic.

- ✔ **Absorption through the skin (or eyes):** Absorbing the substance through direct contact with the substance itself, contaminated surfaces or clothing. Some substances can pass through the skin directly and into the blood stream, almost as if the skin isn't there.

- ✔ **Direct injection through the skin:** Injection through piercing the skin, which is usually accidental (for example, from cuts).

The Health and Safety Executive (HSE) provides a useful case study about a company that was fined after three of its employees suffered with dermatitis as a result of their work with hazardous chemicals. Allergic contact dermatitis resulted from exposure to hazardous chemicals over a four-year period. One employee suffered blistering, cracking, splitting and weeping on the skin because of this condition, and two other employees' fingers and hands became so badly swollen and blistered that one of them couldn't do up his shirt buttons without his fingers splitting open. All three employees had been working with photographic chemicals.

The company was ordered to pay £30,000 in costs and fined a total of £100,000:

- ✔ £30,000 for breaching the Health and Safety at Work etc Act 1974.

- ✔ £60,000 for breaches of the COSHH Regulations 2002 for not making adequate risk assessments, not preventing or controlling exposure of employees to chemicals, and not providing any 'health surveillance' of employees at risk (check out the later section 'Monitoring your control measures' for more on health surveillance).

- ✔ £10,000 for not reporting employees contracting allergic contact dermatitis.

You can find out more about this case study at www.hse.gov.uk/coshh/casestudies/dermatitis.htm.

Factoring in the risk of ill-health

The severity of effect of chemicals in practice depends not only on their hazardous nature (for example, irritant or toxic) and their physical form (routes of entry) but also how you're using them. Depending on the exposure pattern, substances can have *acute* (short-term) and *chronic* (long-term) health effects:

- ✔ **Acute** effects occur quickly after exposure (that is, in seconds, minutes or hours) and are often caused by large amounts of a substance – for example, inhaling high concentrations of chlorine gas causes immediate respiratory irritation. These effects are often reversible.

- ✔ **Chronic** effects take time to appear (that is, months or even years), and usually occur after repeated exposure to smaller amounts of a substance over a longer period of time – for example, when working with lead, it can take months to accumulate high levels of lead in the blood. These effects are mostly irreversible.

You also need to take into account some additional issues, for example:

- ✔ How much of the hazardous substance do you store, use or create on your site?

- ✔ How long are employees exposed to the substance? What are the quantities of the substance and the time duration of employee exposure?

- ✔ Do you use the substances neat or dilute them? When thinking about dusts and powders, what's the concentration in the air?

✔ How many people can potentially be exposed? Are any of them vulnerable groups or individuals, such as expectant mothers or the infirm?

✔ Do you have any existing data to suggest that you have an issue with the substance (complaints, records, monitoring results, any applicable Workplace Exposure Limits)?

Reviewing this information can help you decide if your workplace has a realistic risk of significant exposure to a given substance, leading to ill-health.

The HSE provides a case study where a school cook suffered with respiratory issues following flour dust exposure. She developed breathing problems after working with flour in the school kitchen. The room was small, with poor ventilation, and her breathing problems became so severe that she could hardly walk. She also had to sleep sitting up.

The exposure to flour dust occurred every day while making dough in a large mixer. The council admitted that it hadn't taken sufficient action over the problem despite repeated complaints by the employee to the employer.

The cook became severely asthmatic. She had to retire early on health grounds, and the courts eventually awarded her £200,000 in damages.

You can find out more about this case on the HSE website: www.hse.gov. uk/asthma/schoolcook.htm.

Exposing exposure limits

Workplace Exposure Limits (WELs) represent the maximum allowable concentrations of airborne contaminants and have been devised by the HSE. The idea is to limit your exposure to broadly safe concentrations in the workplace. Actual exposure can be highly variable (it depends on what you're doing, how close you are to the emission source and so on). So, these limits are *time-weighted average values* – which means that you can exceed them instantaneously, so long as on average you comply. A similar analogy is the average speed enforcement cameras you can now find on motorways, which have been steadily replacing the traditional speed camera.

Two main time periods are used for the averaging: 15 minutes and 8 hours. That said, the eight-hour averaging is used more frequently; this is also known as the *long-term (eight hours) exposure limit* (or *LTEL*). This time period is meant to represent a typical working day's exposure – so, if you don't exceed the exposure limit for this time period you should be fine, day after day. The time periods refer to *personal exposure* (exposure that people are realistically likely to experience). So, if someone takes a break, or works in multiple areas, they aren't being exposed at those times (to that substance anyway).

WELs have legal status under the COSHH Regulations 2002 and can be found listed in the HSE's publication *Workplace Exposure Limits, EH40/2005:* `www. hse.gov.uk/pUbns/priced/eh40.pdf`.

WELs are usually quoted on the safety data sheet for a hazardous substance (refer to the earlier sidebar 'Labelling and safety data sheets' for more on what the safety data sheet covers).

You need to be aware of the WELs and have knowledge of any substances within your workplace that have these restrictions. These limits help you with your risk assessment and enable you to ensure that the control measures that you put in place don't put employees at risk.

These WELs are used as reference points to compare against actual exposure levels. The idea is that you measure actual workplace exposure, average it over the equivalent eight-hour period, and compare it with the WEL to see if your process is well-controlled. So, imagine that you're exposed to a certain concentration of a chemical vapour over four hours (and nothing else for the rest of the day). You can halve this to be equivalent to eight hours of exposure (that is, exposure to 100 ppm – parts per million – over four hours is actually an equivalent exposure to 50 ppm over eight hours).

It's best to measure exposure levels after you've installed reasonable control measures (as indicated by your risk assessment). Even then, you don't *have* to measure levels of concentrations (except in specific cases like vinyl chloride monomer). Generally, you only need to measure personal exposure levels where, from your risk assessment, you've concluded that you need to do so to be sure about exposure levels – for example, you don't have enough information to confidently decide if your control measures will be adequate, or where you're very reliant on particular control measures (like ventilation) working properly (which may fail and lead to serious health effects). But, if it's obvious that exposure is not an issue (for example, you have exposure once in a blue moon, and the WEL is set very high), it may just be a waste of money to have personal air tests done to give you levels of concentrations.

Keeping Chemicals under Wraps

You've looked at all the available information (the useful detail on the hazardous substance labels and safety data sheets – refer to the earlier section, 'Staying informed with labels and safety data') and considered how you use your chemicals. Labels and safety data sheets can't quite tell the whole story, however, because:

   ✔ They can't be aware of how your *specific* workplace conditions may affect your level of risk.

✔ Substances can affect different people in different ways – some people are very sensitive (we don't mean easily offended, but that they react strongly to certain chemicals known as *sensitisers*). Some employees may not realise that they have a problem until they start using the product.

✔ The information only considers the substance's use in isolation, when in reality it may be mixed with other substances that can make it even more hazardous.

✔ Scientific knowledge is in constant development – you only recognise that a chemical substance is hazardous when you find out about the issues around its use. It pays to be a little cautious and to review current data every now and then. It's sobering when you realise how much is out there yet to be discovered.

You need to work out the best ways to control chemical substances in your workplace. But no need to feel overwhelmed – help is at hand. In the following sections, we look at the control measures you can implement to reduce exposure.

Practicing the principles of good practice

The *principles of good practice* are a set of overriding approaches set out in the COSHH Regulations 2002 to help control hazardous substances. There are eight in total:

✔ **Principle 1: Design and operate processes and activities to minimise the emission, release and spread of substances hazardous to health.** This principle helps you to design the process to minimise the substance contact with employees or change the operation to do the same. Elimination is ideal but not always possible, so look to substitute one of your nasties with a less hazardous option or introduce other controls to reduce the impact of the substance if you just can't eliminate the risk.

✔ **Principle 2: Take into account all relevant routes of exposure – inhalation, skin and ingestion – when developing control measures.** The safety data sheet for each substance provides you with some information, but remember to consider the way you use the product. For instance, heating the product (by mixing it with hot water, perhaps) may increase the inhalation risk (and thus get you into hot water!).

✔ **Principle 3: Control exposure by measures that are proportional to the health risk.** Don't start using complicated local exhaust ventilation or glove boxes (enclosures with holes, where rubber gloves can poke through) for bleaching the toilet; these solutions aren't proportional to the risk.

✓ **Principle 4: Choose the most effective and reliable control options that minimise the escape and spread of substances hazardous to health.** Engineered options such as extractor fans, vacuums and glove boxes are more effective than PPE as they don't rely on your employees to do something to make sure that they're protected. Of course, they do require maintenance, training and possibly procedures to be in place, but they should already be in place and should work when the relevant machine or process is started.

✓ **Principle 5: Where adequate control of exposure cannot be achieved by other means, provide, in combination with other control measures, suitable PPE.** If you need to use the hazardous substance and suitable engineered options aren't available, you need to implement procedures around handling and finally, PPE. Don't make PPE your first line of defence. In many cases, you use PPE (like gloves) in combination with other measures, such as using the hazardous substance in well-ventilated areas (rather than in a broom cupboard).

✓ **Principle 6: Check and review regularly all elements of control measures for their continuing effectiveness.** Monitoring the use of control measures and ensuring that they're maintained is the only way to ensure that they continually work.

✓ **Principle 7: Inform and train all employees on the hazards and risks from substances with which they work, and the use of control measures developed to minimise the risks.** The more your employees know, the more likely they are to take the hazard seriously; if they're unaware of the issues, they may feel that the control measures are over the top and decide not to use them. Knowledge is power – and 'with great power comes great responsibility' (or was that a quote from *Spiderman*?).

✓ **Principle 8: Ensure that the introduction of measures to control exposure does not increase the overall risk to health and safety.** Control measures shouldn't cause other hazards or mitigate other controls, such as using rubber gloves when the chemical reacts with rubber. Humans have a terrible tendency to focus in on one small facet of a problem or situation and to make the whole thing worse as a result. It takes a bit of thinking to look at the wider aspects.

These principles are in place to help employers control the risks posed by chemicals. They show the hierarchy of control you need to implement for chemicals when you use them, or you're looking to use them.

Implementing common control approaches

You must follow a special order, known as a *hierarchy of controls,* when deciding on the control measures required for your workplace (this hierarchy is essentially an expansion of the principles of good practice explored in the preceding section). The ones at the top are considered more effective and the ones at the bottom less effective.

You need to consider the initial item on the hierarchy first, 'eliminate the exposure', before then moving onto the subsequent items. This doesn't always make business sense, however; for example, if the replaced substance isn't effective, or outsourcing introduces an extortionate cost, you may need to consider some of the subsequent methods of control in the hierarchy.

Here's the hierarchy of controls for managing the risk from chemicals:

1. **Eliminate the exposure.** This is the best way to control risk. This approach has generally been adopted within the manufacturing process for certain chemicals, like carcinogens, though it's impractical in many situations when you take into account the requirements of working processes, and indeed how useful some chemicals are to humanity. You can, therefore, rarely just cease the operation or remove the substance entirely. But you can instead, for instance, screw items together rather than glue them, thus eliminating the glue.

   Your process changes (to eliminate a substance) may inadvertently introduce other hazards into the mix (such as using power tools for drilling/screwing instead of glue), so be careful not to end up increasing your overall level of risk.

   If you lack in-house expertise, you may want to consider outsourcing a process that requires the use of the substance or creates the substance; for example, outsourcing a paint-spraying operation to a specialist paint sprayer. It doesn't actually eliminate the risk (someone has to do it), but it does put the operation into the hands of an expert who knows what they're doing (of course we wouldn't dare accuse you of not knowing what you're doing – but this is more about finding the best person for the job). This is an example of *risk sharing/transfer* (refer to Chapter 4 for more on this).

2. **Substitute the substance for one less hazardous.** It still needs to be able to do the job, but can you find a less hazardous substance for the job? For example, you can now use low-volatility, low-hazard water-based paints instead of solvent-based paints. You can also substitute a substance by changing its physical form (for example, using a slurry, solution or pellet instead of a dusty powder) or you may be able to get away with using a less concentrated (and so less hazardous) form of the substance (diluting the substance or using one that's classed as an irritant rather than corrosive because of the levels of the hazardous chemical).

3. **Change the process you use.** For example, you can use brush painting rather than spraying, and you can dampen down dusts and powders to reduce the amount of dust (many modern concrete saws come with water-spraying attachments for this very purpose).

Use a vacuum cleaner to clean up dust, rather than sweeping it up.

4. **Enclose the process by using glove boxes or something similar.** It can be practical to enclose your employees to ensure that they remain segregated from the hazard; for example, in a control booth or by using a remote handling device. However, this solution isn't always practical, because it may be necessary to frequently access equipment or material within your work area.

5. **Remove the airborne particles.** Local exhaust ventilation works like a vacuum cleaner – targeted suction, like being kissed by a camel. It's widely used for dust-creating machines and processes, so it draws the airborne substances away from the individual.

These controls are good if they're maintained, but they don't eliminate exposure.

6. **Improve ventilation.** General workplace ventilation works by mixing the substance with air, therefore reducing the concentration. Exposure still exists, but the quantities are reduced. This control option is pretty useless for processes that quickly produce high volumes of airborne contaminants, but it can be useful for processes that have very low rates of substance generation.

7. **Reduce the time of exposure for employees, either through job rotation or regular breaks.** It's personal exposure (what people inhale, for example) that counts, not the background concentration in the room. If no one's in the room, no one's being exposed to the substance.

8. **Encourage employees to practise good personal hygiene.** This is vital to reducing the chance of ingesting a substance. Examples include washing hands, especially before eating; covering wounds; and banning eating/drinking in contaminated areas.

Good hygiene practices are essential when it comes to highly toxic substances or ones that, with repeated small doses, can lead to long-term health issues (like cancer).

9. **Provide employees with PPE.** Examples include gloves, goggles/safety glasses, overalls and visors, and respiratory protective equipment such as filtering face masks and breathing apparatus.

You can use the HSE's COSHH Essentials e-tool to take the pain out of considering all these control measures. This uses simple information from the safety data sheet to determine the hazard from using the substance (how dusty or volatile it is) and considers how you're using it (pouring it, say), how much you're using and so on. You fill in a simple online questionnaire and it leads you to a basic range of control measures as a starting point. If anything too complicated arises, it tells you to seek further specialist advice, and for some common processes (like paint spraying), you can go straight to some worked-out procedures called 'direct advice sheets'. To find out more, visit www.hse.gov.uk/coshh/essentials/index.htm.

Monitoring your control measures

After you put your control measures in place, you need to make sure that these measures remain effective. Your control measures require maintenance (making sure that your local exhaust ventilation, glove boxes, barriers and PPE still work) and some judicious monitoring.

Monitoring is checking to make sure that your control measures are working – it's sometimes called 'surveillance', but that seems a bit sinister to us.

You can monitor atmospheric contaminants by measuring their concentrations and comparing them to the WELs (as we discuss in the earlier section, 'Exposing exposure limits'). These measurements can give you only information about what's in the air (and it isn't love). It's quite common to get specialists in to take these measurements (such as occupational/industrial hygienists) – not (just) because it's a bit boring, but because they have all the specialist equipment that you need to get the measurements right (and it is a *bit* boring . . . especially if you have to drill holes or something).

You may also want to conduct some *health surveillance* too – checking the health of your exposed employees.

The problem with health surveillance is that it informs you when something's already gone wrong. Before you even consider tackling health surveillance, remember that it's only worth doing where:

- ✔ You're aware of an adverse health effect or disease linked to workplace exposure, **and**

- ✔ It's likely that the health effect or disease may occur, given what you're doing, **and**

- ✔ You know of valid techniques for detecting early signs of the health effect or disease, **and**

- ✔ The techniques themselves don't present a risk to employees (so, if you can only detect an issue by autopsy, you may not get any takers).

Taking a look at biological monitoring

A more invasive form of checking is *biological monitoring,* where samples of blood, urine or breath are taken to check for the substance. For example, you can check operatives working with lead for cumulative levels of lead in their blood. This indicates the total uptake of a substance into the body by all routes (not just through inhalation), so tends to be used where you suspect that exposure routes other than inhalation are significant, such as absorption. Another example is for employees who work in the water industry. The workplaces tend to be underground, confined spaces and employees may potentially be exposed to gases such as sodium hydroxide. Exposure can be monitored through urine samples.

Some forms of health surveillance are very easy – you don't need a five-stage medical examination to check for dermatitis in a hairdressing salon; you just need to look at your employees' hands. (Dermatitis is well-known in the hairdressing industry and is associated with 'wet-washing' and all the chemicals that hairdressers put on your hair. It's also pretty common in catering too.)

Cutting out cancer

Exposure to hazardous substances can cause cancer, asthma or damage to genes (that's genetic material, not denim). You need to prevent exposure wherever possible but, if this isn't always possible, you need to adopt control measures.

Consider these control measures in the following order:

- Totally enclosing the process and its handling systems
- Preventing eating, drinking and smoking in contaminated areas to reduce the chances of ingestion
- Cleaning floors, walls and other surfaces regularly to prevent contact with the substance
- Designating at-risk areas that may be contaminated by using warning signs and telling people about the hazards associated with these areas
- Implementing, monitoring and maintaining safe storage, handling and disposal procedures; for example, carrying hazardous substances in closed containers

Getting to Know Asbestos

Asbestos is a natural mineral of fibrous nature that is still mined and used in some countries. You can get many different types of asbestos but all types are dangerous. Over 2,000 deaths occur per year due to asbestos exposure, and it still appears in the news despite its use being banned in the UK since 1999.

Although it's been banned, you can still find it in properties built before 2000. Asbestos has been widely used over the years, often mixed with other things, like cement. You can commonly find asbestos used as (or in):

- **Insulation board:** Originally used for fire protection and sound insulation purposes. You can find this board in ducts, ceiling tiles, fire doors and all sorts of places you'd never have thought.
- **Pipe lagging:** Used as thermal insulation around boilers and pipes.
- **Fire blankets** (well, old fire blankets, anyway): Used in homes and commercial catering kitchens.
- **Floor tiles:** Very similar in appearance to ordinary vinyl or plastic tiles.
- **Sprayed coatings used for insulation:** Used inside roofs, lofts and so on.
- **Roofing felt:** Used on the top of roofs to protect from weather.
- **Decorative paints and plasters:** For example, Artex ceiling coatings.

Asbestos-cement products include:

- Corrugated roofing sheets
- Guttering and drain pipes
- Cold water tanks and toilet cisterns

Asbestos is another example of something that people used to think was wonderful, before they discovered its dangers (much like mercury being used to stiffen hats and cigarettes being used to combat asthma!). However, asbestos does have its own set of regulations (the Control of Asbestos Regulations 2012). The basic principles are quite similar to dealing with any highly toxic chemical but with the added issue that it's been used in buildings for years.

The only way to confirm that a substance is asbestos or an asbestos-containing material (ACM) is through laboratory testing.

When asbestos was originally used there was little concept of the health implications, but now the significant health implications are widely understood. Asbestos can lead to the following potentially fatal conditions:

✔ **Asbestosis:** Very fine asbestos fibres are inhaled into the lungs, causing scar tissue to form, which leads to breathing difficulties and irreversible damage to the lungs.

✔ **Lung cancer:** The intrusion of asbestos fibres into the lung can trigger the development of cancerous growths in lung tissue.

✔ **Mesothelioma:** Asbestos fibres travel from the lungs through the surrounding tissue and into the cavities around the lung. This triggers the development of cancerous growths in the lining tissue around the lungs, the heart and the lining of the abdomen.

Asbestos exposure isn't immediately obvious; it takes 5 to 10 years for asbestosis and 20 to 50 years for mesothelioma symptoms to become apparent.

As tempting as it is to think 'Wow, that's really bad, I need to get rid of any asbestos in my workplace now', you need to consider the dangers of removing asbestos too. It's nasty stuff, and there's no legal requirement to remove asbestos from buildings if the building's in good condition and is properly managed. Disturbing asbestos is your biggest concern, especially if you may disturb ACMs during any maintenance or demolition works.

If you do have asbestos within your workplace, do you know what to do to control the risk and safely manage your buildings? If not, we explore this in the following sections.

Containing asbestos

You must ensure that asbestos is, and remains, contained when you find it in your workplace. It has to be protected from damage impact; for example, asbestos-containing insulating board wall panels can be damaged by trolleys, fork-lift trucks and so on.

You can contain asbestos in the following ways:

✔ Boxing in pipework without disturbing the surrounding asbestos.

✔ Fixing a replacement panel (board or partition) over the top of the asbestos panels, ensuring that you fix the replacement panel to nonasbestos materials – you can then use nails or screws.

✔ Using adhesive to attach replacement panels to ACMs.

✔ Sealing the cavity and providing adequate fire barriers.

✔ Warning the building owner about the presence of ACMs, so that it can be managed properly.

We're not going to go into any detail about how to work with asbestos. There's no point. Unless you're dealing with really simple stuff, any work done with asbestos (like removing it) is highly regulated and has to be done by licensed contractors – they know what they're doing and have all the equipment required to do the job safely.

Managing asbestos in buildings

You (or your landlord – whoever's responsible for the building) need to undertake a survey if your building was built before 2000, to see if asbestos is present in the building. If you're in doubt about whether your premises contain asbestos, you must assume that they do, unless you have proof that they don't (the *precautionary principle*). You can conduct one of two types of survey, which should be provided for those who may expose asbestos during their works (for example, maintenance staff and tenants putting up shelves):

✔ **Management survey:** This survey is for normal occupation of a building and doesn't include maintenance works. In simple and straightforward premises, the *duty holder* (that's the person responsible for the building) can do this, as long as they're aware of likely places that asbestos may be; otherwise, you need an asbestos surveyor to do the job. The idea is to confirm that:

- Nobody will be harmed by any asbestos remaining in the premises or equipment.

- The ACMs remain in good condition.

- Nobody can disturb ACMs by accident.

✔ **Refurbishment/demolition survey:** These surveys are required where the premises (or part of them) need upgrading, refurbishment or demolition. This *must* be done by an asbestos surveyor. The idea, again, is to make sure that:

- Nobody is harmed by work on ACMs on the premises or in the equipment.

- Required works are completed by a suitable contractor in an appropriate, safe way.

Once you know exactly where the asbestos is, and whether or not it can be affected by the planned works, you can make a decision about whether you need to remove it (using a competent or HSE-registered contractor) before starting work.

Even with surveys in place, you need a procedure that covers the actions to take if you discover asbestos, by accident, in unknown locations as part of any works. A basic procedure is to:

✔ Stop work immediately.

✔ Prevent anyone entering the area.

✔ Make arrangements to contain the asbestos – seal the area by closing windows, shutting doors and so on.

✔ Put up warning signs – they should state 'possible asbestos contamination'.

✔ Inform the site supervisor immediately.

✔ Decontaminate and dispose of all contaminated clothing, equipment and so on (dispose of these as 'hazardous waste').

✔ Undress, shower, wash hair and put on clean clothes.

✔ Contact a specialist surveyor or asbestos removal contractor.

As long as you enclose asbestos and maintain it (check that it hasn't been disturbed) you can keep it in the building (unlike Elvis, who has already left the building).

Chapter 16

Making Waves: Tackling Noise, Vibration and Radiation

. . . .

In This Chapter

▶ Reducing the volume in your workplace

▶ Protecting your employees from vibration

▶ Delving into the problems presented by ionising and non-ionising radiation

. . . .

*N*oise and vibration are all around you and are two things you can immediately recognise – such as noisy neighbours (or perhaps *you* are that
noisy neighbour), that huge HGV truck passing by as you wait to cross the
street, or a wonderful muddy evening at the Glastonbury festival trying to
find your tent between raucously loud performances. You also know, from
that deep-down trembling in your chest that you feel at a rock concert, that
where you have noise, you also get vibration.

Moving on to a different kind of energy, in this chapter we balance the
intense impact of noise and vibration by shedding a little light on the more
subtle world of radiation. Radiation can be a bit of a nerd-fest. You really do
need some specialist advice.

In this chapter, we cover noise, vibration and radiation, offering you plenty
of useful information for assessing and controlling the associated workplace
risks. (If at any point you feel overwhelmed with information, you may like to
relax with a little music – the Beach Boys' 'Good Vibrations', perhaps?)

Dealing with Noise and Vibration in the Workplace

Too much noise can cause a whole host of problems. Some well-known effects
are deafness (especially in the long term) and ringing in the ears. These
effects can have a big impact on your employees' work and personal lives.

Noise and vibration go hand-in-hand – noisy equipment is likely to vibrate and vibrating equipment is likely to be noisy. Partly as a result of legislative requirements but also because of the relentless march of technology, manufacturers have been working to reduce equipment noise and vibration for some time, resulting in a corresponding decrease in noise-and-vibration-associated ill-health cases over the last ten years.

Unfortunately, however, after the damage from noise and vibration is done, it's irreversible, and some people are never able to work again.

The following sections help you to establish whether you have a noise and/or vibration problem and identify control options that can help you manage these issues.

Listening out for problems

If you've ever been to a rock concert or nightclub, you may have noticed that your hearing seemed a little strange during the evening. You may have had to ask people to speak up so that you could hear them properly. You may even have gotten a strange buzzing in your ears. The next morning, however, your hearing probably returned to normal. This is a well-known effect that results from a one-off exposure to high noise levels. You get a temporary loss of hearing – *sensitivity* – due to disturbing the receptive hairs in your ears (check out the nearby sidebar 'Hearing what?' for more on the inner workings of your inners ears) but after a few hours, the hairs bounce back. (It's nice when you can explain an experience you've known your whole life.)

If you keep going to rock concerts every day for years (say, for example, you're a rock legend), it can eventually lead to permanent damage – known as *noise-induced hearing loss*. The loss gets worse over time and is unnoticeable at first, and it can make you permanently deaf. You may get other symptoms too, such as *tinnitus* – a persistent ringing in the ears. You may think that tinnitus would be quite manageable to live with, but remember that it's with you constantly, so it can really begin to distress you and can lead to depression (and even suicide).

You may think it would be easy to tell if you have a noise problem in the workplace. How hard can it be, you may wonder, to identify a really loud noise – one where you can't hear yourself think? But damaging noise isn't just about really *loud* noises. Lower sound levels can also damage your hearing if they go on for too long or are repeated frequently every day.

Hearing what?

Your hearing works by you receiving a *sound* (a vibration through the air) into the outer ear. It passes through the ear canal and makes contact with the eardrum. The eardrum moves, which transmits the signal through small bones to the *cochlea* (a small sensory organ in the ear that translates sound into nerve signals that are then transmitted to the brain). The cochlea contain millions of microscopically small sensory hairs – these hairs move back and forth with the sound waves and convert the sound into nerve signals. When the sensory hairs are exposed to excessive noise, they're pushed too far in one direction and are unable to bounce back, which means that you lose that part of your hearing.

You won't notice the effect of just a few of these hairs not working. It's only when you experience damage to a lot of these hairs that you start to notice a problem – not being able to hear certain sounds or things sounding muffled.

The UK's Health and Safety Executive (HSE) has come up with a few simple questions to ask yourself to help you decide if your noise is a hazard in your workplace. You're at risk if you can answer 'yes' to any of these questions:

- ✔ Is the noise intrusive – like the noise from a busy street, a vacuum cleaner or a crowded restaurant – for *most* of the working day?

- ✔ Do you have to raise your voice to have a normal conversation with someone when you're about two metres apart for at least part of the day? (This is known as the 'two metre rule' – and no, this isn't a restraining order issued by a court or a theme-park height restriction.)

- ✔ Do you use noisy power tools or machinery for *over* half an hour a day?

- ✔ Do you work in a noisy industry, such as construction, engineering or manufacturing?

- ✔ Do you experience noises because of impacts from hammering, guns or explosive sources, such as cartridge-operated tools or detonators?

- ✔ Do you have muffled hearing at the end of the day, even if it's better by the next morning?

For more information, check out the HSE's website here: www.hse.gov.uk/noise/worried.htm.

Noise doesn't just cause long-term hearing loss. It also directly interferes with safety because you may not be able to hear vehicles, alarms, instructions or warning sirens. Nuisance and background noise can also increase errors, because your employees are unable to concentrate through the noise.

> # Noise travels
>
> Sound (or noise) travels through the air as a pressure wave. When the wave hits an object (like a wall or your eardrum) it can make the object vibrate too – some of this vibration gets reflected back, some gets absorbed and some gets transmitted right through to the other side of the object.
>
> Different materials reflect, absorb and transmit these vibrations to different extents. (You may have noticed this in common phrases like 'the walls are paper thin' and 'the walls have ears'.)

Managing workplace noise

Understanding how noise is absorbed in your working environment, how it travels and how you can measure noise levels provides you with all the information you need to manage noise exposure in the workplace.

Estimating noise levels

Noise has its own vocabulary. You may have heard some of these terms before, but it's worth reviewing them before you consider your control options in detail (at the very least, they're very useful to impress your friends with at parties):

- **Decibels (dB):** Just as length is measured in metres and weight in kilograms, noise levels (technically, *sound pressure levels* or SPLs) are measured and quoted in *decibels*: the more decibels, the louder something sounds. However, it's not a straightforward measure like metres or kilograms. You know that 12 metres is twice as long as 6 metres, so you may assume that an SPL of 12 decibels is twice as loud as 6 decibels – when actually, 12 decibels is about 4 times louder than 6 decibels! (The sound level doubles about every 3 decibels.) This is because decibels use a *logarithmic scale* – in other words, a scale that compresses a large range of values into a more manageable range.

  A loud TV is usually 65–75 decibels loud, and a jet aircraft at 25 metres is approximately 140 decibels loud. However, having two TVs on at the same time in your room doesn't mean that you're exposed to the noise levels of a jet aircraft!

- **Frequency (Hz):** A sound's *frequency,* measured in *hertz* (Hz), tells you the number of times a second that a sound pressure wave hits your eardrum or another surface. Humans are only sensitive to certain frequency ranges. But a typical person can hear sounds in the range 20–20,000 hertz, whereas dogs can hear up to 50,000 hertz. Your hearing sensitivity changes with age, but it's no surprise that people are most sensitive to frequencies in the so-called speech range – around 4,000 hertz.

✔ **Noise weighting:** Humans are more sensitive to some frequencies than others. *Weighting* (or skewing) the measured noise levels is a way to reflect this.

You can get several weighting scales depending on the type of noise (for example, a constant noise versus a one-off loud bang), but 'A-weighting' and 'C-weighting' are the most common and can be measured by instruments. It's easy to see which weighting is used as it's shown in brackets after the value (for example, 80 dB(A) is A-weighted and is used to show the *average* noise level; 135 dB(C) is C-weighted and is used to show the *peak* noise level).

✔ **Daily personal noise exposure ($L_{EP,d}$):** This level refers to the equivalent noise 'dose' that a person is exposed to over an eight-hour working period. (You can also get an equivalent one for weekly exposure – $L_{EP,w}$.) These exposure levels are used to decide what you need to do to control noise, and they're expressed like this because noise exposure can be highly variable for each person throughout the day. For example, a violin player in an orchestra pit may be exposed to noise during their time in the pit, but may have no exposure before or after this time (maybe they're wearing a noise-cancelling headset). Therefore, it makes sense to convert exposure to a standard equivalent so that you can compare like with like.

✔ **Peak sound pressure levels (L_{CPeak}):** This exposure level refers to the peak (maximum) noise level an employee is exposed to in the day. (The noise standards also make reference to these exposure levels, so it helps to have an idea what they cover.)

Noise issues are not just about how loud it is (the sound pressure level in decibels). You also need to know how long you're exposed to it (its duration) to estimate someone's actual exposure to noise. Remember, noise levels for each employee may differ throughout the day, so you need to estimate the daily (or weekly) equivalent exposure ($L_{EP,d}$ or $L_{EP,w}$). You also need to estimate the likely peak exposure (L_{CPeak}).

We know that these measurements may seem complicated at first, but you only need a 'reliable estimate'. A good starting point may therefore be information that you already have about the noise output of your machines (manufacturer data) and how long people spend exposed to the noise. The HSE have developed some noise exposure calculators designed to help you work out your daily and weekly noise exposure and to estimate the performance of your hearing protection. Some of these calculators are based on Excel spreadsheets (with formulae) and others use a handy points system (like Weight Watchers). Check out the HSE website to try out these calculations: www.hse.gov.uk/noise/calculator.htm.

In some cases you may still need to do some measurements, but you can enlist the help of a noise specialist to do the work for you.

The noise *dose* (the combination of how loud a noise is and how long it goes on for) is the key factor. Short exposure to a loud noise is considered to cause equivalent hearing damage to a longer exposure to a lower level of noise – known as the equivalent dose. Here's an example – a noise dose of 85 dB(A) for eight hours has the same equivalent dose as 88 dB(A) for four hours (88 decibels is twice the sound level, because it's 3 decibels greater; so, being exposed for half the time gives the same dose of noise).

The Control of Noise at Work Regulations 2005 look at *exposure action values (EAVs)* – equivalent noise doses where you need to take some action. In short, they're *triggers for action*, and you have two layers of action – a lower and upper (just like shoes have). Each layer is based around the daily/weekly and peak measurement levels we talk about earlier in this section. Neither layer takes into account the use of any hearing protection.

Table 16-1 provides a summary of the EAVs and what you need to do – we look at some of the specific details in the next section, 'Controlling noise exposure', which outlines how to achieve these requirements.

Table 16-1	Exposure Action Value Requirements	
	Lower Exposure Action Value (dB)	*Upper Exposure Action Value (dB)*
Daily or Weekly Equivalent Exposure ($L_{EP,d}$ or $L_{EP,w}$)	80	85
Peak Exposure (L_{CPeak})	135	137
What Do I Need to Do?	Carry out a risk assessment, and if this indicates a risk to health, carry out health surveillance. Provide information, instruction and training to those likely to be affected. Make hearing protection available.	Carry out a noise assessment. Reduce noise exposure as far as possible (using a range of techniques we look at in the next section). If you still can't get your noise exposure below 85 dB(A), you need to: – Set up special 'hearing protection zones'. – Provide information, instruction and training. – Provide hearing protection and make sure that it's used in noisy areas.

The Control of Noise at Work Regulations 2005 cover the *exposure limit values (ELVs)* – these are expressed by two types of weighting values. One is a maximum for A-weighting (average exposure limit), 87 dB(A), and the other is C-weighting (a maximum peak limit), 140 dB(C). Unlike EAVs (which tell you what to do if they're exceeded), these must *not* be exceeded. The other difference is that these ELVs take into account any hearing protection you're using – so it's the exposure at the ear itself rather than for the person or room. If, at any point these levels are exceeded, you need to investigate, find out why it happened and make sure that it doesn't happen again.

Controlling noise exposure

In the preceding section, you discovered how to find out what your workplace noise levels are (either through reliably estimating them or by getting a noise specialist in to measure them – or both). You can see how they compare with the legal standards and whether, as a result, you need to do anything about your noise levels.

If you do need to do anything, you can take three approaches to controlling noise (approach these in the following order):

1. **Source – tackling the noise at its source.** You may be able to get rid of the noisy equipment/process altogether, outsource noisy processes, replace noisy equipment with something quieter, make changes to maintain the equipment properly (sometimes a drop of oil can do the trick), use noise damping techniques on machine parts and use silencers (mufflers) on machines that expel air or gases (think about how your car sounds when the exhaust pipe gets a hole in it).

2. **Pathway – putting something in the way between your employees and the noise source.** Common methods include enclosing the noisy equipment in some kind of sound-insulating cover or isolating the equipment from other structures using noise-absorbent mats or spring-mounts. For example, consider the inside of your car – a lot of effort goes into insulating the mechanics within your engine to stop the sound from travelling through to you in the cabin. Another technique is to use barriers, walls or fences that are designed to reduce transmission.

3. **Receiver – focusing on your employees.** You can put a machine operator into a sound-proof booth (rather than the equipment) or ask them to use hearing protection (such as ear plugs/muffs). (Some of the employee-focused techniques take a similar approach to tackling noise through interrupting the pathway – either way, you provide a barrier between employees and the sound source.)

   Like all other forms of personal protection equipment (PPE), you generally use these items as a back-up – your priority is to reduce sound at the source and, if you can't, to interrupt the sound's pathway. PPE isn't quite a last resort, but something you turn to when you haven't had much luck getting the noise levels down to where you need them to be. So, it's often part of the hearing protection mix.

You can get many different types of personal hearing protection, and they can offer different levels of protection. When choosing hearing protection, you need to consider more than just protection levels. You need to think about protection both holistically and practically and consider things such as:

• Do you need to communicate with others regularly on the job?

• Do you need to wear other PPE too – like goggles and hard hats?

Either way, talking to employees who do the job (it's called consultation – and communicating in this way isn't an option; it's the law to consult with your employees – refer to Chapter 3) can help you to choose hearing protection that best suits your workforce's needs. You don't want your employees to be completely isolated from all the sounds around them, but you don't want them to be exposed to noise levels that can impact on their health either.

In Table 16-1 we mention *health surveillance*. That just means regularly checking (or surveying) the health of 'at-risk' employees – but in this case, you check specifically for any of the conditions known to be related to excess noise exposure, such as loss of hearing. If you're at the EAV or the ELV, you need to get a specialist involved to check your employees' hearing (known as *audiometry*).

The HSE provides an illustrative case of implementing control measures in a workshop. A mobile electrical company's workshop had a bench-top grinder and linisher (a mechanical belt used to smooth wood/metal) that were producing noise levels of 95 dB, which is known to significantly impact hearing.

The company purchased noise-cancelling pedestals (that is, rubber mounts) to prevent direct contact between the machinery and the floor, costing the company approximately £80. The pedestals eliminated the noise caused by the metal cabinet the machinery had previously been placed in and the adjacent wall. The operator's exposure was reduced by 4 dB.

You can find out more about this case on the HSE's website: www.hse.gov.uk/NOISE/casestudies/benchgrinder.htm.

Although the drop in 4 dB meant that the noise levels were still significantly higher than the EAV, they'd actually dropped the noise level by over half (every 3 dB represents a doubling in noise). Also, the machine wouldn't have been used for a full eight hours, and the A-weighting may be less than the EAV. This case study shows how you can easily and cost-effectively make significant changes.

Feeling your way towards the problem

To assess vibration risks in your workplace, you take the same basic approach as for noise (refer to the earlier section, 'Listening out for problems'). You need to:

- ✔ Identify any equipment you have that's likely to cause vibration and establish where this equipment is used.

- ✔ Identify the employees who may be affected (those who use that equipment).

- ✔ Estimate vibration exposure – take the vibration magnitude of the equipment (available from the manufacturers' information), and how long it's used for (this is the actual time of use – the 'trigger time' – and not how long it's held while thinking about using it). We cover more on vibration exposure in the later section 'Estimating vibration levels'.

- ✔ Think about any aggravating factors, such as working in low temperatures (which decreases blood flow, therefore causing more damage for those with prior medical conditions, whose exposure may antagonise their medical conditions).

This information can then be placed into a risk assessment for vibration. If you find that your employees are exposed to vibration and those levels are potentially harmful, you need to increase your control measures (you may, of course, find that you've already done enough). For further assistance on risk assessments, refer to Chapter 4.

Protecting your employees from vibration

Noise and vibration are similar both in terms of physical characteristics and what you have to do to control them. As with noise, vibration has a significant impact on your employees' health.

The health effects associated with vibration exposure fall into two main categories: Whole-Body Vibration and Hand-Arm Vibration Syndrome.

Whole-Body Vibration (WBV) is typically associated with construction and agricultural vehicles going over rough terrain. It leads to knee, hip and back injuries. The vibration and/or jolting from the vehicle or machine passes through the seat and into the driver's body through the buttocks. Standing on the platform of a vibrating machine has the same effect (but not through the buttocks).

Hand-Arm Vibration Syndrome (HAVS) is a painful and disabling range of disorders of the blood vessels, nerves and joints caused by holding vibrating tools, such as road-breakers and grinders. The condition known as *Vibration White Finger (VWF),* a disabling vibration disease that causes the fingers to lose blood, followed by them filling with blood in a painful way, is probably the most well-known example of HAVS. With VWF, you experience blanching, tingling, numbness and pain in the fingers, especially in the cold and wet.

HAVS is a disease that appears following years of exposure to vibrating equipment. It's incurable and further exposure can make it worse, eventually making it too painful or difficult to do the work.

The HSE provides a helpful case study on HAVS. Over a 17-year period, an employee used a range of vibrating tools within a motor company's body shop and was diagnosed with the early stages of VWF. Unfortunately, this diagnosis wasn't taken seriously and following continued use of the tools over the next two years the employee developed Carpal Tunnel Syndrome (a condition caused by compression of one of the nerves that controls sensation and movement in the hands; symptoms are tingling sensation, numbness and sometimes pain) in both wrists and also HAVS.

The vibration levels that employees had been exposed to was approximately double the recommended allowance, and the company was fined £10,000 with costs of £28,000.

You can find out more about this case on the HSE's website: www.hse.gov. uk/VIBRATION/hav/casestudies/enforceex.htm.

Estimating vibration levels

Vibration levels are measured in three dimensions (vibration doesn't just happen in one direction). Its level or magnitude is quoted in units of m/s^2 (metres (m) per second (s) squared – or movement per second every second). You may recognise that this unit is also used for *acceleration* – the rate at which speed (well, velocity) changes. This unit is used by both vibration and acceleration because vibrating parts move rapidly, a bit like a hyperactive spring (up and down, side to side), and the damage potential from vibration for humans is mostly about acceleration, as well as how long you're exposed for – a 'dose'. Think of the vibration magnitude as the equivalent of the noise level we cover in the earlier section, 'Estimating noise levels'.

Again, just like with noise (which is measured using an A-weighting to show a daily exposure), you have an equivalent daily exposure for vibration (given the symbol A(8) – A for 'average' and (8) for eight-hour equivalent acceleration exposure).

You get EAVs for vibration that, if crossed, require you to do something about it, and ELVs as well, which aren't supposed to be exceeded ordinarily.

The daily EAV for hand-arm vibration is 2.5 m/s² A(8) and for WBV is 0.5 m/s² A(8). If an employee reaches these levels, you need to do a thorough vibration risk assessment and make sure that you reduce vibration exposure as much as you can, and also provide information, instruction and training for your employees.

The daily ELV (which must not be exceeded) for hand-arm vibration is 5.0 m/s² A(8) and for WBV is 1.15 m/s² A(8). If an employee reaches these levels, you must do a thorough risk assessment (refer to the earlier section, 'Feeling your way towards the problem' for more) and immediately reduce exposure below the ELV. Further assistance with risk assessment can be found in Chapter 4.

The HSE, in the spirit of helpfulness, has also produced a vibration calculator to help you establish vibration exposure levels: www.hse.gov.uk/vibration/hav/vibrationcalc.htm.

Controlling vibration exposure

After you estimate your business's vibration exposure level, you can compare this with the EAVs and ELVs and take any action you need.

When it comes to sorting out your hand-arm vibration problems, you can find some tried and tested approaches, such as:

- Changing the tool or equipment for one that vibrates less. Modern equipment is designed to vibrate less than older equipment, so you may find that upgrading your tools resolves the issue.

- Finding support for your tools (for example, something to balance them on or suspend them from) that allows the operator to reduce their grip on the tool (the tighter you grip something, the more vibration is transmitted to your hand from the tool).

- Adding anti-vibration mounts (such as rubber feet) to machines or furniture – this can stop vibration from being transmitted through, say, the floor or attached parts/furniture, and to the operator.

- Conducting regular and thorough maintenance – keeping moving parts properly adjusted and lubricated, sharpening your cutting tools, replacing vibration mounts before they wear too badly, and ensuring that you check rotating parts for balance (to reduce vibration in machinery).

- Sharing the work fairly through job rotation techniques – this also helps to ensure adequate rest breaks during the work.

- Providing PPE – protective clothing like gloves may not actually protect against vibration (though some claim to) but they can protect employees from cold and wet, both of which are major aggravating factors.

Here are some things you can do to minimise WBV from vehicles:

- ✔ Plan your site routes to use the smoothest terrain.

- ✔ Fit a suspension seat, correctly adjusted for the driver's weight (we know, weight's a sensitive issue).

- ✔ Make sure that you use correct tyre pressures – yes, some solutions are as simple as that.

- ✔ Ensure that drivers are trained to slow down over rough terrain.

Just as for noise, you may have to consider doing a bit of health surveillance to check the health of your employees who are exposed to vibration. You're looking for concerns relating to vibration-related conditions (such as HAVS and WBV) in this case. You're not going to pick up on any issues until a health problem has developed, but at least you can pick up on issues early enough to do something about them and to prevent further damage. You may need to engage a specialist to conduct a suitable health check.

You need to complete HAVS health surveillance for employees who are regularly exposed above the EAV of 2.5 m/s^2 A(8). Even if they aren't regularly exposed to this level of vibration, you may still need to provide a suitable health check in some case (for example, for employees who already have a diagnosis of HAVS).

HAVS health surveillance can range from a simple questionnaire to a full health assessment, where you need the services of a medical professional. The HSE provides a quick screening questionnaire to help you decide the level of health surveillance that you need for each employee and what further action you need to take; to find out more, check out `www.hse.gov.uk/vibration/hav/advicetoemployers/inscrquest.pdf`.

Addressing Radiation Concerns in the Workplace

Radiation is energy that's transmitted in the form of waves (like sunlight and X-rays) or particles (you may have heard of alpha particles from radioactive decay). This energy can cause considerable damage to humans who get in its way for long enough.

Radiation can be artificially generated but it can also be naturally occurring. For example, the Brazil nut is one of the most radioactive foods in the world. The roots of the tree grow so deep into the ground that they absorb massive levels of radium, a naturally occurring source of radiation.

In the following sections we look at the different types of radiation, how they affect the body and how you can control them.

Differentiating between ionising and non-ionising radiation

Radiation can be characterised in different ways. You get two basic types of radiation: ionising versus non-ionising radiation.

Non-ionising radiation

Non-ionising radiation is waves of energy that aren't able to break down molecules. Non-ionising radiation sources include:

- ✓ **Ultraviolet (UV) light:** Found in sunlight, arc-welding and oxy-fuel welding/burning, UV curing of paint in manufacturing and vehicle painting processes, and curing of inks in printing.

- ✓ **Visible light:** Found in laser levelling devices and laser pointers.

- ✓ **Infra-red light:** Created in red-hot steel in a rolling mill, glass manufacturing and ceramics (clayware) manufacturing.

- ✓ **Microwaves:** Found in food-processing equipment (that is, in microwave ovens) and telecommunications equipment (that is, mobile phone masts).

- ✓ **Radio waves:** Found within radio, TV or radar transmitters.

Non-ionising radiation health effects depend on and differ with the types of non-ionising radiation:

- ✓ UV causes redness and skin burns (for example, sunburn), pain and inflammation to the surface of the eye (leading to temporary blindness – often called 'arc-eye' or 'snow-blindness'), and an increased risk of skin cancer and premature ageing of the skin.

- ✓ Visible light, if intense, can cause temporary blindness (disability glare) and permanent eye damage if very intense (for example, a high-powered laser), as well as burns to exposed skin tissue.

- ✓ Infra-red light (including artificial optical radiation) causes redness and burns to the skin and can cause eye cataracts over time.

- ✓ Microwaves can be absorbed into the body and cause internal heating, which in high doses may cause internal organ damage and can be fatal.

✔ Radio waves can also be absorbed and cause internal heating (in the same way as microwaves).

✔ Lasers are classified according to intrinsic safety and power output. *Class 1* lasers present little risk – common examples being laser pointers and bar-code readers – but *Class 4* lasers (which are used to rapidly cut through metal in manufacturing) are rather good at cutting through you too, and can easily cause instant skin burns and eye damage.

Ionising radiation

Ionising radiation is where particles have enough energy to break molecules into bits called *ions*. Ionisation of molecules in the body can lead to all sorts of health problems, like cancer. Ionising radiation sources include:

✔ **Alpha particles:** Found in smoke detectors and science labs.

✔ **Beta particles:** Found in science labs and thickness gauges.

✔ **X-rays:** Found in medical radiography, baggage security scanners, and non-destructive testing of equipment and machinery.

✔ **Gamma rays:** Found in industrial radiography.

✔ **Neutrons:** Found in nuclear power stations.

✔ **Radon:** This form of ionising radiation is a radioactive gas that originates from uranium that occurs naturally in rocks and soils. Radon levels are much higher in certain parts of the UK. The highest levels are found in underground spaces such as basements, caves, mines and utility industry service ducts, and in some areas in ground floor buildings, as they're usually at a higher pressure than the surrounding atmosphere. Radon usually gets into these buildings through gaps and cracks in the floor. All workplaces can be affected by radon in these areas.

Ionising radiation can cause severe health effects if an employee is exposed to high doses. Effects include sickness and diarrhoea, hair loss, anaemia due to red blood cell damage, and a compromised immune system due to white blood cell damage.

All of the cells in the body can be affected by radiation, but some more so than others (such as the skin and the lining of the gut, as those tissues divide most frequently), causing cancer, genetic mutations and birth defects. A large enough dose can kill in hours or days. You may not have heard of radon, but it's the second largest cause of lung cancer in the UK (after smoking), accounting for 2,000 fatalities a year.

Getting specialist help with radiation worries

Ionising radiation safety has its very own detailed set of regulations. It's a rather specialist area and is therefore usually the preserve of experts. If you work in a nuclear facility, you're probably going to be inundated with expertise, but it isn't just in nuclear facilities that you deal with radioactive materials. If you use radiation for any of your processes, you may need to consult with external *radiation protection advisors* (that is, a person who has gained a certificate of core competence from an assessing body recognised by the HSE and can advise you on the best procedures and processes), albeit ably assisted by some keen radiation champions (an internal person with specialist knowledge). It's highly unlikely that you're using radiation without your knowledge, as you can't just buy it in the supermarket!

You can't set a safe level of exposure to ionising radiation, but you do find a clear relationship between dose and risk – the higher the dose, the higher the risk.

Working with strategies to control radiation hazards

We're not going to delve into the detail of the regulations in this book because they're very technical (and life is just too short). Instead, we provide an overview so that you can at least nod convincingly when you meet a proper radiation protection advisor (check out the nearby sidebar, 'Getting specialist help with radiation worries' for more on these vital experts).

If you work with ionising radiation, you must notify the HSE at least 28 days prior to works commencing for one-off or short-term projects (if you work with it all the time, you need to ensure that the HSE are aware that it's a key part of your business). You can fill in a standard form on the HSE's website, which you can find here: www.hse.gov.uk/radiation/ionising/notification.htm.

If you're using radioactive substances, make sure that you use sealed sources (as far as is possible). This is a type of containment design that helps you to ensure that the radioactive source can't leak out (where it can present much more of a problem).

In addition to using sealed sources, you can control exposure to ionising radiation using three key factors:

✔ **Time:** Spend as little time as possible exposed to the radiation source. The dose is proportional to time: if you halve the time, you halve the dose.

✔ **Distance:** Get as far away as you can. The *inverse square law* applies here (at least for a source that's radiating radiation in all directions): the dose gets lower the further away from the source you get. If you increase the distance from the source to the person, the radiation dose decreases for that person.

✔ **Shielding:** Place something between you and the source. What you can get away with depends on the type of radiation. Relatively thin shields can be used with alpha and beta particles, but X-rays and gamma rays need thicker, denser shields, such as lead.

You may also need to consider using PPE, for example:

✔ Gloves and overalls can prevent exposure from low-energy beta particle emitters, and prevent skin contact.

✔ High-density materials can provide shielded body protection for anyone at risk from penetrating radiation, like radiographers.

✔ Eye protection may be used if the head is at risk from exposure to beams of radiation.

✔ Respiratory protective equipment, such as breathing apparatus, may be needed as an additional precaution to prevent inhalation of radio-active materials (such as radioactive dust blown by ventilation from a process).

You also need to wrap all that together in a safe system of work (refer to Chapter 7 for more on these), which needs to include rules for handling the radioactive source material and emergency plans. If you have a risk of contamination (for example, some radioactive materials may be in the form of liquids or powders and are therefore more likely to become airborne or attach to clothing or equipment) you also need washing and changing facilities.

Radon is a bit of a special case. It's a natural source of radiation – so it's already out there (like the truth, fans of *The X-Files*). Research your location to give you an idea of the potential levels where you are, and follow this up by asking employees about potential symptoms if you find that you're in an affected area.

Engineering solutions are the best way to reduce high radon levels, such as installing positive pressure air fans to prevent the radon gas from seeping from the ground up into the workplace.

Typical control measures to protect against non-ionising radiation include:

- Placing the equipment in a restricted area. Allow only certain people into the workspace (like an exclusive club). You can use a card-access system to control this, for example.

- Avoiding reflective surfaces (so you don't get stray beams everywhere). Use dark, matt colours (like those in a gothic horror film).

- Being careful with metal objects near any radiating Radio Frequency (RF) device, as localised high field strengths may be generated around such items. Take care to remove rings, watches or bracelets when working close to radiating sources.

- Using an alternative, safer light source (instead of laser light, for example) that can achieve the same result.

- Using filters, screens, remote viewing, curtains, safety interlocks, clamping of work pieces, dedicated rooms, remote controls and time delays to remove employees from exposure (or decrease exposure through distance).

- Training employees in best practice and providing appropriate information.

- Organising work to reduce radiation exposure to your employees.

- Issuing PPE (like goggles).

- Displaying relevant safety signs.

Although non-ionising radiation is seen as less dangerous and you can generally deal with it using PPE (like UV-protective or laser-protective goggles) or barriers, you may need warning signs, access restrictions and limited exposure times for prolonged exposure to UV radiation. You need to consider if you have any non-ionising radiation sources in your workplace and, if you do, you need to complete a risk assessment for the types of non-ionising radiation and the possible exposure risks. For assistance on risk assessment, refer to Chapter 4.

If you work with radiation you're probably fully aware of the requirements of the Ionising Radiations Regulations 1999 and the *Work with Ionising Radiation: Ionising Radiations Regulations 1999 Approved Code of Practice and guidance* document (www.hse.gov.uk/radiation/ionising/legalbase.htm). You're required to reduce exposure as far as is reasonably practicable and have suitable risk assessments and control measures in place. Non-ionising radiation is covered by the Control of Artificial Optical Radiation at Work Regulations 2010, which require employers to recognise sources and ensure that they're controlled. Further guidance can be found here: `www.hse.gov.uk/radiation/nonionising/employers-aor.pdf`.

Part IV
Going the Extra Mile

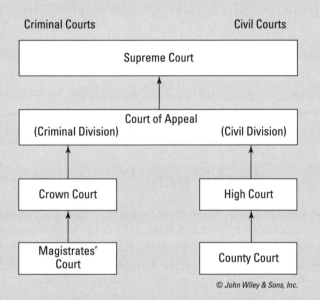

Criminal Courts   Civil Courts

Supreme Court

Court of Appeal
(Criminal Division)   (Civil Division)

| Crown Court | | High Court |

| Magistrates' Court | | County Court |

© John Wiley & Sons, Inc.

Check out how Approved Codes of Practice (ACoPs) can help you navigate health and safety legislation at www.dummies.com/extras/healthandsafetyuk.

In this part . . .

- Understand how the health and safety legal system works – be amazed by the Health and Safety at Work etc Act 1974 and the Management of Health and Safety at Work Regulations 1999.

- Go deeper into safety culture, and use your newfound knowledge to improve your organisation's safety performance.

- Discover why safety is different in 'high-hazard' process industries such as chemical manufacturing, and oil and gas.

Chapter 17

Wrestling with Health and Safety Law

In This Chapter

▶ Operating within the law

▶ Staying legal with the Health and Safety at Work etc Act 1974

▶ Making sense of the Management of Health and Safety at Work Regulations 1999

*M*any people perceive health and safety law to be excessive and too 'woolly' – leaving employers unable to decipher what they actually need to do. Despite this perception, however, it turns out that most health and safety regulations are okay and fit for purpose – the government has paid for at least two reviews in recent years, and that's been the main conclusion (refer to Chapter 1). Okay, some regulations may need tweaking and consolidating in places, but doesn't everything require a little maintenance?

The UK has a regulatory body called the Health and Safety Executive (HSE) that tries to ensure safety remains sensible. It has initiated a myth-busters panel to address these issues, ranging from the humorous to the bizarre (check out Chapter 1 for some entertaining examples from the HSE's archives).

It's accepted that the standards of what's considered acceptable or achievable (and the law that may set them) may change over time. We suspect that in 100 years' time, the people of the future will gasp at what we consider acceptable or safe. The same is true today. What was considered a safe workplace in 1960 is very different to that which is expected today. Societal expectations and tolerances, as well as technology, move on.

In this chapter, we introduce you to the UK legal system and how the law works in terms of health and safety. We also explore, with sheer unbridled joy, the idiosyncrasies of the Health and Safety at Work etc Act 1974 and the Management of Health and Safety at Work Regulations 1999.

Judging What's Right: The UK Legal System

The nature of health and safety law is very different to that of a 'true crime', such as stealing, where the prosecutor needs to prove that the person is guilty. Instead, you're guilty until you prove yourself innocent. Health and safety law is a category of regulatory law that aims to ensure that desirable behaviours for running a business are achieved. Most (but not all) duties under health and safety law are strict *liability* offences, which means that there doesn't have to be any intent on the part of the defendant. This is like most motoring offences, where it's no defence to say, 'I didn't intend to break the speed limit'. Ignorance may be bliss, but it's not a defence.

Many laws start out as moral imperatives. In terms of health and safety, the key moral driver is that you don't want to see anyone harmed by your work or affected by your actions (or the actions of your employees). You want people to remain healthy and therefore able to work.

But instead of staring at people strongly (like Paddington Bear) to persuade them to do the right thing, the UK government takes a formal approach and enshrines these moral imperatives into law.

In the following sections we look into the nature, sources and types of UK law – by doing this, it helps you to understand the UK's legal system and its requirements.

Understanding the law: Criminal, civil, statute and common law

You can describe how the law works and the different types of law in several ways. Some emphasise the type of law – or rather the *type of court* that deals with it (civil versus criminal – see the later section 'Courting disaster: The court structure' for more on these courts); some emphasise how the law developed – that is, the *sources of law* (common versus statute). But these systems aren't perfectly distinct – for example, some courts deal with a wide range of things that appear to cross the boundaries of civil and criminal law, and you have a whole world of specialist courts (like *tribunals,* for example) that deal with particular aspects of life. But at the end of the day, the legal system offers a way for either individuals or the wider state to get justice.

Both criminal law and civil law can draw from both statute and common law sources. However, in health and safety terms at least, most criminal cases deal with statute law (from acts and regulations), and most civil cases deal with common law (like negligence).

In the following sections, we break down the law into these different systems and sources: the criminal and civil legal systems, and the statute and common sources of law.

The criminal and civil legal systems

The *criminal* legal system is in place to punish individuals and companies who 'break' the law. When you read laws like this (though not all are written down as some are based on past decisions made previously by the courts), the language uses words like 'breach', 'offence', 'guilty', 'penalty', 'fine' and 'imprisonment'. The punishment is intended to put you off from committing the offence.

These laws also specify who enforces them. The police ultimately enforce a good deal of UK law, but when it comes to health and safety law, most of the enforcement is handled by the HSE and local authorities (together, they effectively police health and safety). In fact, they have more power than the police, because they can enter a building at any point and remove anything even without a warrant. In practice, the HSE enforces the law in more complex, higher-risk premises (such as factories and construction sites), whereas local authorities enforce the law in lower-risk premises, such as offices and shops (using their Environmental Health Officers). Some aspects of health and safety are also enforced by the fire service (to enforce general fire safety, in this case). You also get other government regulatory bodies for specific industries, like the Office of Rail Regulation and the Office for Nuclear Regulation. (Chapter 22 introduces some of the key websites that can help you with health and safety issues, and many of these have a governmental and/or regulatory role.)

Crimes are often committed against a victim (either an individual or, conceptually, society in general). But criminal law doesn't intend to provide any significant financial compensation to the victim (for example, the injured employee in the case of health and safety), though it can provide some. Instead, the *civil* legal system deals with compensation.

Civil law provides a way to resolve legal difficulties between individuals, or between organisations and individuals; therefore, the aggrieved party is the one who brings the civil case. A large area of civil law is concerned with *negligence*. Essentially, civil law concerns owing people moral duties of care. (If you are careless, you can expect to have to put the situation right with wads of cash or some other remedial action.)

Your head may be spinning with these legal concepts, but don't fret – we're going to try to illustrate the complexities of the law with a simple example.

One of your employees falls on a slippery floor (maybe some oil was spilled) in the entrance of your workplace. They appear to have hit their head in the fall, and they're taken to hospital unconscious. In this scenario, you may be facing both criminal and civil legal action.

Under criminal law:

✔ Since this is work-related, the accident may be investigated by the local authority or a HSE inspector.

✔ The HSE may decide to prosecute your organisation.

Any prosecution is conducted on behalf of the State (in England and Wales this is the government, and in Scotland this is referred to as the 'Crown') and the court papers would reflect this; the case would be recorded as Regina (the Crown) versus the organisation, and go on public record.

✔ If your organisation is found guilty, you would most likely be fined (obviously, you can't imprison a business). If an individual employee, manager or director of the business is found guilty (yes, it can and does happen) they may also be fined, and for very serious offences even imprisoned.

You can't generally insure against fines or write them off against tax. (Criminals aren't meant to be seen to profit from the proceeds of their crimes.)

Under civil law:

✔ The injured employee sues your organisation for compensation (they instigate legal proceedings for a remedy, usually compensation).

To do this, the employee instructs a solicitor to act on his behalf. The letter of claim to the employer generally has to be sent within three years of the date of the accident (or if it were an illness, three years from the date they became aware that they had the illness – not all health-related ill-health problems are immediately apparent).

✔ If the case goes to court, the court papers reflect that the employee is suing you (his employer); their name versus your organisation's name appears in the case records.

✔ In the court, the employee's legal team can use common law and perhaps statute law to support their case (see the later sections, 'Statute law' and 'Common law' for more on these sources of law).

✔ The employee needs to show that your organisation is liable for his accident on *balance of probabilities* (that is, the standard – or burden – of proof test in such cases. It means looking at the evidence, evaluating whether the incident is more likely than not to have happened and deciding if the organisation will be liable. This is a lower threshold than criminal cases, which have the standard of 'beyond reasonable doubt').

✔ If the employee wins, the court decides how much compensation you need to pay him. This compensation is paid from your organisation's insurance policy.

Most civil cases are settled before they get to court to avoid the costs of defending a case.

Statute law

Statute law is legislation that is *codified* (written down) in Acts of Parliament – as regulations and similar 'legal instruments'. Statute law is created, or at least agreed to, by elected representatives (Members of Parliament – MPs – in the UK). A great deal of statute law is created through the UK implementing European Union (EU) directives (agreed to by MEPs – Members of the European Parliament – in Europe), but the UK government does sometimes go it alone and create laws for the local issues it faces – for example, the Mines (Medical Examinations) Regulations 1964.

The main act in the world of health and safety is the Health and Safety at Work etc Act 1974 – which is actually vague in its requirements. It makes statements such as 'must provide a safe workplace' – but doesn't provide any detail about how to do this and what a safe workplace is. But it does set objectives for organisations to meet, leaving the detail to the regulations made under its authority. (That's why it's often called an *enabling act* or *umbrella legislation* – not just because it rains a lot in the UK. . . .) Key aspects of this act are to ensure the safety of your employees and anyone who may be affected by your works or the products you provide.

The regulations made under an Act of Parliament are called *delegated legislation* – Parliament delegates authority to a specific minister to go away and fill in the detail, provided it's in keeping with the objectives and scope of the enabling act. The minister then delegates the job of coming up with the regulations to others (usually through a committee of ministers, industry specialists and advisors, such as doctors).

Regulations made under the authority of an Act of Parliament are generally enforced by the same regulator as for the act itself (for example, the HSE when it comes to safety). The UK government has thousands of regulations. Think of any aspect of health and safety and you can find an accompanying regulation (for instance, regulations exist for manual handling, working at height and construction). Regulations give you more detail (and a severe headache) on the requirements and what's expected of you and your organisation.

Many laws also come with their own stack (and we do mean a stack) of Approved Codes of Practice (ACoPs) and guidance documents to help you interpret what it all means. Guidance has no legal status – but you'd be foolish to ignore it. *ACoPs* have a special legal significance – while they aren't laws, they are guidance provided by the HSE and can be used as evidence in a court of law as to the sorts of things the act or regulation intended (so you'd need a very good reason for not following them).

Common law

Common law is sometimes called 'judge-made' law. However, the judges don't actually make this law but rather refine the interpretation of the law. Common law can be quite a tricky beast, because it isn't written down in the same way as statute law; instead, judges produce a 'summing up' at the end of a court case. The judge decides on the outcomes for a given case and then provides the reasons for her decision in this summation. The reasons can go on for many pages, and the judge's decisions may influence future court cases because they set a *precedent* (that is, they make decisions that can be used to guide courts in the future). Future judges can then look back at these cases to help them make decisions on similar cases that they're hearing.

In addition, judge-made decisions exist within a hierarchy of courts – the lower courts (Magistrates' Court for criminal law and County Court for civil law) are generally bound by the decisions of the higher courts (Crown Court for criminal law and High Court for civil law). However, as each case is taken on its merits (and cases can vary considerably in detail) an apparent precedent may find itself ignored simply because, although it may look superficially the same, the facts of the current case differ materially (through differences in the occurrence, event or information) from the preceding case.

In essence, a precedent is only really a precedent if you can show that it clearly relates to pretty much the same scenario.

Courting disaster: The court structure

The structure of the UK court system is based on the two different types of law: criminal and civil. In terms of health and safety at least, criminal courts are made up of Magistrates' Courts and Crown Courts; the civil system goes through the County Court and High Court (see Figure 17-1).

Role of Common Law

Before an employer's duties to its employees were enshrined as criminal law in the Health and Safety at Work etc Act 1974, employers were meant to adhere to broadly similar common law duties of care (which had been established by the Donoghue v Stevenson case in 1932). However, these were famously refined in the case of *Wilsons and Clyde Coal Co Ltd versus English (1938)*. The judgment established the common law duty of all employers to provide

✔ A safe place of work with safe access to and from it.

✔ Safe plant and equipment.

✔ A safe system for doing the work.

✔ Safe and competent workers.

✔ Appropriate supervision, information, instruction and training.

This case was also important because it stated that those duties were owed personally by the employer to each employee and were *non-delegable* – that is to say, the performance of those duties could be delegated but the responsibility for their correct discharge could not.

The court system is a bit different in Scotland and Northern Ireland; here, we provide a brief overview of the system used in England and Wales, but you can find out more about the Scotland and Northern Ireland court systems online at www.scotcourts.gov.uk/ and www.nidirect.gov.uk/the-justice-system.

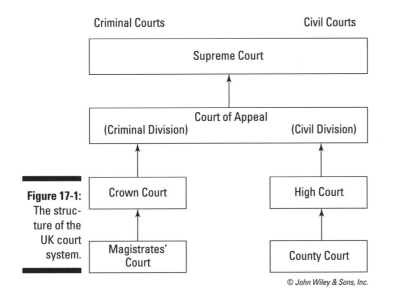

Figure 17-1: The structure of the UK court system.

© John Wiley & Sons, Inc.

All criminal cases are initially heard in the *Magistrates' Court* (the lower of the criminal courts). If you ignore that speeding ticket, you may get an invitation – perhaps best not to try it though! Just about every town has its own Magistrates' Court – with *Magistrates* (local community members who've been verified as suitable) sitting in it. Magistrates are also called *Justices of the Peace* (or JPs).

More serious cases may then be sent up to *Crown Court* (the higher of the criminal courts). If there is an appeal on the decision, it goes first to the *Court of Appeal (Criminal Division)*, which reviews the decision made by the Crown Court.

Civil cases either go to the *County Court* (a lower-value claims court) or *High Court* (a higher-value claims court). Any appeals go first to the *Court of Appeal (Civil Division),* which reviews the decision made by the High Court. The *Supreme Court* is the court of final appeal in almost all instances and can set precedents for all other courts. It deals with both criminal and civil appeals.

Taking responsibility: Criminal and civil liabilities

Breaches of criminal health and safety law have different penalties, depending on the offence and court involved. Different courts have different limits on their powers. Some offences can be dealt with in a Magistrates' Court, and some need to progress to the Crown Court. Some can be dealt with in either – referred to as 'either way' offences. Usually a decision needs to be made on which court they'll be heard in by a 'mode of trial' hearing (held in a Magistrates' Court; this hearing decides if the case should be heard in a Magistrates' or Crown Court). However, if in the Magistrates' Court the defendant pleads guilty, the Magistrate may choose to hear the case straight away without passing it up to the Crown Court.

The following sections cover criminal and civil court proceedings, and also take a closer look at statutory duty – where a breach is liable to criminal penalties but is used to claim damages to the injured person.

Contemplating criminal proceedings

Criminal courts can make a compensation award to a person who has been injured or has suffered loss, but this is unusual, and although criminal courts have the power to award compensation, the injured party usually gains compensation through civil action (see the next section).

In the case of a workplace death, you and/or your organisation can be charged with manslaughter. This is a very rare but very serious criminal offence:

- Individuals can be charged with *gross negligence manslaughter* (or culpable homicide in Scotland), where their conduct falls well below the standards of a *reasonable person* (how a typical member of the community would act in the situation). Conviction carries a maximum sentence of life imprisonment.

- Organisations can be charged with *corporate manslaughter* (corporate homicide in Scotland). There has to be a very serious failing in the way that you and your senior managers manage or organise your business activities, and the prosecution needs to show that this mismanagement substantially contributed towards the death. The sentence is an unlimited fine, and the organisation may be ordered to publicise its offence; there may also be a court remedy order, which is essentially a court-issued improvement notice. Failure to comply with this can deem you to be in contempt of court.

Health and safety legislation is set out differently to most other criminal legislation because the onus is on you to show that you've done enough (fulfilled your legal duties adequately). It's almost a case of guilty until proven innocent, rather than the other way around.

Considering civil proceedings

In civil courts, a compensation award is intended to return the claimant to the position that she was in before the injury occurred. You obviously can't turn back the clock and repair the damage of an injury, but a court can award money to compensate for that injury. The compensation that courts award is split into two categories:

- **General damages:** For pain and suffering, loss of amenity (for example, you're no longer able to do a hobby or pastime that you used to be able to do), loss of future earnings and so on. The court decides on these amounts.

- **Special damages:** For loss of earnings up to the trial date, travel expenses to hospital and so on. These amounts have to be justified by the injured party (the claimant).

Civil claims are usually brought under a legal concept called the *tort of negligence* (a *tort* is a civil wrong – don't get confused with a torte, which is a rich and delicious cake!). The injured party believes that the organisation (or an individual) was negligent (that is, seriously careless) in its actions.

A claimant has to prove three things to bring a tort of negligence claim to court:

1. That a *duty of care* was owed to the claimant by the defendant (the person or organisation that they're claiming against).

2. That the duty of care was *breached* (that is, the defendant didn't do what reasonable people would expect him to do).

3. That the claimant suffered a loss or injury as a direct result of the breach.

Breaching a duty of care may seem a bit mystical at first, but if you think about it, you owe lots of duties to lots of people all the time. Society lays on everybody certain reasonable expectations of behaviour. When you act in a careless (or even reckless) way, or fail to act when you could and should have done something to intervene, you can expect to face consequences. For example, when you drive your car, society expects you to drive it with due care and attention. If you drive like an idiot, you may not only be hauled in by the police, fined or put in prison; you may also have to compensate people (via your insurance) for any damage and/or injury that you cause.

When it comes to health and safety, you owe a duty of care to the people who may be harmed by what you do (your *acts*) or what you don't do (your *omissions*). These things have to be *foreseeable* – that is, a reasonable person has to be able to predict that harmful consequences may follow the act or omission.

Outcomes often seem much clearer after the event – *reasonable foreseeability* concerns whether you can see a harmful consequence coming before and during the event. If you block a fire exit (for any significant length of time at least) you can easily see how that act can stop people getting out in a fire. If you fail to replace a fire detector that you know is damaged, that's an omission that can result in people not being warned about a fire developing.

When defending claims of a breach of your duty of care, you can use three basic arguments:

1. You didn't owe a duty of care – for example, the UK office of a large company with offices in the UK and Spain will consider its UK employees. A UK issue is unlikely to affect those in Spain, so you'd probably be forgiven for not having them in mind.

2. You owed the duty but you didn't breach it (you did the right thing) – this defence means that you did everything that a reasonable person may have done in the same circumstances. For example, if someone

falls off the roof, having forced their way through locked access doors and ignored clear warning signs (that confirmed the danger/restricted access), you may be able to argue that you did enough to protect your employees.

3. The claimant experienced no injury or loss as a direct result of the breach, for example where the nature of the injury or loss cannot be substantiated, or the injury or loss has occurred but can't be linked directly to a breach of duty by the defendant. A simple paper cut can't be linked to a broken leg.

Whether you're successful in any of these defences really depends on the circumstances of the case. What is considered reasonable can rely on specific details. The appropriate court system can help to determine a fair outcome.

Another defence available for the breach of a duty of care claim is through *contributory negligence* (when someone has contributed to the harm they suffered). Contributory negligence is only a partial defence against a claim of negligence where a part of the blame for the injury can be attributed to an individual (often the claimant herself) or organisation other than the defendant. This defence is usually used to pass some of the blame for the injury back to the claimant, but other parties may also be held responsible. The outcome usually reduces the claimant's compensation award. The nearby sidebar 'Considering a case of contributory negligence' considers an example.

When is a duty of care claim not a duty of care claim?

If you run a business undertaking high-risk activities, like a parachuting activity centre, and participants try to make a claim, you may have a defence in that the claimant was a willing volunteer and accepted the risk of personal injury when taking part in the activity. But, this defence can't be used by you to defend a claim from your employees, because you're expected to provide your employees with enough information, instruction and training and to ensure their competence.

In much the same way, you wouldn't employ a trainee mechanic to undertake brain surgery. As part of the recruitment process, you check that you've selected the right person for the right job and provide them with information, instruction and training to ensure that they understand your procedures, equipment and hazards. It's down to you as an employer to ensure that you give employees the correct information so that they can highlight any issues they have.

Considering a case of contributory negligence

You may be able to claim contributory negligence in a case where an employee is making a claim against your organisation for breach of duty of care, but they've failed to comply with their training, failed to use the PPE that you provided and failed to heed warning signs, so they may have contributed to their injury. If the claimant can then demonstrate that there was a complete failure to provide adequate supervision in the workplace (which would have ensured that they used the PPE), she may be able to claim compensation for her injury. You may admit partial liability for the injury because your organisation failed to provide adequate supervision. But you can also claim contributory negligence because the employee had been trained, provided with PPE and you had warning signs in place. If the judge accepts this argument, he can award reduced damages to the claimant in proportion to the allocation of the blame.

Vicarious liability is where you can be held liable for the negligent acts (or omissions) of someone else. Parents can be held liable for acts committed by their (underage) children, even though the parents themselves didn't do anything. In the health and safety world, an employer can be held liable for the acts of its employees. So, if an employee is negligent and injures another person while performing his work activities, the injured person can claim compensation through the civil legal system from the employer (rather than suing the individual employee who actually caused the injury). For example, if an untrained, unauthorised driver runs over a member of the public while the driver is trying to move a loaded pallet with a fork-lift truck, the injured member of the public can sue the employer for the injury.

Breaching statutory duty

Although civil claims are usually based around negligence, they can be based on another type of tort, that of *breach of statutory duty*. This is a bit weird, but basically a breach of a bit of criminal law (an act or regulation) can be used to launch a civil action.

The claimant must prove that:

- ✔ The statutory duty was placed on the defendant. That is, that a health and safety law exists that obliges the defendant to do something, such as provide instruction, equipment and so on.

- ✔ The statutory duty was owed to that claimant, and the law had the claimant in mind (he was someone that law aims to protect).

- ✔ The defendant was in breach of the statutory duty, so it didn't do what was expected of it.

- ✔ The breach of statutory duty caused the injury; that is, it led directly to the injury.

- ✔ The injury was of a type that the statute existed to prevent. This proof is really about the scope of the statute in question. It's no good trying to use a law designed to prevent back injuries when you have a noise-related illness.

Drawing Out the Health and Safety at Work etc Act 1974

The Health and Safety at Work etc Act 1974 is the main piece of statute law that covers all workplaces. It's so famous (in health and safety circles, at least) that it's usually just called 'the Act' and refers to all workplaces and all work activities in Great Britain. In Northern Ireland, the Health and Safety at Work (Northern Ireland) Order 1978 achieves the same end.

The Act creates *duty holders* (people or organisations that have duties laid on them, whether they like it or not) and the duties they owe. Generally speaking, employers owe a duty to employees to ensure, 'so far as is reasonably practicable' (to fathom this bit of jargon, check out the nearby sidebar 'Saying hello to the Act's jargon!'), their health, safety and welfare at work. Employers also owe a duty to others (non-employees, members of the public) to ensure that the organisation's work activities don't put them at risk. It also places duties on employees to look out for themselves, as well as others, and requires them to co-operate with their employer (which comes as a relief to all employers). In fact, the Act probably represents the first time in health and safety legislation that the co-operative approach between the different parties is so clearly phrased (well, for legal-speak anyway).

The Act doesn't give specific detail about exactly what must be done to safeguard health and safety; instead, it provides general aims for employers and employees to achieve. It has been designed to be 'goal-setting' legislation rather than 'prescriptive' legislation.

The Act contains 80 sections – but you don't need to know them all. We cover the relevant sections of the Act in the next two sections of this chapter, first getting familiar with the fundamentals before we consider the sections relevant to criminal offences.

Saying hello to the Act's jargon!

Before you tackle the key sections of the Act, it may help to understand some key terminology. The two most common (and head-spinning) phrases or terms you encounter are 'so far as is reasonably practicable', and 'shall':

✔ **So far as is reasonably practicable:** This means balancing the size of the risk against the effort required to control or reduce that risk. In other words, *being proportionate* – scaling your efforts (money, time and so on) in proportion to the risk. You don't need to wrap everything in cotton wool or provide a risk-free workplace (which isn't actually possible) because risks are involved with all workplaces and activities; even simple tasks such as putting on clothes involve an element of risk to safety (the number of people visiting the Accident and Emergency department at their local hospital because of injuries sustained when getting dressed in the morning is quite surprising!). Similarly, people are exposed to health risks all the time (like exposure to exhaust fumes while walking down the street).

No one worries about the risk of paper cuts in an office environment because the risk is trivial when considering the controls you can put in place – what can you do? Make all your employees wear cut-resistant gloves? But you do have to avert the risk of falls from height (for example, when employees are fixing the roof to a large steel-frame building) because the risks are clearly significant. To weigh up the risk, you make a decision using scales (imaginary ones, that is). On one side of the scale, you think about how likely someone is to be harmed and how serious that harm may be. On the other side of the scale, you put in control measures (which balance the scales).

When you decide on the controls, consider not just the cost but the time and trouble of implementing them. Don't overbalance the scales on either side. If your employees are concerned about leaving the office late at night, you may suggest that they leave in pairs – this takes little time and trouble to organise, and you've got no implementation costs. However, you wouldn't employ bodyguards to escort each employee as the cost, time and trouble is grossly disproportionate to the risk involved. This is what is meant by *reasonably practicable*.

✔ **Shall:** This is a descriptive phrase within the Act that gives an absolute duty: you must do it unless further terms qualify this (such as 'shall so far as is reasonably practicable').

Grasping the fundamental duties

We start with Section 2 here, because Section 1 just introduces the Act – which you may of course read at your leisure!

Section 2 covers the duties on you, as an employer, towards your employees. This section is broken down into a number of subsections.

Section 2(1) states your general duties towards your employees:

To ensure, so far as is reasonably practicable, the health, safety and welfare at work of all his employees.

(See www.legislation.gov.uk/ukpga/1974/37/contents for more on this section of the Act.)

Section 2(2) outlines what you need to provide:

- ✔ **2(2)(a):** Safe plant and systems of work (for example, equipment and procedures).
- ✔ **2(2)(b):** Safe use, handling, storage and transport of articles and substances (for example, chemicals, asbestos and so on).
- ✔ **2(2)(c):** Information, instruction, training and supervision.
- ✔ **2(2)(d):** A safe workplace and safe access to it and egress from it; that is, a safe workplace, no matter where this is, and a safe way to get to it and back from it.
- ✔ **2(2)(e):** A safe working environment with adequate welfare facilities (for example, toilets, drinking water and so on).

Section 2(3) requires you to have a written statement of general policy (refer to Chapter 2 – this is usually about one page) and the organisation and arrangements for carrying it out (a few more pages relevant to your business activities). This policy must be revised as necessary (usually annually) and brought to the attention of employees, for example through notice boards or handed to them.

Section 2(4) covers the appointment of safety representatives by recognised trade unions. You don't have to have union representation, but if you do, you need to work with them.

Section 2(6) requires you to consult with safety representatives, if you have them.

Section 2(7) says you have to establish a safety committee. Best practice is to have a committee chaired by senior management and made up of a mixture of managers and employees (although this is only required if two or more safety reps request for a committee to be established).

Section 3 places a duty on you to ensure, so far as is reasonably practicable, that non-employees (clients, visitors, contractors, the public and so on) aren't exposed to risks to their health and safety through your business operations. Think about what you do and where you do it, and then think about who may be affected.

If you're self-employed you also need to consider this duty – you must carry out your work so that you don't create a risk to yourself or to others.

Section 4 imposes duties on those who have some degree of control over non-domestic premises (that is, workplaces) that they're making available for others (non-employees) to use as workplaces or for work activities. These people can be referred to as *controllers of premises* but in general terms they're landlords or commercial property management companies that own or rent an office block for various other companies to occupy. The controller of premises' duties are to ensure, so far as is reasonably practicable, that:

✔ The premises are safe.

✔ The means of access and egress are safe.

✔ Any plant or substances provided by them for use on the premises are safe.

Section 5 says that employers shall provide arrangements, appropriate to their work activities, for the effective planning, organisation, control, monitoring and review of the control measures in place for prevention and protection. If the employer has five or more employees (including directors), these arrangements must be written down.

Section 6 details the duties on any person who designs, manufactures, imports or supplies any article or substance for use at work – so, this section is about equipment and chemical manufacturers for the most part. These organisations need to make sure that:

✔ Any article or substance is safe to use.

✔ Adequate testing takes place to ensure that it is safe.

✔ The end user is provided with information on safe use.

✔ The end user is provided with revisions of that information as necessary.

It's not just those in charge who have to play ball – **Section 7** of the Act states that it shall be the duty of every employee to:

✔ Take reasonable care for the health and safety of themselves and of other persons who may be affected by their acts or omissions at work.

✔ Co-operate with their employer to enable compliance with legal requirements.

That is what *has* to be done, but the Act also considers what *shouldn't* be done:

Section 8 states that no person shall intentionally or recklessly interfere with or misuse anything provided in the interests of health, safety or welfare in pursuance of complying with legal requirements. The expression 'no person' implies that the duty isn't limited to employees.

So, if you're told to wear personal protective equipment, you must wear personal protective equipment. If a guard is in place to prevent you from coming into contact with dangerous parts, you can't remove the guard without good reason (such as maintenance).

Section 9 states that you can't charge your employees for things done to achieve legal compliance – though this prohibition on charging has many caveats!

If an employee needs safety training or equipment for a work activity, it must be provided by the employer.

Exploring the offences

In later sections of the Act, you wade into a huge section all about *offences* – that is, clear language about criminal legislation. Sections 36 and 37 are of particular interest:

✔ **Section 36** states that where an offence committed by an organisation is due to the act or default of some other person (say, advice from a consultant), the consultant may be charged with and convicted of the offence (whether or not proceedings are taken against the organisation itself). All that means in practice is that if you make a mistake on the advice of someone else, a prosecutor may look to take action against the person giving the advice.

✔ **Section 37** states that senior members of the management of an organisation, as well as the organisation itself, may be personally liable for breaches of the law. Directors and senior managers can be prosecuted for offences committed by the organisation if the prosecution can show that these senior staff members consented, connived or were negligent in their duties to enable the offence to be committed.

Breaking into the Management Regulations

As well as 'the Act' (refer to the earlier section, 'Drawing Out the Health and Safety at Work etc Act 1974'), another key piece of legislation is the Management of Health and Safety at Work Regulations 1999. These regulations apply to all workplaces and give, in more detail than the Act, what you're required to do to manage health and safety.

These regulations consist of 30 regulations, but we just cover the key ones in this section (because we know you have a life):

- ✔ **Regulation 3** states that you need to do risk assessments, but it gives a little more detail than that. The risk assessments need to be meaningful, not just a collection of paperwork, so they need to be:

  - **Suitable and sufficient:** They identify significant risks, either in the workplace or associated with work activities, and help you identify your priorities for risk management.

  - **Recorded:** If you have five or more employees, you have to write down your risk assessments (you can do this electronically, of course).

  - **Reviewed:** You review your risk assessments when you think they're no longer valid. This may be when something significant has changed – or you may set a standard review period, such as annually (it can be sooner or longer depending on the risks).

  Chapter 4 explores risk assessments in more detail.

- ✔ **Regulation 4** states that you must follow the *principles of prevention* (the ones we look at in Chapter 4). So, in reducing order of effectiveness: eliminate hazards where possible, substitute the hazard with something less hazardous, provide engineering controls (mechanical solutions) so that employees don't come into contact with the hazard, establish administrative controls (procedures) and provide PPE. PPE is at the bottom of the list as it relies on someone wearing it properly; if you can remove that requirement, and invest in more collective measures (things that protect everyone equally, without relying on individuals' behaviour), it reduces the chance of someone being hurt.

- ✔ **Regulation 5** requires you to 'make arrangements for the effective planning, organisation, control, monitoring and review of the preventive and protective measures'. Basically, it requires you to have an effective safety management system in place (refer to Chapter 6).

- ✔ **Regulation 6** outlines that you must ensure that employees are provided with appropriate health surveillance (if your risk assessment shows this to be necessary). Consideration of health surveillance is usually a legal requirement of the regulations governing specific hazards. For example, depending on the level of exposure, audiometry (a specific type of health surveillance) is a legal requirement under the Control of Noise at Work Regulations 2005 (refer to Chapter 16).

- ✔ **Regulation 7** states that you must appoint one or more competent persons to assist with undertaking the measures needed to comply with health and safety law. Though it can't quite bring itself to say it, this in practice means that you must appoint a safety advisor and other people who may be given specific health and safety responsibilities. This person can be internal to the business so long as they have sufficient training, knowledge and experience, and they understand the risks and what they're expected to do.

✔ **Regulations 8 and 9** say that you must develop procedures to be implemented in the event of serious and imminent danger – basically, procedures to cover fire or first aid requirements and so on. As part of these regulations, you must also nominate a sufficient number (decided by risk assessment) of competent persons to implement these procedures (fire marshals and first-aiders) and ensure that any necessary contacts with external services are arranged, such as with firefighters, emergency medical care staff and rescue workers.

✔ **Regulation 10** requires you to provide your employees with comprehensible and relevant information on:

- The risks to their health and safety

- Preventive control measures

- Emergency procedures

✔ **Regulation 11** covers shared workplaces, even if you occupy an entire floor; if another floor is occupied by another employer, you must:

- Co-operate and coordinate with the other employers to ensure health and safety, and make sure that you don't expose each other to undue risk.

- Swap information about health and safety risks that may affect the other organisation (essentially, a further application of co-operation and coordination).

✔ **Regulation 12** requires you to provide other workers who aren't your employees with information on the risks to their health and safety and preventive control measures. This means that contractors working on your premises must be provided with essential health and safety information (fire procedures, key information on the work area and so on). Also, think about any temporary staff you may use – you must provide them with information about any specific qualification and health surveillance requirements (for example, if the work is high up then they mustn't have vertigo).

✔ **Regulation 13** outlines the need for you to take into account the capabilities of employees when allocating tasks. You must also provide training when employees are first recruited and exposed to new or increased risks. This training should be repeated periodically where appropriate and should take place during working hours.

Don't worry, it's not all on you. **Regulation 14** states that employees must:

- ✔ Use equipment and materials in accordance with any instructions and training given (so, use these items in the way they were told to).

- ✔ Inform you of any work situation that represents serious and immediate danger to health and safety or any shortcomings in your arrangements for health and safety.

A few more regulations are worth keeping in mind before we draw this exercise to a close. These regulations cover your obligations to assess risks and reduce the hazards for new and expectant mothers and young people (in other words, vulnerable people):

- ✔ **Regulations 16–18** cover new and expectant mothers.
- ✔ **Regulation 19** covers young persons.

These regulations remind you of the need to ensure that you cover vulnerable people in your risk assessment (we cover the risk assessment process in Chapter 4). You need to identify, as part of this process, who may be harmed and how. Certain people are clearly more open to injury in a given setting than others.

Young people are more at risk because of their general lack of experience. They also tend to have a poorer perception of risk (linked to this lack of experience) and, in some cases, may be quite immature in their mental development (that is, prone to larking about) and physical development (that is, not as strong as you may think).

Chapter 18

Developing a Positive Safety Culture: Factoring in Human Behaviour

· ·

In This Chapter

▶ Improving performance by developing your safety culture

▶ Understanding how behaviour can influence your safety culture

· ·

Safety culture is a topic we touch upon earlier in this book (check out Chapter 3), and here we delve into the intricacies of your organisation's safety culture. Companies that have a strong, ingrained, shared safety ethic (we're not talking about surface rules here) are likely to have lower rates of accidents or work-related ill-health. Organisations strive to create a strong, positive safety culture because where this culture exists, it has a direct and lasting influence on employee behaviour.

Your organisation's safety culture is linked to its health and safety performance through organisational values and behaviour (and how these can influence each other). Safety culture is fundamentally about human interactions – the way you behave (errors, mistakes, violations and all) and how this behaviour is influenced by your personal and organisational motivations, values and beliefs.

But what is culture? More importantly, how do you influence it? In this chapter we help you develop a clear sense of what defines a strong safety culture, how it can help to improve your organisation's safety performance, and how human behaviour (good and bad) plays an integral role in developing and growing your organisation's safety culture.

Evolving Your Organisation's Safety Culture

Every business has a culture – its way of doing things. *Culture* covers a multitude of characteristics, so it can also be applied to aspects of the way people go about their business: in this case, the way they go about managing safety.

Safety culture can be defined as the shared attitudes, values, beliefs and behaviours relating to health and safety.

The safety culture of an organisation is the way that everyone within the organisation thinks and feels about health and safety and how this translates into their behaviour. Partly, in a relatively immature organisation driven more by rules, this may be what people think they can 'get away with' and what will be 'frowned upon'. In a more mature safety culture, instead employees look out for themselves *and* for each other. They work safely because they want to, not because they're told to – it's the way that things are done in the organisation and a reflection of how everybody else is behaving, too. We explore the fundamentals of an organisation's safety culture in Chapter 3.

Even in a well-developed, positive safety culture, not everyone shares the same values equally. You may come across employees who don't 'get with the programme', but they tend to be few and far between and are likely to either come round to the group way of thinking and acting, or leave because they don't feel that they fit in. Of course, they may be forced to leave in the end (you may have to sack them for persistently flouting safety rules, for example).

Because your safety culture is value-, belief- and behaviour-based and it involves people, it's forever shifting and adapting to new challenges. In the following sections we look at how you can use the evolving nature of your safety culture to enhance safety performance and influence the development of a positive safety culture.

Improving performance

Improving means getting better, and so one of the characteristics of a mature safety culture is being a *learning organisation* (that is, one that wants to learn from its mistakes). Therefore, you need to understand what your employees think of your safety culture in order to learn from this knowledge and enable you to track subsequent improvements in performance.

Taking a snapshot of your organisation's safety culture

A good start is to use a checklist or questionnaire to survey your employees' perception of your existing safety culture.

We provide a few questions to help you get started. Ask your employees:

- ✔ Do you think that health and safety is important?
- ✔ Have you received training in health and safety?
- ✔ Was the training important to you?
- ✔ Do you think that managers think health and safety is important?
- ✔ Do you think that managers consider health and safety in their decision-making?
- ✔ Do employees work safely?

You need to encourage your colleagues to think of the entire organisation or department and answer 'yes' or 'no' to each of these questions. If your employees answer 'yes' to all these questions, your safety culture is generally positive. If you have some 'no' answers in the mix, your organisation has some room for improvement. If your employees don't feel that health and safety is important, their standards will be low and their behaviour will be poor, and accidents may occur as a result.

Your employees may not be able to provide you with clear 'yes' or 'no' answers to the preceding list of questions. Life can be a little more up and down. Maybe some managers support safety effectively, while others don't appear to. Your employees may have received some health and safety training, but perhaps only some of it was important to them, so they don't recall it in as positive a way as you'd like. As a result, expect measured answers like 'mostly' and 'sometimes' and emphatic responses like 'never' as well as a 'yes' or a 'no'.

Effective leadership is integral to your organisation's perception of safety, and the strength of your leadership team is reflected in the responses from your employees when it comes to this kind of checklist. Turn to Chapter 3 for some great tips on strengthening your safety culture through strong leadership (for example, establishing responsibilities and accountabilities across your management structure).

Getting an indication of your organisation's safety performance

The checklist that you considered in the preceding section is an initial filter. It barely scratches the surface. However, you can use more sophisticated techniques to look at a wide range of safety culture indicators and target your efforts.

In a positive safety culture, most employees think and feel that health and safety is important. They adhere to a clear safety policy and have strong leadership straight from the top. These elements are fundamental to a positive safety culture; however, you can consider many more indicators or characteristics than these to develop a full picture of your organisation's safety culture. Saying that, your safety culture can be tricky to assess. Asking people is a good start (refer to the preceding section), but moods and attitudes can change daily (ask any angst-ridden teenager).

You can only measure what you can measure (the *tangible outputs*). Try to capture the major issues and, importantly, the bits that you can identify and change. Tangible outputs consist of quantifiable data rather than opinion or emotion. You can use tangible outputs to draw conclusions about your safety culture. For example, you can measure, through observation, how many people are wearing the correct personal protective equipment (PPE); or through discussion, find out if people know how to report an accident.

Assessing accident records

A useful tangible output to consider is your accident records. You can use these records to:

- ✔ Benchmark your organisation against industry averages (try the scintillatingly upbeat Health and Safety Executive's (HSE's) statistics for your industry at www.hse.gov.uk/statistics/).

- ✔ Look at trends within your organisation – see how this year's accident rates compare to previous years'.

When you look at accident statistics and trends, you need to think about them in context. Think of the whole cycle. A decreasing accident rate may not mean what you think. It may instead mean that people aren't reporting accidents (maybe because you told them you don't want to see any more accidents). Therefore, human behaviour may explain some of the numbers you're reviewing (check out the later section, 'Anticipating the Impact of Human Factors' for more on how behaviour can impact safety).

It's an old saying, but the only accident type that employees are likely to report accurately are fatalities.

A good indicator of a learning organisation (one that wants to learn from its mistakes) is the standard of investigation that follows an accident and how much effort is put into preventing it from happening again. The standard of this investigation is dependent on your organisation's safety culture:

- ✔ **A positive safety culture:** You put time and effort into investigating accidents, writing investigation reports and introducing follow-up actions (which are followed through) to prevent a recurrence. Alerts based on these reports may be shared with other sites too so that they don't suffer the same incident (so, the organisation learns from its mistakes).

✔ **A negative safety culture:** You either do nothing or conduct 'cheap and nasty', superficial accident investigations, with reports that just address the symptoms (the immediate causes) rather than the root issues. And, as for follow-up action – what's that?

Refer to Chapter 8 for more on accident investigation procedures.

Negative business cultures (safety or otherwise) burn themselves out because people don't like working within them. You only work within a negative organisational culture if you have to. You can't expect to retain a tiptop team if you don't strive to make your organisation a safe, secure and responsible place to be.

Revealing an unhealthy safety culture

High sickness rates (whether through ill-health or people taking sickies) are another tangible output that can also indicate the quality of your safety culture.

If your employees are regularly calling in sick, it may indicate that something is wrong within your organisation's culture (perhaps within your safety culture, though it may also indicate issues with management or colleagues where employees don't feel they can address issues). If you dig deeper into the issue, it may indicate problems such as poor morale.

Poor employee morale is often linked to high staff turnover and may be indicative of a negative safety culture. In contrast, in a positive safety culture, staff turnover is low, people feel safe, their morale is high, they get trained well and they're consulted about their working conditions.

Look around you and at documentation (procedures, records and so on) to establish whether your safety rules and procedures are being followed. In positive safety cultures people tend to follow the rules (probably because they were consulted on them and involved with working them out). In negative cultures, people are less inclined to follow the rules, either because they don't know what they're doing (perhaps due to poor training) or because they know the rules but don't want to follow them (the rules may well be ridiculous, unworkable or unnecessary). There may even be no incentive to follow the rules and no consequences if they break them (so, no effective supervision or discipline).

A company and its officers were fined a total of £245,000 and ordered to pay costs of £75,500 at the Crown Court in relation to the removal of asbestos. The company employed ten, mostly young, temporary workers; they weren't trained or equipped to safely remove the asbestos, nor were they warned of its risk. The company's two directors were also disqualified from holding any company directorship for two years and one year, respectively. (You can find out more about this case on the HSE website at www.hse.gov.uk/leadership/casestudies.htm.)

If a business's directors don't take safety seriously, how can the employees? If a business is run through a 'getting the job done, no matter what the consequences' mentality, the directors will trip up sooner rather than later and be heavily fined for the outcomes (they may even be imprisoned).

Encouraging employee complaints helps to maintain a positive safety culture. People feel that they're listened to and that their views will lead to positive change – or they appreciate that this open two-way communication can reveal an understanding about why something can't be changed. A negative safety culture may actively discourage workers from complaining when many of the complaints may be legitimate and serious.

Checking on your progress

If you think of safety culture as being a living object, it will change and adapt as your business does. This also means that you need to keep a close eye on your safety culture (or at least the visible indicators of it) to ensure that it doesn't get forgotten or overlooked. Refer to Chapter 8 for more on the different types of monitoring available.

The HSE provides this useful good safety culture checklist to help you assess whether your business is maintaining a positive safety culture (see Table 18-1). Consider whether the statements in the table apply to your organisation.

Table 18-1	Reflections of a Good Safety Culture
Managers regularly visit the workplace and discuss safety matters with the workforce.	
The company gives regular, clear and concise information on safety matters.	
We can raise a safety concern, knowing the company will take it seriously and tell us what they are doing about it.	
Safety is always the company's top priority; we can stop a job if we don't feel safe.	
The company investigates all accidents and near misses, does something about it and gives feedback.	
The company keeps up to date with new ideas on safety.	
We can get safety equipment and training if needed – the budget for this seems about right.	
Everyone is included in decisions affecting safety and is regularly asked for input.	
It's rare for anyone here to take shortcuts or unnecessary risks.	
We can be open and honest about safety: the company doesn't simply find someone to blame.	
Morale is generally high.	

Source: HSE Human Factors Briefing Note No. 7: Safety Culture: www.hse.gov.uk/humanfactors/ topics/07culture.pdf. *The HSE Human Factors Briefing Note No. 7: Safety Culture document contains public sector information published by the Health and Safety Executive and licensed under the Open Government License.*

Influencing your peers

Chickens have a 'pecking order', which is literally the high flyers (sorry that was cruel – they can't really fly) pecking the other chickens to show them who's boss. People can act in a similar way (though luckily not with pecking!). Some people (probably you, as the business owner/manager) may end up dominating a group (or at least having a good deal of influence); others may disappear into the shadows (demonstrating little influence). You call this organisational 'structure' a *hierarchy*, and although it may reflect your business's management structure, it can exist separately to the administrative hierarchy of a business and be a personality-based form of influence.

In any group of people (like The Beatles, Queen or Fleetwood Mac, say), a 'norm' or default set of behaviours becomes apparent over time. These behaviours are usually dictated by the dominant *influencers* (the 'movers and shakers' in the group, who make decisions and direct the business). If you want to join the group, you probably have to fit in with this set of behaviours. When you're talking about an organisation, it means toeing the line or 'complying with the organisation's norms'.

The desire to conform is very powerful – it's rooted in a need to fit in. That feeling also goes by the name of peer pressure (do you remember your parents warning you about it?). It may be why you started drinking or smoking (even if you didn't like the taste at first).

The same thing works in safety too. If your group is already working safely and this is the group norm, any new people joining the team will tend to conform. Of course, this works in exactly the opposite way too – if the group is working unsafely, peer pressure may force more and more employees to relax their attitude to safety in an attempt to fit in with the group's norms. People may well know that what they're doing is wrong – it may even make them feel uneasy because they want to act the right way, deep down. But the pressure to comply with (and belong to) a social group can be hard to resist.

If unsafe working is the norm for your organisation, you need to challenge it. You may need to closely supervise your employees, especially at first, to make new rules stick, but it will be worth it in the end. A positive health and safety culture will become the norm over time, and no one will think to do it any other way (though yes, we do appreciate that it can take a while for your employees to change their behaviour – it won't happen overnight).

To give health and safety a high priority, Mid and West Wales Fire and Rescue Service recognised that it was critical for its leadership to demonstrate to its staff that accountability for health and safety was a fundamental element in the success of its overall service delivery. The director of service policy and planning was nominated as the health and safety director for the service in order to clearly define the importance this subject held within the organisation. The director implemented a revised health and safety framework, which included a programme of fire station visits to engage the workforce, and placed a renewed emphasis on improving incident reporting, investigation and monitoring procedures. The service reported the following safety culture improvements:

- A £100,000 reduction in insurance liability premiums in one year through improved corporate strategic risk management
- A 50 per cent reduction in sickness absence through work-related injury over a two-year period
- A 50 per cent reduction in injury incidence rate over a three-year period

You can find out more about this case at www.hse.gov.uk/leadership/casestudies.htm.

As this example shows, leadership action can significantly impact on a business's safety culture through making financial savings for the organisation and improving morale. It doesn't just change behaviour at the top level of an organisation; changes are felt throughout the business, and these can be reflected using tangible results.

Anticipating the Impact of Human Factors

When you look at accident statistics for any industry, the majority of accidents can be put down to *unsafe acts* – people doing something that they shouldn't be doing and putting themselves (and possibly others, too) in danger. Why do people commit these unsafe acts?

Most people don't deliberately do stupid things – they instead tend to do what seems entirely reasonable at the time, although they may not be thinking it through carefully enough.

If you really need to cut the hedge but you haven't got a hedge cutter, it may seem reasonable at the time to turn your gaze to the nearby hover lawnmower. You may think that it's pretty much the same thing . . . except, when you lift it up against the hedge it's heavier than you thought, and overbalanced, and . . . where did Fluffy the cat go?

The following questions may baffle and amaze in your workplace, no matter how strong your safety culture:

✔ Why is it that one employee behaves safely at work, but another doesn't, even though the working conditions for both employees are the same?

✔ Why is it that an employee may behave safely doing one job, but then unsafe practices start to creep into her behaviour when they're switched to another job?

✔ Why is it that an employee behaves poorly when working for one organisation, but when she leaves and starts to work for another organisation, she behaves in an entirely different manner?

Surely it can't always be solely down to the employee? The following sections try to examine the many human factors that can affect employee behaviour and thus impact on your safety culture.

Understanding the human influences on safety behaviour

Three key factors can influence your employees' safety-related behaviour at work:

✔ **Organisational factors:** What is and isn't acceptable behaviour for the business, and whether these standards are enforced. Shouting in a commercial kitchen environment is usually more acceptable than in an open-plan, professional office environment.

✔ **Job factors:** The actual job role and expected safety implications. An office worker is less likely to be injured at work than a police officer on the beat (it goes with the job).

✔ **Individual factors:** The employees' personality (are they shy, bold, ruthless, passive?) and experiences. A shy person is more likely not to question what she's been told, and a person with a back injury tends to lift correctly to prevent further harm.

The HSE has published a checklist for these organisation, job and individual factors to give you a guide on what to look for: www.hse.gov.uk/pubns/priced/hsg48.pdf.

The following sections look in more detail at what you can do to improve your employees' behaviour in each of these three areas.

Improving safety culture

An external health and safety audit at Sainsbury's identified a need to develop a unified approach, and also recommended more direction from the board, to develop an effective strategy for managing health and safety.

The result was a radical revision of the company's approach, including:

✔ The group human resources director created a health and safety vision, supported by a plan with targets over three years.

✔ Training on health and safety responsibilities was introduced for all board directors.

This resulted in:

✔ The board providing a role model for health and safety behaviour.

✔ A 17 per cent reduction in sickness absence.

✔ A 28 per cent reduction in reportable incidents.

✔ Improved morale and pride in working for the company.

✔ A raised health and safety profile, so that it's embedded in the culture of the organisation.

Read more about this case on the HSE's website at `www.hse.gov.uk/leadership/casestudies.htm`.

Organisational factors

Your organisation is a beast in itself. Understanding and knowing your beast is the best way to influence it:

✔ Know where your safety culture is currently and make a commitment to making it better. Use indicator data (the tangible outputs from the earlier section, 'Getting an indication of your organisation's safety performance') to help figure out which areas need the most improvement.

✔ Lead from the front – do what you say and lead by example.

✔ Put workable (not fairy-tale or idealistic) policies and procedures in place and make sure that you tell people about them (rather than hide them in a drawer).

✔ Supervise your employees and make sure that you deal with negative behaviour (like rule-breaking), and 'encourage' people to do the right thing (for example, by making it easy to report issues and ensuring that employees know their report will be taken seriously and that something will be done about it).

✔ Don't underestimate the power and danger of peer pressure when it comes to changing behaviour. Positive role models and norms can encourage good behaviour in your employees (refer to the earlier section, 'Influencing your peers' for more on peer pressure).

✔ Consult with your staff and make sure that you listen to them (refer to Chapter 3 for more on the value of consultation). You still need to manage your team, but you should at least consider and respect what they have to say.

✔ Communicate safety messages clearly to the right people, at the right time and in the right way. Posters may work better in noisy areas, whereas emails may be more effective for desk-bound employees.

✔ Train staff so that they're well-informed and competent. But (please!) make sure that the training is worth doing – and not just a box-ticking exercise because you saw it on a training matrix somewhere (Chapter 3 has plenty to say on making wise employee training decisions).

✔ Make your work patterns work. Shift work, work at night or extended hours can lead to tiredness. Tiredness can make concentration a bit difficult, so if the work requires particular concentration, for example, take this need into account (if you can). You may need to add more rest breaks if this type of work is required.

Job factors

Some jobs come with inherent risks; some have risks added as the job role changes or the business grows:

✔ Adapt the work and the workstation to the person (for more on ergonomics, check out Chapter 11). So, if you need to bend or stoop over when carrying out a task, think about how you can adapt it to best suit your employees' needs (we aren't all the same height, either). You may be able to adapt the workstation for different people. If you can't, people tend to find the most comfortable way of working – and this may not be the safest way.

✔ Give thought to better organisation of the amount of work, rate of work, deadlines and variety of work that individuals have to do (refer to Chapter 9 for more on stress). Provide reasonable workplace conditions such as space, lighting, noise, temperature and humidity (refer to Chapter 5 for more on making your workplace employee-friendly). If your workplace is too hot and the work requires a lot of physical labour, your employees may suffer dehydration, heat stress and heat stroke. Being too hot can affect concentration levels and make employees more prone to making mistakes.

✔ Use well-designed displays and controls. If they're poorly designed, errors are more likely. If critical displays are difficult to view or outside the operator's normal field of view, he may strain to see them or completely miss a critical requirement – either way, not good news.

✔ Develop good-quality working procedures. If you develop poor procedures or they're poorly written, out of date, overly complex, impractical or not provided at all, don't be surprised if people don't bother following them (or anything resembling good practice). Make procedures accurate, concise, understandable and realistic. For more information on developing procedures, refer to Chapter 7.

Individual factors

People genuinely believe the saying 'it will never happen to me'. They don't want bad things to happen to them or their colleagues, but getting them past being 'invincible' can be difficult:

✔ Don't try to change people's personalities. Mostly, you can't. Each person brings different knowledge, experience, skills, attitudes and personality to your business.

It's impossible to change someone's personality completely, but you can help to adjust key areas of behaviour associated with safe working practices.

✔ Do look to change attitudes through education and training. Help people understand the reasoning behind your safety decisions. If your attitude to a machine guard is that the guard is great because it's there to stop your arm being cut off, you're unlikely to remove the guard in any circumstance. But if your attitude is that the guard is unnecessary, over-the-top, put there to tick a box or to make the job harder or slower, you're more likely to remove the machine guard at the earliest opportunity.

The managing director of a manufacturing company with around 100 employees was sentenced to 12 months' imprisonment for manslaughter following the death of an employee who became caught in unguarded machinery. The investigation revealed that, had the company adequately maintained the guarding around a conveyor, the death would have been avoided.

The judge made it clear that whether the managing director was aware of the situation was not the issue; he should have known about the poorly maintained guard as it was a long-standing problem. An area manager also received a custodial sentence. The company received a substantial fine and had to pay the prosecution's costs.

You can find out more about this case at `www.hse.gov.uk/leadership/casestudies.htm`.

✔ Give the right motivators and incentives. Motivation as an influencer can be summed up as 'risk versus reward'. People weigh up what the risk of an action is and what the potential reward is. If you can make more money by taking an unsafe short-cut, you're far more likely to take that short-cut if you think you can get away with it. If you're told that there's a bonus for finishing fast, you may decide to take the risk.

✔ Appreciate that different people see risk differently – you need to help your team better understand workplace risk.

Children don't fully appreciate risk (they have *low risk perception*). Their appreciation grows as they find out more about the world they live in and 'bank' that experience. Adults have a deeper appreciation of risk – but that doesn't apply for everything. Your knowledge and training in a particular subject or topic has a key impact on how well you can perceive specific risks (or, 'you only know what you know' – refer to Chapters 1 and 4 for more on the nature of risk and risk assessments, respectively).

Risk perception also depends on human senses (for example, carbon monoxide gas is colourless, odourless and tasteless, yet deadly at relatively low concentrations) and sensory impairment (for example, a partially sighted person may not be able to see trip hazards on the floor, so she's at greater risk from these hazards than her sighted colleagues). In safety-critical roles, eye tests may be required as part of the recruitment process (for example, for airline pilots) for both sight and colour-blindness (where differentiating colour is key to keeping employees and others safe). Of course, any form of sensory impairment, whether it is sight, hearing, smell, touch or even taste, may mean that a person is unable to correctly perceive the world around her. This may have health and safety implications.

Your individual risk perception can also be affected by illness, stress, fatigue, drugs (prescribed or otherwise) and alcohol. Picking up on these changes in perception quickly is key to ensuring that harm doesn't occur.

Learning from errors and mistakes

People make errors and mistakes all the time – they're only human. Although you may like to believe that your employees are thinking about work from the moment they walk through the office doors, they may be distracted by other things in their personal lives, and a lapse in concentration can lead to an error. These aren't intentional, but they can lead to accidents. You don't just do this at home either. If displays and controls are poorly laid out (for example, the 'up' button on a control panel is below the 'down' button) you may mistake what you see or make an assumption, especially if you use different sets of controls regularly. Your mind comes to expect things to work in a familiar way. For example, you're 'set' to thinking that up is higher than down, therefore you expect a control panel to be laid out this way. Ensuring that controls are logical helps to prevent these types of mistakes.

Lapses in attention can also cause errors, where employees get distracted and forget where they've got up to. Checklists are a good way to prevent this occurring.

Everyone is liable to make mistakes, whether because he has made an incorrect judgement and doesn't have the training to make the right decision, or through accidentally hitting the wrong button (to go back to the control panel example). In this case, supervision and good layout of controls are the best way to prevent mistakes.

It helps to understand how people think and behave when they work. You can find plenty of theories about work behaviour (the world is full of people trying to develop theories of how people work, and most of these theories have at least some truth in them). They all oversimplify the process, however, because humans are so complicated!

Saying that, one popular theory suggests that people have three basic levels of behaviour (skill-based, rule-based and knowledge-based) when it comes to tackling jobs. It says that people differ largely in the amount of effort they use to think about things and to make decisions. This theory was developed by Danish safety expert Professor Jens Rasmussen in 1983, and looks at how processes are influenced:

✔ **Skill-based behaviour:** Practice makes perfect! Skill-based behaviour refers to (usually) physical actions in which you use virtually no conscious monitoring. They can be triggered by a specific event – for example, the requirement to operate a valve, which may arise from an alarm, a procedure or another individual. The practiced operation of opening the valve can then be completed largely without conscious thought.

An example here is driving. If you have many years of driving experience and you know the operations inside out, you pretty much drive on automatic. You don't have to think about changing gear (especially if you have an automatic car!). You only need the odd few 'attention checks', like the odd glance at the speedometer or rearview mirror. This allows you to direct your attention to the road ahead.

✔ **Rule-based behaviour:** The next level up in your thinking is rule-based behaviour. This is where you have a whole stack of sets of actions worked out (that are well-practiced) already and you just have to select the right one – so you need to 'pattern match', that is, to diagnose the situation and select the right set of actions to follow (a bit like following a recipe). You think, 'If I see this, I need to do that . . .' – for example, if you see a red light, you need to apply the brakes, slow down, change gear and come to a stop. Each of these sets of actions is well-practiced, but you need to recognise which set to choose based on all the signals you get from around you.

You're taught to respond to emergencies by using rule-based behaviour. You have to diagnose what emergency it is (smoke, flames, alarm – must be a fire) and then select the appropriate action (evacuate, go to assembly point and so on). This approach is quite efficient if you're well-practiced in each of these sets of actions, so it's no surprise that emergency responders use this strategy when training these behaviours.

✔ **Knowledge-based behaviour:** The top level is knowledge-based behaviour, which is where you have to give your full attention. This approach is common in brand-new situations when you haven't a clue what to do and have to work out what's going on and how to proceed, often by trial and error.

Remember the first time you started to learn to drive and how you had to give all your attention to working out how to change gear? Because your attention was diverted, you probably started to drive the car into the curb – simply because you can't look everywhere, and nothing is second nature at that early stage when you don't have stored patterns of action.

Errors and mistakes can arise easily, depending on how well-practiced you are and how much attention you require. The biggest potential for error occurs when you're thrown into a new situation and you have to work out what to do. If you don't fully understand what's going on, it's easy to make incorrect assumptions and thus make the wrong decision. Even when you're in rule-based mode, you can misdiagnose what's happening and select the wrong 'recipe' to follow.

Distractions are a common issue even at the skill-based level. You can get distracted and then forget where you are in the process, possibly doing the same step twice (adding two lots of a chemical to a mixture, for example) or even miss out a step (not adding the chemical to the mixture at all).

Most people's brains can't really focus on more than one or two things at a time, so people have a tendency to try and move elements of their behaviour to automatic mode (that is, skill-based behaviour) so that they can concentrate on more complex processes. This tendency means that new behaviours that start off as knowledge-based end up as skill-based. You probably remember very little of operating your car on a journey, because it's mostly automatic. But if something unexpected or unusual happens, you jump out of this skill-based, automatic way of thinking and give the unexpected incident far more attention – and from this diversion come potential errors and mistakes.

Try driving in a foreign country for the first time (wrong side of the road!) or going somewhere unfamiliar. This experience can put you out of sorts, and you may forget which gear you're in or leave your indicator light on, for example, as you adjust to the new terrain.

An error or mistake can occur for all sorts of reasons – distractions, lapses of memory, misinterpretations and so on. Taking account of this normal human behaviour when designing your tasks and processes is therefore a good idea. Simple things like observing how someone does a task can help you identify the potential for error. You can then put simple measures in place to help reduce the likelihood of error (for example, by providing checklists to help in case people forget something or get distracted).

Detailed training may be required for high-level jobs (like operating a complicated chemical process) where it's essential to fully understand the process and, importantly, the consequences of any action you take.

You can never stop all accidents or errors, but you can influence how often they happen and how severe they are. Accident and ill-health reporting occurs after the event, and if you investigate these incidents well (that is, to get at the root cause, not just the symptoms) you should be able to prevent similar things from happening again (refer to Chapter 8 for more on investigating accidents). Of course, prevention is better than cure.

Violating the rules

Sometimes people deliberately break the rules – they *violate* them (known as *violations*). Rules may be broken for all sorts of reasons: maybe you fundamentally disagree with the rules (they may be unfair or unworkable, or maybe you just weren't consulted on them).

Following the fatal injury of an employee maintaining machinery at a recycling firm employing approximately 30 people, a company director received a 12-month custodial sentence for manslaughter. The machinery wasn't properly isolated and started up unexpectedly.

HSE and police investigations revealed that there was no safe system of work for maintenance, and that instruction, training and supervision were inadequate. The HSE's investigating principal inspector said: 'Evidence showed that the director chose not to follow the advice of his health and safety adviser and instead adopted a complacent attitude, allowing the standards in his business to fall.'

The director probably didn't agree with the safety advisor, or had worked in the industry for so many years that he just believed that such an incident couldn't happen. Therefore, sorting out a proper procedure and appropriate rules to follow, and supporting that with good training, instruction and supervision, may not have seemed important or urgent. Any unwritten rules and good practice guidance from advisors that did exist were therefore not treated seriously. This filters down through an organisation, so eventually not following the rules may almost be condoned (or, at least, people aren't taken to task for not following the rules, so, to them, the rule is no longer considered 'strict'). Breaking the rules isn't always as simple as a deliberate action; it often occurs because a belief is held within the organisation that it isn't a 'serious' rule.

You can find out more about this case on the HSE's website here: `www.hse.gov.uk/leadership/casestudies.htm`.

Sometimes rule-breaking becomes routine – it becomes the norm if it largely goes unchecked and employees have an incentive (like cutting corners to save time). It doesn't take long for such behaviour to permeate the safety culture – turning your positive safety culture negative.

But most people, even when they knowingly break the rules, do it for a reason that seems good to them at the time. Sometimes it will be justified by the situation. For example, you're fitting a new pump and the supplier has given you the wrong type of seal. It's almost the same specification as the one you need. It would take too long to get the right one, so you fit the one they have and leak test it. It works okay. However, after a few weeks of operation, the seal fails because it's not designed for that pump. Similarly, you need to get a job done, but maybe you've run out of protective gloves. You do the job without the gloves and injure yourself, even though the rule is that you use protective gloves. You figure that your decision was demanded by the situation you were in.

An extreme example occurs when things go badly wrong, like in emergencies – where you can feel like you just have to act in a certain way to save the day, even though you know you're breaking the rules (a real-life example occurred during the Piper Alpha oil rig fire and explosion in the North Sea, where some of the survivors escaped because they disobeyed the emergency rules).

 Because many violations have an apparent justification, to stop them you may need to act beyond supervision and disciplinary action. You have to tackle the *attitude* and challenge the 'justifications'. If people don't feel that they have any choice but to break the rules, it may be that they need better training to understand what their choices are for a given scenario. If they believe the rules are out of date or plain wrong, maybe they are – so review them and get your team involved to help make useful changes. (Refer to Chapter 7 for more on reviewing your safe systems of work.)

If your employees are breaking rules because they figure they just can't get the job done otherwise, maybe you're sending the wrong messages from the top. So, be realistic and understand that your employees are human too.

Chapter 19

Cracking Process Safety

*T*his chapter introduces something you may hear about every now and again – process safety. But the term 'process safety' may be eclipsed by something far more headline-grabbing (and perhaps more fitting), like 'disaster' or 'catastrophe'. Such serious stories may involve a chemical plant explosion or oil refinery fire – or even a nuclear meltdown. You may even hear terms like 'process safety management' too.

Process safety has to tackle the complexity of large industrial processes, where small slips can accumulate and be bad news on a large scale. If you're not working in such industrial processes, you may think that this chapter doesn't apply to you. But the effects of something going wrong can reach a very wide area, such as the surrounding community, whether you work on the site or not. Factories and production units also have offices, which you may be working in (technically low risk in themselves, but not when next to 50 tonnes of highly flammable fuel).

In this chapter we help you appreciate what process safety is, and how process safety is a little different from personal safety and why it has to be.

Approaching Safety Differently

Process safety is safety applied to the so-called 'high hazard' process industries. It aims to stop the potentially major accidents associated with such industries, like huge fires, explosions and toxic gas releases, and if they do occur, it seeks to greatly limit their consequences. Technically, process industries include any large manufacturing process (continuous production or in batches – so including many food manufacturing operations), but process safety is only concerned with the *high hazard process industries*, the ones that store, process or produce dangerous chemicals (usually in large quantities, but some chemicals are so toxic that even very small quantities can lead to major disasters). Examples include chemical manufacturing and the oil and gas industry (a very diverse industry ranging from exploration to refining, the latter referring to a specialised chemical plant). The processes in these industries are often very complex – a series of interconnected activities where the processing conditions may need to be closely monitored to keep them under control.

These process industries are often called high hazard process industries because they use, process or produce substances that are highly hazardous. That is, they have the potential to do a lot of harm (and damage), not only to the people on the site but also to the community around the site.

A *hazard* is anything (a substance, object activity, process or situation) with the *potential* to cause harm. *Risk* is the chance that harm will happen as a result of the hazard (Chapter 1 explores these definitions in more detail).

But you may wonder why process industries take a different approach to safety, or at least a different emphasis. In the following sections, we explain why they've had to do this. Essentially, it's a lesson from history.

Learning from history

When it comes to the high hazard process industries, accidents can be catastrophic but are thankfully very rare. As a result of their rarity, they can be rather complicated and difficult to predict (all accidents are easy to predict *after* the event, but we're talking about the useful bit – stopping them before they happen).

You can be lulled into thinking that rare events will never happen. You can become complacent and start focusing on the wrong things – the things that don't matter quite as much – and that's precisely when accidents happen (when you relax your guard and stop paying attention). If you think an event will never happen, you don't tend to put much resource into averting it – or, you may find it difficult to justify the investment cost.

To look at this in a different way, over recent decades the UK has had milder winters in many areas, with less snow and ice. When an unusual and protracted snowstorm appears, people may complain that they've been caught off-guard and that they haven't stockpiled enough road salt or don't have enough snow ploughs (hindsight is a wonderful thing). But these same people may also have been against committing large amounts of money for the eventuality in preceding years. It's far easier to make the case for investment in, say, New England (a region on the northeast coast of the United States), which has more frequent and severe snowstorms.

Large fires and explosions have occurred in the UK. Consider this relatively recent example.

In 2005, an oil/petrol storage depot at Buncefield (north of London) experienced a major fire and a series of explosions. There was a great deal of damage to surrounding business and residential properties and 40 people were injured, but fortunately no one was killed (due largely to the fact that it happened early on a Sunday morning when fewer people were on-site and hardly anyone was working in the nearby industrial/business park).

Here's what happened. A tank was being filled with petrol. Theoretically, there were several 'layers of protection' against overfilling (for more on layers of protection, check out the later section, 'Attending to the little things'). For example, there was a gauge (that was monitored by employees) and an Independent High-Level Switch (IHLS) that was supposed to automatically shut down the filling operation if the tank was close to being overfilled. Unfortunately, on this occasion the gauge became stuck and the IHLS didn't work. Therefore, no one knew that the tank was about to overfill. The fuel spilled out from the top of the tank, the vapour subsequently ignited and exploded, and it took the fire service about five days to put the fire out.

Although clearly the IHLS should have worked properly, there was a whole chain of other events that contributed to the accident. Fundamentally, the scale of the explosion was 'unexpectedly high'. In other words, an explosion that big was never considered realistic. In addition, there was a distinct failure in the maintenance process for safety-critical items like the IHLS not working. The design of the *containment systems* (the systems that stop petrol leaking everywhere) was also flawed. The work culture was pretty pressured too – people felt they had to keep the fuel storage and distribution operation going no matter what.

The accident reports are available free from the Health and Safety Executive's (HSE's) website at `www.hse.gov.uk/comah/accidents.htm` (look down the list for the Buncefield reports, released at various stages of the four-year investigation, with a final summary after legal proceedings were concluded).

You can find plenty of other such incidents over the years (for example, the BP Texas City Refinery explosion in the United States in 2005 or the Barton Solvents explosion in Kansas, United States, in 2007).

None of the companies in these examples are uniquely cavalier or accident-prone – they just happen to have had a catastrophic failure. So, if your business hasn't had one yet, don't sit there smugly thinking 'it'll never happen to me', because the truth is that, if you look more closely, you may be surprised to discover that your business suffers from the same underlying series of deficiencies but, because of chance, they haven't quite come together yet and caused anything serious. If so, take action before it's too late.

Hanging up hard hat safety

Personal safety is sometimes called *hard hat safety*. Hard hat safety is mostly all the obvious stuff – slips, trips and falls (refer to Chapter 5); machinery guarding (refer to Chapter 12); fire precautions (refer to Chapter 14) . . . in fact, the majority of this book covers this kind of traditional safety detail. It tends to focus on sensible risk management considerations like reviewing personal accident rates and near misses to get a handle on how well you're doing (though you may also find some information on health and safety relating to culture, ownership, consultation and human behaviour thrown into the mix too – refer to Chapters 3 and 18 for more on these elements).

Just focusing on personal safety doesn't work well for process safety hazards. Personal safety is still important, but it doesn't help you predict major accidents, mostly because they're infrequent (you'd worry if they weren't) and occur on a catastrophic scale. These major accidents are also often a result of lots of seemingly small issues coming together (like neglected maintenance of instrumentation, or heating a process chemical a bit too much or too unevenly). These issues are not nearly so important in other contexts, as the consequences may be much smaller. But if you know what you're looking for, you can often notice the early signs of things going wrong. The fact that you've not had (or nearly had) a catastrophic process accident doesn't mean that you're running the plant safely!

Process safety is instead focused on preventing catastrophic events like the ones we discuss in the preceding section. These are mainly major fires, explosions and the release of toxic chemicals. Process safety places strong emphasis on analysing *credible* (that is, realistically possible) major accidents – things that can happen. Of course, a valuable source of information on what can happen is that on previous major accidents, either in your own business or in similar industries. You review such incidents and learn from them, considering how the same thing could possibly happen to you.

The problem is that, due to the rarity of catastrophic failures in process safety, it's a challenge to predict what *can* happen – in these very rare cases, it's always much easier to assess the incident after the event.

In most cases, process safety isn't so much to do with the type of industry but more the types (and amounts) of chemicals that a given organisation deals with. High hazard process industries carry large amounts of quite dangerous chemicals (or even small quantities of *really* dangerous substances). If things go wrong, these dangerous chemicals can spread very quickly – not just on the site of the incident but into the surrounding areas, affecting towns, villages, schools, rivers . . . the list goes on. As a result, you end up with mass poisonings (such as those at Bhopal in India and Seveso in Italy – for more on the Seveso incident, see the later section 'Producing an onshore

Safety Report: Visiting Seveso') or alarming explosions and daunting fire-balls (like those at the Piper Alpha oil and gas platform in the North Sea, the Buncefield oil depot (refer to the preceding section, 'Learning from history'), the Feyzin Refinery incident in France and the Flixborough chemical plant incident in England).

Attending to the little things

In the high hazard process industries, processes are often highly complex in terms of the interaction of hardware (equipment, plant), software (to control and monitor said hardware) and people (yes, people are still useful). They typically involve careful control of factors such as chemical reactions and distillations, which often occur under high temperature or pressure. Some chemical processes are ultra-sensitive – they really don't handle going outside their normal operating conditions well. And, like ultra-sensitive people, they may react very badly over seemingly small details.

Process safety relies on what's often termed *layers of protection* or multiple 'barriers' – this means having lots of different controls in place that either prevent processes from going pear-shaped or, when things do go wrong, limit how bad the outcome may be (that is, they *mitigate* the effects).

The process safety approach relies on using lots of layers because history has shown that no single protective measure is 100 per cent reliable all the time. The chemical plant (or other industrial site) doesn't become vulnerable to fire or explosion just because of one thing not working (like a broken IHLS to prevent overfilling, or an operator accidentally doing the wrong thing) – you design the process so that you need many things to go wrong together for that to happen (and the chances of everything going wrong at the same time, and not being detected or corrected, should be much lower than if a major incident required just one thing to go wrong). These catastrophes are nearly always just that – the result of multiple small failings in critical systems all coming together (which is why they're rare events and thus difficult to predict).

Inattention to seemingly small details designed to keep the plant in good working order and under control (like lack of maintenance) can often lead to serious consequences. It can be difficult to fully appreciate the value of paying attention to the little things, however, especially if you've never had a serious incident in your own workplace.

In principle, process safety isn't really any different from traditional safety; it's more a question of emphasis. That means paying more attention to some things that, in lower risk workplaces (like offices), would probably make little impact. But in a high hazard establishment, neglect of several seemingly insignificant things can lead to disaster, so you need to focus your mind on the things that matter for keeping processes under control, rather than neglecting these important things and being distracted by other things.

Breaking Down Process Safety Management

Process industries are highly regulated in most countries. Nearly all laws we can think of that relate to process safety (and that's a lot!) have arrived after a major accident somewhere.

These laws are based on an approach that is termed either a *Safety Case* (for offshore installations, such as oil rigs) or a *Safety Report* (for onshore installations, such as refineries or chemical factories). Despite the difference in wording, these documents are similar – they require you to show that your processes are being closely managed to make sure that the chances of a disaster are reassuringly small. These documents are based on evidence and logical consideration of what may lead to a disastrous incident. In practice, in order to produce these documents, you need to be aware of the hazards on your site, what can go wrong (in terms of events that may lead to major accident scenarios), how likely an incident is to happen, and what you have in place to prevent or mitigate it.

You also need a robust, comprehensive plan to monitor essential stuff that can give you an early warning of deviations from your process. Learning from previous incidents (either your own or from a similar industry or scenario – refer to the earlier section, 'Learning from history' for some examples) can be pretty helpful too.

Process safety management (PSM) is the application of safety management to the high hazard process industries to prevent disasters. It seems to be an idea that's developed over many years as people have learned from major accidents around the globe. PSM has therefore become a collection of elements that make up good management in process safety, allowing industrial companies to stop catastrophic events in their tracks.

The way we like to view PSM is as being made up of two parts, which have to work together:

- **Technical risk controls:** Relating mainly to plant and equipment used in the (chemical) process

- **Safety management system:** Relating mainly to how the technical risk controls are monitored, maintained, used and developed (for example, your systems/procedures and your people/organisation)

As you may know from looking at safety management systems in personal safety scenarios (refer to Chapter 6), a big emphasis over recent years has been safety cultural issues of competence and also leadership (for more on leading from the front, refer to Chapter 3).

Some process safety regimes in the world tend to focus on technical risk control (though a safety management system is always implied), but the UK regime of Safety Cases and Safety Reports explicitly integrates technical risk controls and the safety management system, recognising that you need both to make PSM work.

In the following sections, we look at the Safety Report regime, which formally imposes PSM to regulate onshore (land-based) high hazard sites, like large chemical factories, chemical storage depots and refineries. We then look at the Safety Case regime, which regulates offshore high hazard installations, such as oil rigs.

Producing an onshore Safety Report: Visiting Seveso

The current UK legislation for controlling high hazard sites on land (that is *onshore*) is based on a European Union (EU) directive known lovingly as the *Seveso III Directive* (now in its third edition, hence the 'III'). It's named after a serious incident in Seveso, Italy, which involved the release of large quantities of a very toxic material (dioxin).

The Seveso III Directive has been transposed into UK law as the Control of Major Accident Hazards Regulations (or COMAH, for short – which is more memorable). There are separate COMAH regulations for Great Britain (England, Scotland and Wales) and Northern Ireland, but they both go by the same name and basically have the same requirements.

COMAH is an enlightened bit of legislation. It cleverly integrates health, safety and environmental protection (disasters always lead to severe pollution, either directly though spills or releases or through fighting the fire – so-called fire-water run-off. For those with a penchant for old John Wayne films, fire water may mean something else entirely).

Because of this dual interest (health and safety, and the environment), COMAH is jointly enforced by both the health and safety regulator and the environmental regulator who are together referred to as the 'competent authority' in the regulations. Who the competent authority is depends on where you are in the UK. England, Scotland and Wales all have the same health and safety regulator, the Health and Safety Executive (HSE; or the Office for Nuclear Regulation in the case of nuclear sites). But for the environment, it can be different. If you're in England, the regulator is the Environment Agency. If you're in Wales, it's Natural Resources Wales. For Scotland, it's the Scottish Environment Protection Agency. Northern Ireland has its own set of regulations, the competent authorities being the Health and Safety Executive for Northern Ireland (HSENI) and the Northern Ireland Environment Agency (NIEA).

COMAH only applies to the more hazardous sites – those that have amounts of dangerous chemicals above certain thresholds (identified in Schedule 1 of the regulations). Though the thresholds are listed for each chemical (or chemical hazard type), you also need to take account of aggregation – that is, to consider the total amounts of hazardous materials, even though you may be below the thresholds for each individual chemical or hazard type. Large overall quantities of these chemicals present a potential threat to local communities if things go wrong.

Like a wedding cake, COMAH categorises *installations* (that is, a site or unit where you produce, handle, use or store dangerous chemicals – including all the equipment, vessels, pipelines and so on that you need) into two tiers, unimaginatively called *lower-tier* and *upper-tier*. Which tier you fall into largely depends on the amounts and types of dangerous chemicals listed (at great length) in the regulations. Lower-tier sites are those that have lower quantities of dangerous substances (though obviously enough to be considered dangerous). They have correspondingly less onerous requirements than the upper-tier sites. However, because the categorisation is based on chemical hazard types (as well as specific substances), it's perfectly possible to find yourself being brought into COMAH (as a lower-tier site, when previously you were outside the regulations) or moving from lower-tier to upper-tier (if you change the quantity of chemicals that you store or use, or something new is discovered to change the status of a particular hazard). Knowledge of hazards isn't static; it evolves.

The COMAH regulations require an upper-tier site to:

1. **Tell the competent authority that you're intending to start operations.** These regulators need to know not only where you are but also what chemicals/materials you have on your site, how much, what you're doing with them, what your site's surroundings are like and so on.

2. **Put together a Major Accident Prevention Policy (MAPP).** The *MAPP* describes your overall aims, principles, management roles and responsibilities, and provides a commitment to continuous improvement. Basically it's a *leadership* commitment (which sounds a bit like the equivalent of the statement of general policy in a safety management system).

The MAPP must be implemented by a safety management system. It can't just be an empty piece of paper but must actually be implemented – have all the systems, procedures, organisation (people), checking and so on behind it to make sure that it results in action. As with all safety management systems, it needs to be proportionate to the scale and complexity of the business (refer to Chapter 6).

The regulator may tell you about possible knock-on/escalation effects (*domino effects* – that is, where one COMAH site may cause another nearby COMAH site to experience a disaster such as an explosion . . .) relating to other COMAH sites that it knows about in your neighbourhood. Therefore, they expect you to share information and take account of these domino effects in your MAPP and plans.

3. **Produce a Safety Report.** This is major part of the requirements, and it's a big task for most companies. You're justifying (or making the case) that you're actively controlling your risks to a standard called 'as low as reasonably practicable' (ALARP).

ALARP is a bit like limbo dancing – how low can you go. It's the standard for keeping risks under control and proportionate, taking account of the time, effort and resources needed to reduce risk compared to the level of risk reduction that you can achieve. But it's also a shifting goalpost. What's not reasonably practicable today may well be in a year's time, as technology moves on. So, implied in ALARP is that you keep your risks under review.

You have to submit your Safety Report to the competent authority (who, for a small fee – well a large fee actually – reviews it and decides if you can operate). The detail you need can be extreme. The HSE has produced a good deal of guidance on Safety Report writing and assessment on its website: www.hse.gov.uk/comah/guidance.htm.

Amongst other things in your Safety Report, you need to demonstrate that you have:

- A working safety management system in place (refer to Chapter 6), not just a paper chase.

- Identified major accident hazards, the potential scenarios they may cause and the prevention/mitigation measures you need (often called *process hazard analysis* – refer to the later section, 'Analysing process hazards' for more on this).

- Incorporated reliability and safety in design, construction, operation and maintenance of the site installation (as well as making sure that you design and build plant to good design standards – that means you need to consider things like operating procedures, contractor control, management of change, maintenance of assets, training and so on).

- An *emergency response plan* that's a workable on-site plan, including how you're going to clean up and restore the site after an environmental incident. In fact, you also need to provide enough information so that an off-site emergency plan can be developed (by others).

All the requirements in the preceding list apply in full if you're an upper-tier COMAH site. If you're lucky enough to be a lower-tier site, you don't have to produce a Safety Report (you only need a MAPP), and you also don't have to produce a detailed emergency plan (though you're required to take all necessary measures to avoid major accidents – which surely requires some kind of emergency plan). You also don't need to provide information to people likely to be affected by a major accident (like the surrounding community).

The regulators have the responsibility for joining up the dots and seeing the bigger picture. They need to take into account any domino effects and think about safety distances between your site and nearby schools, and so on (some sites are historic and residential areas have crept closer over time). But they can also stop you dead in your tracks if they think you're not running a safe site. They expect to inspect you every now and then too.

Making a Safety Case offshore

As with onshore sites (refer to the preceding section), you require PSM plans for offshore installations such as oil and gas installations (typically oil rigs). However, the terminology differs with offshore sites – you have a Safety Case instead of a Safety Report (so, it's not a massive deviation from the Safety Report). The law differs a little more (you have the Offshore Installations [Safety Case] Regulations 2005 to contend with), but ultimately the PSM approach amounts to the same thing.

Stacking Up Some Process Safety Management System Elements

PSM systems have some similarities with more general safety management systems (refer to Chapter 6), though of course with a focus on process hazards rather than personal safety. So, here we take a whistle-stop tour of some of the hot topics in PSM. You'll notice many similarities with topics you see elsewhere in this book (such as permit systems and equipment maintenance) but which take on a more critical emphasis when it comes to high hazard process industries. Knowledge around these areas has developed over time as people have discovered the hard way what's necessary for adequate PSM.

Monitoring, auditing and reviewing tools are also essential for the continuous improvement of any safety management system (refer to Chapter 8 for more). That means they need to be applied to all the elements we look at in the following sections, because they each need to be kept under review, and improved with experience, knowledge and learning from incidents.

Analysing process hazards

Process hazard analysis is extreme risk assessment – a central plank of any safety management system. It helps you to identify major risks and set priorities to sort them out. You need to think deeply about the major hazards of the process, plant and equipment. You also need to consider all the major accident scenarios (ask yourself, 'What if . . . ?') and think about the chances of these scenarios happening.

We're not talking about any and every possible scenario here. These situations are foreseeable and credible (realistic) major accident scenarios. So, you don't need to sit there imagining all sorts of fantastical and unlikely events – like Joe eating his lunch, choking on a peanut and spitting out the peanut (which flies out the window); and the peanut hitting an operator in the eye, who falls, trips against 13 critical valves and sets a whole escalating explosion scenario in place, with the output that you're now considering banning peanuts from the site. . . . Be realistic when evaluating potential incidents in order to establish the genuine issues.

Part of process hazard analysis involves conducting a *sensitivity analysis* (that is, looking at how sensitive or intolerant your process is to that component working reliably). You need to look at the elements of the process, plant and equipment that are absolutely critical (so if they fail or behave differently, the consequences may be major). To achieve this, you need to have (or be able to develop) a huge amount of detailed information on plant and process design (such as detailed info about substances, materials of construction and so on).

You also need to figure out what you're going to do about any potential issues that you identify. For the most part, sensitivity analysis is done by a team of experts (engineers, scientists and possibly even safety people). They use advanced hazard identification methods like HAZOP (HAZard and OPerability study), Fault Tree Analysis, Event Tree Analysis and, our personal favourite, the excellently named Bow-Tie Analysis. You may even do a bit of modelling (for example, to explore dispersion of release clouds – we're not talking about standing in front of a camera looking pretty).

Operating with procedures

Plants don't run themselves, even though many processes may be automated. You need to maintain all your operational processes, so, routinely, you still have a good deal of human intervention. Therefore, you need operating procedures, permit-to-work systems (refer to Chapter 7) and so on to cover normal operations (operating within the design intent), as well as to cover the unusual things, like maintenance and emergency scenarios (and that eternal mystery, who's turn it is to make the tea).

Steaming through cultural change

In Chapter 18 we look at how developing competence is an important factor in improving the performance of your organisation – which is why it's an integral part of PSM. These processes are highly technical and complex. If you've got people running them who don't understand how the process interacts, you don't have much hope of performing successfully as a business.

To develop competence in each process, you need to train your team and provide them with the information they require (initially, periodically and when significant changes occur) to understand the whole process itself as well as the specific operations they're performing (and thus the context and potential consequences of actions they may take to control the process).

Contracting work

Process industries make extensive use of contractors. That's because you're dealing with highly specialised work, so you tend to get the experts in. But trying to manage your own employees is difficult enough. Figuring out what's going on with a large team of contractors is even more difficult unless you specifically plan for it (refer to Chapter 7). It's mainly about selection, communication (clear expectations and responsibilities) and monitoring.

Managing your assets

You may think you can run your plant and manage your equipment just like you treat your home – once built, you never touch it again. However, while not (that) much can go wrong with a house, a chemical plant or oil refinery is a bit different. For example, the consequences are far greater if you let your distillation column corrode to hell than if you procrastinate over modernising your kitchen! Therefore, you must first make sure that all your critical equipment is of the right specification to start with, that it's installed properly, and that you regularly inspect and maintain it.

We can't offer you a magic list of what's safety-critical (and how critical it is on a sliding scale compared to other aspects of your operation that require asset management). You have to decide on your priorities based on your hazard analysis. Some common (and important) equipment to watch includes your pressure relief valves/vents and emergency shutdown devices. You can also include any alarm or sensor/monitor to the list of critical equipment (these things send you information about whether your process is operating within normal parameters and, if not, give you a warning so that you have enough time to avert a disaster).

Managing change

When you have a complex process, it can be quite difficult to appreciate the impact of even small changes because things can interact in a way that you may not foresee at the time, unless you have a formal process to force you to think it through systematically and, importantly, get the views of others.

Because even minor changes to a process can have unforeseen consequences, process industries universally have *management of change* (MoC) procedures – a formal system for looking at potential consequences of change (process, equipment, personnel and so on).

Analysing root causes

You learn from incidents by investigating and analysing the causes of them (refer to Chapter 8, which looks at the general approach to why accidents should be investigated). If you have a near-disaster, the temptation is often to think 'Blimey, that was lucky', and then just carry on. But to stop it happening again, you need to dig deeper to find the multiple causes that lie behind it. High hazard process industry accidents tend to be much more complicated, and the underlying or root causes are more difficult to identify as a result.

Ordinarily, you get several telltale indicators that something may go wrong. Major accident investigations have shown time and time again that factors like messing up repairs or failing to correct critical equipment issues, or sensors and alarms going off unexpectedly (and being treated like a nuisance instead of a concern) are early warnings that, someday, another couple of things will fail at the same time – and 'boom', your worst-case scenario occurs.

Just as with management of change (refer to the preceding section), you need people on your team who can understand the process well enough to deduce what the consequences may be if you don't identify the problem in time.

Preventing escalation

You may never stop an event from occurring – the sheer complexity of industrial processes and the nature of chance dictate that things will at some time not work as planned. Therefore, you need a back-up plan – a series of measures that you can activate to stop unexpected events from spiralling out of control. Simple examples are emergency response plans, emergency response teams and equipment (such as breathing apparatus and the ever present gas-tight suit – a favourite at parties).

You need to be able to mobilise your emergency response quickly to cope with credible scenarios (with on-site assistance such as an emergency response team, first-aiders, fire suppression equipment and possibly even off-site assistance, such as from the local Fire and Rescue Service and the Police). Refer to the earlier section, 'Producing an onshore Safety Report: Visiting Seveso' for more.

Part V
The Part of Tens

Explore the top ten secrets of providing effective safety training in our online article at www.dummies.com/extras/healthandsafetyuk.

In this part . . .

- ✔ Avoid common pitfalls when conducting your risk assessments.
- ✔ Discover great online tools that make risk assessments easy and choosing precautions (almost) a joy.
- ✔ Link to fabulous websites that give you tonnes of free guidance, legislation and advice.

Chapter 20

Ten Ways to Get Risk Assessment Wrong

In This Chapter

▶ Overcomplicating your risk assessment

▶ Ignoring guidance and advice

▶ Drowning in paperwork

Risk assessment can be a wonderful thing (refer to Chapter 4 for more on the whole process in intricate detail). It's designed to help you systematically discover what the main risks are in your workplace (that derive from the things you do in them) and work out if you can reasonably do anything more about these risks than you're already doing.

You have a legal obligation to assess the health and safety risks arising from your business activities (which will affect both employees at work and also others, like visitors). This general requirement is in the Management of Health and Safety at Work Regulations 1999 (refer to Chapter 17), but overlapping requirements exist in many other topic-specific laws (like those covering chemicals and noise – refer to Chapters 15 and 16, respectively). You may feel that you always have more than enough to do to keep your business running smoothly, so keeping your risk assessments current may seem like a futile exercise – like you're running just to stand still. But the risk assessment process is very important for your business, as long as you stay focused on doing your assessments properly.

One of our favourite Health and Safety Executive (HSE) reports (published in 2003, so rather elderly now) is *Good Practice and Pitfalls in Risk Assessment* (Research Report 151). This report was prepared by the Health and Safety Laboratory (HSL) bods, who analysed some common risk assessment issues. Many of these may come as no surprise to you, and you've probably come across quite a few of them in practice at some stage.

The topics in this report provide a useful framework for this chapter, so we use these to outline some of the key problems you may encounter with risk assessment. We summarise some of the report's findings (which are extracted mainly from real-life case studies) and embellish these with a few of our own too.

Using a Risk Assessment to Justify Decisions You've Already Made

This is a big temptation. You know in your mind what the risk may be, so you work backwards in your risk assessment to justify it.

Nearly always, you do this to justify doing nothing. This is just good old-fashioned human nature (and a ploy used by politicians everywhere).

This is often known as *reverse risk assessment* – the origin of the term is in line with similar commonly used phrases like 'reverse engineering', where you start with the answer you want and work backwards to the starting point. With reverse risk assessment, you want to do nothing, so you make sure that your risk assessment aligns with that desire!

The truth is, you use risk assessment to help you *make* decisions, not to support a decision you've already made.

Making Your Risk Assessment Too Generic

Many risks can seem generic, at least in principle – for example, most work-places have risks associated with electricity, machinery, computers and so on. But you need to be careful not to ignore the specifics of individual risks.

Proximity and location can make a big difference. If you have two identical factories but one is next to a brook or river, that factory may have a greater potential for causing pollution. If you have two seemingly similar offices but one allows public access (say, it has an enquiry desk), that office may pose a greater risk to your staff (for example, from violence).

That said, grouping similar things and doing things generically has its place – and can save you a lot of time. It can stop you from reinventing the wheel and helps avoid unnecessary repetition. So, in workplaces where the issues are 'the usual suspects' – commonly occurring, simple types of risks – and not particularly unusual, you may find that generic risk assessments do very well. The risk assessment you do in one office will therefore be much like the risk assessment you do in another office. Even where differences exist, a generic risk assessment can be used as a good starting point (like a sort of checklist) – you can then review it, focusing in on the areas where you need to customise it because of specific differences.

In many cases everything will be exactly the same, so you won't need to change anything. If your organisation has larger, more complex workplaces, you'll find that the devil is in the detail and you're likely to have to do far more tailoring.

Overcomplicating Your Risk Assessment

Making your risk assessment too complicated is frighteningly common – but it's unsurprising, because it can be a bit of a minefield to know how detailed to go when you get started. In general, the sophistication and detail you need to go into should be proportionate to the risk. If risks (and their control measures) are reasonably obvious, you don't need to put much effort in before it becomes apparent what you need to do to manage the risk.

You may assume that a more complex and sophisticated risk assessment method is automatically more robust, leads to a more accurate result and is overall better. This isn't true at all. The method needs to be suitable for the risk. The simpler you can make your risk assessment (while still being effective), the better. You don't need to use complicated risk matrices (refer to Chapter 4) that allocate a large number of categories to the likelihood and consequences of a given risk if simple methods will do. For most office (and other low-risk) environments, you don't need to use risk matrices at all.

If you don't know what you're doing, it's easy to prioritise the trivial over the important or miss some risks entirely (that would easily have been identified with simpler methods). So, keep your risk assessment simple – fit for purpose.

When using risk-rating matrices, it's easy to get carried away, but you don't need to make it too complicated. In theory, you have three basic levels of risk when you conduct your risk assessments. These all take account of what precautions you have in place (and how effective they are):

- ✓ **Pure risk:** The 'naked' risk, assuming you have no precautions at all (this is entirely theoretical because you're bound to have something in place).

- ✓ **Residual risk:** The risk you have now, today, when you take account of all the precautions you *already* have in place.

- ✓ **Revised residual risk:** After looking at your residual risk, you may decide to put in more precautions, either because you think the risk is too high or because you can do something easy to reduce the risk anyway. You then have a new level of residual risk (if these precautions work) – your *revised residual risk* (for want of a better term).

Most risk assessments only need to deal with *residual* risk, because this helps you to prioritise any further actions you need to take in the simplest way. By comparing what you already do (in terms of precautions) with regulatory and industry good practice guidance, it's quite possible to make a simple, qualitative judgement as to whether you're doing enough (that is, whether the residual risk is acceptable).

When it comes to looking at risks from slipping and tripping hazards in a standard office (such as slippery floors, trailing cables and other obstacles), imagine that you already have in place a housekeeping policy (keeping the place tidy through weekly checks by managers), rules on eradicating trailing cables/leads, regular cleaning through a contract cleaner, and level floors that are in good condition. You may decide, by looking at the guidance, that you're in the right area when it comes to having low residual risk. But perhaps you also notice the bit in the guidance about considering your lighting levels – and you remember that it was a bit dim in the hallway when you went into the storeroom the previous day (in fact, you remember almost losing your footing, fumbling for the doorknob). As a result, you conclude that making the lighting brighter in the hallway can make a big difference for little cost and effort. That's the stuff of legend . . . actually doing things rather than talking about it.

More complex risk assessment methods do have their place – of course they do. But save them for cases when you need them. In most ordinary, everyday low-risk workplaces, the simple approaches (that is, comparing what you have in place with what it says in best practice guidance) are perfectly adequate. They should be your starting point – make the effort to go deeper only when you need to.

Ignoring Industry Standards and Good Practice

Instead of jumping immediately to complex risk assessment methods (to prove a point, or just because you think you should; refer to our sage advice in the preceding section), stop and think a minute and see if anyone has already worked the problem out elsewhere. You may well find that industry standards and good practice guides are available to help you find your way.

Most low-risk workplaces can simply look at the relevant guidance (from the HSE or professional industry bodies) that advises you on expected good practice. In fact, quite a few *hazard checklists* (a simple checklist you can make up of common hazards you're likely to encounter, as an aide memoire when looking for hazards – refer to Chapter 4) are based on HSE, or other professional body, guidance. What a great, and perfectly legitimate, shortcut!

Even for more complex activities, you can sometimes find industry standards – where someone else has figured out what you need to do to address safety risk in your workplace. Therefore, you don't need to reinvent the wheel. Industry best practice is what the HSE expects you to use – yes, there's still room for innovation, but your workplace needs to either be at or exceed the industry standard, so don't ignore the information that's already there to help you achieve this standard.

Using the Wrong Guidance

You may be tempted to use guidance that fits with your idea of what you require (or what you consider to be the main point). But all guidance has context. For example, for purely practical reasons associated with the nature of the site and the job, the provision of toilets you can expect on a very temporary construction site may be quite different from a fixed office block in a city. Because the building site is in a state of constant change, the toilets are more likely to be portable types, and drinking water may have to be bottled (renewed every day) rather than mains-fed. The official guidance on this topic accepts these practical difficulties (that is, that it's not ideal) in the advice it gives. You can't therefore take the construction site guidance and try to apply it to the office (telling people to use portable toilets), or ask your employees to pop round to the neighbouring office or just store it up all day. . . .

The same would be true of the difference between guidance for welding in a dedicated welding workshop versus doing it elsewhere *in the wild* – out on a job. You have different expectations of what you can practically achieve and a different mix of control measures (for example, if you're away from the workshop you may be more reliant on procedures, like permits, if you're not working in a dedicated, purpose-built and safe area).

Lots of guidance can make certain assumptions of the context. If these turn out not to be the case, you can quickly go down the wrong path. The danger is where there just isn't much guidance about your specific issue in your specific circumstances – if you're doing something a little unusual, you end up clutching at straws.

Research Report 151 (*Good Practice and Pitfalls in Risk Assessment,* published by the HSE) cites the example of a hospital that wanted a refuelling station on top of one of its buildings. The hospital used industry standard guidance – but the guidance was for normal refuelling (not even aero-refuelling, and it certainly didn't envisage this refuelling happening on top of a hospital building, where the consequences of spillages would be very different from a typical refuelling scenario – such as on a garage forecourt).

Knowing Nothing about the Activity You're Assessing

You need to know something about the activity you're assessing. Therefore, it's a good idea to at least talk to the people who do the job – rather than make lots of false assumptions. You need to be careful to consult with the experts on your team when you need to so that you're involved in risk assessment in the most practical way possible.

If you're not familiar with, say, a bench-top grinder, how will you know if it's working properly? More importantly, how will you know if its safety controls, like interlocks and guards, are working properly? If you don't know what you're looking for, you won't be in a position to recognise potential problems with your machinery. (Chapter 12 has the ins and outs of machinery risk covered.)

Most office-based risks are well-known and familiar, so you don't need a team of people to advise you on the safety risks. Even if you're dealing with a less common office-based risk, such as a heat sealer (used to seal documents or books in a plastic film wrapper) or moveable archive storage units (bookcases that run on a track), you can find many checklists these days that can help you ask the right questions to complete your risk assessments. However, don't forget to involve other people when you're dealing with more complex and unusual workplace risks.

Leaving Consultants to the Task without Getting Involved Yourself

You may think that when you delegate risk assessment tasks to hired consultants, you can delegate the responsibility to them too. That's not the case, however. You're still responsible (and liable!) for your organisation's health and safety. The consultant may be culpable – but that's cold comfort. It's like telling your mother that your brother told you to burn the house down and expecting your mother to let you off.

When you use consultants, you need to make sure that you understand what's going on at all times. You need to understand the significance of their findings enough to understand the required actions. After all, it's you and the people who work with you who will be facing the day-to-day risk from your activities, not the consultant. You therefore need to get involved and inform the risk assessment. Consultants bring their expertise to bear to help you work out what your risks are and what the solutions should be, but you need to be part of the process too.

Risk assessment (in its many forms) represents the majority of the work that health and safety consultants do (it's like their staple diet). But unless you're engaged in the process (as an organisation), you're just paying someone to stack your bookshelves with risk assessment records that you're never going to read and have little understanding about. That's why larger organisations with more complex risks tend to employ a dedicated in-house safety expert, such as a safety manager, or a whole safety department.

Safety is everyone's job (safety advisers and safety managers aren't there to hand out the safety goggles – or put them on your head – or put the guards in place before you turn your machinery on). But the more complex your organisation, the more infrastructure you need to make sure that you get the right advice (competent, proportionate advice), which is well understood and implemented effectively.

Getting Bogged Down in Trivia

The law doesn't expect you to record every single risk in a risk assessment. It expects you, instead, to record your organisation's *significant* risks.

But people worry about whether they've missed something and so, in an effort to avoid this outcome, decide that it's easier to write everything down to show that they've considered all the possibilities. And although this identifies some key information, you can take it too far.

One of your authors remembers someone who was worrying about whether or not to take into account malfunctioning aircrafts crashing into the factory as part of their risk assessment. The argument was that the building was on the flight path (but who isn't these days?) and so technically the factory was at risk. However, as much as this raised an interesting point, the eventuality definitely didn't belong on the risk assessment (we've no idea what you could feasibly do to reduce risk either). You have to think about whether something is under your control (or at least partly), because the point of risk assessment is that you're able to do something about the risk.

Of course, this example is extreme – it's almost on a par with worrying about a nuclear strike or an asteroid hitting the earth (and these are problems for governments to worry about, not small businesses!). These events may not be trivial at all, but in terms of risk, they're so unlikely and so removed from your control that they're not worth considering.

Some risks are truly trivial. They may occur frequently but be very minor in terms of impact – for example, getting a paper cut in an office (though this may be a more serious issue in a laboratory when working with dangerous chemicals, bacteria or viruses, for example). You don't need to worry about such trivial events for the most part (though how long has the paperless office been promised?).

Keep your risk assessment realistic and don't spend time worrying about the trivia.

Treating Your Risk Assessment as a Paper Exercise

When you've put so much effort into doing your risk assessment, which has helped you make decisions and set priorities for action, it's rather a pity if your work goes to waste because you fail to implement the outcome actions.

Risk doesn't change if you don't do something about it. Having a risk assessment isn't enough – you need to take action and see your risk assessment as a means to an end.

Assuming That Nothing Ever Changes

When you get through the trauma of doing your risk assessment (only kidding – it's not that bad!), it can be tempting to never look at it again. But – we promise! – the thought of reviewing your risk assessment is usually worse than the review process itself.

 Don't fall into the trap of assuming that a risk assessment is set in stone (that it's 'for life, not just for Christmas'). It isn't like a popular fiction novel (once it's written, it never changes) or like one of your authors' pet tortoise (which spends most of its time in hibernation).

 Think of reviewing your risk assessment as like doing a fitness programme – you need to give it ongoing attention; otherwise, your hard work just turns to fat. If you don't keep your risk assessment current, it will soon be out of shape! And like a fitness programme, you need to respond to change – you're not always going to want to lose weight, for example, because you may then want to tone up your muscles or train your body for an event like a marathon.

 When you do a risk assessment, you make lots of inherent assumptions and you draw on current guidance and knowledge – and these things can all change. Granted, the simpler the risks, the less likely they are to change that much over time. With anything more technological, however, the pace of change can be much faster and the changes that you're expected to make can evolve too. So, if something changes (like a process, chemical, procedure, member of staff, law or guidance document), you need to take these changes into account in your risk assessment.

 You don't have to redo the whole risk assessment again – just adjust the affected bits. Some people even review risk assessments on a scheduled basis (once a year, perhaps). A handy approach if you're disciplined – and if you can't face the looming annual diary date, delegate the responsibility to someone who can.

Chapter 21

Ten Neat Tools to Help You Assess Risks and Choose Controls

In This Chapter

▶ Charting manual handling and repetitive tasks

▶ Calculating noise and vibration exposure

▶ Targeting stress

*T*he UK's enforcement agencies – mainly the Health and Safety Executive (HSE) and local authorities – and professional bodies are sympathetic to your pain: they know how complicated and difficult risk assessments can seem to the uninitiated. Therefore, they provide a few nifty tools to help you. Some aren't risk assessments but checklists to help make life more bearable (a bit like a pet hamster, or chocolate).

In this chapter, we introduce you to some of the most helpful tools available that can help to make workplace risk assessment simple and straightforward.

Office Risk Assessment Tool

The HSE provide this handy way to assess your office-based workplace on the risk section of the main HSE website at www.hse.gov.uk/risk/office.htm. You can get several focused risk assessment interactive tools for different lower-risk workplaces (as well as the office, they also provide charity shop, general shop and classroom tools).

This tool isn't without its flaws, and it's possible to get through it without adding anything yourself (just sticking with the defaults). But if you're careful to consider what the tool suggests, and to compare it to your situation, it's a very good shortcut to considering office-based risks, and it gets you thinking about these risks in more detail (you're only fooling yourself if you cheat).

When you launch this interactive tool, you're faced with two main options: you can either register so that you can come back to it later (so, it saves your assessment for you) or opt for once-only use (which won't save your assessment).

After you launch the tool, it takes you through nine steps, offering a helpful progress bar as you go through. The first seven steps cover commonly encountered office hazards. The tool raises a hazard category (like slips and trips), explaining how someone may be harmed and who it may affect. It then asks if that hazard applies in your workplace. If you select yes, it asks you to consider what you're already doing about the hazard (you can select some standard measures from a list). You then decide what else you may need to do to control the risk from each hazard.

This tool goes the extra mile by pushing you to decide who's going to do what and when by helping you manage and control your risks – it then creates a handy action list for you that's associated with each hazard type.

When the tool finishes cranking through the common office hazards, it turns to manual handling (which may require a more detailed assessment – refer to Chapter 11), working at height, psycho-social issues (that is, stress), computer use (which may also require a more detailed risk assessment – refer to Chapter 11), fire (which points you to a separate risk assessment guide) and work equipment.

When you get to Step 8, you're invited to consider:

- ✔ Office cleaning (mainly relating to the use of chemicals)
- ✔ Vulnerable employees (such as young people, people with disabilities and lone workers)
- ✔ Gas appliances
- ✔ Asbestos in your building

In Step 9, you can add other hazard types that you haven't already considered but that you know are present in your workplace. When you finish it, the tool produces a neat risk assessment summary (as a pdf download). And you get all this detail without the aid of a consultant or a risk matrix of any kind . . . magic!

Risk Assessment Routefinder

The Risk Assessment Routefinder is an offering from that august body, the Institution of Occupational Safety and Health (IOSH) (www. ioshroutefinder.co.uk/). It's been around for quite a while.

Though this is called a Risk Assessment Routefinder, it isn't a straightforward, simple risk assessment tool like the HSE tool in the preceding section. It's got a much broader scope to it – looking at wider business risks and utilising risk management approaches to cover health and safety too. It uses business language and looks at product risks, information risks, environmental risks, and other types of risk as well.

The questionnaires that it includes to help work out the issues in your business are thoughtful and helpful, and much meatier than the HSE's approach – which is a no-frills, quick way in.

You can see this tool more as an online (free) course, with some practical checklists. It's full of resources, such as downloadable questionnaires to provide practical help. These resources enable you to drill into some of the issues that you may raise in your HSE risk assessment (from the preceding section) in much more detail. So, we suggest trying the HSE tool first and then taking a look at this tool in order to drill deeper into other issues.

COSHH Essentials

The HSE provide this online risk assessment toolkit to help you assess chemical risks and find control solutions. It's divided into two basic parts – direct advice sheets and an online COSHH e-tool (see `www.hse.gov.uk/coshh/essentials/index.htm`). (COSHH stands for Control of Substances Hazardous to Health – the COSHH Regulations 2002 apply to working with chemicals. Refer to Chapter 15 for more on COSHH.) You can use this toolkit to assess the risks from any activities you do that involve chemicals that are hazardous to health.

The link to the direct advice sheets is at the top of the webpage. The direct advice sheets provide useful worked-out details for the control of chemicals for typical operations in specific industries. For example, if you follow the welding thread, you get through to a table of choices depending on the metal you're using, your location and so on.

The downloadable advice sheets are 'good practice' guides that tell you everything from how to set up your work area, what kind of ventilation you require and what you need to wear (the type of protective equipment; not, say, a dinner jacket). These sheets then connect you to other sheets on specifications for respirators and so on, as required by the specifics of your COSHH-related work.

As the advice sheets tell you (see also the frequently asked questions section when you get to the COSHH e-tool), the advice is necessarily sometimes a bit generic – the onus is on you to decide if the process described in the guidance properly reflects your activity. If it does, fine. If you do things a little differently, however, you need to see what else you may be required to do.

If you can't find anything relevant in the direct advice sheets, it's time to delve into the COSHH e-tool. When this e-tool was first brought in several years ago, it was a bit of a revelation. It doesn't need too much information about the task and the chemicals you're using:

- ✔ **Task/process information:** You're asked about the number of chemicals you're using, what you're doing with them (for example, mixing), the temperature of the process, how long the task takes and how often you're doing the task in a day.

- ✔ **Chemical information:** You're asked about health hazards (hazard statements), the chemical's physical state, the amounts used, the boiling point (if liquid) and the dustiness (if solid).

   You can take most of this detail from the suppliers' safety data sheet.

You then get a conclusion, generated by the tool, about the recommended control approach you need to use to help you comply with the COSHH Regulations 2002, a downloadable summary assessment and a load of downloadable guidance sheets that give you tips on how to practically implement the controls. Nice!

Manual Handling Assessment Charts (MAC) Tool

Although this tool (another great tool from the HSE) doesn't provide you with a full manual handling risk assessment, it's a helpful filtering tool (that helps you to identify the high-risk manual handling activities as opposed to the simple, straightforward cases). It's designed for certain types of manual handling tasks, including lifting, carrying and team handling. The MAC tool (where MAC refers to Manual handling Assessment Charts) can be found online here: www.hse.gov.uk/msd/mac/.

The MAC tool uses a scoring system (like football, rugby and, well, most sports) and a colour system (the nicely recognisable traffic light system, except it uses four colours – green, amber, red and purple) to grade a combination of the weight of the load being lifted and the lift frequency (you use a chart to do this). You use the tool through a downloadable pdf form that has an interactive score sheet.

In a burst of enthusiasm, the HSE have also provided several manual handling videos for you to practise your scoring on. Because the tool is a bit bewildering at first, the practice videos help you to get to grips with how the tool works before you take the plunge with assessing your own workplace.

Assessment of Repetitive Tasks (ART) Tool

The Assessment of Repetitive Tasks (ART) tool can be found online here: www.hse.gov.uk/msd/uld/art/. This is another filtering tool (like the MAC tool in the preceding section) but it focuses on your upper limbs (in other words, your arms). It assesses tasks against 12 risk factors, which are spread over four risk categories – frequency/repetition, force being used, awkward postures, and other factors (such as duration of the work and breaks).

This tool is best suited to assembly line work, where tasks can be quite repetitive and frequent (you can't use it on your tax self-assessment because, although it's repetitive and seems too frequent, you only do your tax assessment once a year). It's not much good for computer usage assessments either (you can download specific checklists to help with your workstation assessments for computer use; refer to Chapter 11 for more).

In some respects, this tool works in a similar way to the MAC tool; you get some training videos and a downloadable chart to fill in (again, with scores and colours).

The interesting thing about the ART tool is that it stresses how important the input is from the person doing the repetitive task. That means you don't just sit there with your clipboard or tablet recording what you see – you actually have to talk to people and ask them questions about how they're doing the job and what's awkward about it (we're not sure whether this is about trying to humour your poor bored employees – brightening their day through a stimulating chat with you).

Noise Exposure and Hearing Protection Calculators

The HSE has produced a few calculators over the years that enable you to estimate exposure levels or effectiveness of personal protection. You can find calculators that assess noise exposure (daily and weekly) and how effective your hearing protection is here: www.hse.gov.uk/noise/ calculator.htm.

They support the Control of Noise at Work Regulations 2005 (refer to Chapter 16) by helping you estimate noise exposure compared to the legal standards and evaluate the contribution that hearing protection may realistically make towards reducing that exposure.

The noise exposure calculator is an equivalent noise dose calculator (that is, it converts your measured or estimated exposure to a form that can be compared to the way it's quoted in the regulations). You feed it data on the average noise levels (which you can measure using a sound-level meter) or estimate this level (using information on noise levels quoted by the manufacturer of the noisy machine) for each task your operator is exposed to. You also need data on how long the operators are exposed each time. The calculator's cells are loaded with the correct formulae (from the Control of Noise at Work Regulations 2005) to calculate the equivalent eight-hour value for daily or weekly noise exposure. You can then compare this value to the legal limits quoted in those regulations.

These legal limits are essentially action triggers. If you find that the noise levels exceed them, you have to take certain actions (refer to Chapter 16) to reduce the noise level.

An alternative tool uses a points system (read from a chart that the HSE calls a 'ready reckoner') to get the same end result.

The hearing protection calculator is another spreadsheet that's often used with the noise calculator spreadsheet. It's used to identify whether a given set of hearing protectors are adequate for a specific noisy environment. As well as information on the noise levels, it requires you to have information on the noise attenuation rating for the hearing protection. These ratings are standardised methods of reporting the effectiveness of different types of hearing protection and are usually provided by the manufacturer (they're typically printed on the box or even on the hearing protection itself). The calculator is then able to calculate how much the hearing protection reduces (or *attenuates*) the noise level at the ear (assuming that the protection is worn correctly).

Hand-Arm Vibration Exposure Calculator

You use this calculator in the same way as the noise calculators in the preceding section, except this time, you're assessing vibration output. You can find the hand-arm vibration exposure calculator online here: www.hse.gov. uk/vibration/hav/vibrationcalc.htm.

You need to measure (using a device known as an accelerometer) or estimate (using data supplied from the manufacturer of the vibrating machine) the vibration output of the tool, process or task (for example, using an angle grinder to cut concrete blocks), and how long you're exposed for, and key this data into the calculator. The calculator then tots up your scores to see where you are in relation to the legally enforceable limits contained in the Control of Vibration at Work Regulations 2005.

The duration you need to think about is the 'trigger time' – the time for which the machine is on and in use. This time can be very different from the duration of the task (where you often stop and start the machine many times).

Work at Height Access Equipment Information Toolkit

The Work at Height Access Equipment Information Toolkit (otherwise known as the far snappier WAIT toolkit) can be found online on the HSE's website at www.hse.gov.uk/work-at-height/wait/wait-tool.htm (we assume that there may have been an in-joke here about not jumping ahead, and waiting so you can make the right choices . . .).

Like all the HSE's other tools, you need to know relatively little in advance. The toolkit requires you to input information on the following:

- ✔ The height of the working platform (so how far up you need to go to do the work)
- ✔ How long the work is going to take
- ✔ How long you have to wait before you have to move the equipment (so, whether you need to move it along frequently)
- ✔ Whether access is restricted
- ✔ The type of work (light, medium, heavy?)
- ✔ Whether the access equipment needs to be freestanding or fixed

Consider the following sample responses:

- ✔ You need to work up to 6 metres above the ground (up to the top floor height on a standard house, for example).
- ✔ The job is likely to last for no more than half an hour.
- ✔ You need to be able to move the access equipment around a bit as you work.

✔ You have some space restrictions (so it's difficult to get a large vehicle into the workspace).

✔ The work is relatively light (for example, painting).

✔ The access equipment can be fixed or mobile.

The WAIT toolkit then offers up several access equipment choices for you, including:

✔ A standard leaning ladder

✔ A Mobile Elevating Work Platform (MEWP)

You also need to consider maintaining your equipment and training people, among other things, but the WAIT toolkit provides you with a good shortcut to help you narrow down some reasonable access equipment options.

Asbestos Essentials Task Sheets

Asbestos has always been treated as a separate subject from other hazardous substances. It has its own legislation (refer to Chapter 15). But, for all practical purposes, the control approach is similar to the way you treat a highly toxic substance under more general legislation like the COSHH Regulations 2002 (again, refer to Chapter 15).

However, because asbestos is a very specific case and its uses are well known, the approach is much simpler. It uses a system of advice sheets (known as asbestos essentials task sheets, because they're based on common tasks you'd want to do that involve asbestos). So, you can think of this as a specific application of the more general COSHH Essentials toolkit we describe in the earlier section, 'COSHH Essentials'. You can find out more on the HSE website at www.hse.gov.uk/asbestos/essentials/.

The asbestos essentials webpage provides numerous downloadable task-specific sheets (such as on drilling asbestos cement sheets) plus a few generally applicable items too (such as on training or using personal protective equipment). You have plenty to choose from and can expect to find advice specific to your asbestos-related task here.

Stress Management Tools

Stress is increasingly being recognised as a workplace mental health issue, leading to long-term sickness absence (refer to Chapter 9). The HSE provides a range of tools, including a stress indicator tool (in several languages), a stress analysis tool, a model stress management policy and a return-to-work questionnaire. This set of tools helps you identify stress, decide if it's a problem and devise methods to tackle it. These tools can come in handy for anyone – especially as you near the end of this book! You can download them from the HSE website: www.hse.gov.uk/stress/standards/downloads.htm.

The main one is the HSE Management Standards Indicator tool. It's a two-page questionnaire that you can deploy to employees to ascertain whether you have a significant stress problem in the workplace. It asks questions related to such things as how much control you have over your work, whether you're clear on what your role is, whether you feel supported by your colleagues and so on (we're sure it's good fun to fill in at the pub with your mates too – just watch the stress fall away as the evening progresses!). You can even get the stress management standards indicator tool in Welsh (in fact, many other languages too).

The stress management standards indicator tool is used in conjunction with the stress management standards to help you decide whether you have a stress-related problem (well, whether your organisation does). If you do have a stress problem, the tool can help you to determine what you can do about it – and no, burying your head in the sand is not an option (unless you're an ostrich or the sand fairy from *Five Children and It*).

Chapter 22

Ten Great Health and Safety Websites

In This Chapter

▶ Taking a look at health and safety websites provided by the UK government

▶ Looking to Europe and the rest of the world for useful health and safety advice

*W*hen it comes to websites on health and safety, you're spoilt for choice. But top of our list are the websites from the various official regulators and agencies, many provided (or sponsored) by the government.

In this chapter we direct you to ten of the best websites to turn to if you need to know more about health and safety legislation and guidance relevant to the UK. We also include a selection of professional bodies who are jolly helpful too. Towards the end of the chapter we cast our net wider, to the EU, because of its strong influence on UK law, and then to organisations like the ILO and WHO that promote a global agenda.

Health and Safety Executive

The Health and Safety Executive's (HSE) website, www.hse.gov.uk, is the first place you need to start when looking for more information on a given health and safety topic. The HSE is the main health and safety enforcer in England, Wales and Scotland (many other organisations enforce health and safety law in specific sectors, such as factories and shops, or on specific issues, such as rail or offshore oil and gas installations). Other than the HSE, commonly encountered regulators include local authorities (your local councils), Fire and Rescue Services (that is, the local fire services), the Office of Rail Regulation, the Office for Nuclear Regulation and the Trading Standards Institute (Chapter 17 looks at different regulatory bodies in more detail). That said, the HSE produces nearly all the relevant UK guidance, either on its own or in collaboration with other agencies or professional bodies.

At time of writing, the site has a signpost feel to it (quite literally – it uses images of street signposts to help you navigate). It's written in a novice-friendly, businesslike way. It recognises that many of the people who use it aren't going to be health and safety experts, but that they really want to know where to start out to find specific information. So, it has quick links to the typical types of groups using it – for example, it asks if you're 'New to health and safety?', 'A low-risk business?' or 'An employee?'

The HSE's website directs you to quick links for topics that you may be interested in or that may be relevant to the industry that you work in. The front page also has a slideshow of current hot topics, and you can sign up for both sector-specific newsletters and a weekly digest of important changes and updated information.

The website hosts some pretty impressive tools for conducting risk assessments of different types (refer to Chapter 21 for some examples of these). Admittedly, they won't be wholly suitable for complex, high-hazard sites (even so, they're still a good starting point), but they certainly work well for the majority of lower-risk workplaces where things are much simpler and the risks are more obvious.

The HSE's website is also the portal to lots of downloadable guidance – the Approved Codes of Practice that accompany legislation – and better yet, this is all free to access online.

Health and Safety Executive Northern Ireland

Historically, even though Northern Ireland is part of the UK, it has always had its own separate health and safety legislation – to all intents and purposes, it's the equivalent of the Health and Safety at Work etc Act 1974 (refer to Chapter 17) that applies across the rest of the UK. So, instead of the HSE, Northern Ireland has the Health and Safety Executive Northern Ireland (HSENI) as its main health and safety regulator, and this works in partnership with local authorities (local councils) and others in a similar way to the HSE in the rest of the UK.

If you're working in Northern Ireland, you start with Northern Ireland's HSE website (www.hseni.gov.uk) rather than the HSE website (refer to the preceding section). Northern Ireland's HSE website isn't quite as snazzy or well-presented as the HSE website for the rest of the UK, but the information is presented logically. Currently, this website organises its content around a drop-down menu, where you can easily find information based on who you are (that is, your role – such as employer or employee) or guidance based on different health and safety topics. Like the HSE website, it also uses home-page slideshows to direct visitors to hot health and safety topics.

Public Health England

Public Health England's (PHE) website directs you to content from the current regulator for health in England: www.gov.uk/government/organisations/public-health-england.

TIP

PHE is just for England, but you also find local equivalents for other regions (Health Protection Scotland, Public Health Wales and the Public Health Agency for Northern Ireland).

REMEMBER

PHE issues advice on all sorts of health-related things, though radon is its speciality. It can provide you with radon maps of the UK – colour-coded maps that identify 'hot spots' of high concentrations of naturally occurring radon gas (a radioactive gas produced from the radioactive decay of uranium present in the ground). You can even get hold of radon gas test kits from PHE if you're concerned. It also gives you advice on what to do to reduce radiation exposure from radon.

TIP

Navigation of this site can be tricky due to PHE's web content being absorbed into the general government portal (www.gov.uk). The home page has a few quick links, but unless you're into well-being and general health, the most useful approach to finding anything really specific is to use the search bar at the top of the page.

Fire Safety in the Workplace

The Fire Safety in the Workplace webpages (housed under the consolidation of government websites at www.gov.uk, just as with PHE – refer to the preceding section) provide good business-specific guidelines on fire risk assessment: download them for free at www.gov.uk/workplace-fire-safety-your-responsibilities.

These guidelines are produced by the government and are the official, autho-rised guidance. They aren't legally binding, but they give very clear advice on what's considered best practice. The guidelines are specific to different types of workplaces or activities (like offices, factories and places of public assembly, such as football stadiums), so you'll almost certainly be able to find something that applies to your workplace. The webpages also provide a general overall introduction to fire safety in the workplace. Each guide includes helpful checklists after each fire-related topic, so they give you some theory as well as some practical ideas.

Legislation

If you want to consult specific UK health and safety legislation, you can find it all at www.legislation.gov.uk. It has reasonably good search facilities (title and year) and, once found, you can view the legislation on the website or download it for free as a pdf.

Institution of Occupational Safety and Health

The Institution of Occupational Safety and Health (IOSH) is the primary professional membership body for people who work in safety: www.iosh.co.uk. If you're a safety professional, joining IOSH offers you the benefits of networking, a monthly professional journal (keeping you up to date with what's changing in health and safety), an online CPD (continuing professional development) recording system, a legal helpline, and discounts on various products (such as insurance). The benefits change from time to time. As well as encouraging you to join its 44,000 members (or thereabouts), the website offers a good deal of free stuff to download, including easy guides to all sorts of useful things (for example, making a business case for health and safety, introduction to management systems, and the effects of shift work on health) and, if you're an academic, some research-oriented papers. You can also look up training providers that offer IOSH-approved courses.

Occupational Safety and Health Consultants Register

The Occupational Safety and Health Consultants Register is a non-compulsory register for safety consultants: www.oshcr.org. You can use it to find a good quality safety consultant. Consultants on the list must fulfil certain conditions (oh, and, did we mention, pay a fee?), and you can search on specialisms, locations and industries too.

Not just anyone can get on the list as a consultant. Each consultant that applies needs to fulfil certain criteria. For example, they need to demonstrate relevant professional memberships (such as Chartered Membership of IOSH), commit to CPD (keeping up to date on safety developments), abide by the professional body's code of conduct, provide sensible and proportionate advice (that is, be able to show that they're not just in it for the money), and carry professional indemnity insurance (in case they give the wrong advice).

By engaging an OSHCR consultant, you're choosing a well-qualified, up-to-date, pragmatic expert to help you, plus you have some recourse if things go wrong (refer to Chapter 2 for more on selecting qualified help).

European Agency for Safety and Health at Work

Every member state within the EU is required to have an enforcement body (or bodies) to enforce health and safety laws (in the UK, this is mainly done by the HSE and local authorities). The EU also has an additional body – the European Agency for Safety and Health at Work (also known as EU-OSHA) – that creates a good deal of guidance that all member states can draw from: www.osha.europa.eu/en.

EU-OSHA also provides a good portal to EU regulations and directives on health and safety. *EU regulations* are directly acting, binding laws – they apply to all member states in the form they're written. *EU directives* are laws that are also binding, but in terms of the objectives to be achieved; the detail on how these are implemented locally is left up to each member state (so the UK transposes these regulations and directives into local legislation, which is then directly enforced through the courts in the UK). We find that this site is good for some of its no-nonsense guidance, tools and videos, such as its risk assessment tool and its series of language-free safety videos.

If you have a European remit within your job, it's handy to see the source principles of what's then implemented (in a different way) throughout the EU.

World Health Organization

The website for the World Health Organization (www.who.int/en) is worth visiting for its wealth of health-related guidance, including information on radiation (and because its abbreviated name – WHO – happens to simultaneously be shared with a famous rock band and a Time Lord).

The WHO has a global remit, so it's a good source of information on global concerns, such as pandemics and world health statistics. It has many (free) fact sheets on subjects ranging from asbestos to youth violence.

If you're running a health promotion campaign at work as part of a safety initiative, the WHO can offer some useful information to support your activities.

International Labour Organization's Encyclopaedia of Occupational Health and Safety

The International Labour Organization (ILO) provides what's effectively an online book containing lots of health and safety principles and arranged in meaningful topics: www.iloencyclopaedia.org. This Encyclopaedia of Occupational Health and Safety is necessarily general (it's supposed to be widely applicable), but the principles do travel and make for interesting reading.

Catch this while you can! This content was free access for a while, but then the ILO started charging for it; now, in a fit of philanthropy from the ILO, it's free access again.

Index

• *I* •

About the Author

David Towlson is the Director of Training, Development and Quality at RRC International, which specialises in training and consultancy in health, safety, environment and quality.

David initially trained as a physical chemist, researching the delightful areas of nuclear magnetic resonance and liquid crystals (which mainly involved lots of Fortran programming, building equipment parts and late nights). He then worked for several industrial chemical manufacturing companies, gradually moving into health and safety management and training. He spreads himself around a bit, writing blogs, opinion pieces and articles for journals and publications such as the *Safety and Health Practitioner, Health & Safety Matters* and *Health & Safety Middle East,* and he also appears at conferences (especially if there's free food). He also supervises research students on Loughborough University's Occupational Health and Safety Management MSc programme and is a Principal Examiner for NEBOSH, the main health and safety qualification exam board.

David spends his spare time repairing his son's classic Mini, which resists him all the way (this mainly involves welding, grinding, sheared bolts, pain and swearing – but not necessarily in that order).

Vicki Swaine currently works as an associate trainer, consultant and writer for RRC International. Vicki started out in hotel management and then moved into sales before becoming a local authority safety advisor. She has particular skills in fire safety management (that means she's very much in demand on Bonfire night as she has all the best fireworks) and management system auditing (which means she can use a checklist and ask questions at the same time).

Terry Robson also works as an associate tutor and writer for RRC International. He moved into health and safety after working as a development chemist for British Nuclear Fuels. Perhaps unsurprisingly, his favourite topics include chemical safety and radiation protection, although his expertise is wide-ranging. Terry has worked as a NEBOSH Examiner and is Chair of the NEBOSH Diploma panel. He is passionate about tutoring and enjoys helping students to achieve their ambitions.

In his spare time, Terry enjoys running to stay physically fit, playing chess to stay mentally fit, and listening to jazz to stay sane.

Authors' Acknowledgements

The authors would like to thank their respective families, without whose patience they would be out on the streets. They would also like to thank the course development team (Anthea, Rachel, Joanna, Terri, Chris and Cindi) at RRC International, who did a first pass sense check and edit. *Lord* Wenham (the title is aspirational, but if we use it enough, someone will listen) has our thanks for a sterling job as our technical reviewer. Finally, thanks go to the editing team at Wiley (especially Michelle and Kerry), whose help, advice and flexibility made it easier for us to navigate this first foray into the *For Dummies* world.

Publisher's Acknowledgements

Executive Commissioning Editor: Annie Knight

Project Manager: Michelle Hacker

Development Editor: Kerry Laundon

Copy Editor: Kerry Laundon

Technical Editor: David Wenham

Production Editor: Kumar Chellappan

Cover Photos: © DutchScenery/iStockphoto

Take Dummies with you everywhere you go!

Whether you're excited about e-books, want more from the web, must have your mobile apps, or swept up in social media, Dummies makes everything easier.

FOR DUMMIES®
A Wiley Brand

BUSINESS

978-1-118-73077-5   978-1-118-44349-1   978-1-119-97527-4

MUSIC

978-1-119-94276-4   978-0-470-97799-6   978-0-470-49644-2

DIGITAL PHOTOGRAPHY

978-1-118-09203-3   978-0-470-76878-5   978-1-118-00472-2

Algebra I For Dummies
978-0-470-55964-2

Anatomy & Physiology For Dummies, 2nd Edition
978-0-470-92326-9

Asperger's Syndrome For Dummies
978-0-470-66087-4

Basic Maths For Dummies
978-1-119-97452-9

Body Language For Dummies, 2nd Edition
978-1-119-95351-7

Bookkeeping For Dummies, 3rd Edition
978-1-118-34689-1

British Sign Language For Dummies
978-0-470-69477-0

Cricket for Dummies, 2nd Edition
978-1-118-48032-8

Currency Trading For Dummies, 2nd Edition
978-1-118-01851-4

Cycling For Dummies
978-1-118-36435-2

Diabetes For Dummies, 3rd Edition
978-0-470-97711-8

eBay For Dummies, 3rd Edition
978-1-119-94122-4

Electronics For Dummies All-in-One For Dummies
978-1-118-58973-1

English Grammar For Dummies
978-0-470-05752-0

French For Dummies, 2nd Edition
978-1-118-00464-7

Guitar For Dummies, 3rd Edition
978-1-118-11554-1

IBS For Dummies
978-0-470-51737-6

Keeping Chickens For Dummies
978-1-119-99417-6

Knitting For Dummies, 3rd Edition
978-1-118-66151-2

FOR DUMMIES

A Wiley Brand

SELF-HELP

978-0-470-66541-1

978-1-119-99264-6

978-0-470-66086-7

LANGUAGES

978-0-470-68815-1

978-1-119-97959-3

978-0-470-69477-0

HISTORY

978-0-470-68792-5

978-0-470-74783-4

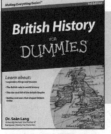

978-0-470-97819-1

Laptops For Dummies 5th Edition
978-1-118-11533-6

Management For Dummies, 2nd Edition
978-0-470-97769-9

Nutrition For Dummies, 2nd Edition
978-0-470-97276-2

Office 2013 For Dummies
978-1-118-49715-9

Organic Gardening For Dummies
978-1-119-97706-3

Origami Kit For Dummies
978-0-470-75857-1

Overcoming Depression For Dummies
978-0-470-69430-5

Physics I For Dummies
978-0-470-90324-7

Project Management For Dummies
978-0-470-71119-4

Psychology Statistics For Dummies
978-1-119-95287-9

Renting Out Your Property For Dummies, 3rd Edition
978-1-119-97640-0

Rugby Union For Dummies, 3rd Edition
978-1-119-99092-5

Stargazing For Dummies
978-1-118-41156-8

Teaching English as a Foreign Language For Dummies
978-0-470-74576-2

Time Management For Dummies
978-0-470-77765-7

Training Your Brain For Dummies
978-0-470-97449-0

Voice and Speaking Skills For Dummies
978-1-119-94512-3

Wedding Planning For Dummies
978-1-118-69951-5

WordPress For Dummies, 5th Edition
978-1-118-38318-6